W0187450

The Changing Gaze

The Changing Gaze

Regions and the Constructions of Early India

Bhairabi Prasad Sahu

OXFORD
UNIVERSITY PRESS

OXFORD
UNIVERSITY PRESS

Oxford University Press is a department of the University of Oxford.
It furthers the University's objective of excellence in research, scholarship,
and education by publishing worldwide. Oxford is a registered trademark of
Oxford University Press in the UK and in certain other countries

Published in India by
Oxford University Press
YMCA Library Building, 1 Jai Singh Road, New Delhi 110 001, India

© Oxford University Press 2013

The moral rights of the author have been asserted

First published in 2013

All rights reserved. No part of this publication may be reproduced, stored in a retrieval system, or transmitted, in any form or by any means, without the prior permission in writing of Oxford University Press, or as expressly permitted by law, by licence, or under terms agreed with the appropriate reprographics rights organization. Enquiries concerning reproduction outside the scope of the above should be sent to the Rights Department, Oxford University Press, at the address above

This volume only contains maps of historical significance and does not cover all the geographical locations. The international boundaries, coastlines, denominations, and other information shown on any map in this work do not imply any judgement on the Oxford University Press concerning the legal status of any territory or the endorsement or acceptance of such information. For present boundaries and other details, please see Survey of India maps.

You must not circulate this work in any other form
and you must impose this same condition on any acquirer

ISBN-13: 978-0-19-808919-3
ISBN-10: 0-19-808919-8

Typeset in Adobe Garamond 11/13.2
by Eleven Arts, Keshav Puram, Delhi 110 035

For
late Professor R.S. Sharma
and
Professor B.D. Chattopadhyaya

Contents

Illustrations

Preface

Regional histories emerged in the early part of the twentieth century in Bengal, Maharashtra, and Tamil Nadu, among other regions, largely as a part of the nationalist response to the process of colonial 'centralized archivization' and production and circulation of knowledge. In these histories small battles were transformed into major wars and local heroes were unduly imbued with great honour in the historians' desire to create glorious pasts. Only from the 1970s have historians begun to address problems associated with a realistic history of the regions and there has been a shift from regional histories to the histories of the regions. Moving away from chauvinistic writings there have been efforts to understand regions on their own terms, leading to the unveiling of the making of multiple regional traditions and trajectories of socio-political developments across regions. In the far south there are differences in environment and landscape between the adjoining states of Kerala and Tamil Nadu, and their bearing on the historical evolution in the two regions is obvious. Examples such as this can easily be multiplied. Works on Rajasthan, Bengal, Andhra, and Tamil Nadu in course of the last thirty years, while unraveling the shaping of these regions, have also demonstrated that regions are a legitimate category of historical studies. They allow for in depth analysis of the data and the mapping of agrarian, non-agrarian processes, political formations and the common woman/man's history. The emergent picture across several regions then provides the basis for wider generalizations. This is unmistakably different from macro-generalizations based on perspectives from either Gangetic north India or the Kaveri valley in the south.

The concept of region is amenable to a variety of meanings. Environment, ethnicity, and language are all useful categories for defining a region. In many cases historians have projected the present day political boundaries into the past and assumed them to be convenient categories of analysis. However, there is an increasing realization that past historical or cultural regions need not necessarily conform to present day state boundaries, which are the result of recent administrative decisions. The regions that the historians are now usually concerned with are historically constituted, they expand and contract through time and are not immutable. Kamarupa, Varendra, Kaliṅga, Dakṣiṇa Kośala, and Mālwa provide some good examples. There are instances where they combined with other entities to constitute a larger region. At varying points in time parts of Kaliṅga, Utkala, Jharkhand, and Dakṣiṇa Kośala were a part of pre-modern supra regional Orissan states. While histories of the regions and their interplay constitute the national they themselves are forged by sub-regional and local histories. Histories of regions cannot be written by assuming them to be already there. Writing the history of the regions therefore involves the understanding of the shaping of regional and pan-Indian patterns and traditions through complex networks of interrelationships between the local, regional and trans-regional elements, mediated by multilateral transactions involving giving and borrowing. Thus, the history of regions is shaped in the context of its relationships with larger units. In these narratives it is futile to look for uniformities. Pluralities across spaces continuously coexist, the differences are not homogenized. Unity in diversity is not assumed to be something natural and given; it is seen as evolving historically. The variety of regional traditions ultimately gave shape to the united colours of India.

This volume comprises about a dozen papers, some published between 1996 and 2011 as well as others presented at seminars/conferences during 2007–11. About half of them are focused on Orissa and Chhattisgarh, while the rest, using evidence and works on the varied regions, have a wider spatial reach. They point to the continued interplay and coexistence of the local and trans-regional elements and comparable trajectories of growth across regions. The basic concern in all the essays has neither been the regional versus the national nor generalizations versus specificities, but how they helped in constituting one another and have lived together as a civilization with a shared moral order. It is about plurality and confluence, as well as change through continuity. It is an effort to understand the creative processes and the common pool of ideas and values that mediated in the network of linkages between the localities, regions and the transregional.

The state of Orissa has very recently been rechristened as Odisha. However, both for the convenience of the general reader as well as the fact that the book had gone to the press before this development we have preferred to continue with the older name. The articles and papers were written on different occasions, catering to diverse requirements; and in situations such as these some overlaps and repetitions are but natural. Readers may kindly bear with it.

In completing this work, I have depended in various ways on the cooperation of many others. Many well wishers and friends within and outside the country first gave an opportunity to try out some of the ideas in their respective universities at seminars and conferences, and I am grateful to them for their kindness. I am indebted to Professor B.D. Chattopadhyaya, and my colleagues Sunil Kumar and Kesavan Veluthat for their generous suggestions and comments on the draft of the Introduction and sections of the work. To Kesavan Veluthat I owe special thanks for his unfailing support at difficult moments. My ideas have benefitted greatly over the past years in reading and interacting with B.D. Chattopadhyaya, and Hermann Kulke, and I continue to benefit from their erudition. For their help in various ways and generous encouragement I am grateful to Sabyasachi Bhattacharya, T.K. Venkatasubramanian, Biswamoy Pati, Martin Brandtner, Daud Ali, Georg Berkemer, Rajan Gurukkal, Upinder Singh, Kumkum Roy, R.P. Bahuguna, Shishir Kumar Panda, and Kumar Amarendra Singh. I am indebted to the editorial team at Oxford University Press for seeing the book through to production. I cannot fail to mention my general intellectual debt to late Professor R.S. Sharma who as a teacher introduced me to the dominant historiography in the later half of the 1970s, and continued to encourage and inspire in the following decades. I have drawn on the patience and indulgence of my family, and my debt to my wife Gayatri and our son Devavrata is of a different order all together. I thank them the most.

Bhairabi Prasad Sahu

Acknowledgements

The author and the publisher would like to thank the following for permission to include these articles in the volume:

Manohar Publishers and Distributors for 'Ways of Seeing: History and Historiography of the State in Early India', in Martin Brandtner and S.K. Panda (eds), *Interrogating History: Essays for Hermann Kulke*, 2006, pp. 63–82; and 'Profiling Dakṣiṇa Kośala: An Early Historical Sub-region?' in H. Kulke and Georg Berkemer (eds), *Centres Out There: Facets of Subregional Identities in Orissa*, 2011, pp. 39–60.

Tulika for 'The Early State in Orissa: From the Perspective of Changing Forms of Patronage and Legitimation' in B. Pati, B.P. Sahu, and T.K. Venkatasubramanian (eds), *Negotiating India's Past: Essays in Memory of Partha Sarathi Gupta*, 2003, pp. 29–51.

Indian History Congress for 'Presidential Address, Section I: Ancient Indian History', *Proceedings of the Indian History Congress*, Mysore, 2003, pp. 44–76.

The Project of History of Indian Science, Philosophy and Culture for 'Brāhmaṇical Conception of Jātis: A Study of the *Manusmṛti*' in B.D. Chattopadhyaya (ed.), *A Social History of Early India*, vol. 2, pt. 5 of *History of Science, Philosophy and Culture in Indian Civilization*, gen ed. D.P. Chattopadhyaya, 2009, pp. 43–52.

Abbreviations

BRW	Black-and-red ware
EI	*Epigraphia Indica*
IAR	*Indian Archaeology—A Review*
IESHR	*Indian Economic and Social History Review*
IHQ	*Indian Historical Quaterly*
IHR	*Indian Historical Review*
IO	*Inscriptions of Orissa*
JBORS	*Journal of the Bihar and Orissa Research Society*
JBBRAS	*Journal of the Bombay Branch of the Royal Asiatic Society*
JESHO	*Journal of the Economic and Social History of the Orient*
JRAS	*Journal of the Royal Asiatic Society*
NBPW	Northern Black Polished Ware
OHRJ	*The Orissa Historical Research Journal*
PIHC	*Proceedings of the Indian History Congress*
RCPW	Russet Coated Painted Ware
SSP	*Social Science Probings*

Introduction

Regions and the Constructions of Early India*

> ... whether it is a question of political sovereignty or of culture, total neglect of localities and regions not only blurs our vision of ground-level patterns but also hinders our understanding of the 'grand plot' itself.
>
> —B.D. Chattopadhyaya, *Representing the Other: Sanskrit Sources and the Muslims*

> Broadly, there have been two differing descriptions of Indian history. One ... sees India as a victim of recurring invasions ... as a series of rude interruptions.... The second celebrates the mongrel character of India's peoples and their histories: instead of hankering for purity, it sees the moments of mixture as the most creative and imaginative ones. It is a view that insists that what was distinctive about India's past was its ability to transform invasion into accommodation, rupture into continuity, division into diversity.
>
> —Sunil Khilnani, *The Idea of India*

The Problem

The ways of understanding early India have undergone significant change since the middle of the 1950s. Unlike the conventional

*This chapter is a revised and enlarged version of the article originally published as 'Perspectives from the Regions and the Construction of Early India', in K.L. Tuteja and Sunita Pathania (eds), *Historical Diversities: Society, Polity and Culture (Essays for V.N. Datta)*, Delhi, Manohar, 2008, pp. 35–55; a modified version of the chapter was presented as the Keynote Address at the National Seminar on Writing Regional History and the Historiography of Jammu, Kashmir and Ladakh, organized by the Department of History, Jammu University, Jammu, 29–30 May 2009.

historiography, the ascendant perspective, which became the dominant one through the subsequent decades, analysed and explained changes as well as the significance of such changes in the socio-economic and political structures, as well as in the cultural domain. Over the last three decades some of the assumptions of this historiography have been refined, particularly with reference to the historico-geographic transformation of the regions outside the Gangetic heartland and the changes coming from within local societies. This historiography emphasizes that for a proper appreciation of Indian history the regional perspective is crucial,[1] largely because any generalization from the perspective of Gangetic north India or the Kaveri valley in the south has its share of problems. One can recognize and accept the significance of the regions, without losing sight of the larger transregional patterns of socio-political and economic processes. The multiple sources of cultural antecedents, varying across spatial segments, the pluralistic tradition of the Indian historical experience and the reality of an overarching cultural ethos and civilizational universe have been mutually interacting, not exclusive, phenomena. It may be useful to draw attention to the enduring significance of the regions, the variegated historically constituted cultural entities,[2] while simultaneously arguing for the reality of a pan-Indian ideology and civilization, emanating from the operation of historical processes which combined elements of the local and the transregional, which in turn helped to universalize aspects of the local and the regional cultures. Monographs and collected works over the last twenty years, more particularly the last decade, have increasingly focused on the making of regions and regional societies in the larger context of their relationships with the transregional and sub-regional and/or local societies.[3] What follows is an effort to locate and understand the changing gaze, where there has been a perceptible shift from the centre to the peripheries.

This brings us to one of the most basic juxtapositions in historical literature—namely, the opposition between the pan-Indian view from the top and perspectives from the regions. Colonialist writings either characterized Indian history in terms of its bewildering variety—constructing exclusive identities on considerations of region, caste, language, ethnicity, etc.—rendering it impossible to be held together as a socio-cultural and political unit or constructed a totalizing and consequently hegemonic picture where the unchanging caste system and 'the village community' were represented as its defining traits. The politics of imperial enterprises and their administrative requirements dictated these shifts in perceptions.[4] Notwithstanding their rebuttal of many aspects of the imperialist reconstructions, the nationalists wittingly or unwittingly accepted the idea of India as an undifferentiated entity and, deriving from it, as a given cultural and political reality. R.K. Mookherji's *The Fundamental Unity of India* is a good example of the tendency to associate modern ideas with India's ancient past. The work was based on geographical evidence underlying the unity, not plurality, of the country. It also drew on the network of sacred sites and *tīrtha*s among the Hindus and Buddhists to make the argument. However, as it has been suitably pointed out '"Fundamental" in a culture is a quality, by implication, essentially embedded, it does not evolve historically.'[5] It has its bearing on ideas such as nation, nationality and nationalism. In the context of the struggle for freedom the compulsions of the nationalist historians, and their reluctance to grant the continuing inheritance of the regions their due is understandable. However, the long shadow it has cast over the dominant historiography in post-Independence India is somewhat intriguing, especially because the uneven patterns in Indian history have been recognized within the same historiography and historians have engaged with the problem since the latter half of the 1950s.[6] However, in charting the history of change interestingly it has also produced large, durable common institutional structures of sub-continental spread; spanning centuries. The meta-narratives of socio-political evolution echoed nationalist sentiments insofar as they imagined the sub-continent as 'India' and not a combination of 'regional particularities'. Not surprisingly therefore this historiography in some quarters has been labelled as Marxist-Nationalist. It makes the more general point that while identifying changes in historiography, one should not lose sight of the continuities. This centrist or epicentric perspective is derived largely from the Gangetic valley and its fringes; it fails to appreciate and address the cultural pluralism of the variegated regions. Paradoxically, the reason for the great popularity and resilience of the dominant historiography now also appears to be its primary weakness. While its ability to generalize allowed for lucidity and easy comprehension, it tended to homogenize the variety of human experiences and ignored the specificity of the regions with their comparable, but not necessarily similar, socio-political trajectories.[7]

Lest anybody should get the impression that this is a clever argument for going back to a different version of a Nationalist historiography, it needs to be quickly stated that there is a difference between writing regional histories and histories of the regions. While the former is consumed by a desire to establish the comparative historical precedence, antiquity or uniqueness inspired by regional sentiments and chauvinism, the latter is engaged in a dispassionate discerning of processes, structures and the trajectory of the evolution of institutions and traditions across regions. The glorification of individual rulers, exaggeration of regional events and the construction and privileging of competitive sub-nationalisms has been long overtaken by time, especially with the advances registered in the discipline since the 1970s. In the past, regions, as in the case of India, were perceived to be given bounded territories and the career and achievements of the kings and dynasties and important literary figures grafted on to these spatial entities in the intellectual climate of the times, which was informed by regional sentiments; reminiscent of nationalist Indology. In brief, the present day linguistic states were sought to be historicized in most of these writings. Regions surely have a distinguishable territoriality but the sense of affiliation and cultural bonding which forges it is shaped historically over time. The chronologies, patterns, and constituent ingredients of the historical regions as they emerged through the early medieval and medieval centuries do not necessarily converge. It is evident that these are also different from the early archaeological cultures represented by the distribution pattern of the deluxe pottery of the times. Many other possibilities apart, it is not possible to distinguish between the material culture and social formations of Magadha and Kośala, for example, on the basis of the Northern Black Polished Ware (NBPW) cultural assemblages in the two *mahājanapadas* (major *janapadas* or localities) in the middle of the first millennium BC, in the mid-Gaṅgā plains. Similarly, the Russet Coated Painted Ware (RCPW) culture in the south was spread over territories which later became parts of distinct historical regions. Briefly stated, archaeological cultures have their own distribution patterns and boundaries, which usually do not correspond with the historical regions as they evolved through the early medieval times and beyond.

Integrating regional histories into the history of India represents a condescending attitude and is not the same as writing history from within and in terms of the processes in operation across regions.[8] Even a casual comparison of some of the works within the dominant historiography and alternative histories produced during the last decade makes the general point more obvious. Besides, regional history calls into question accepted notions of causation, periodization and our understanding of the larger pattern of Indian history. Histories informed by nationalism unwittingly produced largely homogeneous, uniform narratives of India, playing down its multiplicity, vibrant regional variety, and their changing contours. The recent shift towards understanding the regions has been accompanied by a movement away from colonization as the agency of socio-cultural transformations from a privileged centre; to networks of linkages, interactions, and change, and the recognition of the fact that the emergence of the Sultanate in north India did not mark any major departure in the regions outside the Gaṅgā valley and adjacent territories. Flowing from it, the issue of periodization in Indian history possibly needs to be revisited. Complex, plural societies across regions were not held together mechanically, but sustained through processes of emulation, competition and antagonistic tolerance. The richness and vibrancy of the Indian cultural mosaic, constituted by the regions, is beautifully captured in the national anthem. The recognition and tolerance of variety and respect for underlying cultural commonalities is lucidly enshrined in the Indian constitution. It states that India that is Bhārata shall be a union of states. The notion of a monolithic unitarian nation/state is not true. Neither is the concept of India equivalent to a confederation of the regions. There is no conflict here; the two live together, cooperate and enrich each other, though the priority of one over the other is context specific. If the subsumption of the regions under the overarching idea of India does not do justice to the Indian historical experience, the opposite position asserting regionalism to the exclusion of an underlying cultural unity too is a falsification of history. The truth lies in the dynamic interrelationship of the two, in the course of which they constituted each other. Regions have not remained insular from evolutions within a larger unit. Regional history and the larger pattern of Indian history, to use a familiar expression, move in tandem.

Understanding the regions on their own terms or looking at the general pattern of Indian history from the perspective of the regions is not the same thing as encouraging regionalism. Bernard S. Cohn vividly makes the point.

The obvious distinction, conceptually, between the terms 'region' and 'regionalism' is sometimes overlooked. 'Region' with all its difficulties as a concept refers to means of classification of a wide variety of kinds of data, which helps analyse particular or general situations. 'Regionalism' refers usually to conscious or unconscious development of symbols, behaviours and movements which will mark off groups within some geographic boundary from others in other regions for political, economic, or cultural ends. *The term 'region' relates to a form of analysis, 'regionalism' to a call for action....*[9] (italics mine)

In other words, allowing the regions their due in historical analysis need not be viewed with apprehension. It is a necessary academic exercise and entails a corrective to tendencies to generalize from the perspective of Gangetic north India. It may be mentioned that regions are anything but fixed; they evolve historically.[10] While regions interact with and imbibe aspects of the pan-Indian, it is important to remember that localities and sub-regions also cohere in their making.

Regions emerge through the process of the shaping of common shared cultures, collective memories, a consciousness of felt community or a sense of belonging and affiliation which is constituted historically. The markers are spatially distinguishable and culturally identifiable art forms, architectural styles, food habits, dance forms, and language and script, among others. Deriving from it, one may ask how can then one distinguish between a region and a sub-region. Sub-regions are parts of a region with no entity singly constituting it insofar as they interact, overlap and intersect, while still retaining their own identities. To put it differently, it is a relationship which is analogous to that between the region and the transregional or pan-Indian. In this situation of being into it and yet out of it are embedded the historical roots of contestations and negotiations within the regions. Kaliṅga, Toṣala/Utkala, and Dakṣiṇa Kośala in Orissa clearly illustrate it. Sub-regions all through influenced the perceived regional 'centre', while simultaneously getting impacted by it. Unmistakably, identities in the past, as so often today, were not immutable.[11] Locality in historical terms is seen to approximate the *janapadas* in early India, or one may even equate them with the *nāḍus* under the Pallavas and Cōḷas in south India. Conceptually, it is a relational idea dependent on the context of its usage. It could also be either source or subject based, related to an event or episode and its perception from the 'centre'.[12] In that sense the concept of the local keeps changing.

In two articles and a recently edited volume, which focus on the conception of India as gleaned from textual references,[13] it is argued that the idea of India militates against the privileging of one region, community, language or religious group over the others. But then the important question is when and how did this concept of India emerge and crystallize? The works of Amir Khusrau and Abul Fazl, among others, in medieval India represent the richness of India's composite culture and the country as home to different interacting traditions.[14] How is it that despite some references to languages, scripts and territories outside northern India these traits did not attract the attention of Alberuni in the same way a few centuries earlier? Was it simply because his was an outsider's view of India addressed to an exogenous audience, or was there more to it? It is recognized that what one writes is informed by the tradition within which he/she writes, yet the important question to ask is whether the spatial spread of the Sultanate and the Mughal state across the Vindhyas and beyond help in shaping a richer perception of India or, to put it differently, whether the societal processes of change of transregional universality fructify and come into their own around the middle of the second millennium of the Common Era forcing others to pay attention, to take them seriously. The truth may be rooted in the simultaneous interplay of several developments. Greater interaction with other regions and regional societies beyond north India may account for the increasing tendency to take cognizance of them and their cultural practices. The formation of regional polities, evolution of regional languages, scripts and the pursuit of regional historiographies,[15] almost concomitantly, broadly around the first half of the second millennium as significant markers of the evolution of regions perhaps bear out our assumption. The *Rājataraṅgiṇi* in Kashmir, *Keraḷolpatti* in Kerala, and the *Mādaḷā Pāñji* in Orissa easily come to mind. It is equally possible that Amir Khusrau and Abul Fazl employed different registers to explore and capture the idea of India. They seem to have perceived and written about the country as insiders for an entirely indigenous audience, and consequently their works are more lively and enriched with vivid details. Following from what has been already said, it would be logical to ask how and through what stages the regions were constituted, and what relationship they shared with the larger idea of India. Regions like nations did not exist from times immemorial; they were formed through certain configuration of historical forces over time. We wish to develop the argument with reference to two interrelated aspects: first, the evolution of Brāhmaṇical ideology and, secondly the spatial spread of state societies. While the former represents the forging of trans-regional values, beliefs, and symbols, the latter have a bearing on the shaping of the regions.

The Expansion of a Tradition

Admittedly, Brāhmaṇical ideology and Hinduism is not the only route to understand the Indian reality. Indeed, the past was made of a variety of constituents. The heritage of heterodoxy, for example, from the middle of the first millennium BC onwards stares one in the eyes, and the mutual influences and borrowings between the 'heterodox' sects and Brāhmaṇical tradition in fashioning ideas and practices cannot be swept under the carpet. We choose to focus on Brāhmaṇical ideology, because for a large part of our cultural past under discussion, it appears to have been the dominant cultural strand. Besides, through it we wish to also show the gamut of interactions, very often quite complex and nuanced, that went into the making of a unified civilization. The preference for the term Brāhmaṇical as against Hinduism has the advantage of indicating continuity from the later Vedic period onwards. Though Hinduism is seen as a movement from below, involving religious and social practices with local and regional roots, which transformed Brāhmaṇism in the post-Gupta and early medieval centuries,[16] it needs no emphasis that the normative texts while accommodating such changes continued to espouse the core values and the brāhmaṇas never really seem to have given up their dominance, notwithstanding the pressures, compromises and accommodation they had to encounter and endure. Finally, the word Hindu is a later day social construct. Notwithstanding its fuzzy beginnings in *Kitāb-ul-Hind* of Alberuni in the early eleventh century, and its usage in the mid-fourteenth century Sanskrit inscriptions by a Vijayanagara ruler to represent himself as *Hindurāya suratrāṇa* (Sultan among Hindu kings), it is usually seen as a colonial construct or its genesis is at most traced to the thirteenth-fifteenth centuries.[17]

We are charting the progress and development of Brāhmaṇical culture and tradition, which changed in the course of its adoption and adaptation in the varied regions under the influence of the inheritance of the autochthonous people whom it encountered, as it first moved in an easterly direction in the Gaṅgā valley and subsequently beyond the Gangetic heartland. It is generally agreed that the earlier theory that India was colonized by light-skinned migrants from Central Asia is not supported by evidence and that there is a need to discard such history in favour of the evidence for interaction and symbiotic relationships between these migrant groups and speakers of non-Aryan languages.[18] The boundaries of *Āryāvarta* as a cultural region were not very sharply defined. They were porous and flexible, flexible in so far as they extended geographically and incorporated new regions and porous because, contrary to general perception, they were sufficiently open. However, accommodation and assimilation of local cultures did not necessarily take place on a footing of equality. Brāhmaṇical tradition since its early emergence and evolution simultaneously practised integration and hierarchization of peoples, places, customs and rituals by assigning them different positions within its fold,[19] with reference to the dominant structures. Constructs such as Aryan and non-Aryan, *dvija* and śūdra, brāhmaṇa-kṣatriya *versus* vaiśya-śūdra were ingenious devices for ensuring hierarchy as well as incorporation. It is obvious that each preceding category is more inclusive than what follows, which then helps us to understand the governing ideas and society in practice. The sphere of influence of Brāhmaṇical tradition also expanded through the emulation of its rituals by people who considered them to be superior, largely owing to their association with certain cultural and technological attainments. Desirous of raising their own status they started following and participating in Brāhmaṇical rites and rituals. The widening geographical ambit of Brāhmaṇical ideology was thus the result of a two-way process since its inception.

Peoples and regions once considered outlying or perceived with hostility were amalgamated at other points.[20] As one moves from the Ṛg Vedic period to later Vedic times and further through *Baudhāyana Dharmasūtra* up to *Manusmṛti* one gets a sense of the changing contours of the conception of ideas such as *Aryan* and *Āryāvarta*, with their substance and spatial dimensions being constantly modified. Kaliṅga, Vaṅga, Magadha, and Surāṣṭra once placed outside the core were made part of it with the passage of time. The ordering of peoples, places and their customs and beliefs continued over time and it demonstrates the complex processes involved in the spread of Brāhmaṇical ideology as well as the continuous assimilation of disparate groups of people.

Compilers of *smṛti* literature when confronted with practices they did not approve of accepted them as of the other or outlying regions and even dismissed them as belonging to another *Yuga*. However, the very act of the inclusion of local customs and practices ensured their integration with the mainstream over time.[21] The Brāhmaṇical tradition in course of its geographical spread and evolution acquired a composite character, fashioned out of elements derived from different regions. The distinctiveness and specificity of regional contexts, traits, and symbols were many a time subsumed in the process of cultural fusion or the making of a composite cultural tradition.

With the horizontal expansion of state societies, from the Gupta period onwards and the requirements of royal legitimation, local cults associated with different social groups were sought to be assimilated and universalized on considerations of tying legitimacy down and sidewise, within local societies and supra-local contexts, including the fraternity of 'Hindu' *rājās*, respectively.[22] Popular purāṇic religion best illustrates the accommodation and asymmetrical placement of different cults, sects and castes in the socio-religious hierarchy. Local state formation and land grants in regions largely outside the Indo-Gangetic plains created conditions for the interface between Brāhmaṇical ideology and the tribal world, with a bearing on modes of worship, proliferation of deities and developments such as hectic temple building activities and the spread of *maṭhas*. *Tīrthas* in the outlying regions such as Jharkhand, Orissa, Chhattisgarh, Madhya Pradesh, and Rajasthan were the meeting place and melting pot of varied influences and, thus, they provided cultural connectivity and facilitated acculturation and incorporation.[23] The sculptural rendering of purāṇic deities and epic-purāṇic episodes on temples at Bhubaneswar (Orissa), Sirpur (Chhattisgarh), Ellora, Elephanta (Maharashtra), and Mahabalipuram (Tamil Nadu) manifest cultural transactions, involving internalization of ideas and values. The rise of *tīrthas* in a general context of state formation evidently brings out their interrelationship and the former's role in social and political validation. In the Hindu pantheon, comprising Viṣṇu and Śiva, Śakti represented the third stream. The incorporation of *Śākta* (mother goddess) sects into Brāhmaṇical tradition marked an important stage in the transformation of the latter, demonstrating its incorporative abilities and capacity to reach out to those once considered to be on the margins. The absorption of Tantric elements too symbolized the same. In the process of acculturation the Brāhmaṇic tradition both incorporated and Sanskritized aspects of tribal life in the peripheral regions.[24] Vijay Nath vividly portrays this dialogic process—cultic appropriation and extension of Brāhmaṇical ideology on the one hand and its tribalization on the other.[25] However, there is the palpable tension in her work, emanating largely from the mismatch between the conceptual framework she chooses to use and the detailed discussion of the pan-Indian tradition as it played out across different regions and different historical locations. The cult of Jagannātha at Puri, Narasiṁha at Simhāchalam and Viṭṭhala at Pandharpur exemplify Brāhmaṇic adaptability. The appeal of these deities over wide social and spatial segments made them the focus of regional political interest.[26] Examples of this kind can be multiplied. The cult of Ekaliṅgaji in Mewar manifests comparable processes.[27] Structures of legitimation across spaces were not transplants, by their very nature they were culture/region-specific.[28]

Brāhmaṇical ideology gradually acquired a sub-continental presence largely through its socio-political functions such as the production of texts like the *purāṇas*, creation of local mythologies, spread of Vedic-śāstric-purāṇic ideas, invention of origin myths for ruling families, among others, and the use of Sanskrit as a common language. The forging of the 'Sanskrit cosmopolis' over the first millennium has been persuasively argued for by Sheldon Pollock,[29] and even after the rise of the vernaculars in the next millennium it retained its relevance to an extent that in the early colonial encounter the British accessed it to understand precolonial India. The network of temple centric *tīrthas*, mass bathing in holy rivers, *vrata*s, *kīrtana*s, *kathā*s, and the recital of religious texts to collective gatherings not only transmitted śāstric-purāṇic ideas but also prepared the ground for creating and fostering a sense of belonging of different kinds of groups, within and across regions.[30] There was a complex interweaving of the local, regional and national through which attitudes and ideas were produced and circulated. Lest anyone should get the impression of an entirely harmonious situation, it may be added that the process of integration was at play, but as Hermann Kulke puts it, it was 'integration through contestation'.[31] It is also important to remember that in the lived history not every social group or segment of space adhered to the dominant world view. The multitude of cults, sects, castes and beliefs, located in varied social and spatial situations, converged to shape a collective conglomerate; but it did not ever lead to the formation of a monolithic socio-religious identity.[32] The twin processes of fusion and fission impacted the religious and cultural world in the same way as they affected the political domain in the early medieval centuries.[33] By the middle of the thirteenth century Muslim presence in parts of the country was about half a millennium old. Even then they were perceived and represented either in generic terms such as Mleccha, Yavana, and Turuṣka or ethnic or spatial terms like Pārasīka and Tājika, depending on the context of their usage. Significantly, they were not encapsulated within a religious category. The Veraval (Gujarat) bilingual inscription in Sanskrit and Arabic of AD 1264 relating to the construction of a mosque by Nuruddin Firuz, the captain of a ship, of Hormuz after procuring some land in the locality is yet another signifier of the ways in which the 'others' were visualized, and the persistence of differentiated, fluid, multiple identities.[34]

Early Indian texts and inscriptions mention the terms Jambudvīpa, Āryāvarta, and Bhārata, which are usually equated with the idea of India.[35] Even though the self perception of the idea of India contained in these concepts may be inadequate or inconsistent, the authors of the texts seem to have shared a common value system, heritage and language with others of their status. As A.T. Embree aptly notes this is quite striking because Bhārata or India was more often than not a multitude of political formations.[36] The formation of the concept of India, howsoever inadequate and incomplete, sans a unified political enterprise of considerable durability, is significant and needs to be explained.

Spread of State Society

In conventional historiography the Mauryas and Guptas are generally considered to represent the great moments of political unity in early India. Owing to their chronological precedence one may begin the discussion on the interrelated aspects of historical transformation of space and the spread of state societies across regions starting with the Mauryas. Although on the basis of the geographical distribution of Aśokan inscriptions a certain measure of material and cultural uniformity is generally assumed for the subcontinent, recent studies demonstrate that the prosperity in material culture, during the said period, was largely limited to Gangetic northern India and the fringes of Central

India.[37] The processes leading to the emergence of the early historical period in peninsular India are seen to have gathered momentum during and after the Mauryas. The archaeology of early historic settlements in peninsular India largely seems to endorse this argument.[38] The uneven patterns of growth within the Mauryan state as well as the differential levels of interaction between the core (Upper and Middle Gangetic plains) and the peripheral regions have been convincingly argued and, flowing from it, the problems in equating a political formation such as the Mauryan empire with an undifferentiated social formation have been highlighted. The recent perspectives[39] do not negate the existence of an empire, what they do is to bring into relief the different faces of the state in the varied regions (dependent on the socio-cultural levels and revenue potential of the latter) and the overall nature and structure of the polity. The nature of the presence of the state, it is said, had a bearing on the intensity of interactions, which in turn influenced the pace of historical transformation in different regions.

The period under discussion was important in terms of the beginnings of wide ranging interactions across the sub-continent and the opening of communication routes. The distribution of Northern Black Polished Ware sherds (the deluxe ware which originated in the middle Gaṅgā valley around 500 BC and was in circulation up to the end of the millennium) in central India and the Deccan as far as Amaravati, in Andhra Pradesh, and the location of Aśokan edicts at Dhauli, Jaugada, and Amaravati on the east coast point in that direction. The evidence of rouletted ware (a pottery of Mediterranean origin and/or inspiration dated to the post-Mauryan times) on the entire east coast at numerous sites from Bengal to Tamil Nadu together with the Tamil-Brāhmi inscriptions from Tamil Nadu, derived from Aśokan Brāhmi, make the more general point about the network of linkages which seem to have begun during the time of the Mauryas. In the western Deccan and central India donations by craftsmen and merchants from far away places to Buddhist establishments at Nasik, Junnar, Karle, even Sanchi, Bharut, and numerous other centres show the movement of people, goods and ideas over long distances during the post-Mauryan period. Similarly, movements between the west and the east coast, on the Godavari, through the Central Deccan endorse the wide ranging interactions. The archaeology of early historical sites at Kondapur, Dhulikata, and Peddabankur amply bear it out.[40] The

Mauryan presence in the Deccan seems to have paved the way for the subsequent flowering of Buddhism in the region.

It is in these aforesaid interactions and not in the administrative integration under the Mauryas that the transition to the early historical phase in the Deccan is located.[41] The Mauryas spread into the Deccan at a point when the Megalithic communities were on the path to the emergence of internal differentiation. Their subordination to the metropolitan state in the end enhanced the status of the evolving ruling strata because of the said association and they emerged wiser with experience in the management and control of labour as well as produce.[42] The disintegration of the Mauryan state saw the emergence of localities, which corresponded to the earlier *Janapadas* of north India.[43] To elaborate, the Mahārathis and Mahābhojas in the Deccan, for example, represent the evolution of such locality centred ruling elites as a consequence of the internal differentiation within local communities and related changes. Developments such as these not only problematize the question of administrative integration of the Deccan under the Sātavāhanas but also point to the phased socio-political integration of the regions. Continued manifestation of the process of locality formation is discernible in the post-Mauryan period in Kaliṅga, coastal Andhra and northern Karnataka, among others.[44] The process of the formation of localities or secondary state formation, deriving from the combination of autochthonous forces and influences from developed spatial segments, continued throughout Indian history. State formation as late as the late medieval centuries in Chottanagpur and north-eastern India bears testimony to it.[45]

The Kuṣāṇa state in north India, covering large parts of Central Asia as well, comprised numerous socio-cultural entities. The persistence of the *Gaṇasaṁgha* tradition in the Punjab plains from the Mauryan times through the Kuṣāṇa period and beyond, besides indicating weak property rights in land and poor agricultural growth, reflects this reality. Bactria on the west and the Gaṅgā valley to the east only added to the vibrant cultural mosaic. The numerous epithets such as *Mahārāja*, *Devaputra*, and *Shaonano Shao Koshano* (Kuṣāṇa king of kings) that the rulers of the dynasty chose to sport and the accommodation of a variety of deities from different religions on the reverse of their coins (from Śiva to Buddha, even fire cult and the moon) were perhaps products of the recognition of the existing socio-cultural plurality within their domain.[46] Through the adoption of various titles, incorporation of myriad religions and the representation of the rulers in supernatural contexts on the obverse of the coins (with the nimbus behind their head or their being shown as emerging from the clouds, among others) and the practice of *devakula* the Kuṣāṇas sought to reach out to diverse groups and legitimize themselves in a situation of ethnic, linguistic, and cultural plurality.[47] The idea of unity was hung on the state and the state was expected to deliver. It tried to do so by appearing to be culturally sensitive and responsive.

The early medieval centuries were marked by the horizontal spread of state societies, largely into areas with little prior experience of organized state activity. The emergence of the *āṭavikarājyas* and *Pulindarāja rāṣṭra* in different parts of Central India shed light on local state formation in tribal areas and their movement towards complex society. The Maitrakas of Valabhi (Gujarat), the Vākaṭakas of the Deccan, and central India (Maharashtra), Kadambas of Banavasi (Karnataka), Pallavas of Kañchi (Tamil Nadu), Viṣṇukuṇḍins of Andhra, Śarabhapurīyas of Dakṣiṇa Kośala (Chhattisgarh) and the Hill states of Punjab provide good examples of state formation and the extension of state society at the local and translocal levels.[48] They also suggest the introduction of a comparable socio-political structure throughout the country. Local state formation in a big way outside the Gaṅgā valley and the corresponding rise in land grants in the same regions indubitably show the interrelationship between the two phenomena. On the basis of land grant charters it is suggested that there were about fifty political systems spread over Maharashtra, eastern Madhya Pradesh, Andhra Pradesh, Orissa and Bengal between *c.* AD 400 and 650.[49] In the succeeding centuries they were replaced by fewer numbers of subregional and regional states. The evolution of such states point to the emerging configurations, leading to larger, expansive integrated structures. The relationship between the monarch and *sāmanta*s at different levels may have been more complex than is usually conceded. There was certainly more to it than simple loyal submission or affiliation on the part of the subordinates.[50] However, given the fact that early medieval polities were polycentred, graded and characterized by parcellization of sovereignty with integration never complete, they were, as has been suggested, largely dynamic. State formation and socio-economic transformation were interrelated processes. The Gupta and post-Gupta periods were characterized as much by state formation as the gradual concomitant formation of agrarian regions. Agrarian growth led to the emergence of region-specific rich peasants, who were recognized and incorporated into the expanding state apparatuses. The regional polities of the Pālas and Senas of Bengal, Śomavaṁśis and Later Gaṅgās of Orissa, Kākatīyas of Andhra, Hoyśāḷas of Karnataka and Cōḷas of Tamil Nadu from the ninth-tenth centuries onwards thus arose in a wider context of societal changes, which B.D. Chattopadhyaya refers to as the simultaneous operation of multiple interrelated processes of change,[51] involving agrarian expansion and peasantization of the tribes, caste formation, cultic integration and the gradual extension of state society into pre-state areas.

In the course of the simultaneous changes non-Brāhmaṇic ritual practices and ritualists among communities on the margins interacted with Brāhmaṇic rituals and priests at different locations and historical junctures, the latter incorporating elements and diverse practices popularly known as *pūja.* Drawing attention to textual and inscriptional evidence regarding *samāja* (gathering) and *utsava* (gathering/festival) in early India, especially, *Vasantotsava* around the Gupta period at Ujjain and *Śavarotsava* in late early medieval Bengal, it has been suggested that they provided the occasions for the convergence of Brāhmaṇic orthodoxy and popular heterogeneity; as also their interface with the state.[52] Sharing of cultural ingredients between communities, mutual adaptations and the constitution of recognizable shared cultural spaces were at once multidimensional and intricate processes.

Mutuality between the Parts and the Whole

In carrying the story forward let me take up the case of the region with which I have greater familiarity. Early sources do not use the term Orissa to denote the region that is known by that name. The term Kaliṅga is frequently used in the early historic situation to usually represent the coastal segment to the south of the Mahānadī. From the middle of the first millennium AD a number of *maṇḍala*s or sub-regions emerged in different parts of the Oriya speaking region of today. In fact, Hiuen Tsang refers to some of them. From this stage of segmented identities the march towards a larger integrated socio-political formation began under the Bhaumakaras during the eighth-ninth centuries. The formation of a regional agrarian base was more or less achieved by the time of their successors the Śomavaṁśīs and Later Eastern Gaṅgās, though the processes leading to it began much earlier at the level of local societies.[53] It provided the basis for the gradual unfolding of the cultural personality of the region and the attendant larger political experiments. The convergence of influences from multiple sources and the interplay of the sub-regions facilitated the shaping of the region. The first effort at forging a regional state by uniting the different *maṇḍalas* was made by the Śomavaṁśīs who came from Dakṣiṇa Kośala to the Mahānadī delta in the first half of the tenth century. Around the same time a new architectural style developed by assimilating traditions from Kaliṅga, Utkala and Dakṣiṇa Kośala. The regional *rekhā deūḷa* style of temple architecture peaked between the tenth and the thirteenth century. Mukteswara, Rājarāni, and Liṅgarāja at Bhubaneswara, Puri Jagannātha and the Sun temple at Konarka are some of its best manifestations. The region-specific caste system emerged with some measure of clarity most possibly during the Gaṅgā-Gajapati period (twelfth-sixteenth centuries).[54] Although characteristics of the Oriya script began to develop in the thirteenth century, early Oriya inscriptions date between the fourteenth and mid-sixteenth century. The flowering of Oriya literature as manifested in Sāraḷa Dās's writings and those of the *Pañca Sakhās* broadly converges with this time bracket. While the earliest use of the terms *Oḍiśā* and *Oḍiā* are dated to the middle of the fourteenth century, the identification of constituent parts of the region with *Oḍarāṣṭra* and *Oḍiśa rājya* is observed in the *Sāraḷā Mahābhārata* and Gajapati inscriptions respectively in the fifteenth–sixteenth centuries. These simultaneous developments perhaps indicate the formation of a linguistic-historical region in itself, if not for itself. Efforts to reconstruct a trans-dynastic history of the region and a continuous regional tradition through the *Mādaḷā Pañji*, the beginning of which is dated around AD 1600, would have strengthened the attenuated cultural identity.[55] The cult of Jagannātha with its horizontal and vertical linkages with numerous local and sub-regional deities also created a sense of affiliation and bonding and contributed to the making of a regional identity. In the south consequent to the evolution of a regional kingdom under the Kākatīyas and the gradual convergence of language and territory almost during the same period, that is, eleventh–fourteenth centuries Andhra too experienced nascent identity formation.[56] In fact, by the thirteenth century Telugu had come to be accepted as the language of the Andhras. There were symmetrical developments in the domains of agrarian economy and society. Later the emergence of a sense of shared history going back to the Kākatīyas helped to strengthen the awareness of belonging to a region. By then Kerala had already emerged through a different combination of historical forces, and in the post-Perumāḷ era (after AD 1124) was making a self-consciousness assertion of its identity through the use of its language Malayāḷam.[57] Comparable processes operating across regions had a bearing on the formation of nascent regional identities.

The creation of vernacularly bounded domains was a significant new development of the first half of the second millennium. The distribution of the dynastic local language inscriptions from the Cōḷas, through the Hoyśāḷas and Kākatīyas, to the Gaṅgās and Gajapatis facilitated the transmission of the idea of belonging to a region. Geographical spaces got identified with vernacular realms; Tamil, Telugu, Kannada, and Oriya each were broadly territorially bounded. Domains of political authority more often than not sought symmetry with vernacular zones.[58] The correspondence between language, culture, and the political domain helped in the shaping of historical regions. As a reminder to the importance of language in the forging of regions in the period under discussion, it is suggested that political systems which it witnessed may be characterized as 'vernacular polity'.[59] At this point it may be pertinent to mention that caste is essentially region-specific, and these centuries, notwithstanding our cherished notions, also witnessed the congealing of castes and distinctive caste-patterning across several regions.[60] It only reinforces the fact that the history of the formation of regions was not the same everywhere.

These developments were neither entirely unitary nor unilineal. It is difficult to argue for a pattern of uniform validity all over the country. The regions had distinct spatio-temporal trajectories.[61] Further, we may remind ourselves that regions themselves are constituted by sub-regions and localities. Punjab, for example, broadly comprised the Plains and Hills, but closer scrutiny allows for further demarcations.[62] Similarly, the Koṅkaṇ, Khandesh, and Vidarbha constitute Maharashtra, and Jammu, Kashmir, and Ladakh constitute the northern most region of India. Visible manifestations of the importance of localities can be located in the assertion by local chiefs in the last phase of Cōḷa history and the *Nāyakas* following the military incursions of the Sultanate into the Kākatīya territories, and the extension of Vijayanagara to Andhra and Tamil Nadu. Recent works on south Orissa and northern Andhra have reinforced the importance of such studies.[63] Localities, sub-regions or regions were not homogeneous spaces. There were forests and settlements, and in the case of the latter there was immense variety. Historical transformation of spatial segments and their integration with the mainstream is a continuous process. In all periods of Indian history there were spaces outside the orbit of organized state intrusion. Such spaces, however, did not exist in immutable isolation, but in a state of interaction and change.[64] The gradual spread of state societies in Orissa and Andhra, as elsewhere; during the early medieval and medieval centuries make the more general point about uneven development across spatial entities. Regions, thus, in reality were characterized by variability, conflict and change, involving unequal networks of relationships between the centres and peripheries or even the sedentary peasants, pastoralists and hill people; within the wider context of the dialectics of relationships between the sub-regional, regional and the transregional. Deriving from it, regions can also be seen in unbounded relational terms, spatially and socially.

This perspective, deriving from a desire to understand the structure and pattern of Indian history in terms of the regions and transregional processes, focusing on the agency of local societies, and constant interaction and change apparently constitutes an inversion of the dominant historiography; which largely revolves around a mega narrative of assumed epicentre, colonization, crisis, and fragmentation.[65] The alternative perspective has the advantage of presenting a coherent theory of historical change in pre-colonial India. Its emphasis on change through continuity helps to successfully engage with and negotiate the question of transition from the early historical to the early medieval, and the early medieval to the medieval without having to address the curious problem of reconciling the fragmented world of early medieval India, as has been played out in the dominant historiography, with the centralized structures of the Sultanate. One may justly ask where it would leave the *purāṇa* centred idea of Kali Age crisis, which has been invoked to explain the passages from antiquity to the early medieval.[66] The notion of *Kaliyuga* was not symptomatic of a historical crisis, but represented a crisis of confidence; the fear of the loss of status and privileges and related anxieties of the brāhmaṇas in the face of unprecedented all-round growth and prosperity in the post-Maurya centuries. Besides, it alludes to the formation and spread of local states within the framework of Brāhmaṇical ideology.[67] Brāhmaṇical ideology with its focus on the *dharmic* image of kingship had to distance the king from the concept of the Kali, which constituted the negation of *dharma* and all that it stood for. Inscriptions of the Pallavas, Kadambas, Vākaṭakas and numerous dynasties in Orissa yield evidence of it. Constructs such as the Kali Age provide unmistakable evidence for the ascendancy of Brāhmaṇical ideology and its centrality in the making of the strategies of domination across the sub-continent from the Gupta-post-Gupta centuries onwards. The change of perspective in recent years is not necessarily oppositionist in character, it in many ways constitutes the logical extension, fine tuning and adjustment of earlier understandings and positions.

Sanskrit emerged as the language of literature, administration and ideology, or what has been described as the formation of 'the Sanskrit Cosmopolis' took shape largely between AD 300 and 1300 across the sub-continent (and beyond).[68] The transregional spread was actualized through a process of adaptation and appropriation of translocal flows. The early medieval centuries witnessed the spread of Vedic-śāstric-purāṇic ideas in course of the extension of the frontiers of state society. The influence of Gupta symbols, idioms, and notions of power can be gleaned in the inscriptional records of numerous dynasties, across spaces, in early medieval India. The common political culture points to the unfolding of comparable socio-political processes across regions.[69] The question to be asked is how did it happen? The *praśasti* sections with their usually standardized messages of the images of kingship and the benedictory and imprecatory verses in the land grant charters, bearing influence of *Dharmaśāstra* literature, in the process of their being read out on various occasions played an important role in the process of cultural communication.[70] Public records since the time of the Aśokan inscriptions were meant to be read or read out to the people. Numerous temples in peninsular India bear inscriptions charting the achievements of individual rulers and dynasties. Such inscriptions on temple walls as public documents may be invested with similar qualities.[71] Works such as the *purāṇas*, *caritas*, and among other things, incorporated the past and transmitted it to the present and future. In the process they tried to revitalize and reproduce society. Inscriptions, art and literature not only represented society but through a conscious use of ideas and symbols, perhaps, also tried to change it, especially in regions experiencing the interplay of multiple processes of change.[72] In addition to political authority, exchange centres (*māṇḍapikas*, *peṇṭhās*, and *nagarams*), trade and traders,[73] Brāhmaṇic settlements, *maṭhas*, Buddhist and Jaina monasteries, and temples as centres of cultural dissemination and integrative agencies provided the necessary supra local and transregional linkages. The all-India cultural matrix with a predominance of Brāhmaṇical element evolved through these networks of linkages, engaging, and coming to terms with different regions at different points of time. There was a constant appropriation of the local and localization of the translocal flows, which created cultural arenas that went beyond those defined by the localities or regions.

There is no denying the fact that the number of people who thought of themselves as sharing a particular language or culture may have been small and confined largely to the elites. In spite of the fuzzy regional and transregional identities the names of Mughal *subas* such as Bengal, Mālwa and Gujarat remind us of the force of the regions in Indian history. The idea could be elaborated with reference to the history of the *Bhakti* movement, which at one level gives the impression of an inclusive, all encompassing phenomenon and at another demonstrates the region bound specificities, namely, Gauḍīya *Bhakti*, *Bhakti* in the Punjab and Braja.[74] However, simultaneously the depth and reach of an over-arching, unifying cultural domain can be seen in the hierarchies based on *varṇa*, gender and the patrilineal kinship structure, as well as the caste-land-power pyramid through much of the country. The processes of regional/sub-regional identity formation and decentring of identities were at work simultaneously, leading to the making of a composite, pluralist tradition. The evolution of historico-cultural regions by the middle of the second millennium as well as the emergence of the Gaṅgā-Gajapati, Vijayanagara, and later the Maratha political enterprises with all their transregional cultural implications unambiguously demonstrate these developments. Conflicting claims to borderlands by neighbouring linguistic states in modern India seems to be related to the playing out of the twin processes, which have left behind intersecting cultural arenas with overlapping influences.

The Indian entity was forged through multiple inheritances, including diversities of regions and cultures, which were neither contained within nor homogeneous or bounded. They constituted each other through internal transformations and continuous engagements. There are cultural elements that are commonly visible across the sub-continent, while there are others which are region-specific. Unlike the regional festivals like Ōṇam, Gaṇeśa *caturthi*, Ratha yātra or Poṅgal which are celebrated with varying degrees of importance in some regions of India, Dussehrā and Dīwali have more or less a pan-Indian presence. Differences in the stories and rituals apart, these two festivals have basic commonalities throughout; Dussehrā has ten days of festivities and Lakṣmi is worshipped for wealth and well-being at Dīwali. Recently it has been argued that 'imitable models', with varying lives, emerged all through Indian history and provided the necessary connectivity across the country. Buddhism and associated ideas and institutions constituted the framework in early historical times, whereas in the early medieval centuries Brāhmaṇic ideology and structures comprised it.[75] India as we understand it today was not given at any point in history, nor was it even an unchanging entity, it evolved historically with the interaction, entanglement, and overlapping of spaces and cultures; mediated by a plurality of nodes and networks.

NOTES

1. See B.D. Chattopadhyaya, 'Introduction' in *The Making of Early Medieval India*, New Delhi, Oxford University Press, 1994; idem, *Studying Early India: Archaeology, Texts and Historical Issues,* New Delhi, Permanent Black, 2003; H. Kulke, '*The Early and Imperial Kingdom: A Processural Model of Integrative State Formation in Early Medieval India*', in idem. (ed.), *The State in India 1000–1700*, OUP, Delhi, 1995, pp. 233–62; Romila Thapar, *Cultural Pasts: Essays in Early Indian History*, New Delhi, Oxford University Press, 2000, chapter nos 5, 6, 7, and 9 and B.P. Sahu, 'Introduction', in idem. (ed.), *Land System and Rural Society in Early India*, Manohar, Delhi, 1997.

2. The concept of region can be defined in quite different ways. For the problems of definition see Bernard S. Cohn, 'Regions Subjective and Objective: Their Relation to the Study of Modern Indian History and Society', in his *An Anthropologist Among the Historians and* Other *Essays*, New Delhi, Oxford University Press, 1987, pp. 100–35, also B.D. Chattopadhyaya, 'Space, History and Cultural Process: Some Ideas on the Ingredients of Subregional "Identity"', in H. Kulke and G. Berkemer (eds), *Centres Out There? Facets of Subregional Identities in Orissa*, New Delhi, Manohar, 2011, pp. 21–38.

3. See for example, Kunal Chakravarti, *Religious Process: The Purāṇas and the Making of a Regional Tradition,* New Delhi, Oxford University Press, 2001; Cynthia Talbot, *Precolonial India in Practice: Society Religion and Identity in Medieval*

Andhra, New York, Oxford University Press, 2001; Nandini Sinha, *State Formation in Rajasthan: Mewar During the Seventh-Fifteenth Centuries*, New Delhi, Manohar, 2002; Kesavan Veluthat, *The Early Medieval in South India,* New Delhi, Oxford University Press, 2009; Rajan Gurukkal, *Social Formations of Early South India*, New Delhi, Oxford University Press, 2010. Upinder Singh (ed.), *Rethinking Early Medieval India*, New Delhi, Oxford University Press, 2011, too focuses attention on a large number of studies in the context of the regions.

4. See Bernard S. Cohn, 'African Models and Indian Histories', in Richard G. Fox (ed.), *Realm and Region in Traditional India*, Vikas, New Delhi, 1977, pp. 90–113.

5. R.K. Mookerji, *The Fundamental Unity of India*, edited by D.P. Chattopadhyaya with a 'Historical Note' by B.D. Chattopadhyaya, New Delhi, Bharatiya Vidya Bhavan, Chronicle Books, 2003, p. 140.

6. See, for example, D.D. Kosambi, 'The Basis of Ancient Indian History', reprinted in A.J. Syed (ed.), *D.D. Kosambi on History and Society; Problems of Interpretation,* Bombay, University of Bombay, 1985, pp. 27–63; idem, *An Introduction to the Study of Indian History*, Bombay, Popular Prakashan, 1956, early chapters; also see R.S. Sharma, *Indian Feudalism* (*c. 300–1200*), Delhi, Macmillan, 1980 (2nd edition), Appendix 1.

7. For a comprehensive critique see Chattopadhyaya, *The Making of Early Medieval India*; idem., 'State and Economy in North India: Fourth Century to Twelfth Century', in Romila Thapar (ed.), *Recent Perspectives of Early Indian History*, Bombay, 1995, pp. 309–46.

8. Supra, n.1.

9. Cohn, 'Regions Subjective and Objective', p. 119.

10. Ibid., pp. 100–35.

11. See B.P. Sahu, 'Profiling Dakṣiṇa Kośala: An Early Historical Subregion?', in Kulke and Berkemer (eds), *Centres Out There?*, pp. 39–59.

12. I am thankful to Dr Nonica Datta whose presentation at National Nehru Memorial Library, Teenmurti, New Delhi helped to broaden my understanding.

13. Irfan Habib, 'The Formation of India: Notes on the History of an Idea', *Social Scientist*, vol. 25, nos 7–8, Jul.–Aug., 1997, pp. 3–10; idem., 'The Envisioning of a Nation: A Defence of the Idea of India', *Social Scientist*, vol. 27, nos 316–17, September–October 1999, pp. 18–29; Irfan Habib (ed.), *India: Studies in the History of an Idea*, New Delhi, Munshiram Manoharlal, 2005.

14. Ibid. See the articles by Imtiaz Ahmad, Iqtidar Alam Khan, and S.A. Nadeem Rezavi in Irfan Habib (ed.), *India.*

15. For regional historiographies centring on a regional deity and its *kshetra*, see H. Kulke, *Kings and Cults: State Formation and Legitimation in India and Southeast Asia*, New Delhi, Manohar, 1993, ch. nos 9, 10, 11, and 12. In the case of Kerala see Kesavan Veluthat, The *Keraḷolpatti* as History, in idem., *The Early Medieval in South India*, New Delhi, Oxford University Press, 2009, pp. 129–46; and for Jammu and Kashmir see Kumkum Roy, 'The Making of a *Maṇḍala*: Fuzzy Frontiers

of Kalahana's Kashmir', in B. Pati, B.P. Sahu and T.K. Venkatasubramanian (eds), *Negotiating India's Past: Essays in Memory of Partha Sarathi Gupta*, New Delhi, Tulika, 2003, pp. 52–66.

16. See Vijay Nath, 'From "Brāhmaṇism" to "Hinduism": Negotiating the Myth of the Great Tradition', Presidential Address, Ancient India Section, *Proceedings Indian History Congress* (hereafter *PIHC*), Calcutta session, 2001, pp. 26–56.

17. H von Stietencron, 'Hinduism: On the Proper Use of A Deceptive Term', in G-D Sontheimer and H. Kulke (eds), *Hinduism Reconsidered*, New Delhi, Manohar, 2001, (paperback), pp. 32–53; David Lorenzen, 'Who Invented Hinduism?', *Comparative Studies in Society and History*, vol. 41, no. 4, 1999, pp. 630–59; and Philip B. Wagoner, 'Sultan Among Hindu Kings: Dress, Titles, and the Islamicization of Hindu Culture at Vijayanagara', *Journal of Asian Studies*, vol. 55, no. 4, 1996, p. 862.

18. See Romila Thapar, *From Lineage to State: Social Formations in the Mid-First Millenium* BC *in the Gaṅgā Valley*, New Delhi, Oxford University Press, 1984, ch. 2; R.S. Sharma, 'Problems of Continuity and Interaction in Indus and Post-Indus Cultures', *Social Scientist*, nos 320–1, Jan.–Feb. 2000, pp. 3–11.

19. See Kumkum Roy, 'In which part of South Asia did the Early Brāhmaṇical Tradition (1st millennium BC) Take its Form?', *Studies in History*, vol. 9, no. 1, 1993, pp. 1–32; also idem., 'Legitimation and the Brāhmaṇical Tradition: The *Upanayana* and the *Brahmacarya* in the Dharma Sūtras', in *PIHC*, Amritsar session, 1985, pp. 136–46.

20. Roy, 'In which part of South Asia?'.

21. Richard W. Lariviere, 'Dharmaśāstra, Custom, "Real Law" and Apocryphal Smritis', in Bernard Kolver *et al.* (eds), *The State, the Law and Administration in Classical India*, Munich, 1997, pp. 97–110.

22. Kulke, 'The Early and Imperial Kingdom'.

23. See Vijay Nath, 'Tīrthas and Acculturation: An Anthropological Study', *Social Science Probings*, vol. 10, nos 1–4, 1993, pp. 28–54.

24. See Romila Thapar, 'Imagined Religious Communities? Ancient History and the Modern Search for a Hindu Identity', *Modern Asian Studies*, vol. 23, no. 2, 1989, pp. 209–31; also in idem., *Cultural Pasts*, pp. 965–89.

25. Supra, nos 16 and 23.

26. See, for example, A. Eschmann, H. Kulke and G.C. Tripathi (eds), *The Cult of Jagannāth and the Regional Tradition of Orissa*, New Delhi, Manohar, 1978.

27. See George W. Spencer, 'Religious Networks and Royal Influence in Eleventh Century South India', *Journal of the Economic and Social History of the Orient* (hereafter *JESHO*), vol. 12, no. 1, 1969, pp. 42–5; James Heitzman, 'Ritual Polity and Economy: The Transactional Network of an Imperial Temple in Medieval South India', *JESHO*, vol. 34, nos 1–2, 1991, pp. 23–54 and Nandini Sinha, 'A Study of State and Cult: The Guhilas, Pasupatas and Ekaliṅgaji in Mewar, Seventh to Fifteenth Centuries AD', *Studies in History*, vol. 9, no. 2, 1993, pp. 161–82; idem., *State Formation in Rajasthan*, pp. 194–243.

28. For a discussion see B.P. Sahu, 'Legitimation, Ideology and State in Early India', Presidential Address, Ancient India Section, Mysore Session, *PIHC*, 2003, pp. 62–4.

29. Sheldon Pollock, *The Language of the Gods in the World of Men: Sanskrit, Culture, and Power in Premodern India*, New Delhi, Permanent Black, New Delhi, 2006, early chapters.

For later times see Vasudha Dalmia, *Orienting India: European Knowledge Formation in the Eighteenth and Nineteenth Centuries*, New Delhi, Three Essays, 2003.

30. Chakravarti, *Religious Process*, supra n.3, chs 5–7; also see Vijay Nath, *Purāṇas and Acculturation: A Historico-Anthropological Perspective*, Delhi, Munshiram Manoharlal, 2001.

31. H. Kulke, 'The Integrative Model of State Formation in Early Medieval India: Some Historiographic Remarks', in M. Kimura and A. Tanabe (eds), *The State in India: Past and Present*, New Delhi, Oxford University Press, 2006, pp. 59–81; Also see Chattopadhyaya, *The Making of Early Medieval India*, p. 30.

32. See Romila Thapar, 'Imagined Religious Communities?', in idem., *Cultural Pasts*.; also see Suvira Jaiswal, 'Semitising Hinduism: Changing Paradigms of Brāhmaṇical Integration', *Social Scientist*, vol. 19, no. 12, December 1991, pp. 20–32.

33. Ibid. For the political sphere, see Chattopadhyaya, 'Political Processes and the Structure of Polity in Early Medieval India: Problems of Perspective', Presidential Address, Ancient India Section, Burdwan session, *PIHC*, 1983, pp. 25–63.

34. For the engaging details see B.D. Chattopadhyaya, *Representing the Other: Sanskrit Sources and the Muslims*, New Delhi, Manohar, 1998, chs 2 and 3. Also see R. Chakravarti, 'Nakhuda Nuruddin Firuz at Somanātha: AD 1264', in idem., *Trade and Traders in Early Indian Society*, New Delhi, Manohar, 2002, pp. 220–42. Similar examples can be multiplied. The imagery in the Palam Baoli Inscription of the time of Balban is revealing. See Pushpa Prasad, *Sanskrit Inscriptions of Delhi Sultanate, 1191–1526*, New Delhi, Oxford University Press, 1990.

35. Ainslie T. Embree, 'Brāhmaṇical Ideology and Regional Identities', idem., *Imagining India: Essays on Indian History*, New Delhi, Oxford University Press, 1989, pp. 9–27; also see Ishrat Alam, 'Names for India in Ancient Indian Texts and Inscriptions', in Habib (ed.), *India*., pp. 36–44.

36. Embree, 'Brāhmaṇical Ideology and Regional Identities'.

37. See Romila Thapar, *The Mauryas Revisited*, Calcutta, K.P. Bagchi, 1987, pp. 1–31. For a different perspective see R.S. Sharma, *Aspects of Political Ideas and Institutions in Ancient India*, Delhi, Motilal Banarsidass, 1991, pp. 392–402.

38. For example, see the diagram showing the history of sites in R.S. Sharma, *Urban Decay in India (c. 300–1000)*, Delhi, Munshiram Manoharlal, 1987, pp. 192–7. Also see D.K. Chakrabarti, *The Archaeology of Early Indian Cities*, New Delhi, Oxford University Press, 1995, ch. on early historical cities.

39. See for example, I.W. Mabbett, *Truth, Myth and Politics in Ancient India*, New Delhi, Thomson Press, 1972, ch. 6; Thapar, *The Mauryas Revisited*, and G. Fussman, 'Central and Provincial Administration in Ancient India: The Problem of the Mauryan Empire', *Indian Historical Review* (hereafter *IHR*), vol. 14, nos (1–2), 1988, pp. 43–72.

40. See Aloka Parasher, 'Social Structure and Economy of Settlement in the Central Deccan (200 BC–AD 200)', *Social Science Probings*, vol. 5, no. 4, 1992, pp. 1–19.

41. See S. Seneviratne, 'Kaliṅga and Andhra: The Process of Secondary State Formation in Early India', *IHR*, vol. 7, nos 1–2, 1981, pp. 54–69, and B.D. Chattopadhyaya, 'Transition to the Early Historical Phase in the Deccan: A Note', in B.M. Pande and B.D. Chattopadhyaya (eds), *Archaeology and History*, vol. 2, Delhi, 1987, pp. 727–32.

42. S. Seneviratne, 'Kaliṅga and Andhra'.

43. B.D. Chattopadhyaya, Transition to the Early Historical Phase in the Deccan'.

44. For Kaliṅga see B.P. Sahu, 'The Early State in Orissa: From the Perspective of Changing Forms of Patronage and Legitimation', in Pati, Sahu, and Venkatasubramanian (eds), *Negotiating India's Past*, pp. 29–51; also see P.V.P. Sastry, 'Political System in Early Coastal Andhra', in D. Handa (ed.), *Recent Studies in Indology*, Delhi, 1989, pp. 71–6.

45. See Surajit Sinha, 'State Formation and Rajput Myth in Central India', *Man in India*, vol. 42, no. 2, 1962, pp. 35–80; K.S. Singh, 'A Study in State Formation Among Tribal Communities', in R.S. Sharma and V. Jha (eds), *Indian Society: Historical Probings*, New Delhi, People's Publishing House 1977, pp. 317–36 and Surajit Sinha (ed.), *Tribal Polities and State Systems in Pre-Colonial Eastern and North Eastern India*, Calcutta, 1987.

46. See B. Puri, 'Ideology and Religion in the Kushana Epoch', in B.G. Gafurov *et al.*, (eds), *Central Asia in the Kushan Period*, II, Moscow, 1975, pp. 183–90.

47. Even in Gupta and post-Gupta times royal patronage was broad based. The compulsions of political power mostly made it necessary to recognize and address the rich socio-cultural ground reality.

For the Kuṣāṇa state see R.S. Sharma, *Aspects of Political Ideas*, pp. 291–309; A.K. Narain, 'The Kushana State: A Preliminary Study', in H.J.M. Claessen and P. Skalnik (eds), *The Study of the State*, The Hague, 1981, pp. 251–73.

48. See for example, H. Kulke, 'Some Thoughts on State and State Formation under the Eastern Vākāṭakas', in Hans Bakker (ed.), *The Vākāṭaka Heritage: Indian Culture at the Crossroads*, Groningen, 2004, pp. 1–9; Yogender Dayma, 'Political Processes in the Making of the Early Kadamba State', in *PIHC*, Kannur session, 2008, pp. 102–14; B.P. Sahu, 'Characterizing Early Medieval Indian Polity: The Case of Dakṣiṇa Kośala and Beyond', in this volume.

49. R.S. Sharma, *Urban Decay in India*, p. 168.

50. For details of the argument see B.P. Sahu, 'The State in Early India: An

Overview', *PIHC*, Aligarh Session, 1994, pp. 94–5. See the early chapters in Georg Berkemer and Margret Frenz (eds), *Sharing Sovereignty: The Little Kingdom in South Asia*, Berlin, Klaus Schwarz Verlag, 2003.

51. 'Introduction' in Chattopadhyaya, *The Making of Early Medieval India.*

52. B.D. Chattopadhyaya, 'Festivals as Ritual: An Exploration into the Convergence of Rituals and the State in Early India', in H. Kulke and U. Skoda (eds), *State and Ritual in India*, Section IV, in M. Kitts *et al.* (eds), *State, Power and Violence*, Wiesbaden, Harrassowitz Verlag, 2010, pp. 627–45.

53. See B.P. Sahu, 'Agrarian Changes and the Peasantry in Early Medieval Orissa (c. AD 400–1100)', in V.K. Thakur and A. Aounshuman (eds), *Peasants in Indian History*, Patna, Janaki Prakashan, 1996, pp. 283–311.

54. B.P. Sahu, 'The Past as a Mirror of the Present: The Case of Oriya Society', *Social Science Probings*, vol 9, nos 1–4, 1992, pp. 8–23; idem., '*Varṇa, Jāti* and the Shaping of Early Oriya Society', in this volume.

55. For the *Mādaḷā Pañji* see H. Kulke, *Kings and Cults*, pp. 137–91. Regional historiographies elsewhere also seem to have served similar functions. See in the same volume ch. nos 11 and 12. Also see H. Kulke, 'Historiography and Regional Identity: The Case of the Temple Chronicles of Puri', in H. Kulke and B. Schnepel (eds), *Jagannāth Revisited: Studying Society, Religion and the State in Orissa*, New Delhi, Manohar, 2001, pp. 211–25.

56. See Cynthia Talbot, 'Inscribing the Other, Inscribing the Self: Hindu-Muslim Identities in Pre-Colonial India', *Comparative Studies in Society and History*, vol. 37, no. 4, 1995, especially pp. 710–19.

57. See Kesavan Veluthat, 'Presidential Address' on the making of regional identity in Kerala, Ancient Section, Panjab History Conference, Patiala, February 9–10, 2012.

58. Pollock, *The Language of the Gods*, supra n. 28, ch. 10.3; also Veluthat, 'Presidential Address'.

59. Pollock, *The Language of the Gods*, p. 420.

60. See B.D. Chattopadhyaya, 'One Blind Man's View of an Elephant: Understanding Early Indian Social History', in idem. (ed.), *A Social History of Early India* (Vol. II, pt.5 of D.P. Chattopadhyaya (ed.), *History of Science, Philosophy and Culture in Indian Civilization*), Pearson Longman, New Delhi, 2009, pp. XXX1–1; Talbot, *Precolonial India in Practice*, supra n. 3, ch. on society; N. Karashima, 'New Imprecations in Tamil Inscriptions and Jati Formation', in idem., *South Indian Society in Transition: Ancient to Medieval*, New Delhi, Oxford University Press, 2009, pp. 99–114; and B.P. Sahu, '*Varṇa, Jāti* and the Shaping of Early Oriya Society', in this volume.

61. B.P. Sahu, 'Introduction' in idem. (ed.), *Land System and Rural Society in Early India.*

62. See Romila Thapar, 'The Scope and Significance of Regional History', Presidential Address, Punjab History Conference, 1976, reprinted in idem.,

Ancient Indian Social History: Some Interpretations, New Delhi, 1987 (reprint), pp. 364–67.

63. B. Schnepel, *The Jungle Kings: Ethnohistorical Aspects of Politics and Ritual in Orissa*, Delhi, Manohar, 2002; Georg Berkemer, Orissa Revisited: A View from the South, in Kulke and Schnepel (eds), *Jagannath Revisited*, pp. 253–70.

64. See B.D. Chattopadhyaya, 'Autonomous Spaces and the Authority of the State: The Contradiction and its Resolution in Theory and Practice in Early India', in Bernhard Kolver *et al.* (eds), *The State, the Law and Administration in Classical India*, Munich, R. Oldenburg, 1997, pp. 1–14. Also see his 'State's Perception of the "Forest" and the "Forest" as State in Early India', in B.B. Chaudhury and Arun Bandopadhyay (eds), *Tribes, Forest and Social Formation in Indian History*, New Delhi, Manohar, 2004, pp. 23–37.

65. Supra, n. 1; also Kulke, 'The Integrative Model of State Formation'.

66. For envisaging the idea of the Kali Age as a systemic crisis see B.N.S. Yadava, 'The Accounts of the Kali Age and the Social Transition from Antiquity to the Middle Ages', *IHR*, no. 5, vols 1–2, 1979, pp. 31–63; R.S. Sharma, 'The Kali Age: A Period of Social Crisis', in S.N. Mukherjee (ed.), *India: History and Thought*, Calcutta, Subarnarekha 1982, pp. 186–203.

67. See B.P. Sahu, 'Conception of the Kali Age in Early India: A Regional Perspective', *Trends in Social Science Research*, vol. 4, no. 1, 1997, pp. 27–36.

68. 'The Sanskrit Cosmopolis, 300–1300 CE: Transculturation, Vernacularization and the Question of Ideology', in Jan E.M. Houben (ed.), *Ideology and Status of Sanskrit: Contributions to the History of the Sanskrit Language*, New York, 1996, pp. 197–247; idem., *The Language of the Gods*.

69. See Sahu, 'Legitimation, Ideology and State in Early India', supra n. 28, pp. 56 ff.

70. See H. Kulke, 'Some Observations on the Political Functions of Copper Plate Grants in Early Medieval India', Kolver, *et al.* (eds), *The State, the Law*, pp. 237–43.

71. See Georg Berkemer, '"The Centre Out There" as State Archive: The Temple of Simhacalam', in Hans Bakker (ed.), *The Sacred Centre as the Focus of Political Interest*, Groningen, 1992, pp. 119–30.

72. Sahu, 'Profiling Dakṣiṇa Kośala: An Early Historical Sub-Region?', supra n. 11.

73. See B.D. Chattopadhyaya, 'Markets and Merchants in Early Medieval Rajasthan; and Urban Centres in Early Medieval India: An Overview', in idem., *The Making of Early Medieval India.*; idem., *Aspects of Rural Settlements and Rural Society in Early Medieval India*, Calcutta, 1990, ch. 3 and Ranabir Chakravarti, *Trade and Traders in Early Indian Society*, Delhi, Manohar, 2002, chs 9 and 10.

74. I am thankful to my colleague Professor R.P. Rana and friend Dr R.P. Bahuguna for drawing my attention to it.

75. Chattopadhyaya, 'Space, History and Cultural Process', supra n.2.

I

Early Patterns of Social and Cultural Change

1

Brāhmaṇical Conception of the Origin of *Jātis*

A Study of the *Manusmṛti**

The study of caste has attracted insightful inquiries by social scientists for quite a long time. *Varṇāśrama* and caste are seen to be the result of changes that Indian society has undergone over centuries of its existence. The evolution of patriarchy and the spread of state-societies are said to have played important roles in its gradual unfolding. Some recent writings, however, do not share the same perspective, and have an entirely different take on the problem. One influential writing posits that:

> In Pre-colonial India, the units of social identity had been multiple.... The referents of social identity were not only heterogeneous; they were also determined by context ... territorial groups, lineage segments, family units ... occupational reference groups, agricultural or trading associations, devotionally conceived networks and sectarian communities, even priestly cabals, were just some of the significant units of identification, all of them at various times far more significant then any uniform metonymy of endogamous 'caste' groupings. Caste ... was just one category among many others, one way of organizing and representing identity ... Regional, village, or residential communities, kinship groups ... and so on could both supersede caste as a rubric for identity and reconstitute the ways caste was organized. Within localities or kingdoms, groups could rise or fall (and in the process become more or less castelike)...[1]

*Originally published in B.D. Chattopadhyaya (ed.), *A Social History of Early India*, vol. 2, pt. 5 of *History of Science, Philosophy and Culture in Indian Civilization*, gen ed. D.P. Chattopadhyaya, Delhi, Pearson Longman, 2009, pp. 43–52.

This quote intends to show that though caste has been usually perceived as being omnipresent in Indian history and defining the core of social identity and Indian social organization, there are dissenting voices pointing to the historical/colonial roots of our understanding of caste as it is recognized today. Caste was never as standardized and religious as it has been made out to be in textbooks. Nor was Indian society as a whole ever trapped into a fixed and stable hierarchy as has usually been believed in some quarters. Thus, perspectives of caste differ noticeably: from those who see it as a cooperative mechanism to those who identify it with the most important instrument of social dominance; from those who perceive it from a textualized and Brahmanic view to those who locate it in political and social processes.[2] Notwithstanding the differences among a wide range of historians and social anthropologists about the nature of hierarchy intrinsic to caste, it is generally agreed that it is quite central to Indian civilization. This essay is neither about the history of caste in early India nor its detailed representation as is played out in the *Manusmṛti* per se, but about the role of Brāhmaṇical ideology in the construction of caste. It builds on the works of scholars such as R.S. Sharma, V. Jha, S.J. Tambiah, and Suvira Jaiswal who have charted new ways in negotiating the Indian social past and shown that early India was sustained not only by its economic wealth, science and technologies, and spiritual foundations but also by cultural constructs and ideologies of dominance. Through continuous representation of Indian society through the skilful display of rationalizing techniques woven into Vedic, Śāstric, and epic literature, besides other forms, Brāhmaṇical ideology sought to bring about changes more powerful than were perhaps possible through the agency of political power. Hierarchy remains the basic principle behind the caste system and differences in social status or competence are not unrelated to inequities in the economic and political domains. Once Brāhmaṇical ideology had defined what it deemed as social reality or how it was constituted, then society, it was assumed, had to conform to such construction.

Under the influence of anthropological studies the distinction that has been worked out between *varṇa*, meaning scripturally rationalized all-India schema of ritual status, and *jāti*, supposedly representing the actual status of local endogamous groups or castes on the ground, has been germane to the understanding of the social history of early India. The most useful result of this distinction has been that it has helped historians to look into questions relating to the origin of *jātis* and the formation of new castes in terms of historical change in local/regional societies. Issues of social mobility, fissioning of communities, status changes, and differential hierarchical placement of groups with reference to the dominant *varṇa* framework of social structure have been linked to the societal processes of change.[3] Normative texts usually give the impression of attitudes being fixed. However, the possibilities for social change were always there, and historians are increasingly recovering and mapping such changes. The period from the middle of the first millennium BC up to *c.* AD 300, especially the post-Mauryan centuries, was significant for the evolution of ideas and institutions related to polity and society. The concept of *varṇasaṁkara* derived from prescriptive Dharmaśāstric literature, seeking to account for the evolution and spread of castes within the Brāhmaṇical framework, needs to be contextualized and demystified to avoid a skewed (or an entirely religious) perception of the trajectory of caste formation in early India.[4]

The *Manusmṛti* has traditionally come to be accepted as embodying the standard statement of the caste system. It provides an account of the origin of the four *varṇas* and an explanation for the emergence of numerous castes or *jātis*. 'Thus the text has been seen as both prescriptive and descriptive, and the two functions have frequently collapsed into one.'[5] However, historically the origin of *varṇa* and its subsequent evolution into *jātis* have been traced from the Vedic period onwards. These constructs were not a part of the early Brāhmaṇical system alone: they were shared by the Buddhists and Jainas alike. Manu's ideas of *varṇa* and *varṇasaṁkara* thus go back in time and were derived from earlier sources. The importance of *Manusmṛti* derives from its systematic exposition of Brāhmaṇical social philosophy with its built-in notions of division and hierarchy and its effort to ideologically bound *Āryāvarta*, the geography of the text, through a conceptual framework. The text emerges as a manifesto of Brāhmaṇical perception of society and is remarkable for its awareness and articulation of a sense of community culture. It dwells on a whole lot of hierarchies premised on *varṇa*, gender, and age, including mixed castes. Understandably, with the spread of state society during and after the post-Mauryan period it provided the ideological basis for state and society in areas peripheral to the Gangetic plains.[6]

In *Manusmṛti*, the four *varṇa*s are: the brāhmaṇas or priests and teachers of the Vedas; kṣatriyas, whose domain was statecraft and warfare; vaiśyas, constituting the ranks of agriculturists, herders, and traders; and the śūdras, who were relegated to the position of menials. However, the first reference to this schema occurs in the *Ṛgveda* where the Brāhmaṇa is said to have been born from the mouth of Puruṣa (the Primeval Being), the kṣatriya from His arms, the Vaiśya from His thighs and the Śūdra from His feet. It is known that the *varṇa*s crystallized during the later Vedic period. Therefore, it is believed that the creation myth was interpolated into the *Ṛgveda* during that time so as to legitimize the four-*varṇa* order. The upper three *varṇa*s were known as *dvija*s (twice born) because they underwent the *upanayana* (initiation) ceremony at an early age, which represented their second birth, and the śūdras were kept out of it. The differential status and function accorded to the *varṇa*s was embedded in their different points of origin from Puruṣa. The symbolism of the correlation can hardly be missed. Brāhmaṇical ideology since its inception created a series of opposites such as Āryan *versus* autochthons, *dvija* versus śūdra and the brāhmaṇa and kṣatriya power elite versus the vaiśya and śūdra producers to retain hierarchies. The outwardly manifest philosophy was integration, but the operative core was to integrate and hierarchize. The segregation and exclusion of śūdras and the condemnation of many communities, in the early Dharmasūtras compiled between *c.* 600–300 BC, seeking to freeze them at the bottom of an increasingly asymmetrical system provide ample evidence for it. Since its inception the idea of *varṇasaṁkara* was meant, among other things, to drive in a sense of degradation among the lower castes and to perpetuate inequality even in principle.[7]

Notwithstanding the variation in their conception of early Indian society, Buddhist sources too acknowledged the existence of four *varṇa*s. The brāhmaṇas, kṣatriyas, and *gahapati*s were described as *ucca-kula* (superior families) and categories such as the caṇḍālas, niṣādas, veṇas, rathakāras, and pukkasas were assigned inferior status by clubbing them under the head *nica-kula*. In between the superior and inferior sections were placed segments of the vaiśyas and śūdras, and the distinction between these two *varṇa*s is rather vague.[8] This relatively complex picture of society was different from the ideal Brāhmaṇical conception and because of this contradiction many historians invest the Buddhist literature with authenticity.

The *varṇasaṁkara* theory of the origin of castes is largely the product of Brāhmaṇical conception of *varṇas* and related notions of purity and pollution. The concept, appearing in early Dharmasūtra literature, suggests that certain castes emerged from miscegenation among the members of the four *varṇas*. Such castes were perceived to be products of *anuloma* (hypergamous) and *pratiloma* (hypogamous) unions. Though neither of the two forms found favour with the law-givers, *anuloma* marriages (where the status of woman was lower than that of man and therefore less violative of notions of hierarchy), despite reservations, are not entirely disapproved of, while *pratiloma* unions were addressed with prohibition because they were perceived as violative of the sacred law. The progeny of such marriage was placed lower in status than the two parents. The Dharmasūtras go on to dilate on castes which were the result of interbreeding between different *varṇas*.[9]

There are disagreements among the law-givers in matters of details about the so-called mixed castes. Whereas Gautama provides a list of eleven such castes (five *anuloma* and six *pratiloma*), Vasistha mentions six (one *anuloma* and five *pratiloma*). Among the mixed castes only niṣāda in the *anuloma* category and caṇḍāla in the *pratiloma* category are common to all the early Dharmasūtra writers. Beyond this there are differences. While a niṣāda is derived by Baudhayana and Vasistha from a brāhmaṇa male and a śūdra female, Gautama derives him from a brāhmaṇa male and a vaiśya woman. Similarly, the Māgadha, a *pratiloma* caste, according to Gautama, was the progeny of a vaiśya father and kṣatriya mother, but according to Baudhayana of a śūdra father and a vaiśya mother.[10] It needs to be mentioned that in spite of the differences in explaining the origin of particular castes there is no confusion or mixing up in the listing of *anuloma* and *pratiloma* castes. Some kind of concerted effort is visible in this common minimum programme, beyond which the law-givers seem to have exercised their discretion and autonomy in the ascription of origins. Interestingly, Baudhayana derives the kukkuṭa, a *pratiloma* caste, not through the inverse but the natural order of *anuloma* practice, that is, a vaiśya/śūdra male and niṣāda woman. Contradictions such as this bring out the conjectural nature of theorizing and the arbitrariness of the attribution of speculative origins to castes. The concept of *varṇasaṁkara* nonetheless points to the implicit effort to place the different castes at various levels in a hierarchical scale at the top of which stood the brāhmaṇa. Categories like *antya*, its derivatives, and the caṇḍālas indicate that some mixed castes, considered lower than śūdras, suffered segregation.

The formation of agrarian society and the emergence of the idea and practice of untouchability appear to be interrelated developments. In addition to the natural antipathy between expanding agriculturists and forest dwellers, the establishment of peasant society and entrenchment of ideas such as the transmigration of the soul created conditions for fostering a sense of hatred against killing of animals and meat-eating and, flowing from it, their practitioners and allied occupations.[11] The untouchables originated mostly from tribal people who could not complete the transition in lifestyle and ritual behaviour; and were situated on the fringe of advancing rural societies. Though considered impure, paradoxically they were indispensable for the smooth functioning of *varṇa*-based society. The emergence of such categories suited the requirements of the newly emerging state systems in north India. The creation of untouchables seems to have considerably mitigated the disaffection among the wealth producing vaiśya–śūdra communities in the villages, in so far as it enhanced their socio-legal status, and ensured socio-political stability.[12] The *varṇasaṁkara* formulation deprived the *rathakāra* (literally 'chariot-maker') of his favourable later Vedic position by placing him in the list of *anuloma* castes. Similarly, the sūta and māgadha who were bards/charioteers and chroniclers respectively were relegated to the status of *pratiloma* castes. The downward mobility of these groups may, perhaps, be located in the declining fortune of their professions in the changed socio-political situation in the later part of the first millennium BC.

The early law-givers accounted for the origin of a limited number of *jātis*, making the more general point that mixed castes were generated through inter-*varṇa* unions and by the repeated unions of the progeny of mixed unions. The argument has been carried forward in the *Manusmṛti*. It is difficult to conceive of such a major demographic category as the caṇḍālas to be the result of illicit relations between brāhmaṇa women and śūdra men, not to speak of other deprived, numerically substantial, segments said to be born of comparable forbidden unions. However, what this suggests is that the dominant attitudes towards segments of society were implicitly provided a socio-religious justification through the *varṇasaṁkara* construct. The consensus among Dharmasūtra writers on the theory of origin of *jātis* points to their desire to propound an explanation that would accommodate and account for developments on the ground.

Continued manifestation of the concept of the mixing of *varṇas* as an explanatory framework for the origin of castes, occupational, and other groups from the basic four *varṇas* is seen in the *Manusmṛti* and other *smṛti* literature. The idea of *jāti* unfolds elaborately in *smṛti* texts where one encounters expressions such as *jātidharma*. Manu treats the *varṇas* as homogeneous entities and seems to be largely impervious to the question of differentiation within *varṇas* on various considerations, including the processes of fusion and fission.[13] The bounding and explicit ranking of the four *varṇas* was important for the sociological theory of the origin and ranking of mixed castes. Manu produces these numerous, hierarchized castes from different combinations of the four original *varṇas* as well as their progeny.[14] The number of mixed castes presented is over sixty, which includes six *anuloma*, six *pratiloma*, twenty doubly mixed castes, and about two dozen occupations. The desirability of intra-*varṇa* marriages and precedence of men over women is suggested in the use of the seed and field metaphors[15] for men and women. The metaphors are important because, first, they had implications for the status of the progeny, superior seed falling on inferior field is supposed to have produced blemished children and the reverse is met with horror; and is said to have yielded worse. Secondly, the metaphors clearly symbolize a full-blown agrarian economy. A related aspect is the differential access to women by men of different *varṇas* with the scales tilted in favour of the superior *varṇas*. Put differently, the brāhmaṇa could have four wives one from each *varṇa*, while the Śūdra was permitted, within the norms, only one belonging to his *varṇa*. Implied in this arrangement was the interesting possibility of the higher *varṇas* generating more numbers of mixed castes.[16] Similarly, in this scheme the choice of a partner for upper order women was limited because their freedom, it was believed, would have disturbed the purity of caste.

In the background of these general principles which carried forward the ideas of the early Dharmasūtras, the *Manusmṛti* (compiled between the second century BC and second century AD) proceeds to enumerate the numerous mixed castes, ascribing them different positions by trying to define them in terms of their *anuloma* or *pratiloma* origins. What emerges is a formal list derived from different combinations, seeking to explain a complex social reality. Within the permissible *anuloma* framework, children born of wives one degree lower in *varṇa* status were somewhat acceptable as a part of the twice-born,[17] but those born from women separated in status by two or three degrees led to the creation of new groups within the śūdra fold. To elaborate, while the son of a brāhmaṇa male and kṣatriya woman was assigned a *dvija* status, the son of a vaiśya woman by a brāhmaṇa was called ambaṣṭha (associated with healing); and in the case of a śūdra woman the progeny was known as niṣāda (one who subsists by catching fish) or pāraśava.[18] Thus, brāhmaṇa and kṣatriya unions with śūdra women produced degraded occupational *jātis*, signifying the stigma attached to śūdra association. Within the framework of *anuloma* unions further combinations were possible. For example, Ābhīra (a tribal group) was derived from the intermixing of a brāhmaṇa and an ambaṣṭha woman. The text, however, does not go into details of all kinds of possible combinations within the ambit of hypergamous unions. Nevertheless, the acceptability of such marriages is inherent in the unusual statement that by consistently practicing such unions one could secure upward mobility within the seventh generation.[19]

The abhorrent *pratiloma* unions and their progeny are listed at some length. Issues of all such unions are placed at the bottom or beyond the four *varṇa*s. Whereas in the case of *pratiloma* unions between *dvija*s, the *varṇa* status of the parents had some bearing on the social competence of the child, the reverse happened in situations involving a *dvija* and a śūdra, that is, the higher the *varṇa* status of the woman the lower was the progeny placed. In other words, while a brāhmaṇa woman and kṣatriya male's offspring (sūta) was placed higher than a vaiśya male and brāhmaṇa woman's progeny, the śūdra male and brāhmaṇa woman's son (caṇḍāla) was positioned lower than a kṣatriya woman and śūdra man's child (kṣattri).[20] The broad six *pratiloma* categories could produce other loathsome permutations.[21] To elaborate, repeated *varṇasaṁkara* was possible through the union of offsprings of *pratiloma* marriages uniting with women of the core four *varṇa*s or women born of *anuloma* unions. Progeny so born were assigned various low vocations, the practitioners of which can be identified among the untouchables, namely, kārāvara (leather-worker), antyavasāyin (employed in a burial ground), sopāka (follows the caṇḍāla occupation) and paṇḍusopāka (works on cane/bamboos).[22]

In attempting a totalizing perception of society the *Manusmṛti* takes cognizance of numerous groups. There are communities living on the edge of *Āryāvarta* (north India in this case, extending up to the Vindhyas in the south) such as Kambojas, Yavanas, Śakas, and Pahlavas, who are included as fallen (*vrātya*) kṣatriyas; *jātis* associated with crafts and artisanal activities, namely, maitreyaka (rings a bell at dawn), māgadhas (engaged in trade), vaidehakas (in service of women), niṣāda (boatsman), sūta (managing of horses and chariots), āyogava (in carpentry), veṇa (one playing drums), and kārāvara (leather-worker); and ethnic communities such as Āndhras, Cōḍas, Cuñcus, Ābhīras, Licchavis and Mallas, among others.[23] While the Malla, Licchavi, and Draviḍa communities were attributed *vrātya* parentage, the Medas and Āndhras subsisted on the slaughter of wild animals.[24] The discussion on occupation-based *jātis* is not formally meticulous, but there are indications that they emerged from various sources, such as frontier peoples, avocations and autochthonous elements. Those with modest callings were placed higher than those with inferior vocations, the rationale being that the former were perceived to be born from *anuloma* marriages, conforming to male superiority, and the latter from the despised *pratiloma* unions. Thus, numerically more people were segregated. The caṇḍālas and svapākas had to reside outside the village and the kṣattris, ugras, and pukkasas had to dwell in burial grounds, in mountains and in grooves.[25]

A whole range of differentially placed *jātis* are shown to have been born of *varṇasaṁkara*. The whole argument, related to the origin of *jātis*, is remarkably coherent and tidy. It begins with the four hierarchically placed *varṇas* and expands through different permutations and combinations, which are defined as sanctioned or illegitimate unions, with the consequence that ranking imposes itself and hierarchizes the emerging categories, conceptually creating a pyramidal structure in the process. The sheer wholesomeness of the argument and the number of low caste groups that it produces through this systematic scheme raise questions about its efficacy. As S.J. Tambiah rightly observes; 'The rationale of a formula which mixes the basic *varṇa* categories in approved and disapproved ways to produce a classificatory scheme becomes understandable in a hierarchical society which has a steep gradation of statuses.'[26] A related aspect tied to the issue of Brāhmaṇical mode of integration, exemplifying Brāhmaṇical ingenuity, is the visible presence of the brāhmaṇa in various kinds of mixed unions enumerated in the *Manusmṛti*. It is admitted that there was a method in the madness manifest in the apparent laxity on the part of the highest *varṇa*. The brāhmaṇas were not guided by a death wish, but by making themselves a part of the various permutations they were ensuring their dominance[27] insofar as that made them the central reference point and/or placed them at the head of the envisaged pyramidal social structure.

The *varṇasaṁkara* theory incorporated numerous detribalized, ethnic, and occupational groups into the śūdra fold and even beyond it by assigning them imagined pedigrees proportionate to their socio-cultural and vocational competence. The economic advancement and coming of new occupations associated with division of labour and specialization gave rise to the origin of castes from the middle of first millennium BC, especially the post Mauryan centuries onwards. Caste formation was a product of continuous transformation of space and communities through the mutual interaction of many processes of change. Brāhmaṇical ideology accommodated historical reality through the construction of a conceptual device[28] based on fusion. The *varṇasaṁkara* idea was used to explain both the origin of mixed castes and their relation to the four *varṇas*. The very fact of the mention of groups/ communities as mixed castes, notwithstanding the qualities with which they were invested and the context of their occurrence ensured their inclusion in general society.[29] The concept of *varṇasaṁkara* was thus a post-facto rationalization of the origin of *jātis*, simultaneously leaving room for future incorporation, as well as the power and dominance of the 'pure' over the dominated, envisaged to drill into the latter a sense of inferiority by attributing them with impurity. The subordination of numerous occupational orders was achieved by ascribing them a lower status. The idea of purity/pollution was the means of exercising power by distancing 'polluting' castes from the ritually pure and through it siphoning off a significant component of the fruits of their labour. *Jāti* stratification was not detached from the material interests and ideology of the dominant. The strategy of incorporation and relegation structured socio-economic relations to their advantage.

Notwithstanding the generally stringent code of conduct laid down in the text, there is recognition of their being permeable. The flexibility which Manu provides in situations of crises in matters of food and vocation[30] also seems to recognize the possibilities of non-conformity to prescribed and desired norms. This, together with the concept of *varṇasaṁkara* raise questions about the validity of prescriptions as well as the meaning and function of constructs such as *varṇasaṁkara* and *āpaddharma* (*dharma* in times of distress). While focusing on norms there is recognition of the existence of alternatives. *Manusmṛti* seems to create a mutable interface between injunction and social reality on the ground. The idea of *varṇasaṁkara* points to the problems inherent in reconciling śāstric norms with situations which certainly did not conform to them. Like the idea of *kaliyuga* or *āpaddharma* the concept of *varṇasaṁkara* too tried to sustain and perpetuate the ideology of *varṇa*, so indispensable for ruling elites to acquire legitimacy by appearing to and also seen to be appropriating Dharmaśāstric traditions; which were associated with antiquity and prestige. After all, rulers were expected to ensure the preservation of norms, including the implementation of *varṇa-dharma*. Even while recognizing plurality the focus on norms may be seen as a desire to inculcate values which could help in reproducing society in a form that would allow the perpetuation of Brāhmaṇical prescriptions.

Faith in the Brāhmaṇical explanation of the origin of castes through *varṇasaṁkara* cannot answer why the order fractured time and again, and what social forces have altered and modified it over time. The origin of *jātis* and their numerical expansion are related to specific socio-economic contexts. Brāhmaṇic texts, especially Dharmaśāstra literature, provided transregional, totalizing modes of understanding Indian society, which then were projected as real, whereas caste society emanated from heterogeneous foundations and was shaped by political and social processes. Therefore, 'the origins of the caste system should be sought in the material history of India and not in the empyreal recesses of the Hindu mind'.[31] The concept of *varṇasaṁkara* was an afterthought derived from and foisted on familiar social reality, comprising numerous castes.[32] If the spread of iron technology, rise of new crafts, emergence of towns, formation of states, beginnings of trade and the use of metallic money provided the context for the emergence of castes in the mid-first millennium BC, the social dynamism of the post-Mauryan period was rooted in an immense acceleration of these interrelated forces of change. Transformation of spaces and economic growth provided the climate for the movement from tribe to general society and increased differentiation and ranking. The shift across time provides us with the context within which to understand the inconsistencies between the early Dharmasūtras and *Manusmṛti* in their explanation of some of the *varṇasaṁkara* categories. It may also suggest the existence of a not-so-neatly structured society, quite at variance with the prescriptions. The magnitude of social change and the widening geographical horizons of Brāhmaṇical ideology may explain the detailed enumeration of the notion of *varṇasaṁkara* and *āpaddharma*. One is not sure if the inconsistency between the early Dharmasūtras and the *Manusmṛti*[33] can be seen as largely the problem of integrating and placing different castes across north Indian localities in a general scheme. The sweeping and swift socio-economic and cultural changes in the post-Mauryan centuries bearing on opportunities for mobility, social relations and numerical expansion of castes are echoed in contemporary Brāhmaṇical (and non-Brāhmaṇical) literature.[34] The similar social concerns, revolving around ideas such as *āpaddharma*, socio-political pluralism and assimilation, articulated in works such as the *Manusmṛti*, *Śānti Parva* and the *Gītā* can be partly accounted for by their overlapping chronology.[35] Much of the answer for their conspicuous involvement in the aforesaid common issues would perhaps lie in their being seen as Brāhmaṇical ideological responses to the changing times.[36]

The idea functioned as a dominant myth linking power and status. It created and perpetuated the fiction of natural superiority of the Brāhmaṇical vision of society and order, that is, the *varṇāśramadharma* scheme of things, while simultaneously accommodating structural changes such as the visible increase of castes in early Indian society. The concept allowed for incorporation and adjustment while retaining the impression of an inviolable normative order. It facilitated the resolution of the contradiction in theory and practice. Like all myths this one too helped to reconcile the irreconcilable. The point may be elaborated with reference to Medhātithī's reinterpretative commentary on the *Manusmṛti,* situated in ninth century Kashmir. The relative openness concerning certain issues related to *varṇasaṁkara,* women and śūdras, involving modifications of Manu's prescriptions, have been explained in the context of variations over time and space. Societies in early India were surely far more complex than what normative texts would usually suggest.[37] The ability to respond to changing realities, which otherwise would appear threatening, enabled Brāhmaṇical ideology to maintain its dominance over a long period of time.

NOTES

1. Nicholas B. Dirks, *Castes of Mind: Colonialism and the Making of Modern India*, Princeton, Princeton University Press, 2001, p. 13.

2. For a substantial account of both the historiography and history of caste in early India see S. Jaiswal, *Caste: Origin, Function and Dimensions of Change*, New Delhi, Manohar, 1998.

3. See Romila Thapar, *Clan, Caste and Origin Myths in Early India*, New Delhi, Manohar, 1992; B.D. Chattopadhyaya, 'Introduction' in idem., *The Making of Early Medieval India*, New Delhi, Oxford University Press, 1994, and S. Jaiswal, *Caste*, pp. 13–21, 41–7 and Chapter 5. Also see Richard G. Fox, 'Varṇa Schemes and Ideological Integration in Indian Society', *Comparative Studies in Society and History*, vol. 11, no. 1, 1969, pp. 27–45.

4. Several scholars have explored the historical dimensions of the *varṇasaṁkara* concept and their works have provided critical insights into the problem. The names of R.S. Sharma, V. Jha, S.J. Tambiah, and P. Bhattacharyya readily come to mind, and detailed references to their works shall be made later in this chapter.

5. N.B. Dirks, *Castes of Mind*, p. 35.

6. Somadatta, an early seventh-century *sāmanta* of Śaśāṅka in Northern Orissa, for example, states that he followed the Laws of Manu. See his Midnapur plates in S.N. Rajaguru, *Inscriptions of Orissa* (300–700 AD), vol. 1, pt. 2, Berhampur, 1958, pp. 142–3, lines 11–13. Works of a much later date such as the *Jāti Prakāsa* and *Jāti pūraṇas* which carry imprint of the ideas of *Manusmṛti* also bring home the importance of the text. Cited in K.S. Singh, 'Manu and Contemporary Indian Ethnography', in D.N. Jha (ed.), *Society and Ideology in India: Essays in Honour of Professor R.S. Sharma*, New Delhi, Munshiram Manoharlal, 1996, p. 428.

7. For its early manifestation in the Dharmasūtras one may see V. Jha, '*Varnasamkara* in the Dharma Sutras: Theory and Practice', *Journal of the Economic and Social History of the Orient* (*JESHO*), vol. 13, pt iii, 1970, pp. 273–88; also see S.J. Tambiah, 'From Varna to Caste through Mixed Unions', in Jack Goody (ed.), *Character of Kinship*, Cambridge: Cambridge University Press, 1973, pp. 191–229.

8. G. Yamazaki, 'Social Discrimination in Ancient India and its Transition to the Medieval Period', in H. Kotani (ed.), *Caste System, Untouchability and the Depressed*, New Delhi, Manohar, 1997, p. 7. Also see idem, *The Structure of Ancient Indian Society: Theory and Reality of the Varna System*, Tokyo, Toyo Bunko, 2005, chs 7–9.

9. The best examination to date of the problem in the early Dharmasūtras is the study by V. Jha, '*Varṇasaṁkara* in the Dharma Śūtras', pp. 273–88.

10. For details see ibid.

11. See V. Jha, 'Stages in the History of Untouchables', *Indian Historical Review*, vol. 2, no. 1, 1975, pp. 14–31; Irfan Habib, 'Caste in Indian History', in idem., *Caste and Money in Indian History*, Bombay, University of Bombay, 1987, pp. 3–6.

12. Yamazaki, 'Social Discrimination in Ancient India', pp. 11, 16–17. Even in Classical Athens the poor peasant citizens drew solace from the fact that metics and slaves had no nights.

13. For a different perspective on post-Mauryan society see Sibesh Bhattacharya, *Some Aspects of Indian Society—From c. 2nd Century* BC *to c. 4th Century* AD, Calcutta: Firma K.L. Mukhopadhyay, 1978. Also see G. Yamazaki, *The Structure of Ancient Indian Society*.

14. Good discussions of the details are available in the works of R.S. Sharma, Parnasabari Bhattacharyya, among others, but the most lucid exposition of it is found in the contribution of S.J. Tambiah. See Tambiah, 'From Varṇa to Caste through Mixed Unions', pp. 191–229; P. Bhattacharyya, *Conceptualizations in the Manusmṛti*, Delhi, Manohar, 1996, pp. 232–50; R.S. Sharma, *Śūdras in Ancient India*, Delhi, Motilal Banarsidass, 1990 (third edn.), pp. 224–40 and Appendix II, and Sibesh Bhattacharya, ibid., Chapter 6.

15. *Manusmṛti*, X, 69, 71–2. All references to the text are from Georg Bühler's *The Laws of Manu*, (Sacred Books of the East, vol. 25), New Delhi, Motilal Banarsidass, 1988 (rpt) [1886].

16. Tambiah, 'From Varna to Caste through Mixed Unions', p. 198.

17. *Manu*, X, 14 and 28.

18. For the principle assigning varied positions to sons of wives belonging to different *varṇas* see Manu, X, 41, also X, 8.

19. Ibid., X, 64–5. Also see Wendy Doniger with Brian K. Smith, *The Laws of Manu*, New Delhi, Penguin, 1991, p. 243 and notes.

20. Ibid., X, 11–12.

21. Ibid., X, 29–31.

22. Ibid., X, 36–9.

23. Ibid., also see X, 22, 33, 47–8 and K.S. Singh, 'Manu and Contemporary Indian Ethnography', pp. 425–27.

24. *Manu*, X, 22 and 48.

25. Ibid., X, 49–52.

26. Tambiah, 'From Varna to Caste through Mixed Unions', p. 207.

27. Ibid., p. 208.

28. For its capacity to accommodate and change, see B.P. Sahu, 'Brāhmaṇical Ideology, Regional Identities and the Construction of Early India', Presidential Address, Ancient Section, *Punjab History Conference Proceedings*, Patiala, 2001, pp. 12–26; also in *Social Scientist*, vol. 29, nos 7–8, 2001, pp. 2–18.

29. For the larger argument see Richard W. Lariviere, 'Dharmaśāstra, Custom, "Real Law" and "Apocryphal" Smritis', in Bernhard Kolver, Herausgegeben von *et al.* (eds), *The State, the Law, and Administration in Classical India*, Munich: R. Oldenbourg Verlag Munchen, 1997, pp. 97–110.

30. For details of prescribed conduct in times of distress see *Manu*, X, 81–3 ff. Also see Yamazaki, 'Social Discrimination in Ancient India', pp. 5–6, 9.

31. Dipankar Gupta, 'From Varṇa to Jāti: The Indian Caste System, from the Asiatic to the Feudal Mode of Production', in K.L. Sharma (ed.), *Social Inequality in India*, Jaipur, Rawat Publications, 1995, p. 184.

32. It may be mentioned that inter-caste marriages in modern India have not led to the rise of new castes as construed in the *varṇasaṁkara* theory.

33. See P.V. Kane, *History of Dharmaśāstras*, vol. 2, pt. 2, Poona, 1941, Chapter 2.

34. For a vivid account see B.N.S. Yadava, 'Some Aspects of the Changing Order in India During the Śaka-Kushan Age', in B.G. Gafurov *et al.* (eds), 'Central Asia in the Kushan Period', vol. 2, Moscow, 1975, pp. 123–36.

35. The fifth century date suggested by R.S. Sharma for the tenth chapter of *Manusmṛti* does not affect the larger argument here. Sharma, *Śūdras in Ancient India*, Appendix II.

36. For the Purāṇic idea of *Kaliyuga* expressing similar concerns and its contextualization see B.P. Sahu, 'Conception of the Kali Age in Early India: A Regional Perspective', *Trends in Social Science Research*, vol. 4, no. 1, 1997, pp. 27–36.

37. Kumkum Roy, 'Defining the Household: Some Aspects of Prescription and Practice in Early India', *Social Scientist*, nos 248–9, 1994, especially pp. 12–13. Also in Idem, *Power of Gender and Gender of Power*, New Delhi, Oxford University Press, 2010.

2

Conception of the Kali Age in Early India

Perspectives from the Regions*

The idea of the Kali Age entered the domain of serious historical discussions on early India from the late 1970s and after, largely as an explanatory category for change from antiquity to the early medieval times. The earliest versions of the Kali Age appearing in the *Mahābhārata* and the *purāṇas* have been perceived as being symptomatic of an all pervasive social and political crisis in the pre-Gupta, particularly post-Kuṣāṇa and Sātavāhana, period.[1] The associated descriptive details[2] such as the disturbance in the system of four-fold *varṇa*s (*cāturvarṇya*), as evidenced by the upward mobility of the śūdras, insubordination of women, spreading influence of the 'heretical' sects, and precedence of wealth or economic competence over ritual status, among others, resulting in the ideal brāhmaṇical socio-political order being turned upside down, have been construed to suggest *varṇa*/class tensions, degradation and decadence of the early historical society, even a crisis in production relations; which was perhaps not unrelated to changes in the mode of production.[3] Thus, within the framework of the dominant historiography the Kali Age crisis theory is adduced to explain the phenomenon of land-grants as well as the transition from the early historical to the early medieval times, in terms of the intensification of internal contradictions within the earlier society, especially in northern India. However, notwithstanding his preference for the *Kaliyuga* crisis theory as the explanatory framework for the movement towards the early medieval, D.N. Jha has expressed some reservations against its uncritical

*Originally published in *Trends in Social Science Research*, vol. 4, no. 1, 1997, pp. 27–36. This is an extensively revised version.

acceptance and argued for a rigorous examination of the literary evidence.[4] The three sets of the Kali Age descriptions in early India corresponding to the third-fourth, eighth, and tenth centuries, their repetitive nature and the conspicuous absence of evidence in the early epic and purāṇic passages for *Kalivarjyas* (practices forbidden in the Kali Age) are seen as problems which need to be recognized and addressed. More recently B.D. Chattopadhyaya has provided a detailed critique of the thesis and pointed out some of the inherent incongruities in it as an explanatory category.[5] It is argued that the historical roots of the envisaged crisis are far from clear, and that the construct deriving itself from the Brāhmaṇical perceptions of the evils of the Kali Age (a part of the early Indian schema of cosmic periodization) moves on to curiously correlate such perceptions with actual historical changes; not to speak of the anomalous situation arising out of the assumed correspondences between the real, operational and the normative, Brāhmaṇical social order.[6]

Both in the construction of the Kali Age crisis theory, as also the reservations against it, two interrelated aspects seem to have been neglected; if not entirely untouched. There is a need to cross-check and find corroboration for the literary accounts/images in the other contemporary sources such as the inscriptions, and more importantly to examine the problem in the context of the perspectives from the regions. It is necessary to do so because the crisis in the northern heartland is said to have been resolved by land-grants in the peripheral regions.[7]

On the question of the regional dimension of the crisis R.S. Sharma and B.N.S. Yadava appear to have slightly different views. While Sharma observes that 'the general descriptions of the Kali in the texts do point to a state of deep social crisis, possibly in the areas less indoctrinated with the Brāhmaṇical values and teachings', alluding perhaps to the outlying regions, Yadava, adopting a somewhat more cautious tone, posits that 'the tendencies and phenomena noticed above could not have emerged to the same degree everywhere ... The study of the details including the regional and chronological variations, and also of the exceptions, in this regard, still remains a desideratum.'[8] While Jha puts forth that 'the Kali explanation of the transition ... should apparently be applicable only to the heartland of the country and to the areas where Brāhmaṇical order was well established enough to generate a social crisis', all the epigraphic material he adduces as corroborative evidence for the Kali crisis, come from peninsular India.[9] Taking the clues from these above-stated positions of the authors as well as adherents of the *Kaliyuga* crisis theory we intend to look at the problem afresh from the perspective of the regions, and are not overtly concerned here with the debate surrounding the idea of Indian feudalism in the context of northern India. Problematizing the issue may help us to understand it better and see if other alternative interpretations are possible.

There are repeated references to the removal of the stains of the Kali in the inscriptional records of the various ruling lineages at the locality and/or sub-regional levels, in the disparate regions, in early Orissa. Sāmantavarman (Gaṅgā era 64/mid-sixth century AD) of the Early Eastern Gaṅgā family in south-eastern Orissa claimed to have removed the stains of the Kali age by worshipping Gokarṇeśvara (Śiva) at the top of the Mahendra mountain.[10] His successors too make similar statements, up to about AD 900, about providing freedom from the stains of Kali through their worship of Gokarṇasvāmin.[11] The removal of the evils of the Kali is attested in the Jayrampur plates of Achyuta, the *mahāsāmanta* of Gopacandra of Bengal (sixth/seventh century), in northern coastal Orissa.[12] The Midnapore plates of Somadatta (early seventh century) eulogize the overlord Śaśāṅka for being possessed of virtues and dispelling the mass of darkness of the Kali Age. The Patiakella plate of Śivarāja of the same period, in Cuttack district, informs that the sins of the Kali could not approach him because of his virtues and the blessings of God. The Puri plates of the Śailodbhava ruler Mādhavavarman (seventh century) credit him with the removal of the stains of the Kali Age. The Hindol plates of Śubhākara II of the Bhaumakara dynasty indicate that the king provided freedom from the evils of the Kali. His Dharakote plates corroborate the same.[13] The records of Daṇḍi Mahādevī and Dharma Mahādevī of the same family describe them as supporters of virtue against the vices of the Kali.[14] The Bhaumakara charters have been obtained largely from central coastal Orissa and its hinterland in the present-day Dhenkanal district. They belong to the eighth–ninth centuries. Almost during the same period the records of the Bhañjas of Khiñjali *maṇḍala* in central Orissa describe them as removers of or as being unaffected by the stains of the Kali (*nirduta-kali-kaluṣaḥ*).[15] Interestingly, the Nandobhava capital Jayapurakotta, in the Dhenkanal area, is said to have been free from the vices of the Kali. Other records of this dynasty dated around the ninth–

early-tenth centuries describe it as a city resounding with the sound of brāhmaṇas reciting the Vedas.[16] The juxtaposition of Vedic-śāstric ideas and the Kali and its vices makes the general point about the coming of a new order into existence.

The frequent references to the Kali in the inscriptions seem to fall into disuse and mostly go out of circulation from around the middle of the tenth century,[17] coinciding in some measure with the consolidation of the Śomavaṁśī rule and the first efforts towards the creation of a regional polity.[18] The coincidence on closer scrutiny does not appear to have been accidental. By the turn of the millennium multiple, simultaneous, and interdependent socio-economic, cultural, and political processes, unleashed much earlier, were coming into their own and reaching some kind of a new equilibrium; and flowing from it the regional cultural/historical personality was beginning to be shaped.[19] The convergence of multiple societal processes of change, including the intensification of the temple building activities as a part of the strategies of legitimation, at a stage anticipating the making of a regional personality seem to have obviated the need for the continued use of such metaphors of substance as the Kali Age.

The references to the Kali are usually juxtaposed with the virtue and purity of the king, which helped him to confront and obliterate the evil consequences of the said age. On several occasions he is shown to be worshipping or as being close to some deity or the other which helped him to address the problem and accomplish the meritorious act. Significantly, many of the rulers are simultaneously presented as vanquishers of the Kali as well as patrons of Vedic sacrifices such as the *Aśvamedha* and *Vājapeya*, promoters of *varṇāśramadharma,* virtue, righteousness, and *dharma.* Some of them adopted epithets like *paramabrāhmaṇa* and many projected themselves in the image of epic heroes such as Hanūmān, Yudhiṣṭhira, Arjuna, Bhīma, and the other Pāṇḍavas in general, among others.[20] The imagery of the Kali thus has to be understood not in isolation but in relation to the other carefully constructed courtly images of kingship and ideology.

The idiom and symbolism of the Kali Age needs to be contextualized in time and space. The history of early medieval Orissa (*c.* fourth–eleventh centuries) is the history of continuous state formation and agrarian expansion (leading to the formation of a regional agrarian base and political structure), which were interrelated and simultaneous processes, in the disparate sub-regions. While the coastal tracts experienced these developments earlier in course of the fourth–seventh centuries, similar processes manifested themselves chronologically at a later time (particularly, the seventh–tenth centuries) in the dispersed, variegated pockets of the hinterland in central and western Orissa, especially the mountainous terrain inhabited by the tribes. Thus, the notion of the Kali along with the other imageries, which provide significant insights into the contemporary structure of legitimation, were invoked at different points of time in varied spatial contexts to facilitate and signify the transition from pre-state environment to a new kind of socio-political order. The phased unfolding of the historical processes of change in the dispersed sub-regions explains the continued occurrence of the construct of the Kali Age almost up to the end of the first millennium.[21]

Some of the Vākāṭaka inscriptions in the Deccan and central India provide interesting evidence which have a bearing on the problem under discussion. Many of the land grant charters of Pravarasena II (*c.* 420–52), such as the Jamb grant, Belora grant, Chammak plates, Siwani grant, Wadgaon plates, Pattan plates, and Pandhurna grant, suggest that he established the *Kṛtayuga*[22] largely owing to the grace of Śambhu (Śiva). The information contained in these records and their geographical distribution provides certain significant insights. In the purāṇic conception of successive ages and the notion of cyclical change[23] the Kali and Kṛta ages are sharply contrasted, one is represented as the anti-thesis of the other. Therefore, whether a ruler asserted that he destroyed the sins of the Kali or founded the Kṛta Age, he was indicating one and the same thing, that is, the establishment and preservation of an order sanctified by and in keeping with the ideal Brāhmaṇical prescriptions. In other words, what was envisaged to be socially and politically correct and/or desirable in the Brāhmaṇical scheme of things is said to have been fostered and upheld. Besides, more significantly the above mentioned donative records bearing these crucial passages generally come from different areas in the region of Vidarbha, a region which under the Vākāṭakas was undergoing spatial transformation; opening up to new settlements and experiencing the extension of state society or local state formation.[24] References to the *Kṛtayuga*, together with the performance of Vedic sacrifices such as *Agniṣṭoma*, *Aśvamedha*, and *Vājapeya*, among others, and associated aspects of the image(s) of kingship in such a situation would reflect societal changes within the framework of Brāhmaṇical ideology, and the rulers' need to reckon with the compulsions of legitimation in the face of the overall changing cultural milieu.[25] The structure of legitimation reflects on both the cultural basis of power as well as the popular cultural domain.[26] The details in the Nasik inscription suggesting that Gautamīputra Sātakarṇi prevented the contamination of the four *varṇas*, was an *ekabrāhmaṇa*, and comparisons with the heroes in the epics, in the larger context of the detailed construction of his attributes and achievements,[27] point to the changing cultural context in the Deccan under the Sātavāhanas. It also demonstrates the ways in which temporal power was trying to reach out to the temporal domain, and the gradual importance that was being acquired by Brāhmaṇical ideology in the making of the strategies of domination.

Epigraphical material from south India too contains references to the Kali Age. However, for a sober assessment of the evidence it is necessary to examine them with reference to the context. The Kadamba king Śāntivarman (*c.* 455–70) is credited with helping brāhmaṇas in the Kali Age.[28] The purpose in this case may have been to add colour to the portrait of royalty almost in the same way as, for example, the idea of the Kali was resented in the Talagunda pillar inscription of Kākusthavarman to introduce the element of drama in explaining the rise of the Kadambas, beginning with Mayūraśarman (and not to use it to denote the sense of a crisis).[29] Some of the Pallava inscriptions of the sixth-eighth centuries depict them as rescuers of *dharma* from the evil consequences of the Kali age.[30] The expression *Kaliyuga-doṣ-āvasanna-dharm-odharaṇa nitya-sannaddha* or its variants, where the term *avasanna* has been replaced by the word *apahṛta*, occur in conjunction with the other kinds of assertions being made by royalty; such as the many victories they won in the battle field and the performance of various Vedic sacrifices, or their claims to be *paramabrāhmaṇa*, and so on. These notices continue in the early Pāṇḍyan inscriptions too. The Velvikkuti plates call the Kalabhra ruler *Kali-araśan*,[31] but viewed in its entirety it seems that the motive was to highlight the achievements, prowess and virtuous deeds of the *Pāṇḍyādhirāja* Kaduṅgōn by contrasting him with the former. The Vaigai bed record of Cēntan Arikēsari (seventh century) claims that the king surmounted Kali through the *mahādānas*.[32] It may be noted that the Kali was despised, condemned and associated with evil, and the ways of keeping it at bay were through the mediation of sacrifices, *mahādānas*, and comparable acts. However, the relevant verses in the donative records in no way provide an apocalyptic vision, but instead reveal how the ascendant socio-political order, within the Brāhmaṇical ideological framework, with its right side up, was being best sustained.

The Kadamba, Pallava, and Pāṇḍya territories were experiencing local state formation, agrarian expansion, and the movement towards complex society in the post-Saṅgam setting, particularly in course of the fifth–eighth centuries. To put it differently these spatial segments had no prior experience of organized state society and entrenched Brāhmaṇical culture. Therefore, any explanation with reference to the Kaliyuga crisis theory, envisaging that the production relations embodied in the *varṇa* system were disturbed and undermined, on the face of it seems untenable. Scholars have not been able to satisfactorily address and account for the passage to early medievalism, which is usually equated with feudalism, in south India.[33] The early history of the region does not anticipate any aforesaid kind of crisis and it is important to note that the developments in the first half of the first millennium in south India do not seem to have been identical with those in contemporary north India.[34] Taken in their totality the occurrence of references to the Kali in the inscriptions of the various regions in peninsular India in some sense appears to be conventional and repetitive. Kingship was being continuously contrasted with the Kali and its attributes. They need not necessarily be seen as pointers to a crisis. It seems that the claims of the rulers to have defended *dharma* as against the *doṣa* of *Kaliyuga* or ushered in Kṛta indicates that their ideal was to patronize and promote Brāhmaṇical institutions and ideology, in the larger context of internal transformation and the evolution of political society.[35] Thus, it may be inferred that it is the pronouncement and affirmation of the ideological aspirations of the dominant that we get to know from the inscriptional records. Royalty desired to be projected and seen as promoters of *varṇāśramadharma.* In a situation of continued manifestation of local state formation over diverse spaces the phenomenon of land-grants and such ideas make eminent sense.[36]

The language and mode of discourse in matters of the Kali were so conceived as to distance the ruler from a certain stereotype that was visualized to be diametrically opposite to *dharma* or order and constituted the negation of the Brāhmanic tradition; with its belief system, ritual practices, notion of purity and pollution, hierarchically structured *varṇa/jāti* system and gender relations. This sharply, built-in contrast between the *Kaliyuga* and all that the king stood for would have gone a long way in enhancing his cultural/*dharmic* image. The interrelatedness between such cultural signifiers and other contemporary phenomena as the land-grants and state formation is obvious. What is not obvious, however, is the envisaged relationship between land-grants in the peripheral regions and the dissolution of the systemic crisis in Gangetic northern India. State formation in the outlying regions was largely the consequence of change coming from within local societies. It does not appear to have derived itself from the fragmentation of an erstwhile ubiquitous, centralized political structure.[37] Then, flowing from it, it seems to be even more difficult to work out the alleged relationship between the Kali crisis, land-grants to brāhmaṇas, religious establishments and shrines in the regions outside the heartland and the emergence of the *sāmanta*/feudatory system. The continuous process of local state formation and the enormous extension of the frontiers of state society across regions explain the structure of polity and legitimation in early medieval India.[38] What, however, still remain to be answered are how did cultural motifs such as Kaliyuga reach out to the variegated outlying regions, what did it signify in the beginning, and in what ways were the new cultural forms internalized?

The accounts of the Kali Age in the *purāṇa*s and the *Mahābhārata* have been perceived to represent a crisis in north India in the early centuries of the Common Era. The postulation of a crisis may not be unreasonable but one needs to ask what kind of a crisis was it? A survey of the times reveals that it was a period characterized by the peak of early historical urbanization, agricultural growth, improvement in iron and agricultural tools and technology in general, use of metallic money, and long-distance and maritime trade. The said centuries witnessed the growth and prosperity of varieties of guilds, huge patronage of art activities, including Sanchi Bharhut, Amaravati, Karle, Bhaja, and Mathura. In a nutshell, it was a period of immense dynamism, material progress and significant social changes, including the growth and spread of theistic/'heretical' sects. The frontiers of civilization were expanding swiftly and early Brāhmaṇical normative traditions in the course of their consolidation were responding to the changing milieu. B.N.S. Yadava in an important paper on the changing order during the Śaka-Kuṣāṇa times puts together aspects of these developments, focusing on change and their relationship with the later centuries.[39] Interestingly, here the idea of crisis is significantly underplayed. The *Manusmṛti* despite its conservative character recognizes the pluralism of the times and urges the king to recognize the coexistence of diverse traditions and customs.[40] The *Gītā* too besides emphasizing selfless action and personalized theism focuses on integration and assimilation in an essentially pluralistic situation.[41] Thus, contemporary literature, in various ways, suggests the extent, depth and intensity of the changes. In this context, the question whether it was a period of crisis or societal change naturally imposes itself on us. The historical foundations of the crisis are none too clear and it seems difficult to even associate the idea of the *Kaliyuga* with that of decadence, either in the case of north India or the regions beyond it.

Overemphasis on aspects of trade, money, manufactures, and urbanization to the relative exclusion of the agrarian world in the post-Mauryan phase has created the impression of a general decline/break around the late third and early fourth centuries, largely owing to the decline of the Roman empire and the shrinkage of westerly trade and towns, which then conveniently ties up with the Kali Age crisis theory. While the explanation of the transition to feudalism/early medievalism in terms of the collapse of long distance and overseas trade, which is in some ways linked to the paucity of metallic money and urban decay, has been criticized for not being sufficiently responsive to the built-in potential for change in Indian society,[42] the Kali argument which can not be faulted on similar grounds has other kinds of problems. Recently the origins of early medieval India have been alternatively explained with reference to the many simultaneous processes of change such as local state formation and the extension of state society, agrarian expansion and peasantization of the tribes, leading to caste formation, and cultic integration.[43]

Early Indian literature, among other things, represents contemporary notions of power. We have to read our evidence in the context of the larger cultural values so as to grasp the full meaning of their occurrence as a part of the cultural discourse. In traditional Indian political thought there was an obsession with order and stability (which the state/king was identified with) and there was a corresponding fear of chaos,[44] which was defined in terms of *arājaka* as well as the Kali. The sweeping changes during the post Mauryan centuries opened up possibilities and opportunities, leading to greater social mobility; and avenues for worldly competence to contest ritual status ascribed by birth. The ruling elite surely could not have remained entirely impervious to these transformative processes and their implications. The state of Brāhmaṇism was insecure owing to the fear of *varṇa*/caste, class and gender relations being disturbed and the challenge posed by the new theistic religions. It may be pertinent to quote a passage from the *Viṣṇu Purāṇa* which describes the full manifestation of Kali (*Kalivṛddhi*) as follows:

> Whenever there is noticed an increase (in the number) of the heretics, then, Oh Maitreya, should the full swing of Kali be estimated by the wise. Whenever there is a decrease in the number of the good who follow the path of the Vedas, and the efforts of those who cultivate Dharma relax, then, Maitreya, the predominance of Kali should be guessed by the learned. Whenever Puruṣōttama, the God of sacrifices, becomes no longer the object of these (sacrifices), then the force of Kali should be understood. When the people do not show respect to the sayings of the Vedas but are inclined towards the heretics, then, Oh best of the twice-born the augmented influence of the Kali age should be inferred.[45]

There was, it appears, a crisis of confidence. It is quite possible that their fears, apprehensions, even opposition to the scale of changes found expression in apocalyptic ideas such as the Kali. Further, it may not be unlikely that the fear of convulsion, upheaval, and anarchy was to an extent played upon by the traditional elite as a strategy to enforce obedience, in their anxiety to defend the *status quo* and entrenched power relations. Finally, the myth like so many other Brāhmaṇic inventions, *varṇasaṁkara*, and *āpaddharma*, for example, would have perhaps also helped at a certain level to bridge the gap between theory and practice. The idea of the Kali Age broadly seems to be related to some kind of perception of threat to the established order, where the element of exaggeration cannot be discounted. In this sense, hereafter it became a recurrent theme all through Indian history, continuing up to the present times.[46]

The question how did the cultural traditions of the Gangetic plains, including the construct of the Kali, spread to the regions still remains to be answered. The network of linkages in early medieval India was sustained and mediated through brāhmaṇic settlements, temples, *tīrthas*, *vihāras* and *maṭhas*, among others,[47] which were themselves in a regional context largely the product of local state formation, proliferation of ruling houses, the evolving structure of polities in the Gupta and post-Gupta centuries, and the contemporary requirements for validation. These institutions helped the dissemination of Vedic-śāstric-purāṇic ideas, provided connectivity across regions, and contributed towards the making of an overarching cultural/value system, which held together the comparable regional socio-political structures in early medieval India. Nevertheless, it did not lead to the creation of homogeneous cultural spaces; but spaces which interacted, overlapped or even intersected. The idea or the metaphor of the *Kaliyuga*, thus, like many other such symbols, imageries, and idioms,[48] was a product of the times and it beautifully encapsulates the contemporary historical processes of change in the regions.

Notes

1. B.N.S. Yadava, 'The Accounts of the Kali Age and the Social Transition from Antiquity to the Middle Ages', *The Indian Historical Review* (hereafter *IHR*), vol. V, nos 1–2, 1979, pp. 31–63; R.S. Sharma, 'The Kali Age: A Period of Social Crisis', in S.N. Mukherjee (ed.), *India: History and Thought (Essays in Honour of A.L. Basham),* Calcutta, Subarnarekha, 1982, pp. 186–203.

2. R.C. Hazra provides an early account of the details of the Kali Age in his work first published in 1940 from Dacca. Idem., *Studies in the Purāṇic Records of Hindu Rites and Customs*, Delhi, Motilal Banarsidass, 1975 (2nd Edn.).

3. R.S. Sharma, 'How Feudal was Indian Feudalism?', *Social Scientist*, vol. 12, no. 2, 1984, especially pp. 31–2.

4. D.N. Jha, 'Early Indian Feudal Formation: The State of the Art', *Social Science Probings* (hereafter *SSP),* vol. 3, no. 3, 1986, particularly pp. 298–9.

5. B.D. Chattopadhyaya, 'Political Processes and the Structure of Polity in Early Medieval India: Problems of Perspective', Presidential Address, Ancient India section, *Proceedings of the Indian History Congress* (hereafter *PIHC*), Burdwan session, 1983, p. 52, n.29; idem. *The Making of Early Medieval India*, New Delhi, Oxford University Press, 1994, pp. 13–14, n. 29; and idem., 'State and Economy in North India: Fourth Century to Twelfth Century', in Romila Thapar (ed.), *Recent Perspectives of Early Indian History*, Bombay, Popular Prakashan, 1995, pp. 329–32.

6. Neither can the optative character of the Brāhmaṇical sources nor the alternative perspective of society presented in Buddhist literature and inscriptions be brushed aside. Besides, even within the Brāhmaṇical framework the compulsions behind such ideas as *varṇasaṁkara* and its historical role in assimilating people of diverse origins into the *Varṇa* fold can not be missed. See V.N. Jha, '*Varṇasaṁkara*

in the Dharma Sūtras: Theory and Practice', *Journal of Economic and Social History of the Orient*, vol. 13, pt III, 1970, pp. 273–88.

7. D.N. Jha, 'Early Indian Feudal Formation', pp. 299–300; idem., 'Early Indian Feudalism: A Historiographical Critique', Presidential Address, Ancient India section, *PIHC*, Waltair session, 1979, especially pp. 21–2. The logic behind the argument that the land-grants were made in the peripheral regions for the resolution of the crisis in the heartland is neither demonstrable nor clear.

8. R.S. Sharma, 'The Kali Age', p. 198; Yadava, 'The Accounts of the Kali Age', p. 61. In fact, Sharma extends the idea into the Sātavāhana territories as well. Idem., General President's Address, *Proceedings of the Andhra Pradesh History Congress*, XIV session, particularly pp. 6–7.

9. D.N. Jha, 'Early Indian Feudal Formation', p. 299 and n.25.

10. S.N. Rajaguru, *Inscriptions of Orissa (c. 600–1100 AD)*, vol. 2, Bhubaneswar, 1960, lines 4–5, p. 10.

11. Ibid., lines 2–3, p. 35.

12. Rajaguru, 'Jayarampur Plates of the Time of Gopacalndra', *Orissa Historical Research Journal*, vol. XI, no. 4, pp. 206–29.

For inscriptions from coastal Orissa, up to and including the Śailodbhavas, see Rajaguru, *Inscriptions of Orissa (300–700 AD)*, vol. 1, pt 2, Berhampur, 1958.

13. B. Misra, 'Hindol Plates of Śubhākaradeva', *Journal of Bihar and Orissa Research Society*, vol. XVI, no. 1, 1930, lines 9–14, pp. 77–8; and idem., *Orissa Under the Bhauma Kings*, Calcutta, 1934, pp. 21–2.

14. See for example, the 'Ganjam plates of Daṇḍī Mahādevi and the Taltali plates of Dharma Mahādevi', in Snigdha Tripathy, *Inscriptions of Orissa (Inscriptions of Bhauma-Karas)*, Delhi, Gyan Books, 2000.

15. S. Tripathy, *Inscriptions of Orissa*, vol. VI, Bhubaneswar, 1974, line 8, p. 145; line 12, p. 151; line 10, p. 157, etc.

16. K.C. Panigrahi, 'Baripada Museum Plates of Devānandadeva', *Epigraphia India* (*EI*), vol. XXIX, 1951–2, line 1, p. 78; and D.C. Sircar, 'Dasapalla Plates of Devānandadeva', *EI*, vol. XXIX, lines 2–3, p. 187.

17. References to the Kali continue to occur but the context changes. A noble lady of Gaṅgā lineage is for example represented as Kaliyuga Sarasvati. See *South Indian Inscriptions* (hereafter *SII*), VI, no. 1180. The hectic temple building activities from around the same period suggesting a possible shift in the form of legitimation may have had something to do with it. See H. Kulke, 'Royal Temple Policy and the Structure of Medieval Hindu Kingdoms', in his *Kings and Cults: State Formation and Legitimation in India and Southeast Asia*, New Delhi, Manohar, 1993, especially pp. 13–16.

18. Kulke, 'Early State Formation and Legitimation in Late Ancient Orissa', in M.N. Das (ed.), *Sidelights on History and Culture of Orissa*, Cuttack, Vidyapuri, 1977, particularly pp. 11–12.

19. B.P. Sahu, 'The Past as a Mirror of the Present: The Case of Oriya Society', *SSP*, vol. IX, nos 1–4, 1995, pp. 8–23; idem., Agrarian Changes and the Peasantry in Early Medieval Orissa (*c.* AD 400–1100), in V.K. Thakur and A. Aounshuman (eds), *Peasants in Indian History*, Patna, Janaki Prakashan, 1996, pp. 283–311.

20. Such claims relating to the self-images of royalty were made by the rulers of the Śailodbhava and Bhaumakara dynasties and their contemporaries during the seventh–tenth centuries. See, for instance, Banapur plates of Madhyamarāja, Puri plates of Mādhavavarman in Rajaguru, *Inscriptions of Orissa (300–700 AD)*, vol. I, pt. 2; Terundia plates of Śubhākaradeva II in Tripathy, *Inscriptions of Bhauma-Karas*; and Panigrahi, 'Baripada Museum Plates of Devānandadeva'.

21. For a good discussion of the motifs and idioms see Kesavan Veluthat, 'Religious Symbols in Political Legitimation: The Case of Early Medieval South India', *Social Scientist*, vol. 21, nos 1–2, 1993, pp. 23–33. It may be interesting to examine the relationship, if any, between the three sets of Kali descriptions in the *purāṇas* dated to the third–fourth, eighth and tenth centuries and the process of local state formation in the regions outside the Gangetic heartland in the Gupta and post-Gupta centuries, because many of the *purāṇas* do have a regional context.

22. See lines 15–6, p. 12; line 12, p. 19; line 16, p. 24; line 16, p. 30; lines 15–16, p. 55; line 18, p. 60; line 18, p. 66 respectively in V.V. Mirashi, *Corpus Inscriptionum Indicarum*, vol. V, *Inscriptions of the Vākāṭakas*, Ootacamund, Archaeological Survey of India, 1963.

23. It is said that 'cyclical conceptions of time do not, however, necessarily rule out linearity; in this case, there is a linear progression from Satya through Treta and Dwāpar to Kali-yuga. The two can co-exist within the same cognitive system, but generally not on an equal footing....' Sumit Sarkar, 'The Kalki Avatar of Bikrampur: A Village Scandal in Early Twentieth Century Bengal', in Ranajit Guha (ed.), *Subaltern Studies, VI: Writings on South Asian History and Society*, New Delhi, Oxford University Press, 1989, p. 35, n. 118.

24. See K.M. Shrimali, *Agrarian Structure in Central India and the Northern Deccan: A Study in Vākāṭaka Inscriptions*, Delhi, Munshiram Manoharlal, 1987, pp. 22–8, and the maps I to IV; also see H. Kulke, 'Some Thoughts on State and State Formation under the Eastern Vākāṭakas', in Hans Bakker (ed.), *The Vākāṭaka Heritage: Indian Culture at the Crossroads*, Groningen, Egbert Forsten, 2004, pp. 1–9; and Nandini Sinha Kapur, 'State Formation in Vidarbha: The Case of the Eastern Vākāṭakas', *IHR*, vol. 32, no. 2, 2005, pp. 13–34.

25. The claims relating to the performance of various sacrifices and the images of kingship focusing on heroism, righteousness and Yudhiṣṭira like conduct may be seen in the lines which precede the references to the establishment of Kṛtayuga in the inscriptions already mentioned in n. 22. See the early lines in the Indore, Dudia, and Tirodi plates of Pravarasena II. Also see Kulke, 'The Early State and the

Imperial Kingdom: A Processural Model of the State in Early Medieval India', in idem. (ed.), *The State in India, 1000–1700*, New Delhi, 1995, section II.

26. Veluthat, 'Religious Symbols in Political Legitimation'; and B.S. Miller (ed.), *The Powers of Art: Patronage in Indian Culture*, New Delhi, Oxford University Press, 1992.

27. E. Senart, 'The Inscriptions in the Cave at Nasik', *EI*, vol. VIII, 1905–6, no. 8, pp. 60–1.

28. D.C. Sircar, *Select Inscriptions Bearing on Indian History and Civilization: From the Sixth to the Eighteenth Century* AD, vol. I, Calcutta, University of Calcutta, 1965, verse 4, p. 475.

29. F. Kielhorn, 'Talagunda Pillar Inscription of Kakuṣthavarman', *EI*, 1905–6, vol. VIII, no. 5, pp. 32 and 34.

30. For example see Narasaraopet copper plate inscription of Siṃhavarman (sixth century), Vunnaguruvayapalem copper plate inscriptions of Parameśvaravarman (669–70 AD) and the Reyuru grant of Narasiṃhavarman II (700–25 AD), in Sircar *Select Inscriptions*, vol. I, lines 13–15, pp. 470–1; idem., *Select Inscriptions*, vol. II, Delhi, 1983, lines 8–9, p. 606; and lines 8–9, p. 609.

31. N.K. Sāstri, 'The Velvikudi Grant of Nedunjedaiyan: The Third Year of Reign', *EI*, vol. XVII, 1923–4, lines 38–40, p. 300.

32. *EI*, vol. XXXVIII, pt. 1, no. 4, p. 32

33. To have some idea of the problem see Rajan Gurukkal, *The Kerala Temple and Early Medieval Agrarian System*, Sukapuram, Vallathol Vidyapeetham, 1992, pp. 26–9. Compare the text on p. 27 with n. 3 on the same page. Also see Kesavan Veluthat, *The Political Structure of Early Medieval South India*, Delhi, Orient Longman, 1993, pp. 266–7.

34. Gurukkal, 'Towards the Voice of Dissent: The Trajectory of Ideological Transformation in Early South India', *Social Scientist*, nos 236–7, 1993, pp. 2–22; and Veluthat, *The Political Structure of Early Medieval South India*, pp. 12–19. For a recent statement see Kesavan Veluthat, 'Introduction', in idem., *The Early Medieval in South India*, New Delhi, Oxford University Press, 2009.

35. For the significant role played by the brāhmaṇas in these processes of change see Kulke, 'Early State and the Imperial Kingdom', sections II and III.

36. Chattopadhyaya, 'State and Economy in North India', supra n. 5, pp. 332–6.

37. Ibid; idem., 'Political Processes and the Structure of Polity'; and Kulke, 'Fragmentation and Segmentation versus Integration? Reflections on the Concepts of Indian Feudalism and the Segmentary State in Indian History', *Studies in History*, vol. 4, no. 2, 1982, pp. 237–63.

38. Chattopadhyaya, 'Political Processes and the Structure of Polity'; B.P. Sahu, 'The State in Early India: An Overview', *PIHC*, Aligarh session, 1994, especially pp. 94–6; and idem., 'Legitimation, Ideology and the State in Early

India', Presidential Address, Ancient India section, Mysore session, *PIHC*, 2003, pp. 44–76.

39. B.N.S. Yadava, 'Some Aspects of the Changing Order in India during the Śaka-Kuṣāṇ Age', in B.G. Gafurov *et al.* (eds), *Central Asia in the Kuṣāṇ Period*, vol. II, Moscow, 1975, pp. 123–36.

40. *The Laws of Manu*, trans. G. Buhler, Delhi, 1988 (edn), VII, 201–3; VIII, 41 and 46.

41. Ravindra Kumar, 'The Bhagvadgītā: The Text in Historical Context', MPhil dissertation submitted to the Department of History, University of Delhi (unpublished), ch. II.

42. D.N. Jha, 'Early Indian Feudal Formation', pp. 295–6.

43. Chattopadhyaya, 'Introduction', *The Making of Early Medieval India.*

44. Sibesh Bhattacharya, 'Pluralism and Visible Path (*Pratyaksha Mārga*) an Early Indian Idea of Polity', Presidential Address, Ancient India section, Mysore session, *PIHC*, 1993, p. 43.

45. *Vishnu Purāṇa*, VI, I, 44–7; cited in Hazra, *Studies in the Purāṇic Records*, p. 207.

46. The idea has been used several times in the *Harṣacarita*, for example, in juxtaposition to order and prosperity. See *The Harṣa-Carita of Bana*, trans. E.B. Cowell and F.W. Thomas Delhi, 1993 (rpt), ch. III; also Sarkar, 'The Kalki Avatar of Bikrampur', pp. 33–5.

47. A good discussion of the socio-economic and political linkages in early medieval times is available in B.D. Chattopadhyaya, *Aspects of Rural Settlements and Rural Society in Early Medieval India*, Calcutta, 1990.

48. For useful discussions see Veluthat, 'Religious Symbols in Political Legitimation'; idem., *The Political Structure of Early Medieval South India*, ch. 2; B.S. Miller (ed.), *The Powers of Art*; and Sahu, 'Legitimation, Ideology and the State in Early India'.

3

Varṇa, Jāti and the Shaping of Early Oriya Society*

The term caste is of sixteenth century Portuguese origin, while *varṇa* is of much older usage. The expression *jāti*, it is generally agreed, is used to denote the sense of caste or sub-caste. Notwithstanding the fact that ancient texts use the two terms *varṇa* and *jāti* often interchangeably, it is admitted that the latter constituted segmented identities within each *varṇa* largely owing to fission and the integration of tribes with general society.[1] Increasingly *varṇa* is being perceived as the dominant scheme of ideal social order and the *jātis* as the actual operational reality in society. Thus, caste is seen to be central to the reconstruction of the social identities of people and the understanding of Indian civilization. However, in recent years it has been argued that caste in the Indian pre-colonial past was only one among several other equally important markers of identity such as lineage, family, occupation, and sectarian and local affiliations. Besides, it is also said that neither was caste as pervasive as it is believed to be nor was Indian society permanently fixed in an immutable hierarchy.[2] Meanwhile, it has been aptly observed that denying caste hierarchy does not necessarily negate that social order, nor for that matter hierarchy.[3] The issue of social mobility in early India, including the visible rise of region-specific agrarian communities of substance, the emergence of the Kāyasthas and Rajputs as castes in northern India and the Nāthpanthis and Liṅgayats moving on to become castes make the more general point about the Indian social reality being constituted by caste.

*This chapter was first presented as the Professor K.C. Panigrahi Memorial Lecture, organized by the Department of History, Ravenshaw University, Cuttack, 18 May 2011.

From a Brāhmaṇical perspective caste is seen to represent a co-operative, non-competitive, harmonious form of social organization, whereas closer scrutiny has shown that it tries to camouflage economic and political inequities. In the post-Mauryan period the idea of *Varṇasaṁkara* was devised to provide for a post facto rationalization of the spread of castes, largely owing to the spatial expansion of the peasant frontier, the dynamism associated with the non agricultural sector, and the unfolding of patriarchal society. *Manusmṛti*, a totalizing text which tries to bind Indian society of the said times, speaks about communities on the edge of *Āryāvarta* like the Kambojas, Yavanas, and Śakas, occupations and crafts, and ethnic groups such as the Āndhras, Cōḍas, Ābhīras, and Mallas. As one moves into the Gupta and post-Gupta/ early medieval centuries characterized by the integration of chiefly and priestly lineages of tribal background across regions outside Gangetic north India into kṣatriya and brāhmaṇa castes, while the majority of the tribes swelled the ranks of the śūdras, it is usually agreed that the process of caste proliferation came into play.[4] The point could be elaborated with reference to agrarian expansion, the spread of state societies and local state formation, transformation of tribes into peasants and castes, and the appropriation of cults as well as their universalization which were all interrelated, simultaneous processes of change.[5] Nevertheless, the idea of proliferation which means multiplication or fragmentation from a common source has two kinds of problems. First, it has the potential of going back to the ahistorical *varṇasaṁkara* concept to explain post facto the origin of castes,[6] and secondly it can lead to the tacit assumption of the actual movement of people in large numbers to areas beyond north India. In fact, what seems to have happened is that in a situation of the gradual emergence of local and regional societies the evolving social categories came to be perceived with reference to the dominant social schema, which then allowed for varied regional manifestations within the overarching *varṇa* framework. To elaborate, there are potters, weavers, smiths, and carpenters across the modern linguistic states, but they are not necessarily related to each other. Castes and stratified societies have historically evolved across localities and regions, and that they have a regional specificity can be seen even from the Mandal Commission report where the same group is privileged or not privileged depending on the state it belongs to and its structural location. Usually, preliterate societies such as the tribes are outside the ambit of discussions on caste society. However, it needs no emphasis that like the *vana-janapada* continuum there is a tribe-caste continuum. In the background of these issues which have been brought to bear on studies on caste this chapter makes an effort to look at the trajectory of its evolution in the case of early Orissa. The expression early in this case has been used liberally so as to include the period up to and including the imperial Gajapatis. This exercise is essentially based on the study of inscriptions; and admittedly, inscriptions like all texts are not bereft of their share of problems.

It is difficult to be precise about society in Kaliṅga under Aśoka because besides the two sets of Major Rock Edicts at Dhauli and Jaugada and the excavated sites of Sisupalgarh near Bhubaneswar and Jaugada in Ganjam district we do not have any other evidence. The archaeological data indicates the presence of masons, craftsmen, artisans, and traders. Orissa being a natural habitat zone for rice it may be assumed that it could have been the basic cereal. The faunal remains at Jaugada belonged to domestic cattle, buffalo, sheep, goat, pig, dog, and ass.[7] Besides their dietary value some of these species were important sources of non-human labour. That society was anything but homogeneous can be captured from the reference to *avijita anta* in the Jaugada inscription. It suggests the continued manifestation of unconquered autochthons in and around Kaliṅga. It can perhaps be inferred that in the wake of the Nanda-Maurya rule there was a great deal of socio-political flux. Centres of Mauryan interaction would have provided opportunities for the rise of chieftainships, and the local elites with their status enhanced because of the said associations would have now found more meaningful political profiles.[8] The Mahāmeghavāhanas, Khāravela being third in the family, interestingly rose to power around Bhubaneswar and the Mahānadī delta. Again Khāravela's chief queen came from a ruling lineage with three to four generations of history.[9] The expression *Kaliṅga purvaraja nivesitam* in line eleven of the Hāthi-gumphā inscription demonstrates the existence of ruling chiefs prior to the Mahāmeghavāhanas. The use of terms such as *chakravartin, agamahisī, nagara,* and *Bhāratavarsha* in the same record clearly points to the ongoing cultural transactions with North India. The Udayagiri-Khandagiri complex also provide evidence for donations by monks from Dohaḍa and three donations by women. One is by a queen, the second by the wife of a state functionary and the third by Kusama (*pādamulika)*, a mendicant or menial.[10] On their own these pieces of evidence may not mean much. They seem to acquire significance in the light of the copious sculptural representation of women in both private and public spaces. Women's visibility implies the absence of an entrenched Brāhmaṇical society based on *varṇa/* caste ideology and gender hierarchy. Line nine of the Hāthi-gumphā inscription attests brāhmaṇas to be recipients of royal munificence, and flowing from it the existence of brāhmaṇa households. Vedic sacrifices and brāhmaṇas were still not integral to the making of the strategies of domination. Significantly, Kharavela claimed to be a descendant of Rājarṣi Vasu. The basic distinction in an essentially agrarian society seems to have been between the ruling elite and the ruled, and beyond it the differences were not as much structured as in later societies. There is unmistakable evidence for growing technical skill, material prosperity, and cultural networks but beyond it the vagueness that surrounds everyday life and ordinary people is quite striking. One can see depictions of facets of society in contemporary art at Udayagiri-Khandagiri or reconstruct parts of it from the artifacts excavated at Sisupalgarh. But, larger questions related to the structure of society are elusive in the available material.

Land grant documents which begin to surface from the fourth–fifth centuries onwards are the basic source of information on a variety of issues, including society, for the early medieval period. There are seventeen copper plate grants issued by the Māṭhara, Vāsiṣṭha, and Pitṛbhakta lineages who ruled almost simultaneously in parts of modern Ganjam district in Orissa and northern coastal Andhra during the fourth–sixth centuries. The Śailōdbhavas in the north and the Early Eastern Gaṅgās in the south replaced them around the middle of the millennium. The inscriptional data of the early dynasties are replete with information concerning the brāhmaṇas, the beneficiaries of the grants. The branches of Vedic studies they engaged in, their *gotras*, and object of donation are all mentioned. Interestingly, however there is no mention of their immigration at this stage, suggesting perhaps to their local availability. The brāhmaṇas were not internally undifferentiated. Those who received a village were certainly economically more competent than those who got collective grants in a village and had to be co-sharers with other recipients. Again, revenue free *agrahāras* were preferable to the *karasasānas*, howsoever nominal the payment might have been. The Srungavarapukota plates of Anantavarman record the gift of a village to a brāhmaṇa who was already the *bhōgika* of Anantapura-*bhōga*.[11]

Admittedly, one needs to make allowance for the size of the settlements and their varying productivity, but the economic and status disparity within this category can not be ignored. The liberal use of the suffix *varman* by successive rulers is indicative of the spread and popularity of dharmaśāstra ideas, especially the *Manusmṛti*. It prescribes that *sarman, varman, gupta*, and *dāsa* are the suffixes to be used by the brāhmaṇas, kṣatriyas, vaiśyas, and śūdras respectively. In grant after grant a rural category called the *kuṭumbins* have been addressed and informed about the land transactions. This group who usually worked the land with their family labour has been equated with the middle peasants.[12] In addition to the *kuṭumbin* one comes across the section known as *bhōjaka* in some of the records.[13] It has been said that it represents tenants.[14] However, it needs to be mentioned that this category like the *kuṭumbins* are being addressed and intimated about land transactions and happen to immediately follow the said middle peasants in the records. Their context of occurrence would suggest that they were surely better than tenants. The expression *gṛhapatikam* in place of the *kuṭumbins* is mentioned in the Ragolu plates of Śaktivarman,[15] attesting perhaps to the continued or conventional use of the term *gṛhapati*. The manner in which the images of kingship have been captured in the contemporary records tell us something about that society. Śaktivarman of the Māṭhara dynasty is represented as *vasiṣṭhīputra* (son of Vasisthi), whereas Anantaśaktivarman his grandson is seen to have given up on the metronymic appellation in favor of the patronymic imagery which read *bappa-bhaṭṭāraka-pāda-prasād-āvapta-rājya-vibaha* (who obtained the body, kingdom and prosperity through devotion at the feet of the lord the father). Importantly, one of the three lineages called themselves Pitṛbhaktas and in their charters is described as *bappa-bhaṭṭāraka-pāda-bhaktaḥ* (devotee at the feet of his father). In the background of the history of society in the region it appears that together with the spread of monarchy and Brāhmaṇical ideology institutions such as *varṇa*/caste and patriarchy too gradually gained ascendancy.

The early Eastern Gaṅgās of Kaliṅganagara become visible on the political map by the end of the fifth century. They are known from their thirteen land grant records, the last of which takes their story to the middle of the seventh century. They ruled over an area extending from southern Ganjam district to Visakhapatnam district. Mostly brāhmaṇas were the beneficiaries of the grants. There are five collective grants, the donees ranging from two to thirteen. The recipients appear to have come from the neighbourhood and *grāmas* or villages were the object of transfer. The evidence attests to the transfer of certain *halas* of land in a few cases, and the purchase of land by the king in one case (Urlam plates of Hastivarman) for the purpose of donation from *agrahārikas* (peasant proprietors). There is an instance of six *halas* of land with four cottages being constituted into an *agrahāra* and then gifted to the temple of Narayana (Narasimhapalli plates of Hastivarman). The humble cottage dwellers in this case would have served the requirements of the temple. The *kuṭumbins* here too emerge as the addressees in the countryside continuously.

The Sailodbhavas of Kōṅgōda *maṇḍala* ruled the territories around the Chilka lake coterminus with parts of northern Ganjam and parts of Puri district. They are roughly dated between AD 600 and the middle of the eighth century. Thirteen of their sixteen copper plate charters record land transactions. In half a dozen cases a *grāma* was donated, in two instances half a village was transferred and five records bear witness to the gift of some measures of land called *timpiras* to the brāhmaṇas. One is not sure about the kind of influence the brāhmaṇas with a few measures of land would have exercised in a village. When they were numerically tangible they would have facilitated the transmission of śāstric-epic-purāṇic ideas. The Buguda grant of Mādhavavarman refers to the family history of the donee insofar as it records the names of his father and grand father. The Puri plates of Dharmarāja interestingly mention the house of a bronze-smith (*kāṁsakāra*) in the context of the boundary delineation of the donated land. Similarly, the Khurda plates of Madhavarāja mention the transfer of Kumbhāra-*cheda* in Arahanna village to a brāhmaṇa. *Cheda* is usually understood as a part of a settlement, and in this case it seems to have been inhabited by potters (*kumbhāra*). Among the addressees the karaṇas are followed by the brāhmaṇas, who in turn are succeeded by the term *janapadān* (*sakaraṇa-vyvahārin-brāhmaṇa-pūrogādi-vaiśhayika-janapadān*). The karaṇas represent the kāyasthas in this part of the country and here their historical genesis goes back to the seventh–eighth centuries. References to the brāhmaṇas as addressees points to their earlier presence in the territory, and not necessarily their introduction through the instrument of land grants. The term *janapadān* in the context of their occurrence should represent the other inhabitants of the settlement. These records like those of the earlier dynasties also list a range of state functionaries, including the writer, engraver and those who sealed the land grant charters. In comparison to earlier times the list was now longer and titles of substance more numerous. Brāhmaṇical ideology appears to have become quite central to the shaping of the strategies of governance insofar as their inscriptions credit them with the performance of Vedic sacrifices such as *aśvamedha,* and *vājapeya,* compare the rulers with epic heroes and quote benedictory and imprecatory verses from the *Manusmṛti.*[16]

The rise of the Gaṅgās of Śvetaka, who were a collateral branch of the early Eastern Gaṅgās and ruled over northern parts of Ganjam district, coincided with the phasing out of the Sailodbhavas. Their fifteen donative charters carry the story forward in Kaliṅga up to the tenth century. Besides the brāhmaṇas who emerge as the most visible, dominant, but differentiated category in terms of economic competence, as elsewhere and across time; there are some other useful pieces of information that these inscriptions yield. *Janapadān* or the local rural inhabitants are also recorded. In the Kama-Nalinakshapur plates of Jayavarman the northern boundary of the donated area was marked by a *karmakāra-cheda*, and usually the said term is used to denote the iron-smith/artisan.[17] There are some grants pointing to the existence of brāhmaṇa *mahattaras*, the term occurring for the first time in the region of Kaliṅga (Badakhimedi plates of Jayavarman and Bhupendravarma). The emergence of the *mahattaras*, men of substance, suggests increased differentiation in rural society, especially because the *kuṭumbins* continued to be important members of the same society. The *kāṁsakāra* (brazier/bronze-smith) is mentioned in relation to the engraving of the copper-plate charters (Badakhimedi and Bishamgiri plates).

This discussion on Kaliṅga focusing on the trajectory of social evolution in the larger context of continuous state formation and agrarian growth shows how from a situation where society was elusive there was a movement towards complex society characterized by the emergence of ruling houses and substantial agrarian categories as against the ordinary local inhabitants, as well as the gradual unfolding of occupational groups; some of which like the *kumbhāra* and *kāṁsakāra* have continued into the present. It is significant that these changes were happening across spaces and in a phased manner in Kaliṅga largely within the framework of Brāhmaṇical ideology, as can easily be gleaned from the conception of kingship with reference to its adherence to and observance of *dharma* and performance of Vedic sacrifices, while the institution was simultaneously being distanced from the evils of the *Kaliyuga.*[18]

The dissemination of śāstric ideas in north coastal Orissa is discernible in the quotations from Dharmaśāstra verses in the land grant records. A close reading of the Balasore copper plate of Sri Bhanu, Soro plate of Bhanudatta and Soro plate of Somadatta,[19] all located in Balasore district and dated to the seventh century, yields some interesting evidence. In the first two grants the four beneficiaries are the same persons and are all prefixed by the term *mahāmahattara*, while in the third the the donees include Dhruvamitraśvāmin, Arungaśvāmin, who were already mentioned in the earlier grants, and others without reference to any prefix. Whether the expression others (*ādi*) included the two left out donees already mentioned in the previous grants is not clear. Unmistakably, however, these were a group of privileged brāhmaṇas receiving *dāna*s more than once. The use of the prefix *mahāmahattara* in two instances and their absence in one case gives us rare insights into the process of social mobility, most likely related to changing economic competence of the donees. The Asanapat Natarāja image inscription dated around the same period sheds light on the movement of epic-purāṇic ideas into the Keonjhar area. The ruler is said to have studied the *Bhārata, Purāṇa, Itihāsa, Srūti,* grammar, among others.[20] The Ādi Bhañjas emerged on the political scene at the turn of the millennium in Khijjiṅgakoṭṭā *maṇḍala,* comprising parts of Keonjhar and Mayurbhanja districts in northern Orissa and Singhum in Jharkhand. The forest tracts of the region experienced noticeable transition towards complex society during their rule. In addition to the gift of *grāma*s to the immigrant brāhmaṇas, short references to their genealogies, absence of actual boundary delimitations, leaving room for future expansion of the peasant frontier, there is also mention of the weavers, cowherds, brewers and other people (*tantuvāya-gokuṭa-sauṇḍhik-ādikam-prakṛtika*). Notwithstanding the significance of the material attesting to the presence of certain occupational groups it needs to be stated that this is just one lonely case (Adipur plate of Narendrabhañja).[21] Besides the usual officials the other useful occurrences are the town trader/banker (*pūraśreṣṭhi*), scribe (*lekhaka*), and engraver (*khanitaka*).

This brings us to Dakṣiṇa Kośala, comprising the Kalahandi-Bolangir-Sambalpur tract of present day western Orissa and the Bilaspur-Raipur and adjoining localities of Chhattisgarh. Between the sixth and eleventh centuries this area was successively ruled by the Śarabhapurīyas, Pāṇḍuvaṁśīs and the Somavaṁśīs. The brāhmaṇas were familiar with the region from the early centuries of the Common Era. However, they acquired a perceptible presence from around the sixth century AD. Over time they started coming in as recipients of land grants from as far as Rāḍha, Oḍradeśa, Madhyadeśa, and so on. As elsewhere they brought with them the ideas of the calander, agriculture, knowledge of the Vedas, śāstras and *purāṇas* and played their part in agrarian expansion, cultural communication and royal legitimation. The representation of rural society also included the *kuṭumbins, pradhāna-prativāsins,* and *prativāsins.* The later term means inhabitant and by extension *pradhāna-prativāsin* would mean the more important residents. These local notables become visible from the later part of Pāṇḍuvaṁśī rule, particularly the times of Mahasivagupta (Mallar and Bardula plates).[22] Among the professionals the *sūtradhāra* (master craftsman), *suvarṇakāra* (goldsmith), *vaṇik* (trader), *mālākara* (garland maker), *gauḍa* (cowherd/milkman), kāyastha and engraver of records are mentioned in the epigraphs (Gandharesvara temple inscription of Sivagupta and Sonpur plates of Mahasivagupta).[23] The copper plate and stone inscriptions together with the evolving temple architecture, as in Kaliṅga and Khijjiṅgakoṭṭā, provide testimony to the role of the *acharyas,* stone cutters, masons, brick-layers, composers of texts, writers and smiths, among several other occupational groups in practice. The Somavaṁśīs even after their occupation of coastal Orissa in the early part of the tenth century continued to make numerous grants in certain parts of western Orissa; over the next two centuries. A perusal of these records sheds light on the continuation of some of the earlier social categories such as *prativāsin, vaṇik, suvarṇakāra* and kāyastha, while focusing on fresh professionals like *vaidya* (physician), *kālādesin* (astrologer), *vindhāṇi* (engraver), *janapramukha* (important land owners), and *janapadān* (rural populace).[24]

The Khiñjali Bhañjas ruled over a territory called Khiñjali *maṇḍala* which spread from the Baud-Sonepur area to parts of Ganjam district. They ruled from Dhṛtipura and later from Vañjulvaka. This lineage who acknowledged the over lordship of the Bhaumakaras, Somavaṁśīs and perhaps even the imperial Gaṅgās have issued a good number of land grants, which shed light on the problem at hand. Besides the brāhmaṇas the karaṇas are also mentioned in some of the charters.

The relevant expression is *brāhmaṇa-karaṇa-pūrōga-nivasi.* One also comes across references to the *kālādhyasin* (astrologer), *kuṭumbin* and the *janapada nivasi* (rural inhabitants). There are also references to the *vaṇik, suvarṇākāra* and engraver, but the context is important insofar as the *vaṇik-suvarṇākara* is usually presented as the royal engraver too or as the son of the engraver, even at instances as the father of the engraver.[25] We shall soon return to the implications of such occurrences.

The coming of the Bhaumakaras in central coastal Orissa and adjacent territories, popularly known as Tosali, in the middle of the eighth century at the fall of the Śailodbhavas gives us some more evidence for the continued manifestation of occupational groups. There are several records voicing the presence of weavers, cowherds and brewers, and some of the terms used for them with minor modifications have persisted to the present. Sundhi is, for example, used for *śauṇḍika* and Tanti for *tantavāya.* Physicians as a category appear to be gradually emerging as can be seen from the reference to *vaidya* Bhīmata in the Dhauli cave inscription and Gaṇeśagumphā inscription of the time of Santikara.[26] That *vaidyas* were not necessarily brāhmaṇas can be observed from the occupational prefix that is used for them as against *bhaṭṭa* or *svāmī*; generally used for the brāhmaṇas. A large number of their copper plate records mention the average rural subjects as *prakṛtika* or at times as *janapadān.* The well-to-do were known as *pramukha-nivāsin.*[27] The functional groups included the *sutradhāra* (mason), *taṭṭhākara* (brazier), *pedāpāla* (incisor/record keeper), *kavi* (poet), among others.[28] It is interesting that the expression *sva-dharmm-āropita-varṇaśramaḥ* is inscribed in the Neulpur grant of Subhakara, while the Terundia plate of Subhakara II replaces it with *niratisaya-śāstranusāra-pravarṭṭita-kṛitayug-ōchit-asankirnna-varṇāśrama vyavasthā* to convey almost the same intentions. What strikes attention is that around the same time in Dakṣiṇa Kośala Mahasivagupta Balarjuna in his Sirpur inscription was being represented as the protector of the *varṇas* and *āśramas*, as one who prevented the dawn of the *Kali* Age, while simultaneously befriending *Kṛta* Age, as well as the incarnation of *dharma.* The idea was to communicate that royalty stood by and conformed to the *varṇāśrama* order in accordance with the śāstras. The point of inference is that by the late eighth century kingship desired to be perceived as being committed and adhering to the idea of *kṛta yuga*, śāstras, and the *varṇa* order, with its right side up, notwithstanding the patronage of

Buddhism or Buddhist affiliation of the rulers of the different lineages. Comparable tendencies continued under the Somavaṁśīs after their conquest of the Bhaumakara territories in coastal Orissa in the first quarter of the tenth century.

The process of the numerical enlargement of occupational groups is unmistakable during the imperial Gaṅgā-Gajapati times, that is, the twelfth-sixteenth centuries. Their records refer to the *lauhakāra* (blacksmith), *tāmrakāra* (copper-smith), *patakāra* (carpenter), *telikas* (oilmen), *gaṇḍhika* (perfumer), *saṅkhika* (conch-shell dealer), *guḍika* (jaggery dealer), *mālika* (florist), *gopāla* (milkman), *kaivarta* (fisherman), *nāpita* (barber), *rajaka* (washerman), *śilpī* (craftsman), *vaṇika, śreṣḥtin, setti*, and *mahājana*, besides others.[29] The period under consideration was witness to the making of monumental temples and was characterized by enrichment and elaboration in all facets of their activities. The segments of society discussed above largely belonged to the śūdras or were beyond the four *varṇas*. Their association with deities and temples, together with the continuous efforts on the part of the states to integrate the autochthons with mainstream life,[30] had significant bearing on both the structure and nature of Oriya society. Thirty-six professional categories are said to have been deployed to render service in the temples, and the tradition supposedly dates back to the thirteenth century. The institution of Nāyak introduced by the Gaṅgās helps us to understand the emergence of new groups, differentiation within existing ones, and more importantly the process of social mobility within the hierarchical order; insofar as it was constituted by varied social categories, including the brāhmaṇas and kāyasthas.[31] The Sāralā *Mahābhārata* and *Lakṣmi Purāṇa*, belonging to the fifteenth-sixteenth centuries, amply reflect on interrelated aspects of the caste system such as child marriage, *satī*, the suffering of widows, and the segregation of caṇḍālas.

Society in early medieval Orissa is usually perceived through the four-fold *varṇa* framework and not surprisingly there has been a tendency to recreate the Gangetic north Indian model for the region too, which neither appreciates nor does justice to the region-specific social structure.[32] Even today north India has communities assignable to all the four *varṇas*, whereas the same cannot be said about Orissa. As in the other regions of peninsular India[33] in Orissa too a two tiered *varṇa* structure comprising the brāhmaṇas and non-brāhmaṇas evolved. Notwithstanding rare instances of claims to status, for historical reasons the kṣatriya and vaiśya *varṇas* did not take shape in the region. Ruling houses with humble autochthonous origins lost their assumed statuses with the eclipse of power and, even the Khandayats' peasant-cum militia origins would go back to the Gaṅgā-Gajapati times. Realities were the same across peninsular and eastern India. The brāhmaṇa and non-brāhmaṇa *varṇas* were sufficiently differentiated and the social reality was that of a more complex hierarchised structure deriving validation from *varṇa* ideology. Orissa attracted the largest number of brāhmaṇas from outside during the centuries under discussion.[34] Besides the *sāmantas* and *bhōgis* of different grades the brāhmaṇas are the most ubiquitous in the contemporary records. They are seen as a part of the dominant group. It perhaps needs mention that all of them did not share the same competence economically or politically. Some were associated with the royal court in different capacities. Some of them received a full village as donation, while others got half a village or a *palli, pāṭaka*, or *padra*. There are references to plots of land or land measures known variously in the different localities/sub-regions as *hala, timpira, khaṇḍa-kṣetra,* and so on. being donated to the brāhmaṇas. The variations in the quantum of gifts certainly attract attention. The role of the donees with some measures of land in a non-brāhmaṇa settlement or even with a whole village such as an *agrahara* needs rethinking. It is generally agreed that they were important insofar as they disseminated the knowledge of agriculture, invented genealogical linkages for the ruling houses and spread Vedic-śāstric-epic-purāṇic ideas. In doing so they created a subject population averse to questioning authority and in the process promoted the cause of the state.[35] Their places of origin, the Vedic rituals they performed, their *gotras* and related identities could together with their access to or denial of economic and political power influence fission or asymmetrical relations within them. *Varṇa* made immense sense to the brāhmaṇas who were invoked and placed first in the list of local addressees, and in the context of donations are referred to along with their *gotras* and *pravaras*.

Differentially placed diverse peasant and artisanal groups constituted the śūdra/non-brāhmaṇa stratum. *Kuṭumbins* are known from the early records. The *mahattaras* or well-to-do peasant categories and *mahāmahattaras*, men of substance, emerge around the seventh-eighth centuries. Categories like these need to be distinguished from the other inhabitants or lower agrarian order, which are captured through the use of general terms such as *janapadān, prativāsin* and *prakṛtika* in the records of the localities and sub-regions. The *karaṇas* or kāyasthas register their presence from the seventh century onwards in coastal Orissa. In the same zone potters, artisans/iron-smiths (*karmakāras*) and braziers slowly become visible. In Kodalaka *maṇḍala* (Dhenkanal-Angul belt) and Khijjiṅga *maṇḍala* weavers, cowherds, distillers/brewers and fishermen are mentioned along with land donations. Goldsmiths, engravers, and masons too come to light in Dakṣiṇa Kośala around the same period. The patronage extended to temple and *vihāra* building activities in the various *maṇḍalas*, extending well into Dakṣiṇa Kośala, would impose the recognition of several other categories which would have come into play to help in the making of these impressive monumental structures. Hierarchy was natural in a system of social differentiation. With the passage of time occupational groups would have crystallized into *jātis*/castes, with professions becoming hereditary as also endogamous units through imperceptible gradations. However it seems to have been a gradual, continuous evolving process, not necessarily in conformity with the normative Dharmaśāstra prescriptions. Several queens in the Bhaumakara family exercising royal sovereignty, suggesting women taking precedence over male kin in the context of the centrality of the immediate family given the political culture of the times,[36] despite their privileged status, is a case in point. It attracts attention largely because usually royalty would like to be seen and perceived as preserving societal norms. The protracted efforts by royalty to appropriate and internalize kṣatriya rituals of power, including the use of the suffix *varman,* performance of Vedic sacrifices, projecting themselves as the upholders of *dharma* and the concomitant abhorrence for the Kali Age and its evils, appropriation of origin myths, and grand family traditions, not only explains their origins but also tells us a bit about the compulsions of people in power. Kṣatriyaization is seen as change from above so as to strengthen the economic and political basis of the emerging ruling lineages across localities in a situation of the synchronic shaping of a Brāhmaṇic/Hindu socio-cultural milieu to survive.[37] Orissa was not unique in these developments; it happened in Tamilnadu, Raylaseema in Andhra Pradesh, and parts of central India as well.[38] *Varṇa* as ideology and *vaṁśa* and *kula* as identity markers were central to the self-perception of the successive ruling lineages.

The number of occupational and status groups certainly were enlarged during the twelfth–sixteenth centuries as can be seen in the inscriptional records. The emergence of an asymmetrical caste system and the subordination of women are inextricably interrelated phenomena, and that seems to come through in the Oriya *Mahābhārata* of the fifteenth century. That the gradual forging of the caste order in the said period was taking shape can perhaps be seen with the coming of the komaṭis (trading community), leṅkas (army rank) and gollās (herdsmen/pastoralist) from Andhra in the medieval centuries into northern Kaliṅga or present day Gajapati-Ganjam districts and their integration with Oriya society in the making, the emergence of the patras, mahapatras, and pattanayakas from status terms to gradually mean high caste surnames, and the evolution of nāyaks and paikrays from military ranks to represent graded khandayat or peasant-cum-militia castes in central and south coastal Orissa. All these castes continue to be present even today in the said localities. The basic problem confronting the historian is to unveil how or when did the occupational groups acquire qualities like endogamy and commensality or discretely got graded on considerations of ritual purity and pollution and came to be perceived as castes/*jātis*. It may be difficult to discern the stages step by step, but one can intellectually conceive of it to be unfolding in a phased manner in time and space, across the localities and sub-regions.

Peasantization of the tribes, hierarchization of the segments and their organization with reference to the dominant schema of society need to be situated in the wider context of the multiple contemporaneous processes of change, including agrarian expansion and state formation at the locality and sub-regional levels. The spread of temples and popular association with them in matters of rendering services and extending patronage had a bearing on the forging of an asymmetrical society, characterized by antagonistic cooperation. The shaping of caste structures was facilitated and not constrained by the formation of sub-regional or *maṇḍala* identities. After all occupational groups and/or castes had local roots. Variation in terms of the visibility of occupational groups across the sub-regions makes the more general point. For example, while the kāyastha, astrologer and *janapramukha* are discernible in the records of Dakṣiṇa Kośala, karaṇas, and *mahattaras/mahāmahattaras* are more common in Kaliṅga and Tosali. Continuous trans-local interactions and the shaping of regional identity, involving the subsumption of earlier affiliations, under the Somavaṁśīs and beyond (as in the other cultural regions in the sub-continent) also impacted the physiology of the regional caste society insofar as they accommodated influences from the varied sub-regions like Dakṣiṇa Kośala and southern Kaliṅga, among others, in the movement to historically cohere the segmented identities.

Perceiving society through the *varṇa* and/or *jāti* categories is not entirely unproblematic. Pannaka/Panaka is represented as an engraver in one inscription but the Nibinna plates of Mahasivagupta Yayati of the Somavaṁśī lineage show him titled as *thākkura*. Kāyastha Devagana figures as *rupakāra siromaṇi* (the crest jewel among sculptors), who built a Śiva temple at Samba in Chhattisgarh. There is an instance of a *vastavya* as *taṭṭhakāra* (brazier) in the Bhaumakara inscriptions. Again, one comes across Padmanabha, the engraver, who was the son of *vastavya vaṇika* Pandi in the Khiñjali Bhañja records. Similarly, the Rajim stone inscription refers to Jalahastin, a *śilpasalin*, whose son *sādhu* (virtuous) Durgahastin engraved the document.[39] Evidence such as these unmistakably demonstrates that specializations were not rigid, and people could engage in more than one occupation simultaneously, entailing competition and upward social mobility in some cases. Therefore, to simply view the artist within the encompassing category of the śūdra will not help in recognizing the social intricacies, including the fact that social relations were not unalterably fixed.

It emerges from the preceding discussion that neither normative dharmaśāstra literature nor northern Indian parallels can be accepted as paradigms in the reconstruction of Orissa's past. Achieved occupational status rather than ascribed positions mattered in everyday operational situations in society. Society does not appear to have functioned on *Varṇa* lines. There are a few instances of people in periods of economic prosperity such as under the imperial Gaṅgās claiming their assumed vaiśya ranks,[40] and ruling lineages usually asserting their kṣatriya status through invented lunar and solar links or the adoption of other significant symbols and metaphors. The words *kula* and *vaṁśa* reflect the assumed and/or achieved status aspirations of the ruling elite. With the loss of power these categories melted into general society. The term *jāti* is hardly encountered in the inscriptions of the region at least till the early part of the imperial Gaṅgās (twelfth–mid-fifteenth century), suggesting that it was not considered to be an important feature of the identity of a person so as to be recorded in his/her public transactions. Occupations were more meaningful and relevant for use in the public domain. The term nāyaka under the Gaṅgās represented military leaders in Kaliṅga to begin with. Other status terms of the Gaṅgā-Gajapati times like mahapatra, pattanayaka, etc., had much to do with professional affiliations and excellence; pointing to the centrality of occupations in classifying people and not *varṇa* and *jāti*. Caste, as we understand it today, perhaps had not emerged in a well articulated manner among the occupational communities in the region. This is nothing unusual insofar as similar patterns have been obtained for Tamil Nadu under the Cōḷas (AD 850–1279) and Kākatīya Andhra (1175–1325).[41] The process of congealing of castes in neighbouring Bengal and Kerala in the south under the Cēras (AD 800–1100) and beyond also provides a symmetrical trajectory.[42] That said, it needs to be admitted that inscriptions do not necessarily capture society in its entirety. Their purpose being more specific, they can not be expected to dwell on castes. They mostly tell us about those who were important to certain types of transactions, involving land transfers, devolution of privileges, temple committees, or incidentally happened to be there. Even here only the relevant facet of their identity is recorded and not the totality of identities, that is, sectarian, spatial or kin ties. A combined use of inscriptions and vernacular literature for the fifteenth–sixteenth centuries should provide a corrective to tendencies to generalize across cultural regions from the perspective of the dharmaśāstras.

NOTES

1. For different perspectives on the issue see Suvira Jaiswal, *Caste: Origin, Function and Dimensions of Change*, Delhi, Manohar, 1998; Cynthia Talbot, *Precolonial India in Practice: Society, Religion and Identity in Medieval Andhra*, New York, Oxford University Press, 2001, chapter on society; and Upinder Singh, 'Interrogating *Varṇa* and *Jāti* in Ancient and Early Medieval India', Presidential Address, Ancient section, *Panjab History Conference Proceedings*, 40th session, 2008, pp. 11–21. For the fluidity of the *varṇas* in everyday life see G. Yamazaki, *The Structure of Ancient Indian Society: Theory and Reality of the Varṇa System*, Tokyo, Toyo Bunko, 2005.

2. See Nicholas B. Dirks, *Castes of Mind: Colonialism and the Making of Modern India*, Princeton, Princeton University Press, 2001.

3. See B.D. Chattopadhyaya, 'Introduction: One Blind Man's View of an Elephant: Understanding Early Indian Social History', in idem. (ed.), *A Social History of Early India*, History of Science, Philosophy and Culture in Indian Civilization, vol. II, pt. 5, Delhi, Pearson-Longman, 2009, pp. xxxi–l.

4. R.S. Sharma, *Early Medieval Indian Society: A Study in Feudalisation*, New Delhi, Orient Longman, 2001, pp. 186–213.

5. B.D. Chattopadhyaya, 'Introduction', *The Making of Early Medieval India,* Delhi, Oxford University Press, 1994.

6. Chattopadhyaya, 'Introduction: One Blind Man's View'.

7. B.P. Sahu, 'Ancient Orissa: The Dynamics of Internal Transformation of the Tribal Society', in *PIHC,* Annamalai session, 1984, pp. 148–60.

8. S. Seneviratne, 'Kaliṅga and Andhra: The Process of Secondary State Formation in Early India', *Indian Historical Review* (hereafter *IHR*), vol. 7, nos 1–2, 1981, pp. 54–69.

9. R.D. Banerji, *Epigraphia Indica* (hereafter *EI*), XIII, 1915–16, p. 160.

10. B.P. Sahu, 'The Early State in Orissa: From the Perspective of Changing Forms of Patronage and Legitimation', in B. Pati, B.P. Sahu and T.K. Venkatasubramanian (eds), *Negotiating India's Past: Essays in Memory of Partha Sarathi Gupta,* New Delhi, Tulika, 2003, p. 31.

11. For the early dynasties up to and including the Śailodbhavas see S.N. Rajaguru, *Inscriptions of Orissa (300–700 AD)*, vol. I, pt. II, Berhampur, Orissa State Museum, 1958 and Snigdha Tripathy, *Inscriptions of Orissa,* vol. I, Delhi, Motilal Banarsidass, 1997. The inscriptions of the Early Eastern Gaṅgās are available in S.N. Rajaguru, *Inscriptions of Orissa (c. 600–1100 AD),* vol. II, Bhubaneswar, Orissa State Museum, 1960.

12. Ranabir Chakrabarti, '*Kutumbikas* in Early India', in V.K. Thakur and A. Aounshuman (eds), *Peasants in Indian History,* Patna, Janaki Prakashan, pp. 179–98.

13. B.P. Sahu, 'Changing the Gaze: Facets of Sub-regional Agrarian Economies in Early Medieval Orissa', paper presented at the Seminar on Inscriptions and the Agrarian History of India (D.C. Sircar Birth Centenary Seminar), Asiatic Society, Kolkata, 16–17 November 2007.

14. See Rajaguru, *Inscriptions of Orissa*, vol. I, Ragolu and Bobbili plates.

15. Tripathy, *Inscriptions of Orissa*, vol. I.

16. B.P. Sahu, 'Rituals, Royalty and Rajya in Early Medieval Eastern India', in H.Kulke and U. Skoda (eds), *State and Ritual in India,* also in Margo Kitts *et al.* (eds), *State, Power and Violence,* section IV, Wiesbaden, Harrassowitz Verlag, 2010, pp. 675–6.

17. See Rajaguru, *Inscriptions of Orissa*, vol I.

18. A conceptual discussion is available in B.P. Sahu, 'Conception of the Kali Age in Early India: A Regional Perspective', in *Trends in Social Science Research,* vol. 4, no. 1, 1997, pp. 27–36.

19. Tripathy, *Inscriptions of Orissa*, vol. I.

20. Ibid.

21. Snigdha Tripathy, *Inscriptions of Orissa,* vol. VI, Bhubaneswar, Orissa State Museum, 1974.

22. A.M. Shastri, *Inscriptions of the Śarabhapurīyas, Pāṇḍuvaṁśins and Somavaṁśins*, pts I and II, Delhi, Motilal Banarsidass, 1995.

23. Ibid.

24. S.N. Rajaguru, *Inscriptions of Orissa,* vol. IV, Bhubaneswar, Orissa State Museum, 1966, pp. 92, 96, 113, 128, 132, 144, 153, 157, 200, 216, 220, 228, 230, and 238.

25. Tripathy, *Inscriptions of Orissa,* vol. VI, pp. 82, 123, 127, 145, and 216.

26. Snigdha Tripathy, *Inscriptions of Orissa: Inscriptions of Bhauma-Karas*, Delhi, Pratibha Prakashan, 2000, pp. 116 and 118–19.

27. Ibid., p. 180.

28. Ibid., pp. 103, 108, 115, 182, and 207.

29. The Nagari plates of Anangabhima III dated AD 1230 mention the inhabitants of a township which included a number of merchants and artisans such as a perfumer, a worker in conchshells, a silk-weaver, a goldsmith and a brazier. There were also three sellers of betel-leaves, one florist, one maker of sugar, two milkmen, two weavers, two oilmen, two potters and three fishermen. See *Epigraphia Indica* (*EI*), vol. XXVIII, pp. 235 ff.

Also see Shishir K. Panda, *Medieval Orissa: A Socio-Economic Study,* New Delhi, Mittal Publications, 1991, pp. 77–90; H.C. Das, 'Socio-Cultural Life During the Rule of Imperial Gaṅgās', in *Orissa Historical Research Journal* (hereafter *OHRJ*), vol. 27, nos 1–4, 1981; M.P. Dash, 'Some Aspects of the Social Life under the Surya-Gajapati Rule (1435–1540)', *OHRJ,* vol. 27, nos 1–4, 1981; P. Mukherjee, *The History of the Gajapati Kings of Orissa,* Cuttack, 1981 (2nd edn.); and L.K. Mahapatra, 'Gods, Kings and the Caste System in India', in B. Misra and J. Preston (eds), *Community, Self and Identity,* Hague-Paris, 1978.

30. Hermann Kulke, 'Royal Temple Policy and the Structure of Medieval Hindu Kingdoms', in idem., *Kings and Cults: State Formation and Legitimation in India and Southeast Asia,* Delhi, Manohar, 1993, pp. 1–16.

31. See Shishir K. Panda, 'Nayaka System in Medieval Orissa', in K.K. Dasgupta *et al.*, (eds), *Sraddhanjali: Studies in Ancient Indian History,* Delhi, 1988, pp. 92–107.

32. For recent such statements see P.K. Mishra (ed.), *Comprehensive History and Culture of Orissa,* vol. 1, pt.1, New Delhi, Kaveri Books, 1997, pp. 447–74.

33. Suvira Jaiswal, 'Studies in the Social Structure of the Early Tamils', in R.S. Sharma and V. Jha (eds), *Indian Society: Historical Probings,* New Delhi, People's Publishing House, 1977 (2nd edn.), pp. 124–55.

34. See Swati Datta, *Migrant Brāhmaṇas in Northern India,* Delhi, Motilal Banarsidass, 1989.

35. For the fuller argument see Hermann Kulke, 'The Early and the Imperial Kingdom: A Processural Model of Integrative State Formation in Early Medieval India', in idem. (ed.), *The State in India 1000–1700,* New Delhi, Oxford University

Press, 1995, pp. 233–62; B.D. Chattopadhyaya, 'State and Economy in North India: Fourth Century to Twelfth Century', in Romila Thapar (ed.), *Recent Perspectives of Early Indian History,* Bombay, Popular Prakashan, 1995, pp. 309–46.

36. Cynthia Talbot, 'Rudrama-devi, the Female King: Gender and Political Authority in Medieval India', in David Shulman (ed.), *Syllables of Sky*, New Delhi, Oxford University Press, 1996, pp. 391–430.

37. Hermann Kulke, 'Kshatriyaization and Social Change: A Study in Orissa Setting', in S.D. Pillai (ed.), *Aspects of Changing India: Studies in Honour of Professor G.S. Ghurye,* Bombay, Popular Prakashan, 1976.

38. For example see Surajit Sinha, 'State Formation and Rajput Myth in Tribal Central India', *Man in India,* vol. 42, 1962, pp. 35–80; K.S. Singh, 'A Study in State-Formation among Tribal Communities', in Sharma and Jha (ed.), *Indian Society,* pp. 317–36; Nicholas B. Dirks, 'Political Authority and Structural Change in Early South Indian History', *Indian Economic and Social History Review,* 1976, pp. 125–57; and S. Nagaraju, 'Emergence of Regional Identity and Beginnings of Vernacular Literature: A Case Study of Telugu', *Social Scientist,* nos 269–71, Oct.–Dec. 1995, pp. 8–23.

39. See Tripathy, *Inscriptions of Bhauma-Karas,* p. 108; idem., *Inscriptions of Orissa,* vol. 1, p. 166; idem., *Inscriptions of Orissa,* vol. VI, p. 123; and for details R.N. Misra, '*Silpis* in Ancient India: Beyond Their Ascribed Locus in Ancient Society', paper presented at the Seminar on Caste: Origins, Evolution, Diffusion, Repression and Resistance', organized by The Aligarh Historians Society, at the Indian History Congress, Malda session, 12–13 February, 2011.

40. See Panda, *Medieval Orissa,* pp. 58–66, 73–75, and 86; also see A.P. Sah, *Life in Medieval Orissa (Circa* AD *600–1200),* Varanasi, Chaukhamba, 1976, pp. 132–3.

41. The prevalence of professional groups rather than castes/*jātis* even in Cōḷa Tamil Nadu has been observed by Y. Subbarayalu, 'The Cōḷa State', *Studies in History,* vol. 4, no. 2, 1982, pp. 265–306; the continuation of this trend into the twelfth–thirteenth centuries in the region has been also communicated by him in a personal discussion. For a recent statement see N. Karashima, 'New Imprecations in Tamil Inscriptions and *Jati* Formation', in his *South Indian Society in Transition: Ancient to Medieval,* New Delhi, Oxford University Press, 2009, pp. 99–114 and n.18. Also see Cynthia Talbot for early medieval Andhra, *supra* n.1.

42. Ronald Inden, *Imagining India,* Oxford, Basil Blackwell, 1990, p. 82; Kesavan Veluthat, 'Congealing of Castes: The Case of Medieval Kerala', paper presented at the Seminar on Caste: Origins, Evolution, Diffusion, Repression and Resistance, organized by The Aligarh Historians Society, at the Indian History Congress, Malda session, 12–13 February, 2011.

4

The Making of an Early Historical Subregion?*

The question of the formation of regional identities, based on a set of region-specific cultural traits, has become a recent concern of historians. The emergence of the regions is being linked to the early medieval phase in Indian history. Many of its defining features in society, polity, language, literature, and artistic style, among others, it is said, begin to emerge broadly around the second half of the first millennium AD.[1] This chapter attempts to analyse the evolution of Dakṣiṇa Kośala during the early historical and early medieval times to examine how the socially unified space came to acquire discernible qualities which more or less defined it as a historico-cultural unit. Up to now the region, like most hinterlands, has not been the focus of any sustained historical research, largely owing to the attraction of the coastal belt, which is not entirely unrelated to its alleged historical priority. The area of study is conventionally referred to as western Orissa or Chhattisgarh, neither of which constitutes a historical region on its own. They are rather the products of administrative decision and represent political units. Taken together, however, they manifest commonly shared traits, derived through a long process of historical evolution, and constitute an organic socio-cultural entity. From epicentric perspectives, it is seen

*Originally published as 'Profiling Dakṣiṇa Kośala: An Early Historical Subregion?', in H. Kulke and G. Berkemer (eds), *Centres Out There? Facets of Subregional Identities in Orissa*, Delhi, Manohar, 2011, pp. 39–59.

I am grateful to Professors H. Kulke, B.D. Chattopadhyaya, and H. von Stietencron for comments on an earlier draft of this paper. I also thank my younger brother, Shri Lakshmi Narayan Sahu, who facilitated my visit to Sirpur, Rajim, Marguda, Budhikomna, and Khariar in the summer of 2001.

as either an extension of coastal Orissa or a buffer or intermediate zone between the coastal tract and northern and central India, and even as a site of contestation between feuding dynasties ranging from the Vākāṭakas and Nalas, through the Kalachuris and Somavaṁśīs, to the Telugu Cōḍas and Chindaka-Nāgas, among others. The question then is, do we continue to perceive it as such or see if it had a personality of its own? In the case of the latter, questions relating to change, agencies of change, cultural forms, and their signifiers will have to be addressed. This chapter therefore seeks to understand the trajectory of socio-cultural transformation in the region from an early phase of segmented 'localities' to the constitution of a larger supra-local community identity bound by a commonly shared cultural system, assuming there is one. With reference to regional specifics, it examines whether the movement towards the formation of an agrarian region, a differentiated and hierarchized caste society, larger political enterprises (extending across the region and beyond), and the role of Brāhmaṇas, among others, in disseminating cultural forms and the creation of cultic centres, which may have performed a unifying and levelling function, facilitated the creation of a sense of felt community and belonging, or, simply put, identity formation. The area is rich in archaeological material and land grant inscriptions, which form the basic evidence in the present case.

Like Vidarbha and Malwa, Dakṣiṇa Kośala is a part of the central India Intermediate Zone, which separates the northern plains from Peninsular India. Though communication across this zone was never easy, there have been slow and steady interactions between these subregions, as well as with the adjacent and peripheral cultural systems through the ages, which have facilitated the integration of the tribes into the caste-peasant base since the early historical phase. Dakṣiṇa Kośala broadly comprised the space between Amarkantak in the north to Kanker (close to the source of the river Mahānadī) in the south, and from the Wen-Gaṅgā Valley in the west to the middle valley of the Mahānadī (extending up to Sonpur) in the east.[2] It was bounded by Mekala in the north, Vidarbha in the west, Bastar in the south and Kaliṅga in the south-east. More specifically, this cultural unit is spread over the modern districts of Bilaspur, Raipur, Durg, and Raigarh in Chhattisgarh, and Sambalpur, Bolangir, and Kalahandi in Orissa.[3] Like other regions, the territorial borders of Dakṣiṇa Kośala were not fixed in the past. The tribal presence in this region was and continues to be strong even today. The tribal situation, together with its physiography, seems to account for the generally late historical transformation of the region. Sites like Malhar (Bilaspur district) and Asurgarh (Kalahandi district) registering early beginnings, instead of disturbing this understanding, point to their favourable geographical location and the uneven patterns of historical growth within the subregion. Notwithstanding the importance of the Mahānadī and its tributaries, the Sheonath and Tel, for irrigation, paddy cultivation, and other activities in the region, this is a land of tanks. The intrinsic importance of both rice and tanks comes from the early inscriptional references to them in this spatial and cultural segment.[4]

The earliest reference to Kośala as a territorial unit, its location in Dakṣiṇapatha in close proximity to Mahākantara and Kaurala (which comprised parts of Bastar and western Orissa), and indications of its manifest socio-political profile come from the Allahabad *praśasti* of Samudragupta.[5] This is listed among a dozen *aṭavikarājyas*, which suggests that it was a post-tribal chiefdom or early state. The forest people of central India known as *aṭavi* find mention in the Aśokan edicts, and after a gap of about six hundred years the addition of the suffix *rājya* unmistakably points to the change that had come from within local societies during the intervening period. Vākāṭaka inscriptions of the fifth century AD and the Aihole inscription of Pulakeśin II successively record the conquest of Kośala along with contiguous territories such as Mekala, Kaliṅga, and Andhra.[6] Hiuen Tsang provides a good account of the region, its people, their manners, and religious beliefs, in the mid-seventh century, among other details.[7] Around the same time the Pāṇḍuvaṁśī king Tivaradeva is represented in the epigraphical records of the family as the lord of the whole of Kośala.[8] In the land-grant charters of the Somavaṁśīs (ninth to eleventh centuries), who succeeded the Pāṇḍuvaṁśīs, the donated area is usually mentioned as a part of some administrative unit in Kośala *deśa*, their homeland and/or area of control. Continued use of the nomenclature and identification of the region with Kośala is discernible even in a seventeenth-century text, significantly titled *Kośalānanda Kāvya*.[9] It is difficult to pinpoint when and how the territory acquired its name, but the existence of a seal from Malhar (dated to the second century AD) bearing the legend *Gāmasa Kośaliya* may possibly suggest its post-Mauryan origins, especially the early centuries AD.[10] It is not certain whether, in using the term Kośala, an already existing name was being appropriated, or whether the process of its continuous usage conferred on the region a discrete identity through imperceptible gradations. It was perhaps a two-way process, involving both the communication and constitution of a spatial cultural image.

The issue of the formation of a subregional identity raises many obvious but interrelated questions—how was it forged, what were its major identifiable constituents, and even, what were the stages, if any, in its creation? Archaeological evidence constitutes the most important source for the reconstruction of the early phase of the history of Dakṣiṇa Kośala. The available evidence suggest that the process of cultural development was mostly dispersed, spread over the river valleys of the Mahānadī, the Tel (which is an important tributary of the Mahānadī), and their tributaries, possibly with interactions of one form or another between clusters of sites and beyond. The reported sites surely did not all share the same history, but rather there were chronological and typological variations across sites.[11] To elaborate, not all known early historical settlements need be perceived as urban centres. It is the cultural assemblage that ultimately determine the character of a site. In introducing these qualified statements, my intention is to make the more general point that not only was the transition to the historical phase in the region, as elsewhere, a complex phenomenon, but also that there were uneven patterns of growth.

Exacavations unveiling the cultural sequence have been carried out at Malhar, Sirpur, Asurgarh, the Marguda valley, Manmunda, and Nehena; and many other sites have been subjected to surveys and explorations. Malhar in Bilaspur district was occupied from the early part of the first millennium BC to the thirteenth century AD. Periods II and III, which are of immediate concern here, have been dated to *c.* 350 BC to AD 300 and *c.* AD 300 to 650 respectively.[12] For Period II the mud rampart remains of a fort have been located. This has yielded black-and-red ware, two pieces of northern black polished ware (hereafter NBPW), red slipped ware, stamped pottery and bricks corresponding to the Mauryan and Sātavāhana types. Punch-marked, cast and Sātavāhana coins have also been reported. There is the interesting seal, already mentioned, dated to the second century AD, which reads *Gāmasya Kośaliya*. Black-and-red ware (suggesting its continued use), red polished ware and kaolin pottery have been identified from Period III. The site also yielded a piece of the rim of a large jar, a baked pendant and a clay seal with

Gupta Brāhmī characters.[13] The seal is particularly important because it bears the legend *Mahārāja Mahendrasya*, who has been variously identified with Mahendra of Kośala of the Allahabad inscription of Samudragupta and Mahendraditya of the Śarabhapurīya dynasty. The remains of Śaivite temples, Buddhist *chaitya*s and *vihāra*s and bricks used in their construction have also been recovered. A huge tank which now covers an area of about 60 acres is dated to this period. Sirpur or ancient Śripura, situated at a distance of 60 km from Raipur, in Raipur district, and associated with the late Śarabhapurīya kings and their successors the Pāṇḍuvaṁśīs, possesses extensive ruins.[14] However, all of it, including the temples, *vihāra*s, sculptural remains, and the associated artifacts, belong to the second half of the first millennium AD.

The excavation carried out at Asurgarh, in Kalahandi district, has laid bare a site whose chronology ranges between *c.* the third century BC and the fifth–sixth centuries AD.[15] From the upper phase of the lowest layer in this fortified settlement, black-and-red ware was found in good numbers, together with black polished ware. A piece of chunar sandstone bearing Mauryan-era polish was also found from this early layer. The second layer contained red glazed pottery, iron objects, and beads of semi-precious stones probably dating to the early centuries AD. Punch-marked coins and a copper coin of Kaniṣka have also been obtained from the site. The top layer contained floors of houses paved with brickbats, and a circular structure between the two trenches was also exposed. It is not certain whether this had anything to do with the autochthonous deity Stambheśvarī mentioned in the Terasinga plates[16] of Mahārāja Tuṣṭikara, who had acquired a visible political presence around the same area in the same period. Budhigarh in M. Rampur Tehsil, located in the same part of the district as Asurgarh, is marked by an extensive mound (1,000 x 500 metres). This has produced a wide range of antiquities, comprising NBPW, fine black ware, black-and-red ware, punch-marked coins, terracotta figurines, copper and iron objects, two seals and semi-precious beads, among other things.[17] The nature of the evidence alludes to its early historical moorings.

The Marguda Valley is situated in Nuapada subdivision of Kalahandi district, bordering Chhattisgarh, on the banks of the Sonk river, which is a tributary of the Mahānadī. The valley is rich in antiquities and monuments. Excavation and explorations have yielded evidence of beads, iron artifacts, sculptural and brick structural remains. The ruins of the settlement, which has a formidable natural fortification, included a Śaivite *vihāra* complex, a palace complex and a Śaktipitha. An interesting archer image of Durgā has been obtained *in situ* from the single chambered brick temple. The image bears an inscription reading Maheśvarī Bhābadā, which has been ascribed to the fourth century AD.[18] The Amguda copper-plate grant of Jayarāja and the Khariar charter of Sudevarāja (both belonging to the Śarabhapurīya dynasty) have been discovered in the vicinity of the valley. The overall cultural complex suggests that the site can be dated from the fourth or fifth century onward. Nehena, 4 km from Khariar town, in the same subdivision, has produced a cultural sequence ranging from the early historical to the early medieval periods. Material remains unearthed from the trial excavation were black-and-red ware with painting in white, red and brown ware, beads of agate and carnelian, bricks and gold coins of Prasannamitra (of the Śarabhapurīya dynasty). Two cultural phases have been suggested for the site. The earlier period, identified with the early historical phase, yielded much of the pottery mentioned above, which in terms of shape and wares compares well not so much with those from coastal Orissa but with the central and western Indian finds.[19] The early medieval sites had no black-and-red ware with a rough surface but contained iron tools, some iron slags and the gold coins just mentioned.

Kharliagarh, located at the confluence of the Tel and Raul in Bolangir district, is close to the eastern border of Kalahandi district. The mounds inside the fort have yielded evidence of copper punch-marked coins, Kuṣāṇa copper coins, beads of semi-precious stones, iron implements, and metal bangles.[20] These, together with the burnt brick rampart remains of the almost square fort, indicate the early historical origins of the site. Manmunda, situated at the confluence of the Tel and Mahānadī in Phulbani district, is an early historical site. Black-and-red ware, black polished ware, polished and red slipped ware, iron objects (including a sickle), a silver punch-marked coin, beads of semi-precious stones, lids with knobs in good quantity (reminding one of similar finds on the coastal sites of Orissa) and burnt brick structural remains are among the important finds from the trial excavation at the ancient settlement.[21] Black-and-red ware was totally absent in the upper two layers. At a distance of about 50 km to the east of Manmunda lies Maryakud, an island in the Mahānadī in the same district of Phulbani, which along with Manmunda was situated on the eastern frontier of

Dakṣiṇa Kośala. Explorations in and around the mound have brought to light sherds of black-and-red ware, black polished ware, red slipped ware, semi-precious stone beads, and pieces of iron slag.[22] It may not be out of place to mention that the eastern part of Dakṣiṇa Kośala or what constitutes western Orissa today is rich in precious and semi-precious stones.

Buddhist remains have been reported from the excavations at Ganiapali and Nagraj, on the left bank of the river Ong, a tributary of the Mahānadī, in Sambalpur district.[23] The finds comprise sculptures of the Buddha and burnt brick structural remains of a *vihāra* dated to the late fourth and early fifth centuries AD. Carnelian beads, terracotta objects and potsherds were the other miscellaneous finds from these sites.

The provenance of the archaeological data, together with the locations of early numismatic finds and Prākrit inscriptions, seems to suggest a pattern in the evolution of early Dakṣiṇa Kośala. The coin finds—from punch-marked coins through local uninscribed copper coins and inscribed Magha coins to the Kuṣāṇa copper and Roman gold coins—in the western part of the region tend to centre in and around Malhar in Bilaspur district, though with a scattering in the neighbouring districts.[24] The Guñji and the (damaged) Kirāri inscriptions, assigned to the early centuries AD, recording the donation of numerous cows to Brāhmaṇas by important state functionaries (like *amātya, daṇḍanāyaka*, and *balādhikṛta*) and a list of administrative designations (namely, *mahāsenāni, pratihāra, bhaṇḍāgarika, aśvāroha, pādamūlika, rathika*, and *gomaṇḍalika*, among many others) are also located in the same district.[25] Bilaspur thus emerges as a bustling 'locality', with Malhar as an important node. At the risk of repetition one may reiterate that Malhar has yielded most of the above varieties of coin, as well as other markers of prosperity from Period II (*c.* 350 BC–AD 300). The site is said to be located on the ancient trade route joining Kausambi with the south-east coast, and that perhaps explains its importance. Influences both from the north and the Deccan and central India, especially under the Sātavāhanas, may account for the long list of official titles in the epigraphic records of the subregion during its formative period. As one moves into the Gupta period, the adjoining districts of Durg and Raipur, to the south, begin to provide material relating to the extension of Gupta influence. In addition to the Gupta coins, there is the Arang fragmentary inscription, assigned to the fourth century, which is perhaps the first Sanskrit inscription in the area, and the copper-plate grant of Bhimasena II, again from Arang, in Raipur district, dated in 182 or 282 in the Gupta Era (AD 502 or 602).[26] The repouse gold coins of Mahendrāditya and Prasannamatra spread over the districts of Bilaspur, Raipur, Durg, and Kalahandi,[27] with the Garuda motif and *Saṅkha* and *Chakra* to the left and right respectively, bear the unmistakable imprint of the Gupta emblem. Such influences extended to the domains of art, culture and polity as well, and will be discussed later.

On the basis of the combined archaeological and numismatic evidence, it may be surmised that there were mutual interactions and communications between Asurgarh, Budhigarh, Kharliagarh, and Manmunda, cutting across the modern administrative divisions in eastern Dakṣiṇa Kośala, with Asurgarh being in some kind of privileged position. The presence of silver and copper punch-marked coins as well as Kuṣāṇa coins and beads at these sites suggests in that direction. If the alignment of sites is any indication, then the Tel played an important role in the emergence and sustenance of the network of exchange and cultural transactions that contributed to the prosperity of the locality. The river valleys emerge as important factors in the socio-cultural development of the region, and the movement towards a complex society.

The trajectory of internal transformation that has been sketched so far demonstrates the formation of localities across variegated spaces. Localities may be taken to approximate to *janapadas*, to use a familiar north Indian term.[28] Development was uneven and segmented, with some areas registering greater visibility than others. But then the question is, how does one explain craft specialization, trade, the money economy and social differentiation, or, to put it simply, the transition from pre-state to state societies? The proliferation of settlements[29] suggests a rise in population and agrarian growth. Change is archaeologically demonstrable during and after the Mauryas. The horizontal spread of the Mauryan state and the subsequent ascendancy and expansion of the Sātavāhanas then constitute the background to the early transformation of the region. Flowing from it, it may not be out of place to argue that the transition itself derived, as in the Deccan and Kaliṅga,[30] from a combination of autochthonous forces and the influences emanating from proximate advanced cultural regions through continuous interaction.

A further stage in the transition of Dakṣiṇa Kośala is discernible from the sixth to seventh centuries onwards, when the first locally organized subregional state was formed. There was no break but an expansion of and acceleration in the historical processes of change, which continued to influence and impact on each other. For example, the extension of political authority was related to agrarian expansion, the spread of Brāhmaṇical settlements, the dissemination of śāstric-purāṇic ideas, and the emergence and spread of sacred centres, including Buddhist monasteries. Like Brāhmaṇical ideology and temples, Buddhism seems to have helped in organizing diversity and the process of socio-political integration. The process of state formation shows the phased territorial extension and structural evolution of states, from their tentative beginnings to the making of a regional state; combining parts of Kośala and central and coastal Orissa.

The stages in the evolution of the structure of the polity can be mapped with reference to the provenance of the land-grant charters, the identification of donated settlements, lists of officials addressed in these records, the privileges and exemptions transferred to the donees, and the titles and epithets borne by the rulers of successive dynasties. The earliest known *rājā* in the region, following those mentioned in the Allahabad *praśasti*, was *Mahārāja Tuṣṭikara*, whose Terasinga plate informs us that he ruled around the fifth to sixth centuries in Kalahandi district, bordering Bolangir. The Śarabhapurīyas were the first local dynasty. They issued most of their land grants from Śarabhapura (not yet satisfactorily identified) and Śripura (Sirpur), their successive seats of power.[31] The geographical distribution of the copper-plate grants and the identification of the donated settlements reveal that their dominion roughly comprised the present-day districts of Bilaspur, Raipur and Raigarh in Chhattisgarh and Kalahandi in Orissa.[32] The spatial spread of the gold coins of Mahendrāditya of the same lineage broadly coincides with this political geography. *Bhōga, bhukti, rāṣṭra,* and *āhāra* were the administrative units above rural settlements. The single instance of the term *āhāra* may have been an inheritance from the Sātavāhanas and the Deccan. The taxes included *bhāga, bhōga, dhānya*, and *hiraṇya*. High officials do not seem to have been addressed while making land grants. However, there are references to *bhōgapati*s urging them to protect the grants, and such other categories as *dūta, adhikaraṇa, cāṭa*, and *bhaṭa*. Towards the end of their reign we come across one *mahāsāmanta sarvādhikṛta* Indrabalarāja. The Śarabhapurīya kings used the title *mahārāja* and at times the suffix *bhaṭṭāraka*, but nothing more grandiose. The construction of a grand genealogy or exaggerated family tradition was conspicuous by its absence. There are several instances of land grants being made by high state functionaries and influential people with the consent of the king.[33] The impression that one is left with is of a state in an early stage of evolution, where power was unobtrusive and the administrative units, taxes and state functionaries were yet to be formally structured.[34]

The Pāṇḍuvaṁśīs, who succeeded the Śarabhapurīyas, made their grants largely from Śripura. The provenance of their records and the location of the place names mentioned in them suggest that their realm broadly coincided with that of their predecessors.[35] While the kingdom was divided into *rāṣṭra*, *bhōga*, *bhukti*, and *viṣaya*, the popular revenue terms were *bhāga* and *bhōga*. However, the remissions to the beneficiaries of land grants were more elaborate and included expressions such as *sarva-kara-sameta*, *a-cāṭabhaṭa-praveśa* and *sarva-piḍā-varjita*. State functionaries were addressed and informed about the grants being made. The list includes *grāmakūṭa*, *droṇagika*, *gaṇḍakanāyaka*, *devavārika* and *cāṭa* and *bhaṭa*. The records of Mahāśivagupta Bālrjuna also informed the *kālādhyasin* (astrologer), *samāhartṛ*, *sannidhātṛ*, *adhikaraṇa*, and *sakaraṇa*.[36] The Pāṇḍuvaṁśīs began to appropriate significant titles and symbols of substance such as *Paramamaheśvara*, *Paramavaiṣṇava*, *Parameśvara*, and *Kośalādhipati* (lord of Kośala). Mahāśivagupta Bālrjuna was represented in his records as *dharmāvatāra* (incarnation of *dharma*), the protector of *varṇas* and *āśramas*, and even compared to the epic heroes.[37] Overall it appears that the subregional state had moved forward and that there was a consolidation of royal authority.

The Somavaṁśīs, who were perhaps a collateral branch or junior line of the same family, followed the Pāṇḍuvamśīs after a gap of about a century. They were the first to move into central Orissa displacing the Bhañjas of Khiñjali (in the Baudh area) in the later part of the ninth century, and then moved on to occupy coastal Orissa, creating a regional kingdom in the process. Their charters were issued from a number of places like Suvarṇapura (Sonepur), Mūrasima (near Bolangir town), Vinitapura (Binka, near Sonepur) and Yayātinagara, among others, indicating their eastward expansion. The sites where their charters have been found are spread over the districts of Bolangir, Puri, Cuttack, and

Balasore, with a conspicuous concentration in the district of Bolangir. Among the settlements identified in the donative records, many are situated in Bolangir district, especially around Bolangir town and the Bolangir-Baudh area, the Bargarh locality of Sambalpur and Kalahandi districts. *Deśa, maṇḍala, khaṇḍa, bhukti,* and *viṣaya* constituted the administrative divisions. The list of privileges of the donees became more detailed, including the transfer of community rights over trees, creepers and forest products. Similarly, the list of functionaries registered a numerical increase, and royal titles were more numerous and pompous.[38] Terms such as *Mahārājādhirāja*, *Paramabhaṭṭāraka*, and *Kośalendra*, reflecting the image or self-image of royalty, were in circulation. Through the instrument of land grants and the transfer of rights, pockets of authority were being created, which would have then spread the message of royal power and helped in extending the orbit of state authority.[39] There was an underlying unity in these developments. The rise in the number of possible sources of revenue and the widening political structure were in conformity with the expanding frontiers of the state. That begs the question, what were the forces or conjunction of forces that made such political enterprises possible?

The early medieval centuries were characterized by the growth of a rural economy, burgeoning rural settlements and the emergence of religious centres and towns. Malhar continued to flourish. At Sirpur, Rajim, Tala, and Kharod in present-day Chhattisgarh and the Marguda Valley, Budhikomna, Belkhandi, and Ranipur-Jharial in western Orissa, for example, there are extant brick temples and their ruins going back to the Gupta and post-Gupta centuries.[40] Urban centres such as Śarabhapura, Prasannapura and Kośalanagara are also referred to in contemporary dynastic records. Centres like Sirpur and Rajim were multifunctional towns, whereas sites like Tala and the Ranipur-Jharial complex, with religious activities dominating the scene, may have been largely unidimensional in nature. It needs no emphasis that, irrespective of their cultic association and function, temples and towns are markers of agrarian growth. The proliferation of temples thus indicates both the spread of purāṇic religions and the moving frontier of peasant society. Vaṭapadra, Khadirapadra, Śālagrāma and Kadambapadrullaka, among others, unambiguously suggest that the names of settlements were derived from local flora, and they allude to the rich, thick vegetation in their surroundings. During the Śarabhapurīya period and even later, the evidence of settlements sharing boundaries with other habitations is sparse. Similarly, the four boundaries or *catuḥsīmā* of the donated land are in many cases not specifically defined,[41] implying thinly scattered rural settlements; interrupted by intermittent woods and forests. This impression is strengthened by references to trees, plants, animals, forests and forest products in the Somavaṁśī inscriptions,[42] in the general context of remissions to the donees. The evidence for collective grants to several groups of Brāhmaṇas throughout the period and the frequency of the occurrence of *padras* or *padrakas*,[43] not *grāmas* (fully settled villages), as the object of the grants up to the Pāṇḍuvaṁśī perhaps suggest an early stage in the spread of plough agriculture and the evolution of rural settlements in many parts of the region. Notwithstanding the early patterns of socio-economic transformation, there is a gradual increase in the epigraphic references to rural settlements. The use of the names of rivers, like Ong and Tel, in demarcating administrative divisions drives home their importance in these developments. The fact that the land grants of the Śarabhapurīyas and Pāṇḍuvaṁśīs were largely distributed over the districts of Bilaspur and Raipur, while those of the Somavaṁśī were mostly concentrated in and around Bolangir district, urges the recognition of phased agrarian expansion, with specific localities being the focus of political interest at different points in time.

The brāhmaṇas, with their knowledge of the calendar, agriculture, the Vedas, śāstras and *purāṇas* and, deriving from it their inherent capacity to provide socio-political legitimacy, appear to have played a significant role in the transformation of autochthonous societies. Though they are known to the region since the early centuries AD, they achieved a noticeable presence from the middle of the first millennium onwards. During this period they were most often the beneficiaries of royal munificence. The Bonda plates of Pāṇḍuvaṁśī Tivaradeva (seventh century) provide perhaps the earliest evidence of the migration of brāhmaṇas, which in subsequent times became a regular phenomenon.[44] Migrant brāhmaṇas from Rāḍha, Oḍradeśa, Madhyadeśa, Śrāvasti, etc., came in under the Pāṇḍuvaṁśīs. Some more social segments (if not all of them) which emerged in the wider context of social change find mention in the copper-plate inscriptions either as addressees or because of their involvement, in one capacity or the other, in the making of the land-grant charters. Besides the brāhmaṇas, rural society comprised other categories, such as *kuṭumbins*, *pradhāna-prativāsins*, and *prativāsins*. While *kuṭumbin* is seen to be the equivalent of the middle peasant,[45] *prativāsin* means inhabitant and, flowing from it, *pradhāna-prativāsins* would then translate as important residents or men of substance. Such esteemed men attained recognition and visibility from the later part of Pāṇḍuvaṁśī rule.[46] Among the occupational groups, the *sūtradhāra* (architect/master craftsman), *suvarṇakāra* (goldsmith), *vaṇik* (trader), *mālākara* (garland maker), *gauḍa* (cowherd), *kāyastha*, and engravers of records find mention in contemporary sources.[47] The numerous temples and copper-plates, for example, bear testimony to the existence of *ācāryas,* bricklayers, stone-cutters, smiths, and composers, among others. Individuals other than royalty were involved in the construction of temples during the early stages,[48] pointing to their accrued economic competence. To make the more general point that there were noticeable disparities; one need not go further than the brāhmaṇas. There were brāhmaṇas enjoying a settlement, others having some shares in a settlement or settlements and still others with only some measures of land.[49] The emergence of new groups helped the transition to a caste society and the unfolding of social complexity, which were gradual, long-term processes. Differential access to economic resources, political power and ritual status contributed to social differentiation and hierarchization within the overarching framework of Brāhmaṇical ideology, and with reference to the dominant schema.

The early medieval period was shaped not just by an expanding agrarian economy and social fluidity; it was equally a period of artistic innovation, cultural growth, and the movement of ideas. The elite showed interest in temple-building activities, and temple towns emerged as important centres of socio-cultural activity. The temple movement can be fully appreciated in the context of the formation of local and subregional agrarian bases and the simultaneous evolution of a complex, hierarchized socio-political structure, where various segments were seeking the confirmation of their assumed or achieved status.[50] Though the construction of temples in South Kośala dates from the late Gupta period onwards, it is only from around the seventh century that there is evidence for royal patronage to temples and Buddhist establishments alike, the reign of Mahāśivagupta Bālārjuna at Sirpur being particularly prominent. Temple rituals became more elaborate, and brāhmaṇas, *ācāryas* and local bodies looked after their management.[51] The growing complexity and addition of details is reflected in the introduction of music and dance in these religious institutions.

At Tala, situated close to the confluence of the Seonath and Manjari rivers in Bilaspur district, are preserved the ruins of two temples of remarkable beauty, known as Jiṭhāni and Devarāṇi, the former being relatively older than the latter. They are assigned to the late fifth and early sixth centuries, and the motifs bear affinities with Gupta art, combined with influences from Vidarbha, especially the sculptural idiom. Despite the analogy of sculptural art with Vākāṭaka and Gupta examples, it is said that 'they definitely breathe an atmosphere of their own'.[52] It is further suggested that this art form evolved from an indigenous tradition in wood-carving and laid the foundation of the Kośala style of architecture.[53] There have been efforts to understand the region-specific traits in the sculptures representing Śaivite affiliation from South Kośala. The integration of animal figures in the main body of sculptures and the carving of the whole body of the deity instead of just the *mukha* on the liṅga in the assemblages at Tala and Malhar are regarded as the regional characteristics.[54] Under the Pāṇḍuvaṁśīs and, later, Nalas, a distinct art tradition evolved in the region. Sripura and Rajim emerged as important centres with exquisite temples adorning these towns. The Lakṣmaṇa and Rājivlochana temples are fine examples. Malhar and Kharod, too, illustrate the growth in patronage and the spread of temples. Ranipur-Jharial in Bolangir district, a predominantly Śaivite complex, came to prominence under the Pāṇḍuvaṁśīs. In addition to the numerous temples, the large number of what appear to be votive shrines around Someśvara suggests that it was a *tīrtha* (pilgrimage centre).[55] Kosaleśvara at Baidyanath, in the same district, and Pataleśvara at Budhikomna (near Nuapada), in Kalahandi district, among others, are placed in the same time bracket of the mid-ninth to mid-tenth centuries. It appears that during Somavaṁśī rule the tradition of art and architecture in the upper Mahānadī moved into the middle Mahānadī Valley and adjoining areas. Some experimentation in art and ground plan were initiated, to which I shall return later. The Kalachuris continued to patronize temples, a large number of which were built between the middle of the eleventh and end of the twelfth centuries. Contemporary records mention the presence of artists and craftsmen such as *sūtradhāras*, *śilpis*, and *rūpakāras*.[56] Under the Kalachuris art assumed a 'provincial' character, and sculptures were marked by excessive standardization, emphasizing an anthropomorphic type in contrast to the earlier elegant simplicity and sensitive rendering of figure work.[57] In the upper Mahānadī Valley the classical tradition faded out by the ninth century. However, it seems to have influenced art later in the middle Mahānadī region, the Śomavaṁśīs being its ostensible carriers.

Brick was the popular building material in the temples of Kośala, from Tala to Budhikomna and from Malhar to Rajim, as was the case with the temples of Vidarbha. As one moves eastwards into coastal Orissa, stone replaces brick as the preferred raw material. Stellate or star-shaped temples, a product of considerable experimentation, were perhaps a typical South Kośala style. They involved the principle of two squares being placed diagonally to one another and intersecting at an angle of 45°. They are known from Kharod, Budhikomna, Kansil (near Ranipur-Jharial), Baudh, and other places, and are usually brick temples dedicated to Śiva. While the river goddesses Gaṅgā and Yamuna flank the doorway of the shrine, the *Navagraha*s with Gajalakṣmi at the centre adorn the lintel.[58] *Daśāvatāra* images embellish the door-jambs in the Lakṣmana temple at Sirpur and decorate the pillars of the Rājivlochana temple at Rajim. The carving of large figures against the pillars in the temple as at Rajim, Sirpur or Kośaleśvara at Baidyanath, near Sonepur, appear to be specific to Kośala. Similarly, knotted snakes decorating the doorways of shrines as at Kośaleśvara, for example, were a characteristic feature of the region, not known in the Lower Mahānadī Valley and the plains of Orissa.[59] Some of these traits, which are common occurrences in Dakṣiṇa Kośala, find visible manifestation at places like Baidyanath and Boudh, largely because they are situated on the border, which helped them to combine influences from both Kośala and Orissa.

The co-existence of multiple forms of religion, beliefs and practices is borne out by the combined evidence of archaeology and inscriptions. Malhar and Sirpur have yielded evidence of both temples and Buddhist *vihāras*. In fact, the *vihāras* at Sirpur were in the vicinity of the Lakṣmana temple. Patronage was broad-based, and the rulers of successive dynasties spent their resources on the temples of Viṣṇu and Śiva as well as Buddhist monasteries. While Bhāvadeva, brother of Nannarāja (a Pāṇḍuvaṁśī king), had a Buddhist *vihāra* repaired, Isāṇadeva, another brother of the same king, built a temple at Kharod.[60] Mahāśivagupta Bālārjuna was equally liberal in his generosity towards Brāhmaṇical shrines and Buddhist establishments. Many rulers, despite their Śaivite affiliations, invoked Vaiṣṇava imageries in their official records. Even Ranipur-Jharial, an ostensibly Śaivite complex, had a Kṛṣṇa temple and at the same site several Vaiṣṇavite figures are present on the walls of Indralath, a temple dedicated to Śiva.[61] It is thought that at Sirpur the same artists worked at temples and Buddhist sites, a situation akin to what was practised in coastal Orissa.[62]

Narasiṁha and Mahiṣāsuramardinī or Śakti appear to have been popular deities. Images of Mahiṣāsuramardinī are present in Sirpur, at the site museum, and Rajim, and a figure of Durgā has been retrieved from the Marguda Valley, while Stambheśvarī is referred to in the Terasinga plates of Tuṣṭikara. Sculptural representations of Narasiṁha are available at Tala, Sirpur and Rajim, while the Lakṣmana temple at Sirpur (as alluded to in the stone inscription of Vāṣatā) was probably dedicated to Viṣṇu-Narasiṁha. The compulsions of political power or the need to win over one's subjects may explain why royal patronage was inclusive, not sectarian. However, one wonders whether the popularity of Śakti, the man-lion deity and later Śivaism, which unlike Viṣṇuism is kin-based, had anything to do with the autochthonous inheritance of local societies in transition. In the context of adjoining Vidarbha, it has been suggested that the popularity of Narasiṁha rested on his being 'a brave heroic deity'.[63] Even while Buddhist institutions were flourishing and were also the recipients of royal favour, the reformed Brāhmaṇical religion with Viṣṇu and Śiva as its two most important gods seems to have increasingly gained court patronage from around the sixth to seventh centuries onward. The shift mostly in favour of Śivaism is more clearly visible under the Pāṇḍuvaṁśīs and Kalachuris, especially in the artistic record of the times.[64] Whether this shift was a result of a swing in popular support or a change in royal patronage or both; warrants careful investigation.

Art and ideas are a product of society and involve particular cultural contexts and specific forms of social organization. The early medieval scene is illuminated by symbols and idioms in contemporary inscriptions, as is temple art, which reflects on these domains. The spread of Vedic, śāstric, epic and purāṇic ideas can be gleaned from the images or self-images of royalty as represented in the *praśasti* sections of the copper-plate and stone inscriptions.[65] The influence of the Dharmaśāstras is easily discernible in the benedictory and imprecatory verses in the land grant charters. The *daśāvatāra* images on door-jambs or pillars in temples at Sirpur and Rajim or the story relating to Skanda in the *Mahābhārata* rendered in art at Tala point in the same direction.[66]

The significant correspondence between Kośaleśvara, the name of the Śiva temple at Baidyanath, and the Pāṇḍuvaṁśīs, who constantly projected themselves as the lords of Kośala, cannot be missed. This is just one instance of the ways in which royalty sought to identify with divinity.[67] Understandably, the appropriation of divinity was couched in a vocabulary which tried to achieve the desired purpose without doing violence to popular sensibilities. The familiar use of similes, metaphors and double entendre was intended to achieve this. For example, in his charters Mahāśivagupta Bālārjuna described himself as the son of Harṣagupta, just as Kārtikeya was of lord Śiva. Various discursive strategies were employed in the making of dominant ideology and techniques of control. Brāhmaṇas and temples disseminated śāstric and purāṇic ideas and values with a view to creating a coherent cultural ethos, a favourable ground for the extension and consolidation of state society.[68] The place of temples as catalysts in this process can be seen from the Senakapat inscription, which besides granting plots of land to a Śiva temple, expected the Śaivite ascetics to arrange for sacrifices (*yāga*) and initiate people into Śivaism.[69] Brāhmaṇa and temple settlements were the 'pillars of the normative order of Hindu Kingdoms',[70] which explains the grants of land to them as a necessary component of state policy. Whatever may have been its other functions, it surely provided the state with ideological and political legitimacy.

In the course of their being read out on several occasions, starting with a public proclamation on the occasion of the grant, the copper-plate charters, with their significant use of śāstric, epic, and purāṇic ideas and symbolisms and focus on legal and moral norms, played an important role in communicating these messages, in the process contributing to the shaping of an overarching value system. As public records, the inscriptions on temple walls, such as the Lakṣmana temple stone inscription of Vāṣatā at Sirpur, among others, were powerful instruments of cultural transmission.[71] The temples and monasteries at Sirpur attracted many devotees of different ideological persuasions, thus investing the stone inscriptions with political meaning.[72] These official records therefore need to be seen not simply as land transaction documents or as being reflective of a cultural milieu, but perhaps as transformatory stimuli in the early medieval social formation of South Kośala, a region which in many areas experienced the transition to historical society largely during the Gupta and post-Gupta periods. By the time of the Pāṇḍuvaṁśīs, especially Mahāśivagupta Bālārjuna, śāstric and purāṇic ideas had been sufficiently internalized by society for artists to express them in stone and poets and scribes to articulate them in their compositions of the drafts of charters so that engravers could transfer these on to copper-plates or stone surfaces. By mediating between the local and the pan-Indian, brāhmaṇas, temples, artists and poets helped in the creation of an intermediate level of cultural identity or belonging, which in the long term bound people together through a common way of thinking and believing, leading to the making of an 'experienced region'.[73]

It may be good to remind ourselves at this point that early medieval regimes were neither monolithic nor omnipresent.[74] Similarly, the coherence of brāhmaṇa enterprises has perhaps been assumed more than is warranted. It may be reasonable to suggest that both agrarian expansion and Brāhmaṇical ideology built on and could not escape opposition and conflict; as such intrusions would have blended coercive and pervasive strategies. At the beginning of the second millennium, then, Brāhmaṇical settlements, temple towns and their influence were not all-persuasive. Agrarian expansion and concomitant developments moved in a phased manner, with unevenness built into the process. On this material and cultural foundation the medieval Rajput kingdoms of the region emerged,[75] but that is not within the scope of this discussion.

The chapter started with the premise that socio-cultural transformations are a product of interaction between trans-regional patterns and local initiatives. Viewed from this perspective, many of the developments in South Kośala appear to be universal, yet it marked a distinctiveness in particular cultural forms. The regional autonomy of art forms was a historical reality, though its extent is debatable. At this point one may ask how the Dakṣiṇa Kośala experience differed from the pan-India or alternatively the geographically proximate Orissan experiences. Notwithstanding influences from the adjoining regions, the cumulative traits of Kośala art and architecture provide a distinctive regional flavour. The important innovations in art forms seem to be an act of self-assurance on the part of the Kośalan people. The projection of the kings as 'Lord of Kośala' (for example, *Kośaladhipati* and *Kośalendra*) and the worship of Śiva as Kośaleśvara (Lord of Kośala) at Baidyanath perhaps derived from, as well as contributed to, the formation of a Kośala identity. The indigenous people may or may not have comprehended the formation of a subregion, but we can perhaps raise and address the issue by suggesting that it emerged from a shared, common historico-cultural, though not necessarily homogeneous experience, which may have provided the local communities with a spatially distinguishable and culturally identifiable identity. Art and culture would have engendered a sense of affiliation among the people, but how many envisaged it that way is a difficult question to answer.

The terms 'regional' and 'subregional' have been used interchangeably throughout, but at this point there is a need for some precision in what is being said. The subregion, like the region, is a category which is easy to understand but rather difficult to define. Like multiple communities, which constitute a plural society with none having a monopoly or privileged position in defining it, subregions are a part of a region but with no single unit constituting it. In other words, they are in it and yet out of it, and in this are embedded the historical roots of contestation and negotiations within regions. In that sense, by the end of the first millennium Dakṣiṇa Kośala was an evolving subregion with features which defined the contours of its personality in the succeeding centuries.[76] Flowing from it, it is necessary to engage in a different evaluation of the subregions than just seeing them as simple extensions and therefore as hierarchically subordinate repetitive images of the epicentre, in this case coastal Orissa. They seem to constitute as much as be impacted by the perceived centre. It appears that both generalizing and essentializing the criteria of the subregion, like the region, have their share of problems. If generalizations subsume subregional historico-cultural specificities, essentializing them tends to ignore the multiple sources of identity formation, as well as the fact that identities in the past, as so often today, were not immutable.

Notes

1. B.D. Chattopadhyaya, 'Introduction', in *The Making of Early Medieval India*, New Delhi, Oxford University Press, 1994.

2. A. Cunningham, *Report of a Tour in the Central Provinces and Lower Gangetic Doab in 1881–82*, vol. 17, Delhi, Archaeological Survey of India, 2000 (rpt), p. 68.

3. All references in the text are to the undivided districts of western Orissa before 1990. Since then, these districts have been subdivided into many more new districts.

4. For early references to *dhānya*, see S.P. Tiwari, *Comprehensive History of Orissa: Dakṣiṇa Kośala under the Śarabhapurīyas,* Calcutta: Punthi Pustak, 1985, section on taxes; for tanks see *Archaeological Survey of India—Annual Report* (hereafter *ASI-AR*), 1930–4, 1936, p. 140, and K.D. Bajpai and S.K. Pandey, *Malhar*, 1975–8, Sagar, University of Sagar, p. 35.

5. J.F. Fleet, *Inscriptions of the Early Gupta Kings and their Successors, Corpus Inscriptionum Indicarum*, vol. 3, Varanasi, IBH, 1970 (3rd edn), p. 7.

6. Cited in S.P. Tiwari, *Comprehensive History of Orissa*, pp. 9–10.

7. Xuanzang, *Si-yu-ki: Buddhist Records of the Western World: Chinese Accounts of India,* vol. 2, translated from the Chinese of Hiuen Tsiang by Samuel Beal, London, Kegan Paul, Trench, Trubner & Co, 1906, pp. 209–10.

8. See Adhabhara Plates of Mahā–Nannarāja, in *Epigraphia Indica* (hereafter *EI*), vol. 31, 1955–6, pp. 220–1, lines 5–9, and Bonda Plates of Tivaradeva, year 5, in *EI*, vol. 34, 1960–1, pp. 115, lines 16–17.

9. See S.K. Panda, '*Kosalananda Kavyam* and the Making of a Rajput Dynasty: A Study of the Chauhans of Western Orissa', in H. Kulke and G. Berkemer (eds), *Centres Out There? Facets of Subregional Identities in Orissa*, Delhi, Manohar, 2011, pp. 133–48.

10. Bajpai and Pandey, *Malhar,* pp. 21 and 34. It may be mentioned that there is a reference to one Kośala *nagara* in the Malhar Plates of Mahasivagupta. B. Jain, 'Malhar Plates (second set) of Mahasivagupta', in *Prachya Pratibha*, vol. 5, no. 1, 1977, p. 52, line 11. Also in A.M. Shastri, *Inscriptions of the Śarabhapurīas, Pāṇḍuvaṁśīns and Somavaṁśīs,* parts I and II, Delhi, Motilal Banarsidass, 1995, p. 139.

11. This has been well argued in the case of early Bengal and it is equally true of the other regions. B.D. Chattopadhyaya, 'Urban Centres in Early Bengal: Archaeological Perspectives', in idem., *Studying Early India: Archaeology, Texts and Historical Issues,* New Delhi, Permanent Black, 2003, pp. 153–71.

12. Bajpai and Pandey, *Malhar,* pp. 33–5. Megalithic remains have been reported from sites in Raipur and Durg districts. Black-and-red ware (BRW) is a common occurrence at megalithic sites, but it continues well into the early historical period.

13. Bajpai and Pandey, *Malhar*, pp. 34–5.

14. S.L. Katare, 'Excavations at Sirpur', *The Indian Historical Quarterly*, vol. 35, no. 1, 1959, pp. 1–8.

15. *Indian Archaeology—A Review* (hereafter *IAR*) 1972–3, p. 29. Also see S.C. Behera, *Interim Excavation Reports,* Sambalpur, Sambalpur University, 1982, pp. 5–6.

16. S.N. Rajaguru, *Inscriptions of Orissa (300–700 AD),* vol. I, pt. 2, Berhampur, Orissa State Museum, 1958, pp. 81–5.

17. P. Mohanty and B. Mishra, 'A Note on a Seal Matrix from Budhigarh, District Kalahandi, Orissa', in *Purattatva*, vol. 30, 2000, pp. 158–60; B. Mishra and M.P. Singhdeo, 'A Unique Seal from Budhigarh, Orissa', *Puratattva*, vol. 32, 2002, pp. 152–5.

18. C.B. Patel, 'Maraguda Valley Excavations', paper presented at the Seminar on Eastern Indian Archaeology, held at Konark during 5–7 April 2001. Also see J.P. Singh Deo, 'Archaeology of Kalahandi and Nuapada Districts, Orissa', in K.K. Basa and P. Mohanty (eds), *Archaeology of Orissa*, Delhi, Pratibha Prakashan, 2000, pp. 418–30.

19. See M. Brandtner, 'Archaeology of Western Orissa: Finds from Nehena', in A. Parpola and P. Koskikallio (eds), *South Asian Archaeology 1993: Proceedings of the 12th International Conference of the European Association of South Asian Archaeologists Held in Helsinki University 5–9 July 1993*, vol. 1, Helsinki, Suomalainen Tiedeakademia (Annales Academiae Scientiarum Fennicae, Ser. B. 271; Suomalaisen Tiedeakatemian toimituksia, Sarja B), 1994, pp. 101–14.

20. H.C. Das, 'Urban Centres in Ancient Orissa', in Amita Ray and S. Mukherjee (eds), *Historical Archaeology of India: A Dialogue Between Archaeologists and Historians*, Delhi, Books and Books,1990, pp. 187–8.

21. S.C. Behera, *Interim Excavation Reports*; *IAR*, 1984–5, pp. 58–9; *IAR*, 1989–90, pp. 80–5 and *IAR*, 1991–2, p. 86.

22. B. Tripathy, 'Archaeology of Boudh', in Basa and Mohanty (eds), *Archaeology of Orissa*, pp. 401–11.

23. S.C. Panda, 'Buddhist Vestiges at Ganiapali and Nagraj on the Ang Valley', in S.C. Behera (ed.), *New Aspects of History of Orissa*, vol. 3, Sambalpur, Sambalpur University, 1981, pp. 47–52.

24. This understanding is based on the discussion in Sangeeta Abhay Chandra's 'Transition to the Early Historical Phase in Chhattisgarh Region of Madhya Pradesh', unpublished MPhil dissertation, Department of History, University of Delhi, 1994, Chapter II.

25. For details, see N.K. Sahu, *Khāravela*, Bhubaneswar, Orissa State Museum, 1984, pp. 377–85.

26. *EI*, vol. 9, pp. 342ff.

27. S.P. Tiwari, *Comprehensive History of Orissa*, pp. 56–7.

28. For details of this idea, see B.D. Chattopadhyaya, 'Transition to the Early Historical Phase in the Deccan: A Note', in B.M. Pande and B.D. Chattopadhyaya (eds), *Archaeology and History*, vol. 2, Delhi, Agamkala Prakashan, 1988, pp. 727–32.

29. In addition to the sites discussed here, archaeological surveys have identified many ruins and mounds in the region, yielding red ware and burnt brick. For example, see *IAR*, 1981–2, p. 54; *IAR*, 1983–4, pp. 61–2; and *IAR*, 1995–6, pp. 60–1. Beglar and Cunningham's Reports also provide a list of sites, though mostly belonging to the later centuries.

30. S. Seneviratne,'Kaliṅga and Andhra: The Process of Secondary State Formation in Early India', in *The Indian Historical Review*, vol. 7, nos 1–2, 1981, pp. 54–69; B.D. Chattopadhyaya, 'Transition to the Early Historical Phase in the Deccan'; B.P. Sahu, 'Early State in Orissa: From the Perspective of Changing Forms of Patronage and Legitimation', in B. Pati, B.P. Sahu, and T.K. Venkatasubramanian (eds), *Negotiating India's Past: Essays in Memory of Partha Sarathi Gupta*, Delhi, Tulika, 2003, especially pp. 35–42.

31. One grant each was issued from Prasannapura and Tilakeswara.

32. S.P. Tiwari, *Comprehensive History of Orissa*, Chapter 2.

33. Ibid., pp. 76–7.

34. The Eastern Vākāṭakas provide a comparable picture. H. Kulke, 'Some Thoughts on State and State Formation under the Eastern Vākāṭakas', in H. Bakker (ed.), *The Vākāṭaka Heritage: Indian Culture at the Crossroads*, Groningen, Egbert Forsten, 2004, pp. 1–9.

35. See, for example, U. Singh, *Kings, Brāhmaṇas and Temples in Orissa: An Epigraphic Study (300–1147 CE)*, Delhi, Munshiram Manoharlal, 1994, the discussion on the Śarabhapurīyas and Pāṇḍuvaṁśīs in Chapter I.

36. See his Bonda, Bardula, Mallar and Lodhia Plates, in A.M. Shastri, *Inscriptions of the Sarabhapurias, Pāṇḍuvaṁśins and Somavaṁśīs*.

37. See 'The Sirpur Stone Inscription of the Time of Mahasivagupta', *EI*, vol. 11, 1911–12, pp. 184–201, verses 12–13, 18–19, and 23–4.

38. U. Singh, *Kings, Brāhmaṇas and Temples in Orissa*, Appendices II and III on 'Official Designations and Fiscal Terms'.

39. H. Kulke, 'The Early and the Imperial Kingdom: A Processural Model of Integrative State Formation in Early Medieval India', in H. Kulke (ed.), *The State in India 1000–1700*, Delhi, Oxford University Press, 1995, pp. 233–62.

40. For details, see J.D. Beglar and A. Cunningham, *Report of Tours in the South-Eastern Provinces, 1874–75 and 1875–76*, vol. 13, Delhi, Archaeological Survey of India, 2000 (rpt), pp. 4–87, 118ff; K.N. Mahapatra, 'Excavation at Belkhandi in the Kalahandi State', in *Journal of Kaliṅga Historical Research Society*, vol. 2, pp. 167–72; J.P. Singh Deo, 'Archaeology of Kalahandi and Nuapada Districts, Orissa', in K.K. Basa and P. Mohanty (eds), *Archaeology of Orissa*, pp. 418–30; D.R. Das, *Temples of Ranipur-Jharial*, Calcutta, Calcutta University, 1990; S.S. Panda, 'New Light on the Brick Temples of the Upper Mahānadī Valley of Orissa', in *Orissa Historical Research Journal* (hereafter *OHRJ*), vol. 35, nos 3–4, 1989, pp. 117–26, and idem., 'Some Archaeological Remains of Bolangir District', *OHRJ*, vol. 40, nos 1–4, 1995, pp. 46–87.

41. B.P. Sahu, 'Aspects of Rural Economy in Early Medieval Orissa', in *Social Scientist*, vol. 21, nos 1–2, 1993, p. 52.

42. Ibid., p. 51.

43. *Padras*, or *Padrakas*, in Orissa even today, are settlements with a sprinkling of houses, clearly separated from *grāmas*, which are full-fledged villages. For a

good discussion of the typology of rural settlements, see A.K. Choudhary, *Early Medieval Village in North Eastern India (AD 600–1200)*, Calcutta, Punthi Pustak, 1971; and B.D. Chattopadhyaya, *Aspects of Rural Settlements and Rural Society in Early Medieval India*, Calcutta, K.P. Bagchi, 1990.

For collective grants, see, for example, Arang Plates of Sudevarāja, Bonda Plates of Tivaradeva, Bardula Plates of Mahasivagupta and Patna Plates of Mahabhavagupta I, in Shastri, *Inscriptions of the Sarabhapurias, Pāṇḍuvaṁśīns and Somavaṁśīs*, pp. 39–42, 102–6, 119–23, and 172–8.

44. Shastri, *Inscriptions of the Śarabhapurīas, Pāṇḍuvaṁśīns and Somavaṁśīs.*

45. R. Chakravarti, 'Kuṭumbikas of Early India', in V.K. Thakur and A. Aounshuman (eds), *Peasants in Indian History*, vol. 1, Patna, Janaki Prakashan, 1996, pp. 179–98.

46. V.V. Mirashi and L.P. Pandeya, 'Mallar Plates of Mahasivagupta', *EI*, vol. 23, 1935–6, p. 120, lines 6–7; P.B. Desai, 'Bardula plates of Mahasivagupta: Year 9', *EI*, vol. 27, 1947–8, p. 290, lines 6–8.

47. See the Gandharesvara temple inscription from the time of Sivagupta, the fragmentary Gandharesvara temple inscription and Sonpur Plates of Mahabhavagupta I, in A.M. Shastri, *Inscriptions of the Śarabhapurīas, Pāṇḍuvaṁśīns and Somavaṁśīs*, p. 152 (line 5), 161 (line 8) and 196 (line 19). Also see R.N. Misra, *Ancient Artists and Art Activity*, Shimla: Indian Institute of Advanced Studies, 1975, pp. 64–5.

48. See S.P. Tiwari, *Comprehensive History of Orissa*, chapter on administration; A.M. Shastri, 'Temple Administration in Chhattisgarh under the Śarabhapurīyas and Paṇḍuvaṁśīs', in *Prachya Pratibha*, vol. 5, no. 2, 1977, pp. 63–9. See also the Pipardula Plates of Narendra, Arang Plates of Sudevarāja and Senakapat stone inscription in Shastri, *Inscriptions of the Sarabhapurias, Pāṇḍuvaṁśīns and Somavaṁśīs.*

49. Inscriptions not only record the grant of a settlement (e.g. *padraka* or *grāma*) to single brāhmaṇas, but also to more than one brāhmaṇa. The Arang plates of Sudevarāja record a grant to nine brāhmaṇas, while the Bonda plates of Tivaradeva mention a grant to twenty-five brāhmaṇas. As mentioned in the Senkapat stone-slab inscription, some of them received certain *hala* measures of land. See A.M. Shastri, *Inscriptions of the Śarabhapurīas, Pāṇḍuvaṁśīns and Somavaṁśīs.*

50. R. Thapar, *Cultural Transactions and Early India: Tradition and Patronage*, New Delhi, Oxford University Press, 1987, pp. 34ff; B.D. Chattopadhyaya, 'Historical Context of the Early Medieval Temples of North India', in idem., *Studying Early India*, pp. 153–71.

51. See the Lodhia Plates of Mahasivagupta, in Shastri, *Inscriptions of the Śarabhapurīas, Pāṇḍuvaṁśīns and Somavaṁśīs*, p. 129, line 11–12 and idem., 'Temple Administration in Chhattisgarh under the Śarabhapurīyas and Paṇḍuvaṁśīs', in *Prachya Pratibha*, vol. 5, no. 2, pp. 63–9.

52. H. Bakker, 'Observations on the History and Culture of Dakṣiṇa Kośala (5th to 7th centuries AD)', in N. Balbir and J.K. Bautze (eds), *Festschrift Klaus Bruhn*, Reinbek, Verlag fur Orientalistische Fachpublikationen, 1994, p. 25.

53. Ibid, 1994, pp. 10 and 22.

54. S.B. Majumdar, 'Tracing the Region-specific Traits in the Saiva Sculptures of South Kośala', *Proceedings of the Indian History Congress* (hereafter *PIHC*), Mysore Session, 2003, pp. 277–85.

55. D.R. Das, *Temples of Ranipur-Jharial*, Calcutta, 1990, p. 49.

56. R.N. Misra, *Sculptures of Dahāla and Dakṣiṇa Kośala and their Background*, Delhi, Agam Prakshan, 1987, Appendix I.

57. Ibid., p. 99.

58. For the temple art of South Kośala, see R.N. Misra, ibid., 99–128; also see J.K. Patnaik 'Stellate Temples of Orissa', in S. Pradhan (ed.), *Orissan History, Culture and Archaeology*, Delhi, D.K. Printworld, pp. 236–40.

59. V. Dehejia, *Early Stone Temples of Orissa*, Delhi, Vikas, 1979, pp. 136–38.

60. See Arang stone inscription and the inscription in the Laksmanesvara temple at Kharod. Also see Bakker (ed.), *The Vākāṭaka Heritage*, p. 14.

61. B.C. Chhabra, *EI*, vol. 24, pp. 243ff; D.R. Das, *Temples of Ranipur-Jharial*, p. 34.

62. On the basis of the style of carving and treatment of figures, it is suggested that the same artists and craftsmen had been at work at both Ratnagiri and Sisiresvara. See V. Dehejia, *Early Stone Temples of Orissa*, pp. 109, 114; S.L. Katare, 'Excavations at Sirpur', pp. 7–8 n 13.

63. H. Bakker, 'Ramtek: An Ancient Centre of Vishnu Devotion in Maharashtra', in idem. (ed.), *The History of Sacred Places in India as Reflected in Traditional Literature* (being volume III of Panels of the VII World Sanskrit Conference), Leiden, E.J. Brill, 1990, pp. 62–85.

64. See, for example, D.R. Das, *Temples of Ranipur-Jharial*; R.N. Misra, *Sculptures of Dahala and Dakṣiṇa Kośala*,, Appendix II, pp. 139–55. For an analogous situation in Bengal, see R.M. Eaton, *The Rise of Islam and the Bengal Frontier, 1204–1760*, Delhi, Oxford University Press, 1997 (paperback), pp. 12–17.

65. See the Lakṣmana temple inscription of Vāṣatā at Sirpur and Mahasivagupta Balarjuna's Sirpur stone inscription, in Shastri, *Inscriptions of the Śarabhapurīas, Pāṇḍuvaṁśīns and Somavaṁśīs*, pp. 141–7 and 150–1.

66. For Tala, see Bakker, 'Observations on the History and Culture of Dakṣiṇa Kośala', pp. 27–9.

67. For a general discussion of the issue in the early medieval context, see B.P. Sahu, 'Legitimation, Ideology and State in Early India', Presidential Address, Ancient India Section, *PIHC*, Mysore Session, 2003, pp. 56–64; A good discussion of the situation in adjoining Vidarbha is available in H. Bakker, 'Throne and Temple: Political Power and Religious Prestige in Vidarbha', in idem. (ed.), *The Sacred Centre as the Focus of Political Interest*, Groningen, Forsten, 1992, pp. 83–100.

68. B.D. Chattopadhyaya, 'Political Processes and the Structure of Polity in Early Medieval India: Problems of Perspective', Presidential Address, Ancient India Section, *PIHC*, Burdwan Session, 1983, pp. 25–63; H. Kulke, 'The Early

and the Imperial Kingdom: A Processural Model of Integrative State Formation in Early Medieval India', in idem. (ed.), *The State in India 1000–1700*, Delhi, Oxford University Press, 1995, pp. 233–62; and B.P. Sahu, 'Brahaminical Ideology, Regional Identities and the Construction of Early India', Presidential Address, Ancient Section, *Proceedings of the Punjab History Conference, 33rd Session, Patiala*, 2001, pp. 12–26; also in *Social Scientist*, nos 338–9, 2001, pp. 3–18.

69. Shastri, *Inscriptions of the Śarabhapurīas, Pāṇḍuvaṁśīns and Somavaṁśīs*, pp. 154–9, verses 15–23.

70. Kulke, 'The Early and the Imperial Kingdom', p. 244.

71. See, for example, the Arang stone inscription, the Sirpur stone inscription, Sirpur Gandharesvara temple inscription and the Senkapat stone slab inscription, in Shastri, *Inscriptions of the Śarabhapurīas, Pāṇḍuvaṁśīns and Somavaṁśīs*, pp. 96–101 and 148–59.

72. For details of this argument, see H. Kulke, 'Some Observations on the Political Function of Copper-plate Grants in Early Medieval India', in B. Kolver (ed.), *The State, The Law and Administration in Classical India*, Munich, Oldenbourg, 1997, pp. 237–43.

73. This has been derived from K. Chakrabarti, 'Cult Region: The *Purāṇas* and the Making of the Cultural Territory of Bengal', in *Studies in History*, vol. 16, no. 1, 2000, p. 14.

74. For a good discussion, see B.D. Chattopadhyaya, 'Autonomous Spaces and the Authority of the State: The Contradiction and its Resolution in Theory and Practice in Early India', in B. Kolver (ed.), *Recht, Staat und Gesellschaft im Klassischem Indien* (The Law, the State and Administration in Classical India), Munich, Oldenbourg, 1997, pp. 1–14.

75. For later developments, see C.U. Wills, 'The Territorial System of the Rajput Kingdoms of Medieval Chhattisgarh', in *Journal of the Asiatic Society of Bengal*, ns, vol. 15, 1919, pp. 197–262; and N.K. Sahu, *Veer Surendra Sai*, Cuttack, Department of Culture, Government of Orissa, 1985, pp. 1–42.

76. It appears that South Kośala which under the later Pāṇḍuvaṁśīs and early Somavaṁśīs was emerging as a region became a subregion of Orissa after the Somavaṁśīs' conquest of eastern or coastal Orissa; and the forging of a regional or supra-regional kingdom.

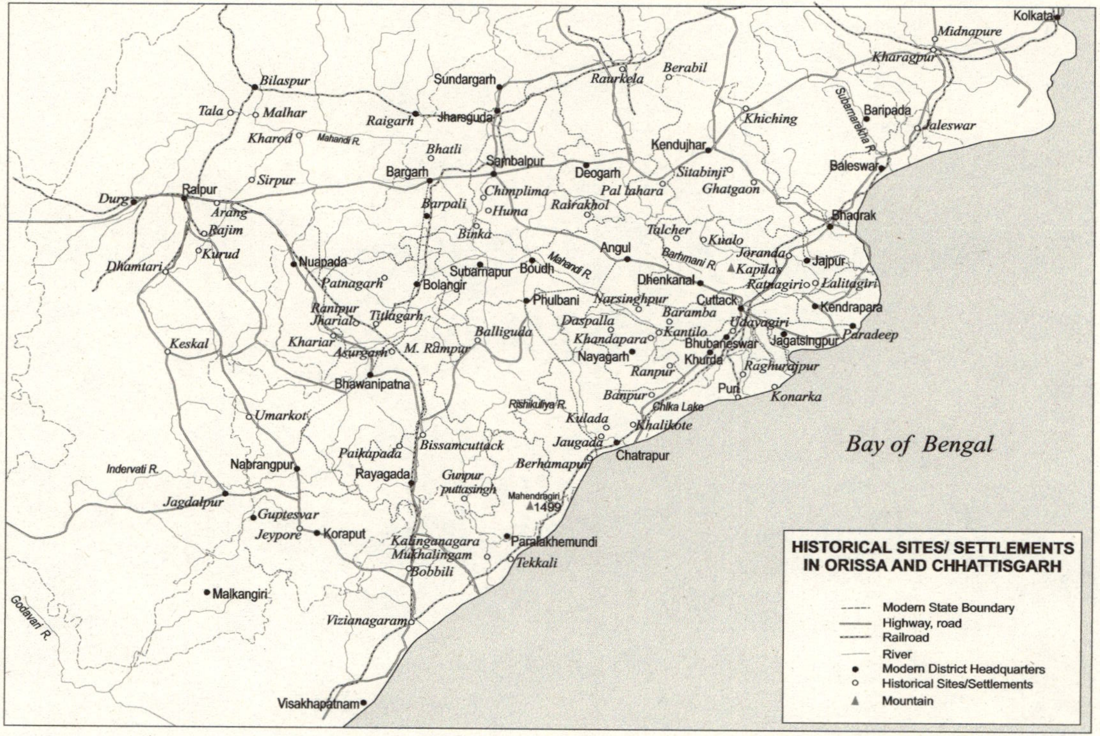

Map 1: Historical Sites in Orissa and Chhattisgarh. Courtesy of Margit Speidel.

II
The Trajectory of Regional Polities

5

Ways of Seeing

History and Historiography of the State in Early India*

The study of the state has been some what privileged in recent years and much has been written over the past thirty years about the state and ideology in early India, which has apart from impacting our understanding of political processes and the structure of polities in ancient and early medieval times, also influenced our comprehension of regional traditions, social formations and the general pattern of early Indian history. An issue of *Studies in History* (1982), four Presidential Addresses to the Ancient India section of the Indian History Congress (1983, 2003, 2009, and 2011), a volume in Oxford University Press's Themes in Indian History series (1995), two collections of essays on State and Society in Pre-modern South India (2002) and *The State in India: Past and Present* (2006) and more recently an entire section of more than two hundred pages in *State, Power, and Violence* (2010), are devoted to the state in early India. One has witnessed in this period a remarkable increase in the number of detailed empirical studies, within more or less sound theoretical frameworks, with different historico-cultural regions as their focus.[1] These writings have partly been produced in India and have partly emerged from Western universities. But then one may ask what accounts for this enhanced interest in the state? In one way or another it is related to the shift from dynastic history towards an understanding of processes and structures, or to the realization that an integrated study of the state provides an entry point to contemporary society and economy.

*Originally published in M. Brandtner and S.K. Panda (eds), *Interrogating History: Essays for Hermann Kulke*, Delhi, Manohar, pp. 63–82.

Admittedly, the state does not exist in isolation; but in a situation of interaction with the other domains and change. Let me elaborate it a bit more. Sedentary agriculture, social differentiation and surplus, among others, are factors which help in the emergence of the state, but once it arises it has the potential of bringing about changes in these very spheres. The role of land grants by the state (from the Gupta period onwards) in agrarian expansion and economic transformation are well known. Similarly, such grants to members of artisanal communities like weavers or potters in lieu of their services to a ritual centre could bring about differentiation within such communities over time. If land grants ensured better economic status, the continued association with a ritual centre enhanced the social position of a group in the long term. The state not only organizes diversity and integrates people with different socio-economic and ritual functions, it also splits up communities.[2] Studies of the state do not just concentrate on issues of how power is shared, distributed or organized, but also tell us something about the socio-economic competence of individuals or groups and their access to or denial of state power, in the general background of the emergence of new social categories (men of substance) and the eclipse of others from time to time.

There are two ways of approaching the subject. One is a constitutional perspective focusing on the definition of the state, derived from texts such as the *Arthaśāstra* or the *Kural*, but that perhaps is a lazy and unexciting way of going about it. The other is to locate states in the past in terms of how they functioned in relation to specific societies and economic situations and, flowing from it, to profile political processes (including legitimation) that had a bearing on their nature and character. The second approach, with a set of questions touching upon issues of state formation, social foundations, typologies of state, the extent of organized political intrusion, and the authority of the state in time and space is surely a more interesting and intellectually rewarding exercise. This shift in the terrain of discussion is of more recent origin. The question then would be, how did we reach here or what has been the trajectory of the studies on the state in early India?

That brings us to the historiography of ancient Indian polities, an area which over the past two centuries has witnessed the making and unmaking (if not the total disappearance) of about half a dozen approaches: the imperialist, nationalist, conventional, Marxist, idealist, and the processual or what Herman Kulke terms processural.[3] Before proceeding further one may make two brief, and fairly obvious, observations. The first is that these labels are somewhat arbitrary categories of convenience and most historians may not be too happy to be slotted as such. Second, no historiography is homogeneous; each comprises a wide range of positions in matters of details.[4] Within the nationalist approach, for example, R.G. Bhandarkar, K.P. Jayaswal, and R.C. Majumdar represent different strands, and in ignoring these differences one will be doing injustice to their individual contributions. Similarly, to paper over the differences in method within the dominant historiography is to simplify and not problematize the issues. Moreover, notwithstanding the differences between the numerous approaches, there are discernible continuities running through some, if not all, of them.

In its early stages this area of study was afflicted by two sets of totalizing and, deriving from it, hegemonic assertions; the imperialist and nationalist perspectives. Colonial Indology marked the beginning of modern writings on ancient India. From James Mill to Vincent Smith, administrator-scholars wrote on a wide spectrum of issues, but did not give any specific attention to political systems. Reflections on it were subsumed under generalities or woven into general discussions on India. In brief, early India was seen to represent a congeries of polities, a conglomeration of peoples (with nothing more than force holding them together) and unchanging despotic monarchies dominating a political map characterized by atomism. We are further told that there was no rule of law, no administered states, popular involvement (not to speak of participation) was absent, moments of larger political unity were rare and civilization prospered only under foreign rule. The situation was compounded by religion permeating all aspects of life. 'The village community' remained impervious to the shifts and turns in the political fortunes of kings and dynasties and persisted throughout, preserving its harmonic character.[5] Continued manifestation of the core formulations, though their lineage extends to James Mill, can be seen even in V. Smith's *Early History of India* (1904). His efforts at writing objective history were dented by the occasional Eucocentric bias, discernible in his treatment of Alexander's campaigns, India in the post-Alexander phase and India after Harṣa. The emphasis on 'the bewildering annals of Indian petty states' and what ensues in the wake of the withdrawal of a supreme authority was perhaps meant to defend the British against charges of despotism at the turn of the century and to turn the idea of Oriental Despotism on its head,[6] making a virtue out of it in the background of this perceived continuous political anarchy; in the process Smith was providing a justification for British rule in India.

The damning indictment of ancient Indian political ideas and institutions need to be situated in the wider context of the shift from 'Indomania' to 'Indophobia', a development not entirely unrelated to the politics and compulsions of the imperial enterprise. It is said that 'Indophobia' was not born, it was made.[7] That explains why the underlying ideological assumption in colonial Indology was the superiority of the European, including British, cultural heritage and conversely the inferiority of the Indian inheritance.

The Nationalist historiography in one way or the other was a response to the imperialist claims, bordering on insistence. Thus, it is the rebuttal aspect of these writings that strikes one's attention. However, in doing so the 'oppositionists' transformed some of the governing hypotheses and formulations to stereotypes insofar as they did not change the terms of discussion, but revolved around the already laid down frames of reference. With the progress of the National Movement, ancient India was called upon to prove the existence of democracy, representative institutions, local self-government, republics and constitutional monarchy (with built-in checks and balances), among a host of other claims. The *abhiśekha* ritual, for example, is said to have symbolized the subordination of power to *dharma* and civil society, and the state's revenue claims seem to have remained mild all through. While K.P. Jayaswal in his by now famous *Hindu Polity* (1918), argued for most of it in the manner of a brilliant defense counsel, Radha Kumud Mookerji urged the recognition of *The Fundamental Unity of India* from the earliest times onwards. In his perception the idea of India as known in the early part of the twentieth century existed in the ancient past too. Further, the construction of the idea of a Golden Age and private ownership of land constituted an inversion of Oriental Despotism. The discovery of the *Arthaśāstra* was a shot in the arm. Armed with it, early India could be credited with a long tradition of political philosophy, large unified political enterprises, a welfare state, and so on.[8] The nationalists recovered and revived dynasties such as the Guptas, Vākāṭakas and Nāgas, and bestowed them with undue honour and glory. They emphasized the great constitutional progress made in early India, which was comparable to the best anywhere; including contemporary England.

The nationalists questioned individual items, but not the basic theoretical presuppositions of the imperialists. Despite all their protests, their approach was rooted in that framework which had set the terms of discussion. There was continuity in the major premises, though they were suitably modified. Thus, we are faced with two kinds of national historiographies, the imperialist and the nationalist viewed from the Indian perspective, trying to prove the presence or absence of a set of political ideas, practices, and institutions in India's past. History was placed at the service of politics, and both were making significant use of the past for opposite purposes. The polemics highlight the role of ideology in historical constructions. They also make the point that unless new questions are asked, or there is a shift in the ground of discussion, historiography does not move ahead.

The writings of the 1940s and 1950s, especially those of K.A.N. Sastri and A.S. Altekar, may be characterized with the advantage of hindsight as traditional or conventional. They were marked by a meticulous concern for accuracy and obsessive avoidance of systemic generalization and evaluation. They usually presented a descriptive account of government and administration at various levels, under numerous dynasties. Administrative details, it was assumed, represented the nature and structure of the state and, flowing from it, they went on to create the picture of centralized, unitarian imperial states with numerous and powerful bureaucracies.[9] In this construction, which equated dynastic and administrative history with the study of the state and largely took its existence for granted, there were a plethora of empires, but little concern for the problem of the origin of states, types of states, and change over time and space. Politics was perceived to be an independent, autonomous domain, abstracted from society. Their engagement with discourses on empire was a carry over from the past. In their enthusiasm to reconcile centralization at the top with the autonomy of the village republics below they failed to see the inherent theoretical inconsistency in the argument. However, one may quickly add that in this apparent conceptual ambiguity was embedded an interesting possibility for future historians, who argued for 'autonomous spaces' within the ambit of the state;[10] with significant implications for understanding the structure of the state, to which we shall return below.

People write histories not in an intellectual vacuum, but in situations they inherit and encounter. Thus, writing history is a dialogic process involving a response to past historiographical traditions and contemporary influences. The problem of reconciling the irreconcilable in the conventionalists' characterization of the state then, can possibly be explained by invoking the shadow of earlier traditions and debates surrounding the making of the Indian Constitution and the nature of the state about to be around the time of India's independence. The Indian Constitution provides for a quasi-federal system with the balance clearly titled in favour of the centre. More or less the basic orientation of inscribing the present continued.

The aforesaid forms of writing political history, in the absence of much analysis of ideas, institutions and historical change, from the later part of the 1950s, and particularly since the 1960s, made way (if not entirely abandoned) for new perspectives. The earliest efforts to understand the state in relation to society and economy were made by D.D. Kosambi and R.S. Sharma; both almost simultaneously inaugurated the Marxist intervention in the historiography of early Indian political ideas and institutions. They were the first to raise discussions to a level of conceptualization, to which we shall soon return.

Meanwhile, there has been a range of writings, incidentally emanating mostly from Western universities, which perhaps for the want of a better term have been classified as 'idealist'. Notwithstanding the differences in the focus of their research interests, treatment of the subject, and style of presentation, what is common to the writings of J. Gonda, Louis Dumont, J.C. Heesterman, Burton Stein, and Ronald Inden, among others, is that they are somewhat abstracted from reality and therefore appear to be ahistorical. Gonda's[11] treatment of kingship in ancient India mixes up the ideal with the real and in generalizing about the institution, based on sources separated in time (and space), ignores the context, or the stages in its evolution. Dumont[12] in subscribing to the Brāhmaṇical view of the caste system, believes that the king having conceded hierarchical preeminence to the brāhmaṇa was perpetually under the shadow and influence of the latter. His notion of 'secularized kingship' not only separated the ritual and temporal domains, but also actually subordinated the political to the moral or social sphere. Dumont seems to have marginalized kingship and replaced it with the idea of 'theocratic despotism'. Proceeding from the understanding that Indian reality was fraught with contradictions, Heesterman segregates power and authority.[13] The brāhmaṇa was endowed with authority because of his association with the transcendental value of renunciation, which was (and continues to be) held in esteem by Indian society. Having said that, Heesterman moves on to argue that 'authority having been siphoned off, the state lacked the means to rise above the essential instability of personal relations'.[14] What we are faced with is the picture of a hapless, permanently incapacitated state, or at best the condominium of the king's authority. It may be of some interest to note that Heesterman extrapolates an atrophied state even from the *Arthaśāstra*, a text which most historians have used to construct the image of a centralized, omnipresent Mauryan empire.

The problem inherent in these works is perhaps partly related to an unwillingness or refusal to concede the role of ideology in the making of early state societies. It also needs to be recognized that the state has a logic of its own, and though it closely interacts with society, it is not necessarily always determined by it. Early Indian ideologues, as in other ancient societies, mystified reality and the relations of power. By continuously according preeminence to the brāhmaṇa or kṣatriya alternately in text after text, they successfully projected the image of endemic conflictual relations between them. However, neither the precedence of one over the other, nor categorical separation of the two; explains their dynamic relationship, or how authority was constituted in ancient India. Competition apart, there was collaboration between them, involving patronage for one and validation for the other. In fact, the brāhmaṇas and kṣatriyas together constituted the power elite.[15] It was in their mutual interest that the secret was not given away and that reality was camouflaged.

Burton Stein's contributions to early medieval studies cannot be underestimated. Through his emphasis on ritual sovereignty and the *nāḍus* (in charting the history of the state during the Pallava-Cōḷa times) he compelled discussion on the role of the sacred domain and local agrarian societies in understanding the structure of polities. Where he seems to have erred is in his preference for a theoretical framework, the segmentary state, which detached the state from its socio-economic foundations, and the absolute distinction he made between political and ritual sovereignty.[16] This analysis was bereft of socio-political substance; as well as of the dynamics of change. Ronald Inden[17] too focuses on the symbols of power, courtly culture and ideational aspects, instead of actual power relations and politics, drawing on perspectives from a text; to the exclusion of the wealth of epigraphical material.

In brief, the 'idealists' appear to believe in changeless, unstable, continuously post-tribal political formations in pre-colonial India.[18] Like James Mill they assume that once the transition from tribe to monarchy was over Indian political institutions lost their capacity to change. They wish away the historical transitions in the realms of ideology, state and society. The envisaged arrested political growth is generally explained with reference to built-in cultural impediments or the religious mentality of the Indians—caste, transcendental value of renunciation or the atavistic, restricted peasant mentality. The cycle had come full circle, from Oriental Despotism, through 'theocratic despotism' and 'oriental desperatism', it was back to the early formulations.

D.D. Kosambi's and R.S. Sharma's interventions in the later 1950s raised discussions of early Indian polity 'from variations in narratives to contending formulations'. They situated the state in the wider context of economy and society and bridged the gap between politics and society, instead of the compartmentalized approach of the earlier traditions. Kosambi was not specifically interested in early Indian polity, but he provocatively suggested a possible relationship between the rise of Magadha, the emergence of urban centres and that of the 'heterodox' sects in the middle of the first millennium BC.[19] The significance of his well-known formulations, feudalism 'from above' and 'from below', and the envisaged relationship between *bhakti* in the *Gītā* and the emergent social formation need no emphasis.[20] Some of his suggested ideas were amended, refined and systematized in later years by Sharma. Sharma's *Aspects of Political Ideas and Institutions in Ancient India* (1959), raised new and thought provoking questions. Did ancient Indians deserve credit for developing nuanced political ideas, intricately weaving the political, social, and the religious? Were ideas and institutions unchanging owing to the continuity of traditions, or do they reflect changes in consonance with change intrinsic to South Asian society, as elsewhere? His evaluation of these issues and delineation of stages in ancient Indian polity (as in the domains of society and economy) were path-breaking.[21] From the Gupta period onwards, Sharma argues, the alienation of state revenues and administrative rights through land grants to brāhmaṇas and officials led to feudal decentralization.[22] The creation of multiple foci of power and *sāmanta*s of various grades (who were held together by grant of privileges, symbolic means, and force), in this perception, were the product of state initiative. In addition, terms denoting different levels in the *sāmanta* hierarchy, graded land rights, hierarchized structure of management in religious institutions, including non-brāhmaṇical establishments such as Buddhist *vihāra*s and Jaina *basaḍis*, and the visible manifestation of hierarchies in temple art, are seen to represent the feudal order.[23] Both Kosambi and Sharma saw religion and religious ideas as a social force, and as ideology providing legitimacy and coherence to the state. In their concern for a theoretical framework to understand early Indian history, or in making systematic generalizations, derived from an ideological position, Kosambi and Sharma provided food for thought.

The works of M.G.S. Narayanan, R.N. Nandi, and Kesavan Veluthat, among others, can be linked to R.S. Sharma's thesis of the feudalization of the state in early medieval times.[24] While Narayanan charts the history of the Cēra kingdom of Makōtai in the context of the problems associated with state formation in Kerala and Veluthat focuses on the structure of polity in south India, Nandi, on the basis of evidence from Karnataka and Andhra, addresses issues related to lord-vassal relationships and the hierarchy of *sāmanta*s.

The Political Structure of Early Medieval South India by Veluthat is an excellent work bearing on religious and political symbols and the structure of legitimation, as well as the socio-economic foundations and the structure of the state, sans the author's preference for a certain model which is ill at ease with the available evidence.[25] The fact that state power was enjoyed by many individuals and corporate bodies at different levels and that there was a great deal of decentralization leads him to argue for south Indian feudalism. However, its genesis remains to be explained. The trajectory of socio-political developments in early Tamiḷakam does not anticipate or explain it. Haziness surrounds the question of the payment of tribute and transfer of resources by chiefs to their overlords. Similarly, political relationships or the hierarchies of domination and subordination do not emerge with unmistakable clarity. The envisaged three-tiered feudal order comprising the Cōḷa overlord, Cēra king and his *nād* chiefs seems to run into rough weather when one realizes that the relationship between the *Perumāḷ* (the Cēra-king) and the hereditary, traditional chiefs of the bigger *nād*s was more flexible than is generally assumed.[26] Again, what Nandi perceives as 'the ceremonial act of vassalization amounting to legitimatization' of ambitious chiefs may equally be seen to represent the incorporation of local chiefs, rising from below. When the state bestowed land grants and honour on a *gāvuṇḍa*, *heggaḍe*, or *pergaḍḍe* for their outstanding military service it was, in fact, reinforcing and strengthening their existing competence. As men of substance already associated with revenue administration, they did not entirely derive their authority from such acts of benevolence on the part of the state. It is possible that through these local elites the state was trying to reach out to newer areas and extend its authority.[27] In discussions on political relations, allusions to the lotus feet of the lord in the copper plate inscriptions, presented in different forms and styles, need not be taken seriously, because there is no dearth of evidence to show that overlords were overthrown by their *sāmanta*s at the first opportunity. At best such evidence may be seen as rhetoric contributing and/or conforming to contemporary images of royalty.

Reality was far more complex and problematic than the perceived neat hierarchies, involving relations of protection and loyalty at various levels.[28] The nature of relations between the king and his subordinates at the intermediate and local levels was not static, but dynamic. Great kings in regional or supra-regional formations were not absolute masters because the lesser kings and chiefs accepted their own subordinate positions largely owing to political compulsions or having entered into mutually beneficial deals. However, this is not to suggest that there were no moments of larger political unity when states tried to intrude as far as possible and achieve vertical administrative integration. The history of the Cōḷas between Rājarāja and Kulōttuṅga is a case in point. So were the efforts at administrative reorganization by the Later Gaṅgās of Orissa under Vajrahastadeva III (1038–70) and Anantavarman Cōḍagaṅgādeva (1078–1152). Such examples also provide a corrective to tendencies to generalize from the perspective of dynastic histories for long periods. The early and later Cōḷa periods provide different histories of the state, pointing to structural changes over time.[29]

There is lack of evidence to support the development of a feudal political structure from around the middle of the first millennium AD. Not that it makes a difference to the larger argument, but incidentally all the evidence that Nandi cites belong largely to the end of the first or early second millennium. To posit that the inability to centrally administer large territorial states led to the feudalization of the state, or suggest that may be the earliest form of state in south India assumed the feudal form[30] amounts to not explaining what needs to be explained. That brings us to the question of what prompted ruling houses to delegate administrative and fiscal rights. The idea of the Kali Age, supposedly representing a ubiquitous crisis, has been adduced to explain the phenomenon of land grants and consequent changes.[31] However, this interpretation has been questioned, and alternatively it is argued that the concept represents the spread of purāṇic and epic ideas and the importance of brāhmaṇas in the making of dominant ideology, in a situation of the formation and spread of local states from around the middle of the first millennium AD. It was not a historical crisis, but a crisis of confidence related to the anxieties of the brāhmaṇas, in the face of unprecedented social and cultural change related to economic growth in the early centuries of the Common Era, which influenced the formulation of the idea.[32] Land grants are mostly reported from regions outside the Gangetic plains. They were issued by kings and chiefs belonging to the newly emerging local states. The spatio-temporal correspondence between land grants and local state formation clearly brings out the inherent relationship between the two phenomena.[33] It then disturbs the epicentric view of land grants and the unmaking of the state in early medieval India.

Generalizations about the state in the dominant historiography tend to homogenize the variety of human experiences and, in doing so; they do violence to the conceptual category (feudalism in this case) by spreading it thin across the varied regions. The characterization of the Mauryan state as a centralized empire with more or less even presence over its territories, and the subsequent Kuṣāṇa and Sātavāhana states as different not so much in form as in scale is closely related to the understanding that the nature of the post-Gupta states was feudal. Post-Gupta political fragmentation could be explained only in the background of some kind of larger unity or wholesomeness. In perceiving the early historic state as being reflective of a certain techno-economic base, insofar as it is related to the iron-productivity-surplus-complex society paradigm, and the state in early medieval India as the prime-mover, which brought about the gamut of significant changes through its decision to make land grants, the dominant historiography does not help the cause of a coherent theory of state. At the level of a long-distance vision of Indian history the fragmented political world of early medieval India does not cohere with the centralized structure of the Sultanate.

The representation of the state within the dominant historiography began to lose some of its lustre as more and more historians moved towards understanding the structure of states in relation to contemporary political processes, in the background of the shift from simple mechanical explanations to locating historical developments in terms of the interplay of multiple forces. Romila Thapar, B.D. Chattopadhyaya, Hermann Kulke, Y. Subbarayalu, and S. Seneviratne, among many others, have documented the way the state structures were varied, flexible, continuously evolving and trying to come to grips with different local and regional situations.[34] An intellectual affinity between these works and those of S.K. Panda, Swapna Bhattacharya, James Heitzman, Cynthia Talbot, Nandini Sinha, the present author, and some of the contributions of Rajan Gurukkal and Kesavan Veluthat is easily discernible.[35] They have addressed concrete specific situations to improve our understanding in terms of the fact that the state is not something of a standard, finished product, which once actualized; would reproduce itself more or less in similar forms across varied spatial contexts. The career of historiographic unease can be traced to Thapar's writings since the late 1960s[36] and the works of B. Stein, Nicholas Dirks, G.W. Spencer, B.D. Chattopadhyaya, and Hermann Kulke in the 1970s.[37]

The processual approach, and within it the integrative model of state formation in early medieval India, emerged formally in the early 1980s, but derived considerably from the intellectual ferment of the 1970s, as well as a different reading of some of the formulations of the dominant historiography and those of Stein.[38] In the early historical context, while Thapar focuses on the origin of the state in north India and the Mauryan state, highlighting the complexities associated with the transition from pre-state to state society; as also the uneven presence and, deriving from it, the different faces of the state in the varied regions. Chattopadhyaya, Seneviratne, Gurukkal, and this author address the trajectory of the evolution of political society in the Deccan, Andhra, Tamiḷakam, and Orissa respectively. The emergence of state society in these regions was the consequence of considerable internal evolution and interactions with Gangetic northern India; in the wake of the Mauryan conquest. The transition derived itself not from administrative integration under the Mauryas, because it did not happen uniformly across regions, but from the network of linkages and internal dynamics of local societies. Chattopadhyaya and Kulke also provide a critique of the other two contending conceptual frameworks for understanding early medieval Indian polity: the 'Indian feudalism' model and that of the 'segmentary state'.[39] The process of integrative state formation shows the phased spatial extension (including territorial integration) and structural evolution of states in areas peripheral to or outside the Gaṅgā valley from the mid first millennium AD onwards. The stages in state formation are expressed either in terms of chiefdoms, early kingdoms and imperial kingdoms, or as local, sub-regional and regional/supra-regional polities. The relationship between the sacred and temporal domains, the changing forms of ideological intervention by the state and cultural integration through incorporation and transformation of regional traditions are inextricably woven into the discussion. The extension of state power and the evolution of the structure of polity, expansion of the agrarian frontier, and the emergence of markets as nodes are continuously treated as simultaneous, interrelated developments.[40] Instead of macro-generalizations the focus is on regional structural changes and within it the sub-regional and local formations get their due. Regional state formation is, thus, situated in the wider context of numerous political processes; and change coming from within local societies as well as from the network of transregional linkages.

There has been some engagement with the intermediate levels of the socio-political order[41] and the issue of legitimation. While the *kuṭumbin*s appear as addressees in the early land-grant charters, the *mahattara*s, *mahāmahattara*s, *gāvuṇḍa*s and other region-specific rich peasants acquired prominence in the later land transaction documents. These groups seem to have shared the confidence and authority of the state. However, the recognition and incorporation of the newly emerging significant local landed categories into the regional state structures and changing forms of legitimation, bearing on state-society interface, are areas which warrant greater attention. This is not the place to go into the details of various approaches, including the one under discussion. However, it may be added that the study of legitimation of power in early Indian societies, which has attracted the attention of Indian and non-Indian scholars in the last forty years or so, is an important area of study; largely because it focuses on the strategies of domination, including the cultural basis of power, over time. The significance of the theme has gained acceptance over the last quarter century and some new questions have been posed.[42]

Chattopadhyaya envisages the existence of 'autonomous spaces' in early India, which were organized differently from the 'administered' territories.[43] They comprised physical spaces as well as alternative centres of authority within the frontiers of the state, such as the village community (with its corporate institutions), localities, castes, guilds, etc., bound by and managing their affairs through commonly arrived at decisions, customs, and *dharma*. It is argued that matters of common concern such as local law and order, policing, defense, and so on were looked after by them to the exclusion of the superior, transcendent authority of the state.[44] However, this did not entirely preclude state intervention. There are examples of the state being invoked to resolve local knotty problems and surely as and when necessary, as in the case of the Cōḷas and the Later Eastern Gaṅgās mentioned above, the state could and did intrude even without invitation. The concept makes two significant points: first, that such spaces did not exist in isolation, but were open to interactions and change; and secondly that any search for homogeneity or a great degree of cohesiveness within the territorial limits of the state will not be rewarding. Apart from the fact that integration was never perfect, it needs mention that the process was not always harmonious; it involved competition and contestation, and, flowing from it, continuous engagement and negotiations.[45] In this perspective the evolution of the state was neither unilinear nor unidimensional, states could and did consolidate and expand, and, similarly, they also suffered shrinkage.

The ways in which the state has been perceived are largely a product of choice and consequence of historiographies rarely questioned on their paradoxes and inconsistencies until recently. In course of the shift from consciously inscribing the present to deciphering the past historians have moved beyond the merely descriptive approach to the subject and developed conceptual tools to sharpen our understanding of institutional structures and society.[46] With the recognition of the possibility of more than one reading of the available source material the understanding of the state, as in other areas, in early India has gained immensely. Similarly, the regional empirical studies focusing on Tamil Nadu, Kerala, Andhra, Orissa, and Rajasthan, and their related issues, have thrown up new questions and modified some of our cherished notions. Recent perspectives of the state on the face of it constitute an inversion of the dominant historiography, but change of perspective need not always mean change of ideological position. The processual model of socio-political change in early India has, in fact, corrected and refined some of the arguments and assumptions in the 'Indian feudalism' model. The authors of the processual model or integrative paradigm cannot be viewed as opponents of the dominant historiography insofar as their writings are embedded in, and form an extension of, the same social formations approach. It only demonstrates the possibilities and prospects inherent in the approach.

NOTES

1. One may mention the works of Romila Thapar, *From Lineage to State: Social Formations in the Mid-First Millennium* BC *in the Gaṅgā Valley*, New Delhi, Oxford University Press, 1984; R.S. Sharma, *The State and Varna Formation in the Mid-Gaṅgā Plains: An Ethnoarchaeological View*, New Delhi, Manohar, 1996; idem., *Aspects of Political Ideas and Institutions in Ancient India*, Delhi, Motilal Banarsidass, 1991 (3rd edn.); S.K. Panda, *The State and Statecraft in Medieval Orissa under the Later Eastern Gaṅgās (*AD *1038–1434)*, Calcutta, K.P. Bagchi, 1995; H. Kulke, *Kings and Cults: State Formation and Legitimation in India and Southeast Asia*, New Delhi, Manohar, 1993; Nandini Sinha, *State Formation in Rajasthan: Mewar During the Seventh-Fifteenth Centuries*, New Delhi, Manohar 2002; C. Talbot, *Precolonial India in Practice: Society, Religion and Identity in Medieval Andhra*, New Delhi, Oxford University Press, 2001; Kesavan Veluthat, *The Political Structure of Early Medieval South India*, Delhi, Orient Longman, 1993; idem., *The Early Medieval in South India*, New Delhi, Oxford University Press, 2009; B. Stein, *Peasant State and Society in Medieval South India*, Delhi, Oxford University Press, 1980 and R.N. Nandi, *State Formation, Agrarian Growth and Social Change in Feudal South India, c.* AD *600–1200*, New Delhi, Manohar, 2000, which focus either entirely or substantially on the state.

B.D. Chattopadhyaya, like Kulke, has contributed substantially to this area of study. See idem., *The Making of Early Medieval India*, New Delhi, Oxford University Press, 1994, chs 2, 3 and 8 and *Studying Early India: Archaeology, Texts and Historical Issues*, Delhi, Permanent Black, 2003, chs 3, 7, and 8. For some other important contributions during the same period see H. Kulke (ed.), *The State in India*, Delhi, Oxford University Press, 1995; H. Kulke and U. Skoda (eds), *State and Ritual in* India, Section IV, in Margo Kitts *et al.* (eds), *State Power and Violence*, Wiesbaden, Harrassowitz Verlag, 2010; and N. Karashima (ed.), *Kingship in Indian History*, Delhi, Manohar, 1999.

2. See, for example, B.D. Chattopadhyaya, 'Political Processes and the Structure of Polity in Early Medieval India: Problems of Perspective', Presidential Address, Ancient India Section, in *Proceedings of the Indian History Congress* (hereafter *PIHC*), Burdwan session, 1983, pp. 25–63.

3. See H. Kulke, 'The Early and the Imperial Kingdom: A Processural Model of Integrative State Formation in Early Medieval India', in idem. (ed.), *The State in India*, pp. 233–62.

4. For a detailed discussion see B.D. Chattopadhyaya, 'Confronting Fundamentalisms: The Possibilities of Early Indian History', *Studies in History*, vol. 18, no. 1, 2002, pp. 103–20.

5. For some good discussions see R.S. Sharma, *Aspects of Political Ideas*, ch. 1; Ronald Inden, *Imagining India*, Oxford, Basil Blackwell, 1990, ch. 5; D.K. Chakrabarti, *Colonial Indology: Sociopolitics of the Ancient Indian Past*, New Delhi, Munshiram Manoharlal, 1997, pp. 86–116 and 'Conclusions', and D. Lorenzen, 'Imperialism and the Historiography of Ancient India', in S.N. Mukherjee (ed.), *India: History and Thought*, Calcutta, Subarnarekha, 1982.

6. See Romila Thapar, 'Interpretations of Ancient Indian History', in idem., *Ancient Indian Social History: Some Interpretations*, Delhi, Orient Longman, 1987 (rpt.), pp. 1–25.

7. For an excellent analysis of the complexities associated with the competing ideas and shifting dominant positions in Colonial India see T.R. Trautmann, *Āryans and British India*, Berkeley, University of California Press, 1997.

8. Good surveys of the nationalist positions are available in Sharma, *Aspects of Political Ideas*, Thapar, supra n. 6, and A.L. Basham, 'Modern Historians of Ancient India', and R.C. Majumdar, 'Nationalist Historians', in C.H. Philips (ed.), *Historians of India, Pakistan and Ceylon*, London, Oxford University Press, 1967 (rpt.), pp. 260–93 and 416–28.

9. See Veluthat, *The Political Structure of Early Medieval South India*, ch. 1.

10. See B.D. Chattopadhyaya, 'Autonomous Spaces and the Authority of the State: The Contradiction and its Resolution in Theory and Practice in Early India', in Bernhard Kolver *et al.*, (eds), *The State, the Law and Administration in Classical India*, Munchen, 1997, pp. 1–14; also in Chattopadhyaya, *Studying Early India*, pp. 135–52.

11. J. Gonda, *Ancient Indian Kingship from the Religious Point of View*, Leiden, E.J. Brill, 1969. For a different perspective see R.S. Sharma, 'From Gopati to Bhūpati: Changing Position of the King', in idem., *Aspects of Political Ideas*, pp. 185–96.

12. L. Dumont, 'Conception of Kingship in Ancient India', *Contributions to Indian Sociology*, vol. 6, 1966, pp. 48–77.

13. For J.C. Heesterman's views, see 'The Conundrum of the King's Authority', 'Power, Priesthood and Authority' and 'Kauṭilya and the Ancient Indian State', in

idem., *The Inner Conflict of Tradition: Essays in Indian Ritual, Kingship and Society*, New Delhi, Oxford University Press, 1985.

14. J.C. Heesterman, 'Power and Authority in Indian Tradition', in R.J. Moore (ed.), *Tradition and Politics in South Asia*, New Delhi, Vikas, 1979, p. 82.

15. See for details Sibesh Bhattacharya, 'Political Authority and Brāhmaṇa-Kṣhatriya Relationship in Early India: An Aspect of the Power Elite Configuration', *Indian Historical Review* (hereafter *IHR*), vol. 10, nos 1–2, 1984, pp. 1–20.

16. B. Stein, 'The Segmentary State in South Indian History', in Richard G. Fox (ed.), *Realm and Region in Traditional India*, New Delhi, Vikas, 1977, pp. 3–51; idem., 'The Segmentary State: Interim Reflections', in H. Kulke (ed.), *The State in India*, pp. 134–61; for a critique see D.N. Jha, 'Validity of the Brāhmaṇa-Peasant Alliance and the Segmentary State in Early Medieval India', in *Social Science Probings*, vol. 1, no. 2, 1984, pp. 270–96 and R.S. Sharma, 'The Segmentary State and the Indian Experience', *IHR*, vol. 16, nos 1–2, 1989–90, pp. 80–108.

17. R. Inden, 'Hierarchies of Kings in Early Medieval India', in T.N. Madan (ed.), *Way of Life: King, Householder, Renouncer, Essays in Honour of Louis Dumont*, Delhi, Motilal Banarsidass, 1982, pp. 99–127. For a recent good, comprehensive discussion, see Daud Ali, *Courtly Culture and Political Life in Early Medieval India*, Cambridge, Cambridge University Press, 2004.

18. Inden, *Imagining India*, ch. 5; also see B.P. Sahu, 'The State in Early India: An Overview', in *PIHC*, Aligarh Session, 1994, pp. 88–98.

19. See D.D. Kosambi, *An Introduction to the Study of Indian History*, Bombay, Popular Prakashan, 1956, ch. 6.

20. Ibid., chs 9 and 10; D.D. Kosambi, *The Culture and Civilization of Ancient India in Historical Outline*, London, Routledge, Kegan & Paul, 1965, pp. 206–9.

21. See R.S. Sharma, *Aspects of Political Ideas*, chs 4, 12, 14, 16, 17, 22 and 23, for example.

22. See, for example, R.S. Sharma, *Indian Feudalism, c. 300–1200*, Calcutta, Macmillan, 1965, and idem., 'How Feudal was Indian Feudalism?', *Journal of Peasant Studies*, vol. 12, nos 2–3, 1985, pp. 19–43.

23. Sharma, 'The Feudal Mind', in idem., *Early Medieval Indian Society: A Study in Feudalization*, Kolkata, Orient Longman, 2001, pp. 266–82.

24. M.G.S. Narayanan, 'The Hundred Groups and the Rise of Nāyar Militia in Kerala', in *PIHC*, Burdwan Session, 1983, pp. 113–19; 'The Cēra Kingdom of Makōtai: Factual and Conceptual Problems Related to State Formation in Kerala', paper presented at the Seminar on State Formation in Precolonial South India, Centre for Historical Studies, Jawaharlal Nehru University, New Delhi, March 1989, and M.G.S. Narayan and Kesavan Veluthat, 'The Bhakti Movement in South India', in S.C. Malik (ed.), *Indian Movements: Some Aspects of Dissent, Protest and Reform*, Simla, Indian Institute of Advanced Studies, 1978, pp. 33–66; Veluthat, *The Political Structure*, R.N. Nandi, 'Feudalization of State in Medieval

South India', *Social Science Probings*, vol. 1, no. 1, 1984, pp. 33–59; also in idem., *State Formation, Agrarian Growth*, supra n.1.

25. Kesavan Veluthat, *The Political Structure of Early Medieval South India*, Delhi, Orient Longman, 1993.

26. See Narayanan, 'The Cēra Kingdom of Makōtai', supra n. 24.

27. See, for example, Kesavan Veluthat, 'Landed Magnates as State Agents: The Gāvuṇḍas under the Hoyśāḷas in Karnataka', in *PIHC*, Gorakhpur session, 1999, pp. 118–23; also in B.P. Sahu (ed.), *Land System and Rural Society in Early India*, Delhi, Manohar, 1997, pp. 322–8.

28. Nandi himself provides evidence for the complex relations between different grades of chiefs and *samantas*, supra n. 24; also B.P. Sahu, 'The State in Early India', supra n.18, pp. 94–5.

29. See, for example, Y. Subbarayalu, 'The Cōḷa State', *Studies in History*, vol. 4, no. 2, 1982, p. 304, and J. Heitzman, 'State Formation in South India, 850–1280', *Indian Economic and Social History Review* (hereafter *IESHR*), vol. 24, no. 1, 1987, pp. 44–61.

30. See Nandi, 'Feudalization of State in Medieval South India', Kesavan Veluthat, *The Political Structure*, p. 267.

31. See R.S. Sharma, 'The Kali Age: A Period of Social Crisis', in S.N. Mukherjee (ed.), *India: History and Thought*, Calcutta, Subarnarekha, pp. 186–203; also in idem., *Early Medieval Indian Society*, supra n.23, pp. 45–76, and B.N.S. Yadava, 'The Accounts of the Kali Age and the Social Transition from Antiquity to the Middle Ages', *IHR*, vol. 5, nos 1–2, 1978–9, pp. 31–63.

32. The initial doubts were raised by B.D. Chattopadhyaya in his 'Political Processes and the Structure of Polity', and 'Introduction' to *The Making of Early Medieval India*, for a detailed discussion see B.P. Sahu, 'Conception of the Kali Age in Early India: A Regional Perspective', in *Trends in Social Science Research*, vol. 4, no. 1, 1997, pp. 27–36.

33. See B.D. Chattopadhyaya, 'State and Economy in North India: Fourth Century to Twelfth Century', in Romila Thapar (ed.), *Recent Perspectives of Early Indian History*, Bombay, 1995, pp. 309–46.

34. Supra nos 1–3 and 28; also see Romila Thapar, *The Mauryas Revisited*, Delhi, Popular Prakashan 1987; S. Seneviratne, 'Kaliṅga and Āndhra: The Process of Secondary State Formation in Early India', *IHR*, vol. 7, nos 1–2, 1980–1, pp. 54–69; B.D. Chattopadhyaya, 'Transition to the Early Historical Phase in the Deccan: A Note', in B.M. Pande and B.D. Chattopadhyaya (eds), *Archaeology and History*, Vol. II, Delhi, Agam Kala Prakashan, 1987, pp. 727–32; and H. Kulke, 'Royal Temple Policy and the Structure of Medieval Hindu Kingdoms', in A. Eschmann, H. Kulke and G.C. Tripathi (eds), *The Cult of Jagannāth and the Regional Tradition of Orissa*, Delhi, Manohar, 1978, pp. 125–38.

35. Supra nos 1 and 28; also see Veluthat, 'Landed Magnates as State Agents'; idem., 'Into the "Medieval"—and out of it: Early South India in Transition', Presidential

Address, Medieval India Section, Bangalore session, *PIHC*, 1997; also in his *The Early Medieval in South India,* supra n.1.; Rajan Gurukkal, 'Towards the Voice of Dissent: Trajectory of Ideological Transformation in Early South India', *Social Scientist*, vol. 21, nos 1–2, 1993, pp. 2–22; Sahu, 'Conception of the Kali Age in Early India', and idem., 'Early State in Orissa: From the Perspective of Changing Forms of Patronage and Legitimation', in B. Pati, B.P. Sahu, and T.K. Venkatasubramanian (eds), *Negotiating India's Past: Essays in Memory of Partha Sarathi Gupta*, Delhi, Tulika, 2003, pp. 29–51.

36. Thapar has always been focusing on the mutual interaction between numerous historical forces. See for example, her Presidential Address, Ancient India section, *PIHC*, Varanasi session, 1969.

37. For Stein and Kulke supra nos 16 and 34. For some of Kulke's other contributions see A. Eschmann *et al.* (eds), *The Cult of Jagannāth*, also see B.D. Chattopadhyaya, 'Origin of the Rajputs: The Political, Economic and Social Processes in Early Medieval Rājasthan', *IHR*, vol. 3, no. 1, 1976, pp. 59–82; N. Dirks, 'Political Authority and Structural Change in South Indian History', *IESHR*, vol. 13, no. 2, 1976, pp. 125–57, and G.W. Spencer, 'Religious Networks and Royal Influence in Eleventh century South India', in *Journal of the Economic and Social History of the Orient*, vol. 12, 1969, pp. 42–56, and idem., 'The Politics of Plunder: The Choḷas in Eleventh Century Ceylon', *Journal of Asian Studies*, vol. 35, no. 3, 1976, pp. 405–19.

38. See B.P. Sahu, 'Early Medieval Orissa: Recent Historiographic Trends', *PIHC*, Dharwad session, 1988, p. 163; and H. Kulke, 'The Integrative Model of State Formation in Early Medieval India: Some Historiographic Remarks', in M. Kimura and A. Tanabe (eds), *The State in India: Past and Present*, New Delhi, 2006, pp. 59–81.

39. For example, see H. Kulke, 'Fragmentation and Segmentation Versus Integration? Reflections on the Concepts of Indian Feudalism and the Segmentary State in Indian History', *Studies in History*, vol. 4, no. 2, 1982, pp. 237–63; Chattopadhyaya, 'Political Processes and the Structure of Polity', and 'State and Economy in North India'.

40. Ibid., also see Chattopadhyaya, 'Markets and Merchants in Early Medieval Rajasthan', in idem., *The Making of Early Medieval India*, pp. 89–119; idem., *Aspects of Rural Settlements and Rural Society in Early Medieval India*, ch. 3; and B.P. Sahu, 'Agrarian Changes and the Peasantry in Early Medieval Orissa (*c.* AD 400–1100)', in V.K. Thakur and A. Aounshuman (eds), *Peasants in Indian History*, Vol. I, Patna, Janaki Prakashan, 1996, pp. 283–311.

41. See Veluthat, 'Landed Magnates as State Agents', Cynthia Talbot, 'Political Intermediaries in Kākaṭiya Andhra, 1175–1325', *IESHR*, vol. 31, no. 3, 1994, pp. 261–89 and Chattopadhyaya, *Aspects of Rural Settlements*, ch. 2.

42. For a recent statement see B.P. Sahu, 'Legitimation, Ideology and State in Early India', Presidential Address, Ancient India section, *PIHC*, Mysore session, 2003, pp. 44–76.

43. Supra n.10.

44. Ibid., also see Rajan Gurukkal, 'Aspects of Warrior Power in Localised Agriculture: The Case of Pāṇḍya Region during the Early Medieval Period', *PIHC*, Srinagar session, 1986, pp. 192–8, and V.S. Elizabeth, 'Hero-stones in the Rāshṭrakūṭa Period: Their Implications for Society and Polity', *PIHC*, Gorakhpur session, 1989, pp. 828–33, and Romila Thapar, 'Death and the Hero', in idem., *Cultural Pasts: Essays in Early Indian History*, New Delhi, Oxford University Press, 2000, especially pp. 690–1.

45. See Chattopadhyaya, *The Making of Early Medieval India*, p. 30 and Kulke, supra n.38.

46. For a good discussion of the idea of 'little kingdom', for example, which was a structural constituent of the expansive, incorporative states see B. Schnepel and G. Berkemer, 'History of the Model'; G. Berkemer and Margret Frenz, 'Hermann Kulke: An Appreciation of His Contribution to the Debate', among others, in Georg Berkemer and Margret Frenz (eds), *Sharing Sovereignty: The Little Kingdom in South Asia*, Berlin, Schwarz, 2003.

6

The Early State in Orissa

From the Perspective of Changing Forms of Patronage and Legitimation*

Preliminaries

Recent perspectives on the state have moved beyond the obvious engagement with its administrative apparatus and resource generation, to include various kinds of interface with society and culture at different locations and contexts, in all their complexities. Power is a broader and more comprehensive concept than authority, which is a form of power but not the only one. Authority is legitimate power and as such, is associated with assured, regular obedience of the subjects. While the distinction between power and authority is an important one, people seeking to sustain and consolidate their power always look for ways to legitimize it. All forms of power, including domination, concentrate on a variety of justifications.[1] Ruling elites find it difficult to justify their power by *de facto* possession of it, and therefore try to find a moral and/or ethical basis for it. Validation of power was necessary not only in communities passing from the pre-state stage to the stage of state society, but also in established complex societies. Legitimation helps in addressing the concerns and compulsions emanating from within local society, as well as in conforming to and becoming a part of the pan-Indian tradition. Legitimation of temporal power and the

*Originally published in B. Pati, B.P. Sahu, and T.K. Venkatasubramanian (eds), *Negotiating India's Past: Essays in Memory of Partha Sarathi Gupta*, New Delhi, Tulika, 2003, pp. 29–51.

I am grateful to Professor B.D. Chattopadhyaya for his comments on an earlier draft of this paper.

making of dominant ideology are issues more complex than have generally been assumed. Legitimation, instead of being perceived in simple reductionist terms, is increasingly located as an arena of continuous engagement, involving contestation and negotiation, and as being constantly restructured and redefined.[2]

Patronage, with its inherent capacity to confer status and influence the domain of popular perceptions, has always been an important factor in socio-political processes, including the legitimation of royal authority. Rulers derived their legitimation through patronage of brāhmaṇas, local deities and religious centres, among others. Studies on patronage and legitimation in early India range from analysis of the brāhmaṇa-kṣhatriya relationship and grant of land and resources to monastic establishments, through the study of purāṇic genealogies and the imageries of kingship in inscriptional evidence, to temple-building activities as well as the formation of cultic centres.[3] In ancient societies, as so often today, patronage was usually not disinterested. The objective implicit in the act, more often than not, was the creation of iniquitous social bonds and interactive networks of asymmetrical relationships, and consequently further strengthening of the prevalent authority structure.[4] The patron, the recipient, and the objects of exchange were the interacting elements in the act. The dynamics of the relationship between the constituent elements were rooted in the particular society, for, ultimately, conceptions of status, power, and authority were culturally patterned. Patronage included not only impressive monuments but also more modest efforts and services, for what really mattered was the perception that such activities created at the popular level and the image that they helped to project.[5] Community patronage, as distinguished from that of the ruling elite, implied among other things, popular acquiescence in the social advancement of individuals and/or groups. Patronage, thus, viewed in a broader perspective, bound people in complex relationships of domination and subordination, and in doing so, institutionalized unequal relations in society. Patronage being a significant component of the dominant ideology and, therefore, of the strategies of domination, its changing forms, it is hoped, will reflect the trajectory of socio-political transformations in early Orissa.

Studies on early Orissa are usually limited to the construction of political and dynastic history. It is presumed that administered bureaucratic states were the normal prevailing condition from the time of the Mahāmeghavāhanas, the first local dynasty. The state is also perceived as something that was natural and given. Such assumptions, deriving perhaps from the imperialist and nationalist discourses on empire, contributed to the image of the all-powerful, omnipresent state in early India, divorced from its material foundations and having little to do with popular opinion.[6] In an effort to re-evaluate some of these questions, this chapter explores the complex links between patronage and legitimation in the particular regional context, its immense variety, changing forms, and the social categories involved in the act. It focuses on the relationships between art, religion, state, and society on the basis of archaeological, sculptural, and epigraphic sources. The period covered is roughly between the first century BC and *c.* AD 600. The lower limit of this time-span is defined by the Hāthigumphā inscription and the group of rock-cut caves at Udayagiri and Khandagiri, on the outskirts of Bhubaneswar. The terminal date perhaps warrants some explanation. By the seventh century, the manifest socio-political profile in many areas, especially in the littoral region, indicated an early stage of the transition to the early medieval period. It then constituted a turning point in the history of the region.

The Beginnings

Udayagiri and Khandagiri provide the earliest evidence of systematically organized rock-cut monuments in the region. The Dhauli elephant sculpted just above the set of Aśokan edicts is perhaps the only piece of incontrovertible evidence of an earlier art form, dating to the middle of the third century BC. The elephant gives the impression of emerging out of the woods, for only the first half has been sculpted. Historians hold diametrically opposite views on the remnant of a lion figure and the bell capital, now placed in the Orissa State Museum, and the *liṅga* identified as a part of a pillar, in the Bhāskareśwara temple at Bhubaneswar.[7] Though these sculptural relics need not have been part of an Aśokan pillar or even contemporary to each other, at the present stage of research it is difficult to be precise about their antiquity and authorship.

The series of caves at Udayagiri and Khandagiri dedicated to Jaina monks are situated not far away from Sisupalgarh, identified with Kaliṅganagara, the ancient capital of Khāravela. The inscriptions in some of them indicate that these were excavated between the first century BC and first century AD, under the patronage of the Mahāmeghavāhanas. Khāravela, the most illustrious of them, is known to us by his lengthy Hāthigumphā inscription. Despite the fact that the data are not voluminous, the donors may be divided into two broad categories. The first includes those belonging to the ruling class, for example, Khāravela himself, his chief queen, king Kudepasiri (probably a successor of Khāravela), prince Vadukha,[8] the town judge (*nagara akhadamsa*) Bhūtti, and Nākiya, the wife of the *mahāmada*,[9] while the second category comprises humble individual donors, most probably lay devotees and monks.[10] In the latter category donations by (*pādamulika*) Kusuma, a servant/menial or even nun, and the monks of Dohāḍa are noteworthy. The donation by Jaina monks is unambiguously stated, unlike the indirect, hesitant references to similar donations at Mathura. In addition, it indicates that, like the Buddhist monks in the Deccan and central India, the Jaina monks too possibly did not renounce all their worldly possessions and could have used these for worthy purposes.[11] Each cave (*leṇa*) was usually a gift by a separate individual and the donations may have been more substantial as compared to those at Sanchi.[12] The possible explanation for this lies in the elite nature of most donations. The paucity of donative records at Udayagiri-Khandagiri may be accounted for by the fact that Khāravela seems to have provided the funds for the construction of most of the caves.[13]

The evidence also provides insights into the socio-political dimensions of art in early Orissa. The fact that the donors considered it necessary to record their gifts, so that they could be read, suggests that they were seeking advertisement for their acts and, flowing from it, recognition and status, apart from religious merit. The donative record of the chief queen also mentions her pedigree, connecting her to another ruling family. She is said to be the daughter of King Lalaka, the grandson or great-grandson of Hastisahasa/Hastisiṁha.[14] It is tempting to invoke parallels with Nāyanikā's marriage to the Sātavāhana king Śātkarṇi in the Deccan, with all its political implications. However, in doing so at this stage, there is the danger of reading more than what is provided in this short inscription.[15] Another aspect of these inscriptions is that they record three donations by women: one by a queen, the second by the wife of a state functionary, and the third by a nun or menial (?) woman.[16] They themselves may not suggest anything significant. However, they acquire meaning in the light of the rich sculptural representation of women at the site in a variety of contexts, both in the private and public domains.[17] The social visibility of women may imply the absence of an entrenched, Brāhmaṇical society premised on *varṇa*/caste ideology and gender hierarchy.[18]

For purposes of piety the recording and display of the donor's name is not necessary, and less so is a lengthy public statement encapsulating the career and achievements of the donor, as in the case of the Hāthiguṁphā inscription. Apparently, the purpose of the Hāthiguṁphā inscription was not merely to record the donation to the Jaina recluses. The image or self-image of Khāravela was also aimed to be projected through it. A carefully constructed image of royalty runs through the length of the record, especially, in the first two and last two lines, revealing the various elements that were invoked in its making. The elements include the picture of a successful warrior, a hero, a conqueror/*chakravartin*,[19] a liberal donor, a benevolent and responsive administrator, a patron of the arts and religions, etc.

In the narrative reliefs on the façade of the caves, particularly those on the lower storey of Rāṇiguṁphā, the representations bear witness to an emphasis on royal actions. In the sculptural arrangement, one finds a corroborative and repetitive image of kingship. This is an early, perhaps the earliest, instance of historical and political allegory in contemporary art. The use of metaphors in lithic art and the spatial spread of such art forms are usually associated with the Gupta period and beyond. The sculptural elements range from war to entertainment on the elaborate façade to carefully select narrative stories, and are focused on themes relating to the career and conquests of Khāravela.[20] The sculptures celebrate the political success of the *chakravartin* king symbolized in the installation of the Kaliṅga Jina after its recovery from Magadha following the defeat of its ruler, who, perhaps, is shown bowing at the feet of Khāravela in one of the scenes.[21] The remarkable correspondence between the visual imagery of the sculptures and the content and spirit of the epigraph is striking, and only the naïve would believe that it was accidental, not designed. Their propaganda and, deriving from it, their legitimation value, cannot be underestimated. These symbols of substance at the Udayagiri–Khandagiri complex vividly convey the self-image(s) of kingship, and are possibly visible markers of the political structure of early Kaliṅga. Monuments are indicators of, as well as mediums for, the control over produce and labour. Their capacity for generating respect and awe, and conferring esteem needs no emphasis. They are thus acts of political wisdom and not merely related to personal religious faith. While the simplicity of the architectural plan conforms to Jaina ethics and ethos, the sculptural arrangement in general has much that is mundane and elaborate. Not everything is religious or Jaina in this case. Scenes of combat, dance, music, songs, festivities, rejoicing, and so on,[22] although they might militate against the self-denying, austere, supposedly Jaina ambience of the site, are still very much there. Khāravela's faith in Jainism notwithstanding, he relentlessly engaged in political aggrandizement, war and booty—indicating perhaps the pragmatism associated with the political compulsions of a ruler.

Khāravela, in spite of his personal faith in Jainism, was liberal to all sects. This catholicity is evidenced by the expression *sava-pāsaṁḍapūjako sava-devāyatana-saṁkārakārako* (the worshipper of all religious orders, the repairer of shrines of all gods) in line seventeen of the Hāthiguṁphā inscription. Royal generosity was widespread and there is a mention of donations to brāhmaṇas as well.[23] Again, this non-sectarian attitude of the ruler is corroborated by sculptural art. Nāga figures are found on the door arches at Anantaguṁphā. Tree worship has been depicted in one of the tympana on the façade of Anantaguṁphā and at Jaya-Vijayaguṁphā in the space between the arches.[24] Interestingly, the six *yakṣa* images and three large images of Nāgarāja reported from sites in the vicinity of Bhubaneswar are broadly dated around the time of the Mahāmeghavāhanas.[25] Miniature *yakṣa*s occur at the Rāṇiguṁphā and Gaṇeśaguṁphā in Udayagiri, and the Anantaguṁphā at Khandagiri.[26] All this evidence, together, point towards religious pluralism, characterized by the coexistence of popular cults and beliefs. Khāravela may be seen to have been responding to the religious and cultural aspirations of a diverse ethno-cultural setting, somewhat like the Kuṣāṇas in north India. Compulsions of royal power made it necessary for the king not to be perceived as being partisan and/or sectarian.[27] The broad-based religious patronage, thus, was not entirely disinterested.

The reconstruction and beautification of Kaliṅganagara, the capital, arrangements for the restoration of the aqueduct, entertainment of the people with music, dance, and festivities, building of the victory palace, and the remission of taxes and cesses,[28] perhaps, were largely acts of benevolence, for they led to the creation of a special kind of a bond between the ruler and his subjects because of their potential to provide for better conditions for agriculture, employment opportunities and such other benefits.[29] Such acts were neither entirely personal acts of charity nor impersonal conduct, as are commodity relations, especially when these were prominently listed as achievements, as part of a lengthy public statement, by the king. Moreover, the poverty and misery of the masses, it is said, is the breeding ground for aristocratic patronage.[30] Thus, the relationship between deprivation and patronage focuses on an important dimension of temporal power and authority.

The evidence suggests that the Udayagiri–Khandagiri complex and the associated projects were products as much of power and politics as of piety. The images of kingship and of forms of patronage as gleaned from the inscriptional and sculptural data may be better understood in the context of the power structure and the nature of the polity.

The earliest manifestation of some form of institutionalized state in ancient Kaliṅga under Khāravela seems to have derived largely from the Mauryan interaction with the region, as were the contemporaneous, similar developments in the Deccan.[31] The details of the processes leading to this are exasperatingly elusive in the archaeological record.[32] The two sets of Aśokan inscriptions at Dhauli and Jaugada suggest that the Mahānadī delta and Riṣikulya valley were scenes of activity during the Mauryan period. Aśokan Kaliṅga roughly extended from the Cuttack-Puri area to the modern Ganjam-Srikakulam districts. Though apparently a digression, it is imperative to mention that the term Kaliṅga had varying connotations at different points of history, and probably covered the area up to the Godavari-Krishna delta along the Andhra coast in the early historical period.[33] Coming back to the Mauryan context, it is difficult to be precise about the administrative details and its consequences, on the basis of the available evidence. We may infer that there was a great deal of socio-political flux after the end of the Nanda-Mauryan experience and the region's interaction with the metropolitan centre. Maximum opportunities for the growth of chieftainships would have arisen at the centres of Mauryan interaction in the wake of such a momentous development. The hitherto co-opted periphery or 'locality' elites, with their power and status enhanced within their own societies because of the said interaction, could acquire a more meaningful and visible political profile.

Sisupalgarh, identified with Tosali, one of the administrative centres in Aśokan Kaliṅga near Dhauli, has produced evidence for continuous occupation between the earlier part of the third century BC and *c.* AD 300.[34] It is situated on the outskirts of Bhubaneswar on the way to Dhauli. Jaugada, identified with Samāpā, the other contemporary political centre in the region, has yielded similar data.[35] It may not be entirely coincidental that the Mahāmeghavāhanas—Khāravela being the third in the family—rose to power around Bhubaneswar and the Mahānadī delta. At the risk of repetition one may reiterate that Khāravela's chief queen came from a ruling lineage with three to four generations of history. The expression *Kaliṅga purvarāja nivesitaṁ* (founded by the earlier rulers of Kaliṅga), in line eleven of the Hāthiguṁphā inscription, implies the existence of ruling chiefs in Kaliṅga prior to the Mahāmeghavāhanas. Inscriptional evidence, thus, indicates the continued presence of 'locality' chiefs in the post-Mauryan period.

Notwithstanding the adoption of exalted titles such as *chakradharo*, *chakravarti*, *Kaliṅgādhipati*, and *mahārāja* by the Mahāmeghavāhanas,[36] the power structure over which they presided seems to have been in an early stage of evolution. It is doubtful if they were able to provide for an 'administered' polity. There is very little evidence for a state exercising control over a precisely delimited territory with the help of a bureaucratic command structure, where the contours of power relations and the jurisdiction of the officials were defined. The *mahāmada* and *nagara akhadaṁsa* are two high state functionaries mentioned in the donative records discussed above. The interpretation of the words *kamma*, *chūlakamma*, and *pādamulika* is far from satisfactory, and one is not sure whether the first two constitute personal names or administrative designations.[37] Even if we concede, for the moment, the latter possibility, our understanding of the administrative structure is by no means enhanced. Certainly, it was not a state with a bureaucratic structure, characterized by officials with distinct and specific jurisdictions. The possibility of individuals holding multiple responsibilities cannot be ignored. Taxes and cesses are mentioned in the context of their remission. Surprisingly, neither Khāravela nor his successors seem to have issued any dynastic coins. More so, because Khāravela refers to colossal state expenditure on his construction projects, among other things.[38] One may consider the possibility of some of the available punch-marked coins being used as the medium of exchange. However, most of the coins from Sisupalgarh, including the silver punch-marked coin, date from *c.* AD 100 onwards. Besides, coins with their motifs and symbols are also signs and statements of royal sovereignty, and their absence cannot be wholly unrelated to the compulsions and nature of the socio-political system. A comparison with the contemporary Deccan makes the paucity of metallic money in Kaliṅga more conspicuous.[39] The rudimentary administrative mechanism and such other associated problems[40] were sought to be compensated, perhaps, by the forging of ties through various forms of cultural transactions in a post-tribal state, as it were.

Khāravela's unusual inscription was an important, and possibly effective, medium of communication. Indubitably, it was a discourse in power and conveys the notion of authority. It eulogizes war, valour, and victory, and highlights the prospects of booty and tribute. However, nowhere does the image of a compelling, assertive or even persuasive ruler emerge, either from the language or tone of discourse. To make a more general point about the importance of such evidence for understanding the nature of contemporary political structures, it may be useful to briefly reflect on the Aśokan inscriptions, for instance. Even a cursory reading of the Aśokan inscriptions reveals that the mode of discourse in such mediums of communication is important and is likely to provide significant insights into the nature of power and authority. The paternalistic attitude and image of a father figure that the Aśokan inscriptions exude, while simultaneously conveying the king's striking self-confidence and notion of authority, are noteworthy.[41] The point of inference is that the state under Khāravela, with an independent socio-political organization, a vaguely defined territory, and centre of government, and an ideology based on the concept of reciprocity, apparently, was an early state. The military successes of Khāravela in general and his victories over such categories as the Bhojakas, Raṭhikas, and the people of Pithuṇḍa in particular, seem to have been overstated.[42] The military campaigns appear to have been plundering raids, because there is nothing to suggest a consolidation of the gains from these conquests. Moreover, such localities/communities were themselves in a stage of transition to the early historical phase.[43] These raids, however, had the potentiality of generating the necessary resources for the extensive patronage at home, which could sustain the ruling elite's strategies of domination and, consequently, help the consolidation of authority.

In spite of the fact that there is a reference to *paurajanapada* and evidence for royal indulgence, the vagueness that surrounds the ordinary people is striking. The community and the common man/woman are elusive. Given the limitations of the data, one can see depictions of society in the art of Udayagiri and Khandagiri and in artifacts from sites like Sisupalgarh. But, as for the larger issue relating to the nature of society itself, the available evidence is not unequivocal. The use of terms such as *chakravartin, agamahiṣī, nagara, rājarsi*, and *Bhāratavarsha*, terms with perhaps northern moorings, is instructive. References to northern political centres in the Hāthigumphā record also indicate the ongoing cultural interactions. The existence of brāhmaṇa households may be inferred from line nine of the said epigraph. It mentions them as recipients of royal munificence, among others. Nevertheless, Vedic sacrifices and patronage of brāhmaṇas were not yet integral to the legitimation process. Khāravela significantly claimed to be a descendant of Rājarsi Vasu. Brāhmaṇas, and Brāhmaṇical ideology, structures and institutions were still not intrinsic to the making of strategies of domination. Society, though largely casteless, was not necessarily classless. Material prosperity, growing technical skill, trade and cultural contacts are demonstrable in the archaeological record.[44] However, there is little on the organizational aspects of manufacture and trade. A casual comparison with the data from the Deccan concerning the varieties of guilds, their activities, and intra-regional and inter-regional exchange networks, shows up the poverty of information in the Orissan context. In addition, the non-issuance of coins by the Mahāmeghavāhanas, among other things, perhaps reveals the state of the market economy and the level of the society. It has generally been recognized that early historical trade was conducted by guilds, cutting across political formations.[45] However, in Orissa during the said period, we do not come across terms denoting traders, commercial centres or guilds. Kaliṅga, because of its geographical location, perhaps acted as a bridge in the eastern coastal trade; but that is far from saying that mercantile activities were in the making in the region.[46] D.D. Kosambi's thesis on the socio-economic role of the cave-monasteries on trade routes[47] is enticing but, given the nature and limitations of the data, it is difficult to ascribe a very active role to the group of caves at Udayagiri–Khandagiri, not far away from Sisupalgarh, in the trade network along the east coast.

Material remains, coins, pottery, ornaments, etc., are more numerous in the second–third century AD layers at Sisupalgarh.[48] The earliest evidence of rouletted ware from the site is dated to the latter half of the first century AD, and the glass bangles and clay bullae belong to the second century. The gold coin of Dharmadāmadara, a Murunda ruler supposedly, and the clay seal of *amātya* Prasannaka belong to the third century.[49] This brief survey does not focus on factual details, important though these may be, but on the overall pattern that emerges from the material remains.[50] Interestingly, defences were in good condition till the mid-first century AD and thereafter were neglected, coinciding perhaps with the decline of the Mahāmeghavāhanas. Under Khāravela, therefore, Sisupalgarh appears to have been more of a political centre than anything else. The cultural sequence and data obtained at Jaugada, to the south, in Ganjam district, broadly conform to the Sisupalgarh evidence.

What emerges from this amorphous evidence is a society in a stage of transition to the historical period where the contours of development were not fully established and, hence, providing conflicting signals. It seems to have been a loosely organized, primarily agrarian society, in which the basic distinction was between the ruling elite and the ruled. Beyond this the differences appear to have been considerably blurred and not hierarchically structured, as in later societies.

Localities Conform

The processes leading to the emergence of ruling elites at the level of 'localities'[51] did not end with Khāravela and his immediate successors. Continued manifestation of the process in the early centuries of the Common Era is discernible in the dispersed data from various pockets of the region. They demonstrate uneven and perhaps dissimilar patterns of growth in the region, while simultaneously revealing the inherent complexities. The expansion of the Mahāmeghavāhanas into the Godavari-Guntur area of modern Andhra Pradesh in the mid-second century AD[52] manifests a continuation of the process of locality formation. Whether this was an offshoot of one of Khāravela's campaigns or a consequence of fission, that is, segmentation of the ruling family, or both, is not clear. The two relevant inscriptions, the Guntupalli inscription[53] and Velpuru inscription,[54] record the donation of two *maṇḍapa*s, one each by the scribe of Mahāmeghavāhana Śri Sada and the lady attendant (Devā, the lamp-bearer) of Aira Mahārāja Mānasada. Though it is difficult to determine the exact relationship between the Mahāmeghavāhanas and this Aira Mahārāja, it is significant that *Aira* as a family name also occurs in the record of the Mahāmeghavāhanas of Kaliṅga, and the title *mahārāja* was used by them as well. The grants were made in favour of, what appear to be, autochthonous deities. Donations to deities and the association of the donors in some capacity or the other with the state attract attention. Commoners, for example, peasants, artisans, and traders, continue to be absent from the scene. The accrued political profile of the said locality, implicit in the inscriptions, may have to be viewed in the context of a further stage in the transition to the historical period. Similarly, the Bhadrak stone inscription of the time of Gaṇa, dated to the second half of the third century AD, recording the donation of a certain measure of land or grains in favour of a shrine or religious establishment,[55] has important socio-political implications. It has a bearing on the question of the evolution of ownership rights in land and/or control over produce. In addition, the tentative political visibility of the locality suggests that its internal transformation, leading to the emergence of the historical phase, was far from complete.[56] The process there, in all likelihood, came into its own during the late fifth or sixth century.[57]

The subsequent emergence of the Bhañjas in the Keonjhar area, and Mahārāja Tuṣṭikara around Asurgarh, in Kalahandi district, will have to be viewed in terms of the continuation of the same trend. However, these localities, far as they are from the coast, help us to appreciate the phased evolution and development of the variegated areas in the region. The patronage extended to the local, autochthonous deity Stambeśvarī by Mahārāja Tuṣṭikara, referred to in his Terasinga Plates,[58] perhaps finds archaeological corroboration in the excavated circular brick structure at Asurgarh. The site yields some very inconclusive, yet significantly suggestive, information on the developments leading to this stage in the fifth century. Fine black polished ware, a broken piece of chunar sandstone with Mauryan polish, red glazed Kuṣāṇa-type pottery, unfinished or broken pieces of stone ornaments and a mould for the preparation of ornaments,[59] among other finds, reflect the earlier history of the site. The fragmentary evidence from Manmuṇḍā, located close to the confluence of the Mahānadī and the Tel in Phulbani district, and Ganiapalli, near the confluence of the Ang and Magar rivers in the district of Sambalpur, relate to the early centuries AD.[60] They suggest the formative beginnings of these areas. In much of western and southwestern Orissa the formation of 'localities' and the transition to the historical period seem to have been generally later than similar developments in the coastal districts.

The Asanapat inscription of Mahārāja Śatrubhañja of the Nāga family records the construction of a shrine (*Deva-yatana*) by the king,[61] while the inscription on the stone image of Śiva from the same site in Keonjhar district describes events during Śatrubhañja's rule.[62] At Sitabinji in the same district, there is a tempera showing a royal procession. The name of the king is mentioned as Rājarāja Sri Diśabhañja. In its vicinity are a *chaturmūkha liṅgam* and boulders, some of which are inscribed with the names of Śaiva ascetics. The associated finds include a female figurine, a ruined brick structure, bronze ear ornaments, pottery and Puri-Kuṣāṇa coins. Khiching, in the neighbouring Mayurbhanj district, has yielded a stone seal with the letters reading *rāgarāja* (*rājarāja*),[63] implying the presence of some ruling chief. There is a visible pattern in the apparently scattered data which conforms to the emerging ubiquitous trend. They focus on the linkages between temporal power and the sacred domain, the networks of patronage and legitimation that rulers with a name ending in 'bhañja' sponsored and participated at the locality level, during the fourth to sixth centuries.

Patronage centred on locality deities and their shrines or establishments may be understood in the context of the need to create larger community identities by transcending kinship considerations. Autochthonous chiefs without the support of a kṣatriya status for legitimacy extended patronage to locality deities. The politics of patronage legitimized power and helped the emergence of a stratum of ruling elites. Consequently, it accentuated differentiation within communities and lead to the formation of complex relationships of domination and subordination.

On the basis of the spatial distribution of punch-marked coins, covering both western and coastal Orissa, and the discovery of the coin mould from Sisupalgarh, the presence of an organized currency system in the post-Khāravela period may be suggested. The chronology of these coins is, however, debatable. While most of the coins have been conventionally dated from the middle of the first millennium BC onwards, the date of the Sisupalgarh find is around AD 100 and the Asurgarh collection of fifty coins came from the upper-most layer assigned to the fifth century.[64] It is not unlikely, therefore, that these coins were in circulation up to the fourth–fifth centuries AD. Hoards of Puri-Kuṣāṇa coins (local Kuṣāṇa imitations), usually in association with some Kuṣāṇa coins, have been reported from different parts of northern and coastal Orissa. The abundance of these coins, among other things, suggests that it was the regional currency during the second–fourth/ fifth centuries.[65] The find-spots of these coins point to the possibility of a trade route from the Singhbhum area of Jharkhand to coastal Orissa and Andhra through the northern districts of Keonjhar and Mayurbhanj. The Mahānadī valley could have been used as a communication route between the littoral and the flood plains of western Orissa. The concentration of both punch-marked and Puri-Kuṣāṇa coins in the coastal districts is perhaps indicative of their growing social complexity. Familiar beliefs about ancient Orissa's transoceanic trade networks may be disturbed but the actual evidence for trade with Southeast Asia is little,[66] and the data for Roman contacts are limited to the rouletted ware and clay bullae from Sisupalgarh and the few Roman coins from Bamanghati in Mayurbhanj.[67] With the available information it is difficult to be precise about the organization, nature and impact of early historical trade in the region.[68]

The details of the processes and stages in the emergence of 'localities', and the transition to the early historical period are not clear. It is, however, obvious that historico-cultural stages were uneven over the region.[69] While some localities, particularly those in the coastal tract, acquired early visibility, others inland were still characterized by ill-defined, at times even exasperatingly hazy, contours of development. However, the early socio-political manifestations even in the relatively difficult terrains of northern and western Orissa suggest that both the movement of men, ideas and goods, and human interactions, including perhaps exchange networks, cut across geographical categories such as heartland, periphery and frontier.[70]

Towards the Early Medieval

Land grants to brāhmaṇas and the growth of temples, the two ostensible markers of patronage since the Gupta period, can be appreciated in the context of the formation of sub-regional agrarian bases and the need to legitimize the emerging political structure and society.[71] Royalty patronized brāhmaṇas, subscribed to the Brāhmaṇical ideology and dispersed their resources as donations to Brāhmaṇical institutions, due to their own compulsions. Such patronage ensured the extension and consolidation of authority.[72] Ruling lineages used the mystique of Vedic rituals, śāstric ideas and purāṇic symbolisms to strengthen their authority. The relationship between the king and the brāhmaṇa was crucial to the processes of state formation and socio-economic transformation. In Orissa, these processes began to operate simultaneously from the fourth–fifth centuries onwards. The formation of agrarian bases at the locality and sub-regional levels was an ongoing process and it introduced a comparable socio-political structure throughout.

The spread and entrenchment of Vedic, śāstric, and purāṇic discourses can be gleaned from the early epigraphic records and sculptures of Orissa. The Māṭhara, early Eastern Gaṅgā and Śailōdbhava inscriptions bear testimony to these developments. These records refer to the Vedas, Vedāṅgas, Vedic sacrifices, *purāṇas*, purāṇic deities, and stories.[73] Kings begin to be compared with heroes of the epics, such as Arjuna and Hanumāna.[74] Moreover, statements suggesting the destruction of the impurities or stains of the Kali age in the early Eastern Gaṅgā and Śailōdbhava records, among others, are suggestive of the cultural and ideological transformation.[75] The references to the Kali age in purāṇic literature have been interpreted to symbolize a systemic crisis in northern India.[76] However, in the context of Orissa, Kali may be perceived differently. Repeated references to the removal of the stains of the Kali age are usually juxtaposed with the virtue and purity of the king, which helped him to accomplish the act. A contextualized analysis of the notion of virtue/purity of the ruler shows that it meant the patronage of Vedic sacrifices, *varṇāśrama dharma* and the śāstric-purāṇic value system.[77] Kali, thus, was a metaphor for a society not conforming to the normative, ideal Brāhmaṇical prescriptions. It symbolized the negation of *dharma* and, flowing from it, the king, representing order, had to be distanced from it. The notion of the Kali, while distinctly highlighting kingly virtues by contrast, unmistakably suggests the formation of monarchial states with reference to the dominant ideology.[78]

The early temples of Bhubaneswar, such as Śatrughneśwara, Lakṣhmaṇeśwara, Parasurāmeśwara, and Suvarṇajaleśwara, depict scenes from the epics and the *purāṇas*. Themes relating to the marriage of Śiva and Pārvatī, Śiva curbing the pride of Rāvaṇa, Śiva begging food of his consort, the discussion between Rāma and Sugriva, Rāma killing the golden deer, Bāli's death at the hands of Rāma, the fight between Śiva as Kīrata and Arjuna, and so on, constitute the subject matter of the narrative panels in these temples. These sculptures indicate the familiarity of the artists with stories from the epics and *purāṇas*, and constitute significant evidence of the process of internalizing cultural forms. The Śaiva *āchāryas* who were associated with this earliest group of temples may be seen as contributors to the propagation of these new ideas and institutions. Brāhmaṇas and temples were thus the agencies for disseminating these ideas. The spread of such ideas would have achieved socio-cultural integration over wider areas, and across communities. Consequently, the associated symbols would be used to exercise domination[79] in a hierarchically structured society in the making.

Accompanying this process of sub-regional state formation and power elite configuration, involving patronage for one and validation for the other, was a process of social change. The community, which had so far been elusive in our records and was therefore presumably in the background, was now becoming visible. The occurrence of terms such as *kuṭumbin*, *gṛhasvami*, *gṛhādhyaksha*, *prajā*, *mahattara*, and *mahāmahattara*[80] in the land-grant charters of the various ruling lineages during the fourth–seventh centuries, in a general context of agrarian expansion,[81] suggests the emergence of a stratified peasantry. The upwardly mobile among them would look for channels of status advancement. The foundations of the early phase of temple-building activities in the region were laid around the seventh century. The royal records convey evidence of donations to temples for repairs, offerings, services and maintenance, but quite strikingly, not one of the early donative charters alludes to their construction by royalty.[82] The beginnings of the temple movement, then, may be credited to the long architectural tradition in the region and to community patronage. Individual or group patronage would emanate from the desire to acquire upward mobility in the asymmetrically structured society in the making and to gain acceptance for the assumed status. Besides, common people, too, perhaps, looked to men of substance for the performance of services that were important for the everyday life of the community. Patronage of religious establishments, thus, provided a major channel for status enhancement to those who wanted to move up within the hierarchical, caste society.

The interacting elements in the act of patronage changed through time. However, the nexus that was created between power, religious institutions and the people continued throughout. The structure of legitimation reflects both on the cultural basis of power and the cultural domain. The shift in patronage from rock-cut monuments and public entertainment programmes to śāstric-purāṇic ideology and temples, through local folk deities/cults, exhibits early forms of socio-cultural transformation. The autochthonous deities had strong local roots. The spatial spread of these deities and/or cults provided the emerging local/trans-local ruling lineages an assured dimension of territoriality; as their principal patrons. The varying forms of legitimation in early Orissa provide insights into the intra-regional variations. These distinctions extended to the domain of art as well. The artists of Kaliṅga and the *śilpi*s of the lower Mahānadī valley did not follow identical traditions in the early phase of temple-building activities.[83] Though the pace and stage of socio-political developments across sub-regions were not uniform, they existed not in immutable isolation but in a state of ongoing interactions and change. The transfer of land as gift (*dāna*) introduced complex agrarian relations and, flowing from it, greater differentiation within society. However, the patronage extended to brāhmaṇas and temples may be understood in the context of the contemporary society, which was beginning to experience simultaneous processes of change—agrarian expansion, state formation, evolution of hierarchized society and cultic integration.[84] Both contributed towards the growth and subsequent consolidation of a hierarchically structured, complex socio-political order.

Notes

1. The ingenuity of the people of antiquity in devising mechanisms to sustain the socio-political order need not be underestimated. For a useful discussion, see the relevant essays in Anton Powell (ed.), *Classical Sparta: Techniques behind her Success*, London, Routledge, 1989; also M.I. Finley, *Politics in the Ancient World*, Cambridge, Cambridge University Press, 1984 (reprint).

2. See, for example, B.D. Chattopadhyaya, 'Political Processes and the Structure of Polity in Early Medieval India: Problems of Perspective', Presidential Address, Ancient India section, *Proceedings of the Indian History Congress* (hereafter *PIHC*), Burdwan session, 1983, pp. 25–63; Hermann Kulke, *Kings and Cults: State Formation and Legitimation in India and Southeast Asia*, New Delhi, Manohar, 1993; idem.,

'The Early and the Imperial Kingdom: A Processural Model of Integrative State Formation in Early Medieval India', in Kulke (ed.), *The State in India 1000–1700*, New Delhi, Oxford University Press, 1995, pp. 233–62; and Kesavan Veluthat, 'Religious Symbols in Political Legitimation: The Case of Early Medieval South India', *Social Scientist*, vol. 21, nos 236–7, 1993, pp. 23–33.

3. Ibid. Also see Sibesh Bhattacharya, 'Political Authority and Brāhmaṇa-Kṣatriya Relationship in Early India: An Aspect of the Power Elite Configuration', *Indian Historical Review*, vol. 10, nos 1–2, pp. 1–20; Romila Thapar, 'Genealogy as a Source of Social History', in *Ancient Indian Social History: Some Interpretations*, Delhi, Orient Longman, 1987 (reprint), pp. 326–60; and B.S. Miller (ed.), *The Powers of Art: Patronage in Indian Culture*, New Delhi, Oxford University Press, 1992, sections I and II.

4. For a good general discussion on authority and patronage in the ancient world, see Finley, *Politics in the Ancient World*, chapter 2, pp. 24–49.

5. For the socio-political dimensions of patronage, see Romila Thapar, *Cultural Transaction and Early India: Tradition and Patronage*, New Delhi, Oxford University Press, 1987, especially pp. 26–8. Also the 'Introduction' by Barbara S. Miller and Richard Eaton, in Miller (ed.), *The Powers of Art*, particularly pp. 1–4.

6. For a statement of this kind, see A.K. Mohanty, *State and Government in Ancient Orissa*, Vidyapuri, Cuttack, 1993.

7. See R.L. Mitra, *Antiquities of Orissa*, vol. 2, *Indian Studies: Past and Present*, Calcutta, 1880, p. 98; K.P. Jayaswal, 'Evidence of an Aśokan Pillar at Bhubaneswar in Orissa', *Indian Antiquary*, vol. 58, 1929, pp. 218–19; N.K. Basu, 'Some Ancient Remains from Bhubaneswar', *The Journal of Bihar Orissa Research Society*, vol. 15, 1929, p. 261; K.C. Panigrahi, *Archaeological Remains at Bhubaneswar*, Calcutta, Kitab Mahal, 1961, pp. 184–7; N.K. Sahu, *History of Orissa*, vol. I, Cuttack, Utkal University, 1964, pp. 273–7; see Debala Mitra, 'A Note on the Bhāskareśwara Liṅga', *Journal of the Asiatic Society*, vol. 1, no. 1, 1959.

8. The upper storey of cave 9, known as Svargapuri, at Udayagiri, was dedicated by the queen. Two of the cells on the ground floor of the same cave, popularly known as Manchapuri, were gifts by *Mahārāja* Kudepaśri and *Kumāra* Vadukha. See R.D. Banerji, 'Inscriptions in the Udayagiri and Khandagiri Caves', *Epigraphia Indica* (hereafter *EI*), vol. XIII, 1915–16, nos I, II and III, pp. 159–61; also H. Lüders, 'A List of Brāhmi Inscriptions from the Earliest Times to about AD 400', *EI*, vol. X, appendix, 1912, nos 1346, 1347, and 1348.

9. Banerji, 'Inscriptions in the Udayagiri and Khandagiri Caves', nos VII and VIII, pp. 163–4; Lüders, 'List of Brāhmi Inscriptions', nos 1351 and 1352.

10. Lüders, 'List of Brāhmi Inscriptions', nos 1344, 1349, 1350, 1353; also see Banerji, 'Inscriptions in the Udayagiri and Khandagiri Caves', nos IV, V, VI, and IX–XIII, pp. 162–5. It is necessary to mention that in inscriptions IX, XII, and XIII, the donors have not been properly identified owing to the poor state of the said records.

11. For such evidence in the Deccan and central India, see Vidya Dehejia, 'The Collective and Popular Basis of Early Buddhist Patronage: Sacred Monuments, 100 BC–AD 250', in Miller (ed.), *The Powers of Art*, p. 37.

12. The exceptions are the donation by the monks and the one by Kamma and Harakshina. Banerji, 'Inscriptions in the Udayagiri and Khandagirai Caves', nos V and XI.

13. The Hāthigumphā inscription points in this direction. K.P. Jayaswal and R.D. Banerji, 'Kharavela's Hātigumphā Inscriptions', *EI*, vol. XX, line 15, p. 89.

14. Some differences are noted in the readings of Lüders and Banerji. See *EI*, vol. X, no. 1346, p. 161, and *EI*, vol. XIII, p. 160.

15. Matrimonial alliances, even later, continued to help the consolidation of power and status elevation of the newly rising ruling families. For an example, see Devangana Desai, 'The Patronage of the Lakshmana Temple at Khajuraho', in Miller (ed.), *The Powers of Art*, p. 79.

16. Lüders, 'List of Brāhmi Inscriptions', nos 1344, 1346, 1352.

17. For details, one may see N.K. Sahu, *Khāravela*, Orissa State Museum, Bhubaneswar, 1984, pp. 109, 111, 117–20, 197; also see R.P. Mahapatra, 'Position of Women as Depicted in the Early Sculptures of Udayagiri and Khandagiri Caves', *Orissa Historical Research Journal* (hereafter *OHRJ*), vols XXIV–XXVI, 1980, pp. 61–4.

18. The hierarchical caste system and subordination of women are inextricably inter-related because the purity of caste is contingent upon the purity of women. See Uma Chakravarti, 'Conceptualising Brāhmaṇical Patriarchy in Early India: Gender, Caste, Class and State', in *Everyday Lives, Everyday Histories: Beyond the Kings and Brāhmaṇas of 'Ancient' India*, New Delhi, Tulika, 2006, pp. 138–55.

19. While Khāravela uses the epithet *Chakradhara* (holder of the wheel of sovereignty) for himself, his chief queen refers to him as *Chakravartin*, *EI*, vol. XX, line 17, p. 80; and Lüders, 'List of Brāhmi Inscriptions', no. 1346.

20. Some of the photographs and sketches are available in N.K. Sahu, *Khāravela*, pp. 63, 65, and 68; and Debala Mitra, *Udayagiri and Khandagiri*, New Delhi, Archaeological Survey of India, 1975, plates IIIA, VB, VIB, etc.

21. For plates and sketches, see Mitra, ibid., plates IIIB and VIIIB; N.K. Sahu, *Khāravela*, pp. 70, 82, 241.

22. N.K. Sahu deals with them at length. See ibid., chapters 6 and 7, especially the sketches on pp. 156, 158–9, 210.

23. Jayaswal and Banerji, 'Khāravela's Hāthigumphā Inscription', line 9.

24. In both instances the tree is within railings, under umbrellas, being worshipped with offerings of flowers. Photographs and sketches of the same are available in N.K. Sahu, *Khāravela*, pp. 146 and 217; and Mitra, *Udayagiri and Khandagiri*, plate XIVB.

25. See B.P. Sahu, 'Ancient Orissan Cultural Relations', *Indica*, vol. 21, no. 1, 1984, p. 6.

26. Ibid.

27. Various dynasties in ancient India addressed the problem by ensuring that members of the royal family, especially, women patronized sects other than those encouraged by the ruler himself. See A.K. Narain, 'Religious Policy and Toleration in Ancient India with Particular Reference to the Gupta Age', in B.L. Smith (ed.), *Essays on Gupta Culture*, Motilal Banarsidass, Delhi, 1983, pp. 17–51.

28. Lines 3 and 5–7 in the Hāthigumphā inscription mention these activities. See Jayaswal and Banerji, 'Khāravela's Hāthigumphā Inscription'.

29. It is recorded in the inscription that such works were paid for and that they were not products of involuntary labour. See lines 4, 6–7, 10, and 16, referring to state expenditure.

30. Finley, *Politics in the Ancient World*, p. 47.

31. The implications of the Mauryan interaction with the Deccan are both convincingly and lucidly presented in S. Seneviratne, 'Kaliṅga and Andhra: The Process of Secondary State Formation in Early India', *Indian Historical Review* (hereafter *IHR*), vol. VII, nos 1–2, pp. 54–69; and B.D. Chattopadhyaya, 'Transition to the Early Historical Phase in the Deccan: A Note', in B.M. Pande and B.D. Chattopadhyaya (eds), *Archaeology and History*, vol. II, Delhi, Agam Kala Prakashan, 1988, pp. 727–32.

32. B.P. Sahu, 'Ancient Orissa: The Dynamics of Internal Transformation of the Tribal Society', in K.M. Shrimali (ed.), *Essays in Art, Religion and Society*, Delhi, Munshiram Manoharlal, 1987, pp. 170–1.

33. The territories of many ruling lineages associated with Kaliṅga encompassed areas of both modern Andhra and Orissa. For a historical explanation, see N.K. Bose, *Culture and Society in India*, Bombay, Asia Publishing House, 1977 (reprint), pp. 25–6. For a recent statement and the most comprehensive treatment of the idea of Kaliṅga, see Martin Brandtner, 'Representations of Kaliṅga: The Changing Image and Geography of a Historical Region', in H. Kulke and B. Schnepel (eds), *Jagannāth Revisited: Studying Society, Religion and the State in Orissa*, New Delhi, Manohar Publishers, 2001, pp. 179–210.

34. B.B. Lal, 'Sisupalgarh 1948: An Early Historical Fort in Eastern India', *Ancient India*, vol. V, 1949, pp. 62–105.

35. *Indian Archaeology—A Review*, 1956–7, pp. 30–1.

36. See Hāthigumphā inscription, lines 1 and 17, *EI*, vol. XX, pp. 79–80; Lüders, 'List of Brāhmi Inscriptions', Nos 1346 and 1347.

37. N.K. Sahu interprets these terms as official designations. He suggests that 'Kamma' stands for *Karma Sachiva* and 'Chūla Kamma' was his junior in the Department of Works. N.K. Sahu, *Khāravela*, p. 91.

38. See B.P. Sahu, 'Ancient Orissan Cultural Relations'.

39. See R.S. Sharma, 'Urbanism in Early Historic India', in Indu Banga (ed.), *The City in Indian History*, New Delhi, Manohar, 1991, pp. 13–14.

40. A good discussion of the administrative organizations of the earliest states and their socio-political implications is provided in Shereen Ratnagar, *Enquiries into the Political Organization of Harappan Society*, Pune, Ravish Publishers, 1990, pp. 162–4.

41. The Aśokan inscriptions portray not only the king's sense of indebtedness to the people and his activities for their welfare, but also define a lot of marginal groups and reveal the king's/state's desire to regulate them, besides contrasting his achievements with the ephemeral activities of earlier rulers and constantly focusing on him.

42. The exaggeration and unduly favourable picture presented in the record is obvious from statements such as his army marching through Bhāratavarṣha for conquest, Line 10 in Hāthigumphā.

43. For the Raṭhikas and Bhojakas, see Chattopadhyaya, 'Transition to the Early Historical Phase in the Deccan'.

44. B.P. Sahu, 'Ancient Orissan Cultural Relations'; idem., 'Ancient Orissa: The Dynamics of Internal Transformation of the Tribal Society', p. 172.

45. For a survey of early historical trade and a good discussion of eastern coastal and trans-oceanic trade, see H.P. Ray, 'Early Historical Trade: An Overview', *The Indian Economic and Social History Review*, vol. 26, no. 4, 1989, pp. 437–57; and idem., 'Early Trade in the Bay of Bengal', *IHR*, vol. 14, 1990, pp. 79–89.

46. For a critical appraisal of the situation in Orissa, see B.P. Sahu, 'Situating Early Historical Trade in Orissa', in K.M. Shrimali (ed.), *Indian Archaeology since Independence*, Delhi, Association for Study of History and Archaeology, 1996, pp. 95–109.

47. D.D. Kosambi, 'Dhenukakata', in A.J. Syed (ed.), *D.D. Kosambi on History and Society: Problems of Interpretation*, Bombay, Department of History, University of Bombay, 1985, especially pp. 198–201.

48. See B.B. Lal, 'Sisupalgarh 1948'.

49. A.S. Altekar, 'A Note on the Kushana Gold Coin', *Ancient India*, vol. V, 1949, pp. 100–01, and 'A Unique Kushano-Roman Gold Coin of King Dharmadāmadara', *The Journal of the Numismatic Society of India*, vol. 12, 1950, pp. 1–4; S.C. De, 'A Peep in the Dark Period', *OHRJ*, vol. 3, no. 2, 1954, p. 106.

50. For details, see B.P. Sahu, 'Situating Early Historical Trade'.

51. Chattopadhyaya explains the term by invoking the *janapada* parallel from northern India. See Chattopadhyaya, 'Transition to the Early Historical Phase in the Deccan'.

52. D.C. Sircar, 'Two Inscriptions from Guntur District', *EI*, vol. XXXII, 1957–8, pp. 83; also see note 2.

53. N.K. Sahu, *Khāravela*, pp. 368–72.

54. Ibid., pp. 373–6; Sircar, 'Two Inscriptions', pp. 82–7.

55. D.C. Sircar, 'Bhadrak Inscription of the Time of Gaṇa, of Regnal Year 8',

EI, vol. XXIX, 1951–2, pp. 169–72; S.N. Ghosal, 'The Bhadrak Stone Inscription of the Time of Gaṇa', *Journal of the Asiatic Society,* vol. 22, nos 1–2, pp. 36–8.

56. The image of goddess Bhadrakāli at Bhadrak is as old as the third century AD. The Bhadrakāli temple inscription suggests that the deity was originally known as Parnnadevati. See A.N. Parida, 'The Sculptural Art and the Early Temples of Orissa', *Utkal Historical Research Journal,* vol. 1, 1990, p. 98 and note 13.

57. The inscription of Gopachandra, the Gaṇḍibedhā copper coins and subsequent inscriptions from the district of Balasore point in that direction. See S.N. Rajaguru, *Inscriptions of Orissa,* vol. 1, pt II, Orissa State Museum, Berhampur, 1958, inscription nos 22, 25, 26, 28, and 29; for the coins, see ibid., p. 57.

58. Ibid., pp. 81–5.

59. S.C. Behera (ed.), *Interim Excavation Reports,* Sambalpur University, 1982, pp. 5–6.

60. Ibid., pp. 9–22.

61. *Indian Archaeology—A Review,* 1974–5, p. 55.

62. See A. Das, 'Asanapat', *OHRJ,* vol. 13, no. 2, 1965, pp. 1–8; S. Tripathy, 'A Note on the Asanapat Stone Inscription', *Journal of Orissan History,* vol. 1, no. 2, July 1980. In all fairness, it should be mentioned that one is not sure if the two Śatrubhañjas were one and the same person.

63. P. Acharya, *Studies in Orissan History, Archaeology and Archives,* Cuttack, Cuttack Students Store, 1969, p. 374.

64. Behera (ed.), *Interim Excavation Reports,* p. 3.

65. For the early coins, see S. Tripathy, *Early and Medieval Coins and Currency System in Orissa,* Calcutta, Punthi Pustak, 1986.

66. See Ray, 'Early Trade in the Bay of Bengal', p. 82.

67. Cited in Acharya, *Studies in Orissan History,* p. 573.

68. For an assessment, see B.P. Sahu, 'Situating Early Historical Trade'.

69. For an analysis of a similar yet clearer situation in the Deccan, see Aloka Parasher, 'Social Structure and Economy of Settlements in the Central Deccan (200 BC–AD 200)', *Social Science Probings,* vol. 5, nos 1–4, 1992, particularly pp. 6–19.

70. For an analysis of such categories, see Shereen Ratnagar, 'A Bronze Age Frontier: Problems of Interpretation', paper presented at the symposium on Frontiers in Indian History, Indian History Congress, Warangal session, 1992, pp. 6–8, 14.

71. For a discussion, see B.D. Chattopadhyaya, 'Historiography, History and Religious Centres: Early Medieval North India, *circa* AD 700–1200', in Vishakha N. Desai *et al.* (eds), *Gods, Guardians and Love: North Indian Temple Sculptures (700–1200),* New York and Ahmedabad, The Asia Society, 1993, pp. 37–43.

72. H. Kulke, 'Fragmentation and Segmentation versus Integration: Reflections on the Concept of Indian Feudalism and Segmentary State in Indian History', *Studies in History,* vol. 4, no. 2, 1982, pp. 247–8; B.P. Sahu, 'Aspects of Rural

Economy in Early Medieval Orissa', *Social Scientist*, vol. 21, nos 1–2, January–February 1993, pp. 56–7.

73. K.N. Mahapatra, 'Purāṇic Stories in the Early Records and Sculptures of Orissa', *OHRJ*, vol. X, pp. 59–74; Debala Mitra, *Bhubaneswar*, Archaeological Survey of India, New Delhi, 1978 (fourth edition), pp. 29–34; and R.P. Mohapatra, 'Krishna Themes in Orissan Sculptures', *OHRJ*, vol. XXXI, nos 2–4, 1985, pp. 77–9.

74. For example, see the Banapur Plates of Madhyamarāja and Midnapur Plate of Somadatta in S.N. Rajaguru, *Inscriptions of Orissa*, vol. I, pt II, lines 45 and 48, pp. 194 and 198, and lines 3–9, pp. 140–1.

75. For Kali references see, for example, Puri Plates of Mādhavavarman, ibid., line 15, p. 179, and Paralakhemedi Plates of Indravarman, ibid., vol. II, 1960, lines 2–3, p. 35.

76. See R.S. Sharma, 'The Kali Age: A Period of Social Crisis', in S.N. Mukherjee (ed.), *India: History and Thought*, Calcutta, Subarnarekha, 1982, pp. 186–203; and B.N.S. Yadava, 'The Accounts of the Kali Age and the Social Transition from Antiquity to the Middle Ages', *Indian Historical Review*, vol. 5, nos 1–2, 1979, pp. 31–63.

77. For the performance of the *Aśvamedha* and *Vājapeya* sacrifices, expressions of reverence to brāhmaṇas and the projection of rulers as *paramabrāhmaṇa*, see for example, *Inscriptions of Orissa*, vol. I, pt 2, p. 220, lines 39–40; pp. 141–2, lines 3–9; p. 55, line 6.

78. For details of the argument, see B.P. Sahu, 'Conception of the Kali Age in Early India: A Regional Perspective', *Trends in Social Science Research*, vol. 4, no. 1, 1997, pp. 27–36.

79. For a good discussion, see Kesavan Veluthat, 'Religious Symbols in Political Legitimation: The Case of Early Medieval South India', *Social Scientist*, vol. 21, nos 21–2, January-February 1993, pp. 23–33.

80. B.P. Sahu, 'Ancient Orissa: The Dynamics of Internal Transformation', pp. 176–77, also see notes 72 and 74. *Mahattaras* and *mahāmahattaras* are addressed in the records of the Early Gaṅgās, Muḍgalas, and Dattas.

81. B.P. Sahu, 'Aspects of Rural Economy', pp. 48–68.

82. Not before the ninth century do we have definite evidence for such constructions by royalty. See Vidya Dehejia, *Early Stone Temples of Orissa*, Vikas Publishing House, Delhi, 1979, pp. 173–4, 183.

83. D.R. Das, 'Śaiva Images on Orissan Temple Walls (from the seventh to the ninth century AD)', *Journal of Ancient Indian History*, vol. 12, 1978–9, p. 107.

84. For a comprehensive discussion, see B.D. Chattopadhyaya, *The Making of Early Medieval India*, New Delhi, Oxford University Press, 1994, particularly the Introduction. Also see the 'Introduction' in B.P. Sahu (ed.), *Land System and Rural Society in Early India*, New Delhi, Manohar Delhi, 1997.

7

Characterizing Early Medieval Indian Polity

The Case of Dakṣiṇa Kośala and Beyond*

Serious efforts at defining early medieval Indian polity in structural terms, historiographically speaking, can be dated to the later part of the 1950s and onwards. As against the earlier narratives, which were variations of the same theme, the writings of D.D. Kosambi and R.S. Sharma together with those of Lallanji Gopal, and B.N.S. Yadava inaugurated a trend which focused on the interrelationship between economy, society, and polity.[1] This enabled historical explanations, including transitions in Indian history, and raised discussions to the level of conceptualizations. Thus was born the school of Indian feudalism, distinguishing the early historical from early medieval society and equating the latter with feudalism.[2] What came to be perceived as feudal social formations is rich in empirical details, be it in the domain of economy or society, thanks to the contributions of many eminent historians. In the process of delineating and accounting for change this historiography created large, durable, common institutional structures with pan-Indian/supra-regional reach, across centuries. By the middle of the 1970s and clearly by the early 1980s the intellectual unease with the feudal framework manifested itself in alternative paradigms such as the segmentary state model authored by Burton Stein[3] and the integrative paradigm of state formation put forward by Hermann Kulke and B.D. Chattopadhyaya.[4] At this juncture two brief but obvious clarifications

*Presented at the International Seminar on State Formation and the Early State in South and Southeast Asia Reconsidered, organized by Asia Research Institute, National University Singapore, Singapore, 21–3 March 2007.

may be necessary. First, we have deliberately refrained from touching upon pre-1950 frameworks of analysis, including the centralized, bureaucratic, imperial type, because these are no more a part of serious discussions and therefore need not engage us here. Secondly, the opposition to Indian feudalism did not wait to surface until the 1970s, almost immediately after the publication of Sharma's *Indian Feudalism* the formulation was contested.[5] The adherents and opponents of the thesis grew in course of time. The ensuing animated but informed debate, it is said, had both empirical and ideological foundations. However, what merits attention is that while the early oppositionists even in arguing against Indian feudalism followed the terms of discussion already set by its advocates and helped in the making of a stereotype, the later exponents of alternative frameworks changed the discursive ground, without necessarily being polemical. That is a story to which we shall soon return. The second major concern of the paper, besides evaluating the state of the competing conceptualizations, is to map the trajectory of the evolution of the structure of polity in early medieval Dakṣiṇa Kośala and parts of Orissa; in the wider context of contemporary material culture and socio-political processes. Juxtaposing the emerging patterns with the on going debate, it is hoped, will help us to have a better understanding of early medieval Indian polity.

Alternative Concepts

There are three different contending explanatory models for understanding early medieval states in the Indian situation. The Indian feudal model of decentralized feudal states; the model of segmentary state focusing on the pyramidal repetition of the structures in the numerous autonomous segments, as were available in the core; and the framework of integrative state formation demonstrating the phased structural evolution of imperial kingdoms or regional/supra-regional states across regions. At present the first and the third formulations are in contention for the minds of people, while the second framework has having had generated interesting debates in the 1980s suffered relative eclipse owing to the dearth of passionate adherents. Notwithstanding their relative merits, these concepts 'succeeded in effectively destroying the "conventional" picture of the medieval regional kingdoms as centrally governed unitary states for North as well as South India'.[6]

The origins of Indian feudalism is located in land grants to brāhmaṇas and temples from the Gupta period onwards, and later to state officials, involving the alienation of fiscal, administrative and judicial rights. The emergence of multiple centres of power and a great deal of decentralization, consequent to continuous, systematic parcellization of sovereignty or state power, which increasingly devolved on to the donees, making them independent lords, has been identified with feudalism. The many, hierarchized foci of power, different grades of *sāmantas* (such as *mahāmaṇḍaleśvara, maṇḍalika, mahāsāmanta, sāmanta, laghusāmanta*), and graded land rights are perceived to be the result of state activity, that is, land grants.[7] Decline of long-distance and maritime trade, paucity of money, and urban shrinkage apparently nicely rounded off the argument. However the decline of trade-towns-money thesis leading to the emergence of Indian feudalism had its share of ideological problems from the beginning, insofar as an external factor such as trade was perceived to account for momentous internal developments; invoking the transition to a new social formation. Not surprisingly therefore in the late 1970s and early 1980s the idea of the *Kaliyuga* crisis was posited as an alternative or supplementary causative factor explaining the passage to feudalism.[8] In this case land grants were allegedly made to neutralize the pervasive social crisis, but it is another matter that they went on to usher in significant socio-political changes. Besides, there is also a tacit assumption that the land grants across regions were made from an epicenter with uniform consequences. While the idea of Kali Age crisis was redeeming Indian Feudalism, almost simultaneously Harbans Mukhia[9] raised important questions relating to the absence of structured dependence of the early medieval Indian peasantry and their subsistence requirements, compared to those in feudal Europe, and queered the pitch. This was soon followed by the works of Stein, Kulke, and Chattopadhyaya. The idea of Indian feudalism in general, with bearing on its political dimensions, have been persuasively argued for and defended by R.S. Sharma, B.N.S. Yadava, M.G.S. Narayanan, D.N. Jha, R.N. Nandi, and Kesavan Veluthat,[10] among others. Nevertheless, the economic and social dimensions seem to have largely subsumed the political. This is not to say that there are no works on feudal polity but the problem I am trying to point to is perhaps best manifested in the entry 'How Feudal was Indian Feudalism?' by R.S. Sharma, in a volume on the state published in 1995.

The origins of Indian feudalism still remain to be satisfactorily explained. The problems concerning towns, trade and money, among other issues, have been discussed earlier by D.C. Sircar, B.N. Mukherjee, John Deyell, and K.M. Shrimali and an assessment of the situation is available in the writings of Chattopadhyaya.[11] That brings us to the theory of *Kaliyuga* crisis. It has been unmistakably demonstrated that the alleged crisis was not a historical crisis. It was at most a crisis of confidence on the part of the brāhmaṇas, related to the issue of patronage in a situation of competition from the 'heretical' sects and/or an ingenious invention of the brāhmaṇas to make people conform to Brāhmaṇical ideological norms in an age characterized by economic growth, social change and the spread of state societies within the Brāhmaṇical framework.[12] The decentralized, fragmented feudal polity rests on the presupposition of an evenly spread Mauryan empire of uniform administrative depth across the country, which did not change much under the Kuṣāṇas and Sātavāhanas; leading up to proto-feudal Gupta times. However, recent writings on the nature of the Mauryan state questioning the assumed degree of centralization and standardization of the empire, and a different perspective of post Mauryan states disturb this understanding.[13] Similarly, the brāhmaṇas and religious institutions instead of being perceived as agents of decentralization have been relocated productively as pace makers of royal authority.[14] The related issues are the object of donation, which were usually a *grāma, palli, pāṭaka, padara,* measures of land, and so on, the quantum of such donations and their relationship vis-à-vis the land under cultivation across regions. These are important for the characterization of the donees and the emergent social formation. One may add that the early assignments were to the brāhmaṇas and religious establishments, while the service assignments followed and did not precede the beginnings of 'feudal' polity. The question then is can the religious donees with a *grāma,* a part of it or less be perceived as feudatories? In case grants to them symbolized the economic and political undoing of the state, it is not intelligible as to why king after king and dynasty after dynasty continued with the phenomenon. That apart, the regional distribution of early land grants clearly suggests their local origins, mostly being made by one local dynasty or another in a general context of local state formation. The spatial and temporal correspondence between land grants and the spread of state societies points to their mutually beneficial, and not antagonistic, relationship.

Questions related to the hierarchy of feudatories and the making of the pyramidal political structure, resource transfer from the subordinate to the super-ordinate and the genesis of feudal polity have not been satisfactorily answered either in the case of north or south India. Likewise, the people have been taken for granted and the need to open bridges or establish a chord with them has not been considered to be sufficiently important within this historiography. There has been some engagement with Bhakti as ideology of the feudal order. However, it needs recognition that legitimation of power or the constitution of authority involves continuous negotiations with popular contestations and engagement with the cultural domain.[15] Peoples and cultures are varied, lively and dynamic, not static. The variations in time and space need to be recognized and appreciated. The problem largely seems to be, as has been pointed out, the consequence of first creating the structure and then looking for processes to explain it, rather than the other way round;[16] and this it appears is being gradually recognized at least in the case of south India.[17] Briefly stated, 'if there is need to look at change in early Indian history, it is necessary that historians too occasionally introduce some change in the way they see the past'.[18]

Burton Stein's segmentary state model in south Indian history is an important conceptual contribution to our understanding of early medieval Indian polity. The basic envisaged argument was published in the form of a substantial article in 1977 and the formulation continued to be a part of his *Peasant State and Society in Medieval South India*.[19] The Cōḷa state, it is said, was characterized by limited territorial authority as one moved from the core to the periphery, through the intermediate zone. In fact, in the periphery it shaded off into ritual sovereignty. In this system of replication of uniformity across the numerous peasant locality units or *nāḍus* the Cōḷa centre had no monopoly of legitimate state authority. To elaborate Stein makes a distinction between political authority and ritual sovereignty, and it is the latter that the Cōḷa kings are supposed to have exercised. Their political competence and precedence was linked to their patronage of Rājarājeśvara or Brihadeśvara at Tanjavur, who enjoyed a preeminent position in relation to the other deities and cults at various levels in the region. The land grant charters with their long *praśastis* seem to have spread the message of royal greatness and augmented the constitution of ritual sovereignty. This explanation of ritual sovereignty, as distinct from political authority, as the major sustaining factor of the state, spread over 400 years, has come in for major criticism.[20] So has the perception of the *nāḍus* as continuous unchanging, autonomous units. The abstraction of the political and economic dimensions of the state and the underplaying of significant issues such as resource mobilization and the sustenance of the political order, especially in a period of enormous agrarian expansion and commercial growth, have attracted the attention of a number of historians.[21] For certain periods of the history of the Cōḷa state empirical evidence provides a different picture.[22] Spencer's[23] idea of the politics of plunder is certainly not a sufficient long-term explanation accounting for the stability of the political structure. It needs to be mentioned that subsequently Stein understood the problems inherent in dichotomizing ritual and political sovereignty. He admitted that in the Indian situation the statement had to be modified because kingship combined both ritual and political authority.[24] Again, he conceded ground on the question of the supposedly immutable *nāḍus*.

Criticisms apart, it needs to be recognized that the model of segmentary state administered the necessary shock treatment to historians of south India in particular and stirred them to the problems and possibilities of early medieval south Indian history. In focusing on the *nāḍus* and ritual sovereignty, Stein drew attention to the peasant localities as the basic building blocks in the construction of the history of the regions, as well as the importance of the sacred domain in consolidating temporal power. He also deserves our gratitude for drawing attention to and highlighting the political function of royal charters.

The integrative model of state formation in early medieval India is an integral part of the processual approach. Unlike the feudal model it locates the political processes at play during different stages in the regions, mostly outside the Gaṅgā valley, and then moves on to work out the emerging structure of polities in time and space. Within the regions the sub-regions and localities receive the necessary attention. This follows from the recognition of the fact that regions are not given but historically constituted entities. In other words instead of simply asserting a paradigm from the top the framework takes cognizance of the developments from below. Integration operated not only at the territorial and political levels, but also in the economic, social and cultural spheres. State formation involves the emergence of organized polities in pre-state territories and their structural evolution in the larger context of simultaneous socio-economic and cultural transformations. The beginnings of the approach may be situated in the early works of Chattopadhyaya and Kulke[25] in the early and mid-1970s, in Rajasthan and Orissa respectively. The first conceptual papers synthesizing the implications of their findings, in the wider context of comparable perspectives from other regions, were published in the early 1980s.[26] Significantly, through that decade it became obvious that there was a remarkable correspondence between these findings and the conclusions drawn from independent researches on the middle of the first millennium BC in the mid Gaṅgā valley, Mauryan and post-Mauryan times. A long-term interconnected vision of Indian history looking at change through continuity began to emerge. Stated briefly, the idea of structurally different *mahājanapadas* converged well with the recent perspectives of the Mauryan state.[27] Similarly, the differential levels of interaction of the core of the Mauryan state with the far flung areas of the empire largely owing to uneven patterns of historical growth tied up quite well with the process of secondary state formation in Kaliṅga, Andhra, and the Deccan in the subsequent centuries. Change in these areas, even if uneven, was a result of their interaction with the Mauryan state and internal evolution of local societies rather than administrative integration.[28] Developments such as these did not end with the coming of the Gupta period, they continued throughout Indian history.

From the Gupta period onwards there was an immense acceleration in the spread of state societies largely owing to the on-going process of local state formation. The Maitrakas of Valabhi, Vākāṭakas in the Deccan and Vidarbha, Kadambas of Banavāśi, Pallavas of Kañchi, Ikṣvākus and Viṣṇukuṇḍins of Andhra, the Māṭharas and Early Eastern Gaṅgās of Kaliṅga, and the Śarabhapuriyās of Dakṣiṇa Kośala are good examples of early local dynasties in the varied regional contexts. Examples such as these can be multiplied. However, the more general point one is trying to make is that these states emerged not from the fragmentation of any erstwhile large kingdom but from change coming from within local societies.[29] The gradual political and territorial integration of the states together with their structural evolution in early medieval India was built on this foundation. The envisaged stages of structural evolution though remain the same are expressed differently, either as chiefdoms, early kingdoms and imperial kingdoms or as local, sub-regional and regional/

supra-regional polities by Kulke and Chattopadhyaya respectively. The compulsions of the *rājās* and other structural features of the state at different stages (such as the coming together of nuclear areas, enlargement of the core region, shifting of the capital to a more central place, change in the structure of legitimation, etc.) have been convincingly addressed.[30] The stages in the evolution of the state converged with many, simultaneous processes of change in the economic, social, and cultural domains. The numerous peasant segments or localities were not unchanging entities; they were continuously integrated with larger units. The legitimatory strategies, which are culture sensitive, also changed with time and context (from autochthonous deities to Brāhmaṇized state deities and monumental temples with wide regional appeal). They did not, and could not, remain the same all through.

Integration was never complete or perfect. Contestations apart, there were always autonomous spaces within the ambit of the state, pointing to the futility of looking for the uniform, homogeneous presence of the state. Nevertheless, such spaces did not remain eternally so. They existed in situations of interaction with peasant/state societies and of course changed with time. Spaces and people transformed from jungles to jungle kingdoms, and even evolved state societies.[31] The state in this perception was not a static entity. It was dynamic, multi-layered, polycentred, and expanding or shrinking regularly; and as Tilman Frasch (of the Manchester Metopolitan University, UK) once remarked it was very much like an octopus. The little king and the little kingdom became structural constituents of such states with the passage of time.[32] The works of S.K. Panda on Orissa, Swapna Bhattacharya on Bengal, Nandini Sinha Kapur on Rajasthan, Cynthia Talbot on Andhra, and James Heitzman on Tamil Nadu,[33] among others, easily tie up with this frame of analysis. The Integrative model did not invent everything anew. What is interesting is that the authors brought new perspectives to bear on some of the already existing ideas. The idea of segments was accepted devoid of its entirely autonomous and immutable character. It now read *segmentation and integration*. The role of the sacred domain in the constitution of political authority was acknowledged. However, it was no substitute for it. Again, brāhmaṇas and religious establishments instead of being perceived as agents of political disintegration came to be seen as factors facilitating the extension and consolidation of royal power insofar as they helped the extension of the agrarian frontier, invented origin myths, provided grand genealogical linkages, and disseminated the dominant ideology.

Theoretically speaking, broadly within this framework there is a coherent explanation of the state from the early historical to the early medieval times and beyond. Neither is the state seen to be the end result of changes in other spheres (iron-productivity-surplus-state) nor is it the harbinger of all other transformations (land grants-political decentralization-feudalism). In this perspective the state was influenced by as well as simultaneously impacting the multiple processes of societal change. Simply put, this marks the movement away from mono-causality towards causal plurality and helps the cause of a long-term vision of Indian history. The transitions in early Indian history, within this perspective, are far more comfortably negotiated, both empirically and conceptually.

Criticisms are the spice of life. Only when empirically valid sound theoretical formulations acquire visibility by entering the domain of contestation as an alternative are they discussed, even criticized. The integrative paradigm in the 1980s itself met with some constructive criticisms. However from the middle of the 1990s onwards when it began to emerge as a serious alternative, especially with the publication of Chattopadhyaya's *The Making of Early Medieval India* and Kulke's *Kings and Cults* and *The State in India, 1000–1700,* the framework has generated, as always with anything new, conflicting responses. It has had both admirers and critics as well. The first, we have already drawn attention to. In the second category there are broadly three kinds of reservations: first, that the economic dimensions need to be addressed,[34] secondly that it is essentially a narrative of regionalism, and finally that one does not get very much about the structural features of the state apparatus.[35] It is widely admitted that the conceptual framework under discussion focuses on the protracted evolution of the state, instead of giving it a spatio-temporal fixity and treating it as static. The question is how else does one address, for example, states such as those of the Cōḷas in the south and the Later Eastern Gaṅgās in Orissa which spanned almost four centuries each. The benefits of such studies discerning structural evolution of the state (instead of freezing it in time) in the above two cases as well as Kerala under the Cēras of Mahōdayapuram and Mewar in Rajasthan are there for all to see.[36] The nature of differences in the organization of chiefdoms and early kingdoms, and the latter and imperial kingdoms have been dealt with in some detail since the mid-1990s, if not earlier.[37] One needs to say what perhaps is obvious. Regions are a legitimate category of historical studies, a way of arranging the data. The emergent picture across several regions then could be culled together to engage in wider generalizations. This is unmistakably different from macro-generalizations based on a part of the country and regionalism. Regionalism has to do with emotions, not reason but human cupidity. From this perspective, localities, sub-regions, and regions are not concepts just denoting scale; they mostly define historically constituted spaces. Kuntala, Vidarbha, Dakṣiṇa Kośala, Kaliṅga, Varendra, Bundelkhaṇḍ, and Mālwa are good examples of such historical and cultural units. Besides, it is not only regional history but also questions related to identity formation, the making of regional and pan-Indian traditions through complex webs of interrelationships between the local, regional and trans-regional elements, mediated by multilateral transactions, involving giving and borrowing, which interest these historians. Admittedly, state formation and socio-economic transformation are inextricably linked, and the point has been convincingly made. Kulke only mentioned it briefly earlier and developed it a bit more later, whereas Chattopadhyaya's writings in the first half of the1990s unambiguously made the state and economy interrelationships clear.[38] The story of phased economic growth and structural evolution of the state can also be seen in the context of Tamil Nadu, Andhra Pradesh, Karnataka, Orissa, Assam, and Rajasthan, for example.[39] The gradual growth of markets and merchants as well as the state's interest in *hāṭṭas*, *maṇḍis,* and *peṇṭhās* has also been worked out. The gradual spread of irrigation networks, opening up of agrarian localities, shift in the boundary markers of donated areas (from stones, anthills and rivers to settlements and others' plots), and the rise in the number of settlements from around the tenth century onwards across regions clearly point to the gentle historical transformation of space.[40]

The debate surrounding the characterization of early medieval polity over the last thirty years has enriched our understanding of the times. Today it is agreed that these polities were graded, multi-centred and continuously waxing and waning. The Indian feudalism model and integrative paradigm derive themselves from the same social formations approach, the latter amending and refining some of the positions of the former. However, that said, it is also necessary to recognize the differences between them. They relate to the movement from processes to structure or the other way round, the idea of India as historically forged and constructed or something given and encountered, and the perception of continuity and change in Indian history as fact and value. The case studies that follow, it is hoped, will open up these issues; and drive home the benefits of this lively, but informed debate spanning about three decades.

Dakṣiṇa Kośala

The territories encompassed by the administrative units of Chhattisgarh and Orissa have attracted greater scholarly attention in recent years. However, neither of them, as in the case of many reorganized states of modern India, constitutes a historically evolved socio-cultural entity. Western Orissa and parts of northern Chhattisgarh together represent an early cultural region/sub-region, which was forged historically and is popularly known as Dakṣiṇa Kośala.[41] That perhaps explains some of the problems associated with the modern state of Orissa, which again is shaped by the coming together of many localities and sub-regions. Much of the work focusing on Dakṣiṇa Kośala revolve around problems of chronology, genealogy, the capital city, and what may broadly be termed as aspects of cultural history.[42] These concerns, important as they certainly are, do not seriously address issues related to political processes and social formations, not to speak of the state and state formation, including its temporal, spatial and least of all structural dimensions. What ever little is available on polity goes on to uncritically reinforce the familiar centralized, bureaucratic and homogeneous constructs, whose genesis may be traced to the Nationalist historiography. Statements such as the Śarabhapurīyas' 'imperial sway over south Kośala' or references to their 'central structure' in an essentially contrived, neat hierarchized construction of the constituents of their polity[43] not only point towards the abhorrence for gaps but also the continued influence of empire centred totalizing discourses. This section attempts to situate the evolution of the structure of polity in early medieval Dakṣiṇa Kośala, with reference to the Śarabhapurīyas and Pāṇḍuvaṁśīs, in the larger context of contemporary socio-political processes.

The earliest epigraphic reference to the region perhaps comes from the Aśokan inscriptions which mention about the forest dwellers (*aṭavi*), and Samudragupta too in his Allahabad *praśasti* refers to these people; but in a different context. The context was the subordination of the *aṭavi-rājyas*. These two sets of evidence are separated in time by about 600 years but more importantly they suggest changes taking place, in local landscape, community structure and ideology, during the said span; leading to the formation of *aṭavi* kingdoms. Such transformation warrants some explanation. Much of the early historical situation in the region is illuminated by archaeological evidence coming from sites such as Malhar (Bilaspur Dt.), Asurgarh and Budhigarh (Kalahandi Dt.), Marguda valley (Nuapada Dt.), and Kharliagarh (Bolangir Dt.), among others. These sites have yielded remains of pottery (BRW [black-and-red ware], NBPW [Northern Black Polished Ware], among others), punch-marked and Sātavāhana coins, interesting seals, two of them reading *grāmasya Kośalīya* and *mahārāja Mahendrasya*, and so on. Chronologically the data range from around 350 BC up to the Gupta period. There seems to have been uneven, dispersed patterns of development spread over the river valleys of the upper Mahānadī, Sheonath, and Tel. The concentration of archaeological and numismatic finds (Punch-marked, local uninscribed, Māgha, Kuṣāṇa, and Roman) together with the Guñji and Kirāri inscriptions suggest that the area around Bilaspur, with Malhar as a node, had emerged as a locality (*janapada*). The trade route from north India to the southeast coast passing through the site only added to its visibility. Asurgarh, in the east, similarly appears to have enjoyed a privileged position. During the Gupta period there is evidence demonstrating the spread of Gupta influence in terms of the symbols on coins (*Garuḍa, saṅkha, chakra*) distributed over the districts of Bilaspur, Raipur, Durg, and Kalahandi. The Arang fragmentary inscription points to the intrusion of Sanskrit, symbolizing the beginning of other related changes, in the region by the fourth century AD.[44]

An expansion and acceleration of the processes of change is witnessed after *c.* AD 500, when the first local state was formed. State formation under the Śarabhapurīyas and Pāṇḍuvaṁśīs, even the Somavaṁśīs, manifests phased territorial extension and structural evolution of polities, or to put it differently the long march from tentative beginnings, through the formative phase, to the making of more elaborate and complex forms. There was change but change not through breaks or any kind of crises. The differences between the drafts of the grants of the two early dynasties, it is said, are of a minor nature.[45] Though the drafts as well as the general framework seem to be quite similar, certain ideas are represented in an expanded and developed form in the charters of the Pāṇḍuvaṁśīs and they seem to have a bearing on our understanding of the evolution of the structure of polity in the region.

Śarabharāja, the founder of the first local dynasty, is known to us from the legends on the seals attached to the Pipardula and Kurud plates of his son Narendra. The first set of plates also indicates that Śarabhapūra their capital was also founded by *rāja* Śarabha. The formative stage of political formation is attested by the early records of the family. The draft of the Pipardula plates, the first known record of the dynasty is strikingly simple. It refers to the illustrious *mahārāja* Narendra without any elaboration. The privilege conferred on the donee was the exemption from the entry of the *cāṭas* and *bhaṭas*. The villagers are asked to pay the donee the taxes (*pratyāya*), including the share in kind (*mēya*) and cash (*hiraṇya*). It is followed by the unusual request to the future *bhōgapatis*, and not kings, to maintain the donated village. The Kurud plates, the second record of the family, were separated by twenty-one years from the first grant. The villagers in this case are asked to be obedient to the donee and to offer him *bhāga, bhōga, dhānya*, and *hiraṇya*. The request for the maintenance of the grant is addressed to future kings and not *bhōgapatis* as in the earlier grant. Significantly the addressees of the charter are now commanded (*samajñāpayati*) instead of being just informed (*bodhayati*) as in the previous charter. The Amgura grant of Jayaraja, the next ruler of the family, mentions *bhāga* and *bhōga* as offerings by the inhabitants to the donee, while his Mallar plates provide a developed description of the king. He is introduced 'as one whose pair of feet is washed by the waters in the form of the flowing forth of the radiance of the crest-jewels of the feudatory chiefs, bowing down before him, subdued by his prowess and as the cause of the tearing out of the parted hair of the women of his enemies, the giver of wealth, land and cows, the devout worshipper of Bhāgavat (Viṣṇu), and mediating upon the feet of his parents.'[46] Later rulers like Śudevarāja are presented in the same fashion (Thakurdiya plates). The grant also records the donee's right to major and minor deposits (*nidhi, upanidhi*) and its exemption from all taxes (*sarva-kara-visarjita*). Kings are described from this time onwards as *sāmanta-makuta-cudāmaṇi*. This was quite an advance from *mahārāja* Narendra's invocation of *paramabhaṭṭāraka-pāda*, that is, the Gupta overlord in his Kurud plates, for reasons of political validation or otherwise. Our intention is not to narrate the story record by record but to make the general point that aspects of polity did not converge with the founding of the first local dynasty, many of them evolved with time.

The distribution of the land grant charters, identification of donated settlements, list of people, and officials addressed in the charters, exemptions transferred to the donees and the titles and epithets borne by the rulers help to mark the stages in the evolution of the political structure. *Mahārāja* Tuṣṭikara who ruled during the fifth or sixth century in Kalahandi District appears to be the earliest known *rājā* in the region, following those mentioned in the Allahabad inscription. The Śarabhapurīyas issued their grants from Śarabhapūra and Śripūra (Sirpur), their successive capitals. The geographical spread of their land grants and identification of the donated settlements suggests that their kingdom included the modern Districts of Bilaspur, Raipur and Raigarh in Chhattisgarh and Kalahandi in Orissa. Their early records as also a major part of their donative grants have been reported from the Bilaspur-Raipur area, alluding to its privileged core status. *Bhōga, bhukti, rāṣṭra*, and *āhāra* were the administrative divisions comprising varied rural settlements. However, given the fact that they occur five times, four times, three times and once respectively, it is neither possible to work out any hierarchy of administrative units nor agree with the suggestion that these were interchangeable categories, as posited by S.P. Tiwari.[47] The revenue terms include *bhāga, bhōga, dhānya, hiraṇya, nidhi*, and *upanidhi*. From among these *bhāga* and *bhōga* seem to have been more frequent occurrences. One encounters the *cāṭa*s and *bhaṭa*s more frequently than the *bhōgapati*s, *dūtaka*s, *pratīhāra* or *adhikaraṇa*. The frequency of the latter categories is rather poor. Towards the end of their history we come across a certain *mahāsāmanta* Indrabalarāja who was also the *dūtaka* and *Sarvādhikarādhikṛta* or Chief Minister. The collapsing of more than one important office in the same person, pointing to the absence of clearly defined jurisdictions, is an indicator of an early state. Kings of the family used the title *mahārāja* and at times the epithet *bhaṭṭāraka,* but nothing more striking. Production of a grand genealogy, ornamented family tradition and curious origin myth were significantly absent. Together, all this tends to suggest a state in the making; where the constituent elements were not yet formally structured.

Land grants were usually royal prerogatives. Nevertheless, there are instances of grants being made by persons other than royalty, which were later sanctified by contemporary kings through the issue of copper-plate charters. While the Pipardula grant of *mahārāja* Narendra approved *bhōgapati* Rahudeva's donation, the Mallar plates of Jayarāja endorsed a grant made by Haḍapagrāha Vatsa, who was an important official. Similar cases of royal approval are registered in some of the charters of Sudevarāja, including one by *pratīhāra* Bhogilla. Such notables seem to have donated land out of their own possessions. During the period under reference there is no evidence of royal land allotments to state functionaries. Taken together with Narendra's exhortation to the *bhōgapatis* to maintain the donated settlement, these facts point to the importance and influence of such local notables in the polity under the Śarabhapurīyas. *Rājā* Śarabha, the founder of the dynasty, could possibly have been one among these local chiefs. With the coming of the state into existence these notables may have been identified and incorporated into the system. The absence of an organized pattern in terms of administrative details, besides the mention of the Gupta overlord in an early dynastic inscription, symbolizes their modest beginnings and a situation where power was not quite obtrusive. The non-invasive nature of power is perhaps also attested by the use of the expression *bodhayati* (informed) in the above mentioned Pipardula grant, highlighting the early compulsions of the state.

The provenance of the Pāṇḍuvaṁśī copper-plate and stone inscriptions and identification of the place names in these records reveal that their territorial frontiers largely coincided with that of their predecessors. Our intention is not to delineate the state structure in detail. What is necessary is an understanding of its character. While the kingdom was divided into *bhōgas*, *bhuktis*, and *viṣayas*, the popular revenue terms were *bhāga* and *bhōga*. Remissions to the donees were more detailed and included expressions such as *nidhi, upanidhi, sarva-kara–sameta,* and *sarva-pīda-varjita* (Baloda, Bonda plates). Rights to collect the fines for the ten offences (*dasāparadha)* and the property of a person dying without a heir (*aputrikaveṇi*) were the added privileges.[48] *Dasāparadha* was there from the beginning to the time of Mahāśivagupta Bālārjuna, whereas the latter was rare. The list of addressees included not only the inhabitants of the rural settlements but also state functionaries like *grāmakuta, gaṇḍakanāyaka, devavārika, pradhāna,* and so on. The records of Mahāśivagupta Bālārjuna, the most illustrious member of the family, also informed the astrologer (*kālādhyasin*), *samāhartṛ, sannidhātṛ,* and *karaṇa.* Admittedly, in his reign of almost sixty years the *pradhāna, samāhartṛ,* and *sannidhātṛ* were more common. All the land grants were made by the kings, though some were issued on the request of certain individuals. Royalty dispensed some of its resources in patronizing different sects and religious establishments, including Buddhist *vihāras.* In contrast to the earlier times the conspicuous growth in this area matched the use of significant titles and symbols of substance, to which we shall return below.

Land grants had implications for agrarian expansion, spread of rural settlements, internal transformation of local societies and the extension and consolidation of state power.[49] They also had ideological functions, especially in a region experiencing late state formation. It is generally agreed that they were a means of spreading royal influence beyond the heartland, particularly with their usually standardized message of the self-images of kingship. In the process of their being read out as and when required they transmitted the image of royal greatness.[50] Thus the *praśasti* section in these documents played a major role in the process of cultural communication. The requests made to the king for grants to brāhmaṇas and religious establishments or their conformation may possibly be seen as indicators of the reaching out of his authority to areas from where such requests emanated as well as the localities where they were executed.[51]

Compared to the Śarabhapurīyas there was an elaboration and refinement in the structure of legitimation. Besides the copper-plates, the lithic public records in and around Sirpur are good examples of it. The point could be elaborated by citing a few examples of the image or self-image of royalty from the donative records. The Bonda plates of Tivara deva describe him 'as an ornament of the three worlds, an auspicious column supporting the mansion that is the family of the kings and the foremost of all the performers of meritorious deeds.... He ... obtained lordship over the whole of Kośala country.... It is said that a number of chiefs who had acquired the five *mahāśabdas* had the ends of their crowns rubbed at his feet.'[52] The Pāṇḍuvaṁśīs traced their lineage to the Pāṇḍavas and *Candra vaṁśa* (*Śasivaṁśasambhuteḥ*). Tivaradeva's identification with the whole of Kośala marks the beginning of a sense of affiliation and formation of a regional/sub-regional identity. Mahāśivagupta Bālārjuna, the last but most glorious ruler in the family, finds more elaborate eulogistic treatment in the sources. He is said to have excelled Bhiṣma, Droṇa, and Karṇa in prowess and the use of arms. Various divinities were invoked and comparisons were sought to be made (Sirpur inscription). If the Śarabhapurīya records depicted them as givers of wealth, cattle and land (*vasu-vasudhā-gopradaḥ),* the details get richer in the case of the Pāṇḍuvaṁśīs. Mahāśivagupta Bālārjuna is said to have been the incarnation of virtue (*dharmāvatāra*). He was the protector of the *varṇa*s and *āśrama*s and prevented the dawn of the *Kali* Age, while simultaneously befriending *Kṛta* Age and perpetuating *dharma.* The construction of courtly ideology had traveled quite a distance since the time of the Śarabhapurīyas when the kings were represented in their human attributes as a devout worshipper of Bhāgavat or as mediating at the feet of the parents. The varied images of a kṣatriya, warrior, hero, and dharmic figure conferred political, ideological, and cultural validation to kingship, and allude to the centrality of the brāhmaṇas in shaping courtly ideology; notwithstanding the strong presence of Buddhism in the region.

Agricultural expansion and the spread of peasant activity leading to growing social complexity, marked by differentiation and stratification, provided the material foundation for the above said developments. Almost half of the grants of both the dynasties under discussion have been identified in the district of Raipur and the remaining, barring a few exceptions; have been located in the districts of Bilaspur and Raigarh. From the distribution of the land grants it emerges that the area around the Mahānadī valley and its tributaries were being opened up for agriculture. That the changes were gradual is also borne out by the evidence for internal differentiation and the visible spread of the state apparatus. The absence of detailed boundary specifications in the land grants suggests low density of settlements and the availability of land for clearance and settlement. Even the Senakapat record while mentioning the boundaries does not refer to other settlements or neighbouring plots. The continued presence of *padara, padraka*, and *pāṭaka* ending rural settlements even under the Pāṇḍuvaṁśīs, and not necessarily *grāmas* (full fledged villages) in almost all cases, may suggest a society in its early stages. The transitory nature of society is manifest in the Prākritism in some words in the Śarabhapurīya copper-plates. In the later charters the language becomes fluent and ornate. The changing forms of the structure of political legitimation were a reflection of these interrelated developments. It needs to be emphasized that the use of śāstric-epic-purāṇic imageries in the charters, alluded to above, especially those on stone in and around Sirpur in a general context of state formation were influencing the negotiations in the cultural domain. The same would hold true for the recent epigraphic finds too. The relationship between text and context, that is, symbols, ideas and the social and cultural domains were possibly dynamic and not just a one way traffic. Whereas the temple towns of Sirpur (Buddhist monasteries included) and Rajim in the heart of Dakṣiṇa Kośala as centres of pilgrimage would have been meeting places and melting pots of varied cultural influences, Kośaleśwara at Baidyanath on the eastern frontier of the kingdom could have provided the kind of pervasiveness and omnipresence that royalty would have craved for. The affinity between *Kośalādhipati*, lords of Kośala, an epithet which the rulers used and Kośaleśwara the deity at Baidyanath strikes one in the face, and it is rather difficult to believe that it was accidental, not designed.

Orissa

The history of Orissa between *c.* BC 300 and AD 350 was characterized by uneven patterns of growth. There is evidence for segmented development comparable to what obtained in Dakṣiṇa Kośala.[53] The early historical phase is better represented in the coastal belt than northern and western Orissa. Various localities/sub-regions in the region experienced internal transformation in the Gupta and post-Gupta centuries.[54] The early medieval polities did not rise on the ruins of an empire because large parts of the region did not have any previous experience of complex society and organized state activity. The sub-regions were known as Kaliṅga, Kōngoḍa *maṇḍala*, Dakṣiṇa Toṣali, Uttara Toṣali, Khiñjali *maṇḍala*, Kōdalaka *maṇḍala*, Khijjiṅga *maṇḍala*, etc. During the fourth–seventh centuries there was a horizontal spread of state societies, particularly in the coastal tract. The Māṭharas and their contemporaries, Early Eastern Gaṅgās, Nalas, Mānas, and Vigrahas, for example, provide good evidence of it. Continued manifestation of the process across spatial segments could be seen between the seventh and tenth century. Most of the ruling lineages such as the Eastern Gaṅgās, Śailōdbhavas,

Bhaumakaras and the Bhañjas of Khiñjali, and Khijjiṅgakoṭṭā had humble local origins. Around the same period the formation of larger political enterprises began under the Bhaumakaras of central coastal Orissa, who after combining Koṅgoda and Toṣala, the lower valleys of the Riṣikulyā and Mahānadī, moved into the hinterlands. The political and historical geography of these dynasties have been already worked out and need not detain us here.[55]

State formation and socio-economic transformation appear to have been simultaneous, interrelated developments. Agrarian and social change was the prerequisite for the consolidation and extension of political authority. The introduction of brāhmaṇas through land grants of various types—individual, collective and scattered—especially in the tribal belts or the maxim of bringing virgin land under cultivation opened these areas to caste-peasant based influences. It stimulated the economic integration of wider areas across localities and sub-regions.[56] Statehood emerged only when a community was capable of producing a surplus sufficient to maintain a non-producing public authority structure. Smaller the surplus less elaborate was the apparatus of the state. One does not have to stretch oneself beyond the cases of the Vigrahas, Mānas, and Māṭharas to make the point.[57] Another aspect of the contemporary political processes was the relationship of the tribal chiefs, who were on the way to becoming Hindu *rājās*, and the local tribes in transition, who had to generate resources and defend the realm. Kulke posits that the problem was largely addressed through the royal patronage of the autochthonous deities as family or tutelary deities of the emerging local or sub-regional states. In the process the *rājās* tried to appropriate the territoriality of the deities and the loyalty of the subjects. The deities were raised to a high level of ritual elaboration along with the consolidation of the Hindu *rājās*. However, the visual aspects of the deity, the tribal priests and related aspects of the rituals were retained and superimposed with brāhmaṇas and brāhmaṇic rituals, facilitating the gradual integration of the deity with the Hindu pantheon. In the process of cultural confluence each contributed to and defined the relevance of the other. The movement of ideas, symbols, and cultural signifiers was a two way process; cultural communication involved both the 'High' and 'Low'. This helped to underline the common identities between the ruler and the ruled within the community and even beyond. In other words, it tied legitimacy down and sidewise.[58]

The Bhaumakaras who began their rule around AD 736 ruled from Jajpur in central coastal Orissa and gradually expanded their sway. *Maṇḍala* territories in the river valleys and hilly hinterland of coastal Orissa became a part of their circle of *sāmanta* domains. These dynasties included the Śulkis of Kōḍalaka *maṇḍala* in the Brahmani valley, Bhañjas of Khiñjali *maṇḍala* in the Baud valley, Tungas of Yamagarta *maṇḍala* and the Nandas of Airāvata *maṇḍala*. The last two *maṇḍalas* were carved out of Kōḍalaka *maṇḍala* after the political eclipse of the Śulkis. The Mayūras of Boṇāi *maṇḍala*, with *varāha* titles, and the Ādi Bhañjas of Khijjiṅga *maṇḍala* (Mayurbhanja, parts of Keonjhar district and adjoining territories in Jharkhand) emerged on the political scene almost contemporaneously and acknowledged the lordship of the Bhaumakaras. Mostly these dynasties used the Bhauma Era in their charters, epithets such as *raṇaka*, *mahāsāmantādhipati*, and proclaimed their having obtained the privilege of *pañchamahāśabda*. These clearly indicate their *sāmanta* status and the rise of a powerful overlord. These semi-independent states while acknowledging the lord's preeminent position, exercised autonomous power in their domains. The fact that the local and sub-regional states emerged from below and were not created by any central omnipresent power may account for their assertion.[59] The Somavaṁśīs, succesors of the Bhaumakaras, rose to power in Dakṣiṇa Kośala following the Pāṇḍuvaṁśīs. In the early stages of their history up to about the end of the ninth century they remained confined to that region and its neighbourhood. By the middle of the tenth century (AD 930) they had conquered Khiñjali *maṇḍala* and subsequently extended their sway over the coastal parts of the Bhaumakara territory. For the first time a regional polity had been forged bringing together several sub-regions, including parts of western Orissa and Chhattisgarh. The process of continued agrarian expansion, especially in the Bolangir area, with all that it entailed continued under them, making the more general point that state formation, agrarian transformation and social change were simultaneous processes in operation.[60] When these developments were actualized straddling across sub-regions and localities over time, they created conditions for the emergence of a concomitant regional state and, flowing from it, the necessary refinements in the structure of legitimation.[61]

On the basis of the smaller number of officials and revenue terms mentioned in the inscriptions, the humble epithets and absence of impressive genealogies and bombastic family traditions it may possibly be argued that the polities presided over by the Śarabhapurīyas, Māṭharas, and Vigrahas, and others, between the fourth–seventh centuries were largely in an early stage of development. The process continued to play itself out in the various *maṇḍalas* during the seventh–tenth centuries. Around the same time the Bhaumakaras began their efforts to integrate some of the sub-regions, which was followed up by the grand Śomavaṁśīs of Dakṣiṇa Kośala and the Later Eastern Gaṅgās of Kaliṅga.

The trajectory of socio-political transformations in the regions discussed above shows that there was change but change through continuity. From the conception of kingship to the constitution of authority, including the structure of the state, all registered continuous evolution and advancement. These processes and institutions were derived not from the undoing of earlier large political systems but from changes coming from within local societies, which were propelled by a network of linkages. The emergence of larger polities was shaped by the gradual territorial and political integration of peasant localities. These communities were asymmetrical and stratified, characterized by the shaping of occupational and caste groups with reference to the dominant Brāhmaṇical framework. Brāhmaṇas and brāhmaṇic settlements, Vedic-śāstric-epic-purāṇic ideas, monasteries (including *vihāras*) and temples provided the necessary coherence to the existing and emerging order. Increasingly there is recognition of the fact that the state tried to incorporate the different grades of well-to-do peasants such as the *kuṭumbins*, *mahattaras*, *mahāmahattaras*, and *pradhāna-prativāśins* into the political structure in different areas and points in time, as in other parts of the country.[62] The context of their occurrence in the land-grant inscriptions makes it obvious. They seem to have constituted the intermediate categories. The cultural dimension though appears to be subsumed under discussions on changing forms of patronage and legitimation is very much visible and was in symmetry with the evolving integrative processes.[63]

Notes

1. See D.D. Kosambi, *An Introduction to the Study of Indian History*, Bombay, Popular Prakashan, 1956; R.S. Sharma, *Indian Feudalism, c.* AD *300–1200*, Calcutta, 1965; B.N.S. Yadava, *Society and Culture in Northern India in the Twelfth Century*, Allahabad, Central Book Depot, 1973.

2. See Sharma, *Indian Feudalism*; idem., *Social Changes in Early Medieval India*, New Delhi, People's Publishing House, 1969; idem., 'How Feudal was Indian Feudalism?', *Social Scientist*, no. 129, Feb. 1984, pp. 16–41.

3. B. Stein, 'The Segmentary State in South Indian History', in Richard Fox (ed.), *Realm and Region in Traditional India*, Delhi, Vikas Publishing House, 1977, pp. 3–51; idem., *Peasant State and Society in Medieval South India*, New Delhi, Oxford University Press, 1980.

4. H. Kulke, 'Fragmentation and Segmentation versus Integration: Reflections on the Concept of Indian Feudalism and the Segmentary State in Indian History', *Studies in History*, vol. 4, no. 2, 1982, pp. 237–63; B.D. Chattopadhyaya, 'Political Processes and the Structure of Polity in Early Medieval India—Problems of Perspective', Presidential Address, Ancient India Section, *Proceedings of the Indian History Congress* (hereafter *PIHC*), Burdwan session, 1983, pp. 25–63.

5. See D.C. Sircar, (ed.), *Land System and Feudalism in Ancient India*, Calcutta, University of Calcutta, 1966.

6. Hermann Kulke, 'The Early State and the Imperial Kingdom: A Processural Model of Integrative State Formation in Early Medieval India', in idem., *The State in India, 1000–1700*, Delhi, Oxford University Press, 1995, p. 257.

7. Sharma, *Indian Feudalism*.

8. B.N.S. Yadava, 'The Accounts of the Kali Age and the Social Transition from Antiquity to the Middle Ages', in *The Indian Historical Review*, vol. 5, nos 1–2, 1979, pp. 31–63; R.S. Sharma, 'The Kali Age: A Period of Social Crisis', in S.N. Mukherjee (ed.), *India: History and Thought*, Calcutta, Subarnarekha, 1982, pp. 186–203.

9. H. Mukhia, 'Was There Feudalism in Indian History?', Presidential Address, Medieval India Section, *Proceedings IHC*, Waltair session, 1979, pp. 229–80.

10. See D.N. Jha, 'Early Indian Feudalism: A Historiographical Critique', Presidential Address, Ancient India section, *Proceedings IHC*, Waltair session, 1979, pp. 15–45; idem., 'Validity of Brāhmaṇa-Peasant alliance and the Segmentary State in Early Medieval South India, *Social Science Probings*, vol. 4, no. 2, 1984, pp. 270–95; R.N. Nandi, 'Feudalization of the State in Medieval South India', *Social Science Probings*, vol. 1, no. 1, 1984, pp. 33–59; and Kesavan Veluthat, *The Political Structure of Early Medieval South India*, New Delhi, Orient Longman, 1993.

11. B.D. Chattopadhyaya, *The Making of Early Medieval India*, New Delhi, Oxford University Press, 1994; idem., 'State and Economy in North India: Fourth Century to Twelfth Century', in R. Thapar (ed.), *Recent Perspectives of Early Indian History*, Bombay, Popular Prakashan, 1995, pp. 309–46.

12. See B.P. Sahu, 'Conception of the Kali Age in Early India: A Regional Perspective', *Trends in Social Science Research*, vol. 4, no. 1, 1997, pp. 27–36.

13. Romila Thapar, *The Mauryas Revisited*, Calcutta, K.P. Bagchi and Co., 1987; G. Fussman, Central and Provincial Administration in Ancient India: The Problem of the Mauryan Empire, *The Indian Historical Review* (hereafter *IHR*), vol. 14, nos 1–2, 1990, pp. 43–72; S. Seneviratne, 'Kaliṅga and Āndhra: The

Process of Secondary State Formation in Early India', *IHR*, vol. 7, nos 1–2, 1981, pp. 54–69; B.D. Chattopadhyaya, 'Transition to the Early Historical Phase in the Deccan: A Note', in B.M. Pande and B.D. Chattopadhyaya (eds), *Archaeology and History: Essays in Honour of A. Ghosh,* Delhi, Agam Kala Prakashan 1988, pp. 727–32.

14. Kulke, 'Fragmentation and Segmentation'; idem., 'The Early State and the Imperial'; Chattopadhyaya, 'State and Economy in North India'.

15. B.P. Sahu, 'Legitimation, Ideology and State in Early India', Presidential Address, Ancient India Section, *Proceedings IHC,* Mysore session, 2003b, pp. 44–76; idem., 'Ways of Seeing: History and Historiography of the State in Early India', in M. Brandtner and S.K. Panda (eds), *Interrogating History: Essays for Hermann Kulke,* New Delhi, 2006, pp. 63–82.

16. H. Kulke, 'The Integrative Model of State Formation in Early Medieval India: Some Historiographic Remarks', in M. Kimura and A. Tanabe (eds), *The State in India: Past and Present,* New Delhi, Oxford University Press, 2006, pp. 59–81.

17. See Kesavan Veluthat, 'Lord of a City; Overlord of a Country: The State under the Cēras of Mahōdayapuram', presented at the Panel on State in Indian History, Indian History Congress, Bareilly session, 28–30 December 2004.

18. Chattopadhyaya, 'State and Economy in North India', p. 346.

19. B. Stein, *Peasant State and Society in Medieval South India,* New Delhi, Oxford University Press, 1980.

20. R.S. Sharma, 'The Segmentary State and the Indian Experience', *IHR,* vol. 16, nos 1–2, 1993, pp. 80–108; for recent statements see N. Karashima, 'The Emergence of Medieval State and Social Formations in South India', in idem., *South Indian Society in Transition: Ancient to Medieval,* New Delhi, 2009, pp. 1–23; also H. Kulke, 'Ritual Sovereignty and Ritual Policy: Some Historiographic Reflections', in H. Kulke and U. Skoda (eds), *State and Ritual in India, Section IV,* in M.Kitts *et. al* (eds), *State Power and Violence,* Wiesbaden, Harrasowitz, 2010, pp. 603–26.

21. Chattopadhyaya, 'Political Processes and the Structure'.

22. See Y. Subbarayalu, 'The Cōḷa State', *Studies in History,* vol. 4, no. 2, 1982, pp. 265–306; J. Heitzman, 'State Formation in South India, 850–1280', *The Indian Economic and Social History Review,* vol. 24, 1987, pp. 35–61.

23. G.W. Spencer, *The Politics of Expansion: The Chola Conquest of Sri Lanka and Sri Vijaya,* Madras, 1983.

24. B. Stein, 'The Segmentary State: Interim Reflections', in H. Kulke (ed.), *The State in India: 1000–1700,* New Delhi, Oxford University Press, 1995, pp. 134–61. Also see H. Kulke, 'Ritual Sovereignty and Ritual Policy'.

25. See Chattopadhyaya, Irrigation in Early Medieval Rajasthan, *Journal of the Social and Economic History of the Orient,* vol. 16, nos 2–3, 1973, pp. 298–316; idem., 'Origin of the Rajputs: The Political, Economic and Social Processes in Early Medieval Rajasthan', *IHR,* vol. III, no. 1, 1976, pp 59–82; Kulke, Early State

Formation and Royal Legitimation in Late Ancient Orissa, in M.N. Das (ed.), *Side-Lights on History and Culture of Orissa,* Cuttack, Vidyapuri, 1977, 104–14; idem., 'Royal Temple Policy and the Structure of Medieval Hindu Kingdoms', in A. Eschmann, H. Kulke, and G.C. Tripathi (eds), *The Cult of Jagannāth and the Regional Tradition of Orissa,* Delhi, Manohar, 1978, pp. 125–38.

26. Kulke, 'Fragmentation and Segmentation'; Chattopadhyaya, 'Political Processes and Structure'.

27. See Romila Thapar, *From Lineage to State: Social Formations in the Mid First Millennium* BC *in the Gaṅgā Valley,* New Delhi, Oxford University Press 1984; idem., *The Mauryas Revisited*; and Fussman, 'Central and Provincial Administration'.

28. S. Seneviratne, 'Kaliṅga and Āndhra'; Chattopadhyaya, 'Transition to the Early Historical Phase in the Deccan'; and B.P. Sahu, 'The Early State in Orissa: From the Perspective of Changing Forms of Patronage and Legitimation', in B. Pati, B.P. Sahu, and T.K. Venkatasubramanian (eds), *Negotiating India's Past: Essays in Memory of Professor P.S. Gupta,* New Delhi, 2003, pp. 29–51.

29. See Nandini Sinha-Kapoor, 'Early Maitraka Land-grant Charters and Regional State Formation in Early Medieval Gujarat', *Studies in History,* vol. 17, no. 2, 2001, pp. 151–73; Kulke, 'Some Thoughts on State and State Formation under the Eastern Vākāṭakas', in Hans Bakker (ed.), *The Vākāṭaka Heritage: Indian Culture at the Crossroads,* Groningen, The Netherlands Egbert Forsten, 2004, pp. 1–9; and Y. Dayama, 'Political Processes in the Making of the Early Kadamba State', *PIHC,* Kannur session, 2008, pp. 102–14.

30. Kulke, 'The Early State and the Imperial Kingdom'.

31. Chattopadhyaya, 'Autonomous Spaces and the Authority of the State: The Contradiction and its Resolution in Theory and Practice in Early India', in idem., *Studying Early India: Archaeology, Texts and Historical Issues,* Delhi, Permanent Black 2003, pp. 135–252.

For good discussions on the transformation of forests into nuclei of state society, see B. Schnepel, *The Jungle Kings: Ethnohistorical Aspects of Politics and Ritual in Orissa,* Delhi, Manohar, 2002; Chattopadhyaya, 'State's Perception of the "Forest" and the Forest as State in Early India', in B.B. Choudhury and Arun Bandopadhyay (eds), *Tribes, Forest and Social Formations in Indian History,* New Delhi, Manohar, 2004, pp. 23–37.

32. Georg Berkemer and Margret Frenz (eds), *Sharing Sovereignty: The Little Kingdom in South Asia,* Berlin, Klaus Schwartz Verlag, 2004, especially the early essays.

33. S.K. Panda, 'From Kingdom to Empire: A Study of the Medieval State of Orissa under the Later Eastern Gaṅgās, AD 1038–1434', *IHR,* vol. 17, 1993, pp. 48–59; Nandini Sinha, *State Formation in Rajasthan: Mewar During the Seventh-Fifteenth Centuries,* New Delhi, Manohar, 2002; Cynthia Talbot, *Precolonial India in Practice: Society, Religion and Identity in Medieval Andhra,* New Delhi, Oxford University Press, 2001; and Heitzman, supra n. 22.

34. D.N. Jha, 'Introduction', in idem. (ed.) *The Feudal Order: State Society & Ideology in Early Medieval India,* New Delhi, Manohar, 2000, pp. 1–58; Kesavan Veluthat, 'Review of M. Kimura and A. Tanabe (eds), *The State in India: Past and Present,* New Delhi, 2006', *The Book Review,* vol 30, no. 5, 2006, pp. 14–15.

35. Daud Ali, 'Review of Nandini Sinha-Kapoor's *State Formation in Rajasthan: Mewar During the Seventh-Fifteenth Centuries,* Delhi, 2002', *Journal of the Social and Economic History of the Orient,* vol. 48, no. 2, 2005, pp. 341–3.

36. See Nandini Sinha, *State Formation in Rajasthan*; Heitzman, 'State Formation in South India'; Veluthat, supra n.17; and S.K. Panda, *The State and the Statecraft in Medieval Orissa Under the Later Eastern Gaṅgās,* Calcutta, K.P. Bagchi and Co., 1995.

37. For example, see Talbot, *Pre-Colonial India in Practice*; Kulke, 'The Early State and Imperial Kingdom'.

38. Kulke, 'Fragmentation and Segmentation'; idem., 'The Early State and Imperial Kingdom'; Chattopadhyaya, *Aspects of Rural Settlements and Rural Society in Early Medieval India,* Calcutta, K.P. Bagchi 1990; idem., *The Making of Early Medieval India.*

39. B.P. Sahu, 'Introduction', in idem. (ed.), *Land System and Rural Society in Early India*, Delhi, Manohar, 1997.

40. ibid.; For the range of rural exchange centres and markets see Ranabir Chakravarti, *Trade and Traders in Early Indian Society*, Delhi, Manohar, 2002.

41. B.P. Sahu, 'Profiling Dakṣiṇa Kośala: An Early Historical Subregion?', in H. Kulke and Georg Berkemer (eds), *Centres Out There? Facets of Subregional Identities in Orissa*, New Delhi, Manohar, 2011, pp. 39–59.

42. A.M. Shastri, 'Introduction', *Inscriptions of the Śarabhapurīyas, Pāṇḍuvaṁśīs and Somavaṁśīs,* Pts I & II, Delhi, 1995; Hans Bakker, 'Observations on the History and Culture of Dakṣiṇa Kośala (5th to 7th centuries AD)', in N. Balbir and J.K. Bautze (eds), *Festschrift Klaus Bruhn,* Reinbek, 1994, pp. 1–41.

43. S.P. Tiwari, *Comprehensive History of Orissa: Dakshiṇa Kośala under the Śarabhapurīyas,* Calcutta, Puuthi Pustak, 1985.

44. Sahu, 'Profiling Dakṣiṇa Kośala'; P. Yule, *Early Historic Sites in Orissa,* New Delhi, 2006.

45. Shastri, *Inscriptions of the Śarabhapurīyas.*

46. Ibid. p. 19.

47. S.P. Tiwari, *Comprehensive History of Orissa,* Section on Administration.

48. Shastri, 'Introduction', *Introduction of the Śarabhapurīyas*, vol. I, pp. 40–1.

49. Kulke, supra n.6, pp. 234–41; Chattopadhyaya, 'State and Economy', pp. 325–37.

50. See Kulke, 'Some Observations on the Political Functions of Copper-Plate Grants in Early Medieval India', in Bernhard Kolver *et al.* (eds), *The State, the Law and Administration in Classical India,* Munchen, pp. 237–43.

51. N. Karashima (ed.), *Kingship in Indian History,* New Delhi, Manohar, 1999, p. 10.

52. Shastri, *Inscriptions of the Śarabhapurīyas.*

53. Sahu, supra n. 28; also idem., 'Ancient Orissa: The Dynamics of Internal Transformation of the Tribal Society', in K.M. Shrimali (ed.), *Essays in Indian Art, Religion and Society,* Delhi, Munshiram Manoharlal, 1987, pp. 169–80.

54. Kulke, 'Early State Formation and Royal Legitimation'; idem., *Jagannāth-Kult and Gajapati Konigtum,* Wiesbaden, 1979, pp. 223–39; Upinder Singh, *Kings, Brāhmaṇas and Temples in Orissa: An Epigraphic Study,* AD, *300–1147,* New Delhi, Munshiram Manoharlal, 1993.

55. Ibid.; also see Malati Mahajan, *Orissa: From Place Names in Inscriptions c. 260 BC–1200 AD (Cultural and Historical Geography),* Delhi, Sharada Publishing House, 2003.

56. B.P. Sahu, 'Agrarian Changes and the Peasantry in Early Medieval Orissa (*c.* AD 400–1100)', in V.K. Thakur and A. Aounshuman (eds), *Peasants in Indian History,* Patna, Janaki Prakashan, 1996, pp. 283–311.

57. For a comparable situation, see Kulke, supra n. 29.

58. See for example Kulke, 'The Early State and Imperial Kingdom'; and B.P. Sahu, 'Rituals, Royalty and *Rājya* in Early Medieval Eastern India', in H. Kulke and U. Skoda (eds), *State and Ritual in India, Section IV,* in M. Kitts *et al.* (eds), *State Power and Violence,* Wiesbaden, 2010, pp. 665–81.

59. Sahu, 'Arguing for Feudalism from Below: A Study in Orissa Setting (*c.* AD 400–*c.*1100)', *Proceedings IHC,* Calcutta session, 1990, pp. 141–50.

60. Chattopadhyaya, 'Introduction', in *The Making of Early Medieval India.*

61. Kulke, 'Fragmentation and Segmentation'; idem., 'The Early State and Imperial Kingdom'.

62. The expanding social foundations of the state are discussed in Chattopadhyaya, *Aspects of Rural Settlements,* ch. on Bengal; Cynthia Talbot, Political Intermediaries in Kākatīya Andhra, 1175–1325, *IESHR,* vol. 31, no. 3, 1994, pp. 261–89; Kesavan Veluthat, 'Landed Magnates as State Agents', in his *The Early Medieval in South India,* New Delhi, Oxford University Press, 2009, pp. 325–31.

63. A very good comprehensive discussion of the cultural aspects of the royal court, including manners, protocols, aesthetics and love on a larger canvass is available in Daud Ali, *Courtly Culture and Political Life in Early Medieval India,* Cambridge, Cambridge University Press, 2004. In the case of the regions under discussion one may see Vidya Dehejia, *Early Stone Temples of Orissa,* Delhi, Vikas Publishing House, 1979; and Thomas E. Donaldson, *Hindu Temple Art of Orissa,* Leiden, 1985.

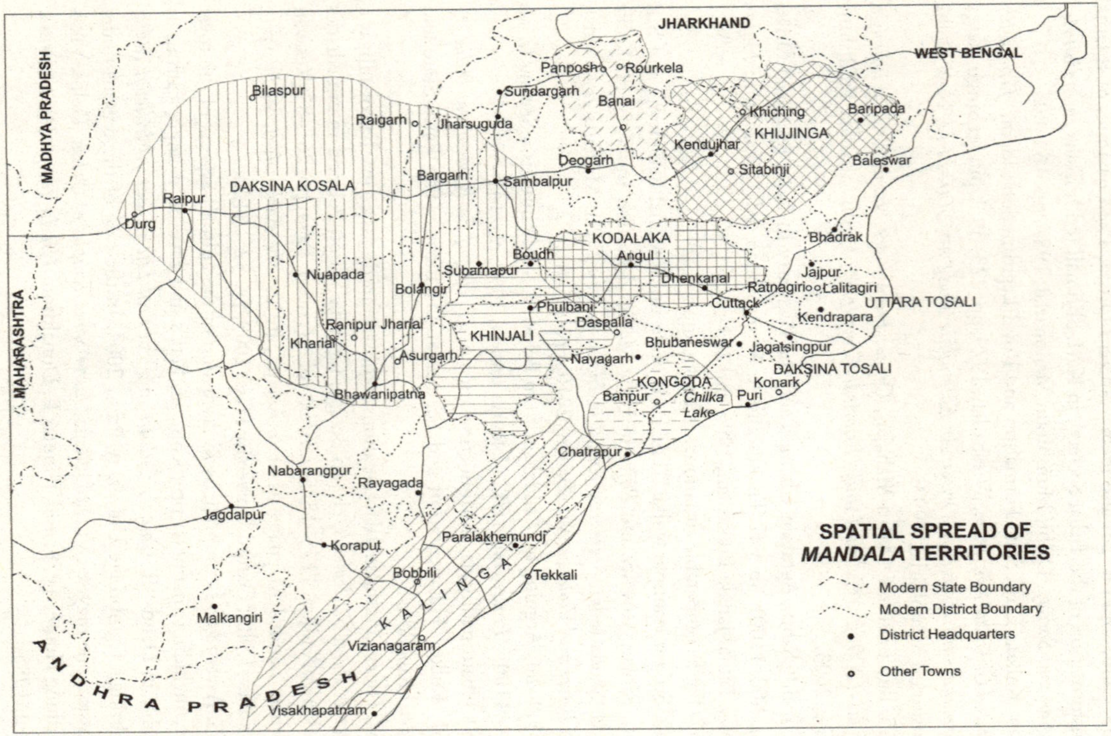

Map 2: Spatial Spread of *Maṇḍala* Territories. Courtesy of the author.

8

Legitimation, Ideology, and State in Early India*

Prologue

The study of political processes and the structure of polity in early India is a recent concern among historians. Some of the early writings around these issues emerged in the 1960s and early 1970s, and disturbed the earlier centralized, powerful, ubiquitous notions of the state, which, it was usually assumed, had little to do with popular perceptions or support. In conventional historiographical usage the expression 'early India' encapsulates both the early historical and early medieval periods. My feeling is that the problem of legitimation in the wider context of state formation and the structure of polities needs greater attention. It may be useful to examine the devices that rulers used to extend and perpetuate their authority over time. A study of the strategies employed and their changing forms can provide an entry point for discerning social processes and structural change in early India, insofar as the system sustaining mechanisms develop and move

*Originally published as 'Presidential Address, Section I: Ancient Indian History', *Proceedings of the Indian History Congress*, Mysore, 2003, pp. 44–76.

I am grateful to Professor B.D. Chattopadhyaya for his helpful comments on an earlier draft of this essay. I am thankful to Professor Hermann Kulke and Dr Martin Brandtner of the University of Kiel and Dr Daud Ali of the School of Oriental and African Studies, London, for their kindness in drawing my attention and providing access to some of the material cited here.

The award of a Charles Wallace India Trust Fellowship in the summer of 2003 provided me the opportunity for utilizing the resources of the British Library and School of Oriental and African Studies Library, London. I offer them all my sincere thanks.

in tandem with social and political processes. This chapter is about legitimation of power in early India; its primary concern will be with the changing forms of patronage and legitimation and the ways in which the question has been approached by practitioners of the craft.[1]

Power is a broad inclusive concept, and includes coercion, domination, and even manipulation. Authority is a form of power, but one which enjoys legitimacy and is associated with obedience and support of the subordinates. The distinction between power and authority is, thus, an important one.[2] Political theory may be concerned with the distribution of power, but the historians are concerned, deriving from the distribution of power between groups and classes in society, with the constitution of authority, its sustenance and changing forms in time and space. Governmentality is constituted in complex ways, involving both the ruling elite and the subjects; it is not one-way traffic. Individuals and groups wielding power and wishing to continue in that position make use of religious ideas, symbols and institutions to cohere the fragmented identities in the realm and validate or consolidate their status. People in power look for a variety of justifications to provide a moral basis for it, and make it appear as deriving from, or rooted in the pool of societal values.[3] Legitimation was necessary for communities experiencing local state formation as well as in complex state societies. Legitimation of power and the shaping of dominant ideology were, as they usually are, complex processes. They were continuously changing, dynamic, and absorptive as against the generally assumed simple reflective and mechanical constructions. This was in consonance with the rich cultural mosaic and change intrinsic to early Indian societies.

Administrative efficiency and control over territories were not the only bases of political systems in early India. Kings displayed support for religious institutions, their representatives and a wide range of other strategies to strengthen their authority. Power was partly related to persuasion, involving distribution of largesse and the practice of deception. The authority that people in power exercised also involved the manipulation of institutions, groups and their belief systems. Conceptions of power and status are culturally determined and therefore the constitutive elements in the structure of legitimation were specific to particular societies. Cultural forms and historical processes may be comparable across cultures or regions, but comparability is not the same as being identical. Patronage and the forging of royal authority were interrelated phenomena. Studies on patronage and legitimation in early India straddle a wide spectrum. In ancient societies, as so often today, it was not disinterested.[4] Rulers participated in and patronized public activities and events, which strengthened their legitimacy as upholders of the socio-political order. Patronage by creating a network of bonds nurtured asymmetrical social relationships and sustained the iniquitous distribution of power in society. It was achieved through engendering a belief that the distribution of power in society and, as a consequence of that, the rules and practices impacting everyday life were just. In fact, 'ideology by systematic distortion naturalizes and reproduces relations of unequal power.' Acts of patronage with their ability to influence the domain of popular perceptions were integral to the legitimation process and strategies of domination. Ruling elites dispensed their resources, stressed their genealogical links, sponsored and shared in impressive rituals and invoked special relationships with Gods in their search for legitimacy, or to put it differently seeking to secure consent to their power. Legitimation allowed those in power to be perceived as 'moral agents, not just self-interested actors'.[5]

Legitimacy comprises three elements: conformation to established rules; rules which can be justified with reference to beliefs commonly shared by the rulers and the ruled (which would vary from one age or society to another); and the evidence of consent on the part of the subordinates to the given power relations.[6] Consent could be expressed through formal or symbolic acts or played out in public on ceremonial or ritual occasions.[7] It is important to recognize that legitimacy could be eroded or contested and, flowing from it, it need not be perceived in absolute terms. Admittedly, legitimation is not the only factor contributing to order and stability in a political system. Organizational capabilities and resource generation are also of crucial importance. 'Emphasis on legitimation alone obfuscates crucial aspects of the exercise of force and of the secular compulsions of state power, but as a part of overall political process it nevertheless offers us a convenient vantage point from which to view the ideological dimension of the state.'[8] Similarly, politics does not exhaust the concept of legitimation; it deals with society as well and in the process is both a social and political concept.[9]

The question of legitimation, like state formation, was not much of a concern until recently, largely owing to the assumption that ruling elites were too immersed in administration, warfare and the mobilization of resources to invest anything in seeking social/moral validation for their rule. The image of an all powerful, unitary, and centralized state, irrespective of time and place, was also not helpful insofar as it took popular support and acquiescence for granted, or did not see the need to examine the complexities and compulsions that people in power had to confront and address. Legitimation studies emerged from historians' recent concern for and engagement with the origin, evolution, and typology of states,[10] instead of the earlier sterile presupposition that states existed since time immemorial or experienced no structural change over time. At this point a brief statement of the historiographical trajectory of studies of the state, which have characterized the work of Indian and non-Indian scholars in the last half a century or so, may help to situate the genesis and evolving contours of the related theme of legitimation.

Changing Perspectives

State formation and legitimation in early historical and, more particularly, early medieval India have attracted considerable scholarly attention since the middle of the 1970s, involving critical engagement with the role of ideas and institutions in the shaping of authority and the sustenance of political systems. During this period there have been several detailed empirical studies focusing on different historical situations across regions, unmistakably though the beginnings of this development, in one form or the other, can be traced to the early influential writings of D.D. Kosambi, R.S. Sharma, Surajit Sinha, Romila Thapar, Burton Stein, G.W. Spencer, and N.B. Dirks.[11] These writings and those that followed drawing inspiration from them shifted the discursive ground insofar as they emphasized that historical states, comprising different communities, groups, institutions, and differentiated spaces did not necessarily conform to theoretical ideal types and, thus, had to be studied not as abstract phenomena divorced from society, but within the framework of state-in-society.

Notwithstanding the recognition of the need to bridge the gap between state and society for a proper understanding of political processes, including ideology and legitimation, and the structure of polities, the dominant historiography in the course of providing an explanatory historical perspective illustrating change, slided towards macro-generalizations, spanning centuries. In the process the specificity of the historical and regional experiences was subsumed under overarching theoretical frameworks. This typically modernist project of constructing large, durable, common institutional structures is characteristic of several mid-twentieth century intellectual endeavours. Admittedly, its lineage extends to the colonial writings through the nationalist hegemonic constructions. It only demonstrates that the historian's craft is a dialogic process and that the weight and influence of earlier generations cannot be easily wished away. The commonalities between different approaches perhaps need as much attention, if not more, as the differences.[12] Whatever their differences and they are considerable, both Kosambi and Sharma have played influential roles in the formation of the dominant historiography. While Kosambi stands out for focusing on the possible affinity between several historical processes during the age of the Buddha and in and around the Gupta period,[13] and Sharma deserves credit for locating political ideas and institutions in society and accounting for change and continuity in ancient India,[14] the latter's generalizations about legitimacy and ideology from a theoretical position simplified and stereotyped the perceptive ideas of Kosambi.[15] Bhakti in north and south India, deriving from Kosambi's stimulating observations, has been shown as the ideology of the feudal order.[16] Religious cults and institutions in early medieval Deccan and south India, with a political imprint early in their history, have been perceived within the feudal model.[17] It is different from examining the socio-religious importance and popularity of certain sects and institutions, which then are seen to have attracted royal patronage for political purposes. In perceiving Bhakti as being reflective of a certain socio-economic reality, insofar as it is related to the land grants and feudalism as ideology of the new order, this historiography manifests a tendency for simple mechanical corelations. The same holds true for the envisaged relationship between Buddhism and the socio-political order in the middle of the first millennium BC.[18] Kingship and state are categories which encompass an infinite variety of political relationships, and it is difficult to study them in a unitary way.[19] In this regard the changing modes of legitimation at different stages and in different spatial contexts would be of particular interest.

It should hardly cause any surprise that in the meantime alternative perspectives of the state and legitimation began to emerge, partly from the intellectual ferment of the late 1960s and early 1970s and largely propelled by the desire to understand the structure of states, from the perspective of the regions, in relation to their genesis and the political processes in operation, rather than vice versa.[20] This shift can be appreciated in the wider context of the movement away from largely mechanical and stereotyped explanations towards situating Indian history in terms of the operation of several mutually interacting processes of change. Within this processual approach, or what Hermann Kulke prefers to designate as the processural approach,[21] one must add, there are different strands of writing. The works of Romila Thapar, B.D. Chattopadhyaya, H. Kulke, Burton Stein, G.W. Spencer, and James Heitzman represent different strands within the processual framework[22] and, these differences need to be recognized. Any effort which homogenizes their treatment of the subject would be fraught with problems. What binds them is their common concern to delineate the structure of polity and legitimation, deriving from an understanding of the region-specific political processes (as against the generally posited binary opposites of centralization and fragmentation), but beyond it there are serious differences between them of method, approach to the role of religious ideas and institutions and, flowing from it, the overall characterization of the state.[23]

Stein and Spencer subscribe to the segmentary state model investing the segments with timelessness and invoking 'ritual sovereignty' rather than political authority as the major incorporative factor accounting for stability, effectively subordinating the political to the ritual dimension of the state.[24] Heitzman despite arguing for change and pointing to the pitfalls of generalizing for whole periods, in this case the Cōḷa state spread over almost four centuries, is close to Stein's position.[25] Chattopadhyaya and Kulke while acknowledging the importance of the segments/localities in Indian history do not see them as immutable entities. In ascribing the localities their due and simultaneously focusing on change, coming from within local societies as well as a consequence of interactions through the network of translocal linkages, they seem to be arguing for segmentation and integration.[26] Having recognized the importance of the localities they chart the history of their phased integration with the imperial kingdom or regional/supra-regional polities, through the stage of early kingdoms or translocal polities.[27] In a system of multipolar, graded administrative, and fiscal control legitimation operated at different levels. The interrelationship between temporal power and the sacred domain is seen not in static or reflective terms, but as dynamic and continuously evolving; involving constant engagement and negotiation. Integration, both political and cultic, in this perspective is never perfect, nor bereft of competition and contestation.[28]

The historiographical shift charted above is of relatively recent origin. The question then would be how was the issue of legitimation treated in earlier or other historiographies? Nationalist and traditional scholarship for their part seem noticeably disinterested in the questions of ideology and legitimation, either because they viewed the state as a constant variable or took popular support for granted, or were even apologetic about the use of religion for political purposes under the impact of colonial writings, which characterized ancient Indians as a people steeped in religion and irrationality. The failure to recognize structural changes in the historical evolution of the state unmistakably had its bearing on the neglect of the ideological dimension. Whatever the limitations of their notions of polity in early India, these ideas provided the basis for fresh historiographic interventions that addressed the problem of the relationship between the temporal and the sacred domain.[29]

Interestingly, some of the views that replaced the old formulations lead us to an erroneous understanding of temporal power and political authority. While Louis Dumont encloses the political within the social (and religious), J.C. Heesterman sees a permanent conundrum in the king's authority; owing to the inherently conflictual nature of the relationship between temporal power and transcendental authority.[30] Such characterization actually misses the dynamic relationship between the two. It is fine to argue that the textual tradition expresses the idea of irreconcilability in Brāhmaṇical thought, but to extend it to actual historical situations is problematic. One needs to rethink about such analysis, especially against the background of the texts themselves.[31] The concern in such Neo-Indological perspectives is to demonstrate continuity, in complete disregard to the transformative developments that characterized Indian society through the ages. There is no effort to see the ideas and relationships that constitute the political as creative or dynamic. The influence of this vision of weak, atrophied political authority has cast its shadow on recent works, which continue to recount in terms of an 'elusive' king or 'hollow crown', political authority as being detached from its social and economic foundations.[32] In addressing the question whether kingship in India was primarily political with ritual or ideological justifications or 'ritual sovereignty' with political imprints the answer lies in the first part of the alternative. There could be 'kings without a kingdom', but not kingdoms without a king.

Historians instead of binding themselves with the familiar conventions are beginning to analyse by reasoning in terms of the variational patterns derived from regional contexts. Generalizations from the perspective of the patterns obtaining in northern India were for far too long treated as unambiguous statements of the Indian reality. The energetic pursuit of regional studies now provides a corrective to that tendency.

The Early Historical Situation

We enter the discussion of the legitimation process in early India beginning with the Mauryan period when the evidence for writing, in the form of royal inscriptions, makes its first appearance. That *dhamma* represented the ideological dimension of the Mauryan empire under Aśoka has been long acknowledged.[33] However an examination of the discursive content of the Aśokan inscriptions, which have conventionally been used to map the territorial extent of the empire, provides an opportunity to study their other possible functions. The inscriptions provide useful information, in addition to administrative organization, about the ways in which the emperor tried to reach out to the people (in search for justification of the imperial enterprise). The Major Rock Edicts are found in the frontiers of the empire, while the Pillar inscriptions are located in the core territory of northern India. There is a concentration of the Minor Rock Edicts in the south with a scatter elsewhere. The overall distribution pattern of the inscriptions reveals their absence in most of interior peninsular India,[34] which endorses the recent revaluations of the structure of the Mauryan state, focusing on uneven patterns of growth within the empire and different levels of interaction between the metropolitan centre and the outlying regions.[35]

The Aśokan inscriptions regularly contrast the deeds and exertions of the emperor, including the promotion of *dhamma*, for the welfare of the people with past rulers and their activities.[36] Images of a good administrator, donor, and concerned emperor run through the records. In spite of his personal faith in Buddhism the proclaimed policy of *dhamma* was not identified with it. More importantly the brāhmaṇas and śramaṇas, people who mattered (as opinion makers), are continuously referred together in the inscriptions, and the Ājivikas were also not discriminated against. The inscriptions define a lot of people such as the Yavanas and Aṭavikas,[37] for example, and even threaten some with state intervention. The picture of a strong, confident ruler in control of his empire emerges from these records. What the emperor perhaps intended to achieve was to assure the people of good government and win their confidence. The inclusion of the Separate Edicts, which communicate encouraging intentions, and the exclusion of Rock Edict XIII, relating to the Kaliṅga war and its aftermath, in Kaliṅga as well as at Sannathi in Karnataka have been seen not as matters of local initiative, but conscious state policy.[38] Flowing from it, there is reason to interpret the records as statements and symbols of royal authority intended to empower the ruler with popular awe, respect, and support. The location of the inscriptions at nodal points and on important communication routes, with easy visibility, also invests them with political significance.[39] The set of Major Rock Edicts at Dhauli is situated in the vicinity of the site of Sisupalgarh in coastal Orissa, which is identified with Toshali, one of the Mauryan administrative centres in Kaliṅga. That said, the question of literacy and communication still remains to be answered. However, it has been argued by Romila Thapar that even if an undefined majority were not able to read the records themselves, in a primarily oral society, it did not really make a big difference because they were meant to be read and translated by state officials to the local people so as to convey the royal message.[40] Besides, the conversational tone and often repetitive nature of the statements too indicate in the same direction. Finally, irrespective of whether they were read or read out, the inscriptions, particularly the Pillar Edicts, had the potential to visually transmit the authority of the emperor.[41]

Eclecticism and toleration that characterized the religious policy of the Kuṣāṇas is known from their coins and inscriptions and confirmed by the archaeology of the period. Notwithstanding their Buddhist leanings, the Kuṣāṇas patronized Brāhmaṇical sacrifices and brāhmaṇas; including the entrusting of *devakula*s to brāhmaṇas.[42] These symbolize not only their respect for Brāhmaṇism but also efforts at incorporation. Mathura, which was an important multi-functional urban centre, and its surroundings have produced evidence for Jaina art and antiquities, together with the wealth of Jaina inscriptions.[43] Naga worship is also attested. The reverse of the Kuṣāṇa coins bear Indian, Zoroastrian and Greek deities and symbols, indicating their syncretic religious ideology. Archaeological and epigraphical evidence reveal that several sects later associated with Śivaism and Viṣṇuism flourished alongside Buddhism and Jainism under the Kuṣāṇas in northern India. The obverse of their coins depicts the kings in religious or supernatural contexts. They are shown as engaged in rituals before a fire altar or the bust emerging from the clouds or flames emanating from the shoulders, or even with the nimbus around the head. The institution of *devakula* under the Kuṣāṇas, involving the housing of the statues of dead rulers in temple like structures, also suggests their efforts to appropriate divinity. The high sounding titles such as *mahārāja, rājātirāja, devaputra, shaonanoshao* or *ṣāhanuṣāhi*, and *kaisara*, derived from a variety of cultural contexts, which they adopted ties up nicely with the emergent picture.

The focus on the religious aspect and its zealous pursuit warrants an explanation. It has been said that in the absence of the Vedic source the Kuṣāṇas had to work towards a new ideology.[44] However, that does not tell the full story. It may be rewarding to situate their non-sectarian, broad-based syncretic religious policy in the background of their territorial extent and the socio-cultural situation obtaining within the empire. The Kuṣāṇas ruled over a far-flung empire, extending from Bactria in the west of Varanasi in the east and from around the Pamirs in the north to the fringes of the Gaṅgā valley in the south. Within these spatial limits persisted numerous languages, religions and cultures. The culture in Bactria was already composite by virtue of having integrated varied influences. North Indian society was characterized by rich diversity, the Upper and Middle Gangetic plains being different from the ancient Punjab. In the Punjab and adjoining regions there were a number of *Gaṇasaṁgha*s or 'communities as states', which outlived the Kuṣāṇas and continued up to the Guptas, suggesting insufficient socio-economic integration and uneven patterns. The official language of the state was Bactrian written in Kuṣāṇised Greek script. Sanskritized Prākrit too was in use and records were written in Brāhmi and Kharoṣṭhi as well. The extensive territory inhabited by various ethnic groups, speaking different languages and practicing diverse religions generated their compulsions. The Kuṣāṇa state was responding to this plural situation, trying to create a level playing field for all, by being non-sectarian, accommodating variety and fabricating a syncretic ideology. The state tried to sustain and perpetuate itself by being responsive to the cultural aspirations of the people. That explains the rulers' occupation with legitimation and the use of devices ranging from the adoption of multiple titles to the accommodation of numerous deities, from various traditions across the empire. This was in keeping with the non-intrusive incorporative nature of the Kuṣāṇa state. In the end what strikes attention is the clever or imaginative use, like the Guptas later, of the limited space on coin surfaces for political purposes.

The evidence for religious patronage by the Sātavāhanas comes from the Nanaghat and Nasik inscriptions. Whereas the Nanaghat inscriptions record the performance of Vedic sacrifices, after the salutation to *dhamma*, Indra, Vāsudeva, and Saṁkarṣaṇa (brahmanic and popular deities), the inscriptions from Nasik speak of their patronage to Buddhist monks as well as inclination for Brāhmaṇical values. Thus, dynastic patronage, irrespective of the rulers' personal religious affiliations, was broad based.[45] Individual choices did not cloud, least of all envelope, the public face of political authority. If brāhmaṇas and Brāhmaṇical sacrifices bestowed ideological legitimation, Buddhist monasteries endowed the rulers with wider social approval. The linkages between guilds, Buddhist monasteries and rulers to their mutual advantage have been highlighted in a work on the Deccan.[46] Monasteries had established channels of communication in newly settled areas and these could be used by the state to extend its authority.[47] The location of the donative records, especially the strategic placement of the Nanaghat inscription in a cave (with representations of the early members of the dynasty) at the head of a pass connecting the Konkan and Junnar (a Buddhist monastic site) is significant. The patronage to Brāhmaṇism apart, which indicates the gradual spread of *dharma* and *varṇa* ideals, the analogy drawn between Gautamiputra Śātkarṇi and Rāma, Keśava, Arjuna, and Bhima seeking to emphasize the king's heroic qualities alludes to the infiltration of epic ideas. Sātavāhana legitimation strategies sought to engage with and shape popular perceptions. This was possible in a context where the socio-cultural situation was fluid, the Deccan during the Sātavāhanas being in a state of transition to the early historical phase.[48] The lengthy Hāthiguṁphā inscription of Khāravela of Kaliṅga, placed in the later part of the first century BC and the Junagarh inscription of Śaka Rudradāman, dated to the middle of the second century AD, recording their conquests and achievements are other examples of similar public documents with political functions.[49] The Junagarh record is the earliest Sanskrit inscription of importance and it points to the use of Sanskrit as a court language, as also the preferred medium for making statements of power. These were precursors of the *praśastis* in the land grant charters of the early medieval centuries.

Alongside the socio-political transformations in early Tamiḷakam the shifts in the ideological domain has also been worked out. The cult of war as ideology of the early heroic society, dominated by values of heroism, valour and victory and prospects of booty gradually made way for Brāhmaṇical ideology.[50] The bardic element was replaced by Brāhmaṇas. The pangs of transition, from warring chiefdoms towards complex society, are beautifully captured in parts of the Saṅgam literature. These peasants' voices of dissent came from the *marutum* or agricultural tracts.[51] The *tiṇai* folk deities were specific to the ways of life in the different ecozones, that is, while Ceyon or Murukan, the warrior deity, was worshipped in the *kuriñci* or woodland segments, Mayōn, the cowherd deity, represented the *mullai* or pastoral localities. The brāhmaṇas entered at a crucial stage in the development of society and their services were welcomed by the three *vēndar*s (Cēras, Cōḷas, and Pāṇḍyas) to enhance their prestige by inventing genealogical connections or appropriate rituals for their legitimation. The performance of Vedic sacrifices symbolized the transition from tribalism and kinship considerations to larger community identities and territoriality.[52] Buddhism and Jainism predated the coming of Brāhmaṇism to the south, yet it appears that the latter succeeded where the former failed, that is, the construction and dissemination of a ruling ideology. From a situation where they were not intrinsic to the legitimation process, the brāhmaṇas with the passage of time because necessary to the making of the strategies of domination.

Dharma was the source of validation of kingly power, but it could not speak for itself. The brāhmaṇa by systematically projecting the image of a recluse and renouncer emerged as the guardian or interpreter of *dharma*. Through symbolic acts and the use of significant legends and figures of speech they posited a theory of duality of power and placed themselves in the very source of royal authority.[53] The brāhmaṇa-kṣatriya relationship, however, cannot simply be understood either in terms of precedence of one over the other or the rigorous separation of the two.

It needs to be located in terms of the dynamic relationship between the two, involving patronage for one and validation for the other, leading to the emergence of a power elite in a situation of early state formation.[54]

The king's duty was to protect *dharma* and, it empowered him to govern. However, protection involved not only physical protection but also protection of the social and moral orders. The king in ensuring the march of *dharma* on earth and adherence to it was known as *dharmātman, dharmarāja*, and so on. Transcendental *dharma* as an inclusive concept impinged on and influenced both society and politics.[55] But *dharma* was not immutable. It was context specific/sensitive. One encounters disparate *dharmas*, from *jātidharma*, through *sreṇidharma* to *deśadharma* and more. The *āpaddharma* section in the *Śāntiparva* poignantly drives home the point. That the execution of *dharma* did not mean the homogenization of beliefs and practices is amply borne out by Dharmaśāstra literature. The king is continuously advised to respect local customs and traditions.[56] They enjoined that plurality was respected. Dharmaśāstra literature evolved through a long drawn process of incorporation of local customs. This aspect is obfuscated by the idiom of the texts, which gives it the appearance of being eternal and timeless. The Vedic mystique provided it with validation and a veneer of orthodoxy. The compilers of the Dharmaśāstras when confronted with practices that they did not approve of presented them as belonging to another *yuga* or as practices of the depraved. Nevertheless, the recognition and mention of such customs or behaviour allowed for their future incorporation.[57] The spread of state societies from around the Gupta period onwards facilitated the dissemination of *dharma* through the agency of brāhmaṇas and related institutions. These developments not only provided a central focus and familiarized people in the areas emerging to limelight with norms of state society, but also through continuous engagements *dharma* and local customs mutually impacted each other. *Dharma* with its conspicuous stress on duty, to the relative exclusion of rights, sought to create a subject population averse to challenge authority.[58] It tries to perpetuate the ideology of *varṇa* which was necessary for ruling elites to acquire legitimacy by appearing to be conforming to traditions. In preserving norms rulers were expected to ensure the perpetuation of *varṇāśrama-dharma*. In spite of the recognition of plurality the focus on norms may be seen as a desire to superimpose ideas and values which could cut through the medley of norms of varied communities and create conditions favourable for the sustenance of monarchical states.

The idea of *Kaliyuga* referred to in the land grant inscriptions from the middle of the first millennium AD too projects the king as conforming to and promoting *dharma*. The references to *Kaliyuga* occur in the *praśasti* section of the land grants of the Pallavas, Kadambas and several dynasties in Orissa, in a situation of local state formation, where the king's piety, righteousness and other deeds are juxtaposed with it.[59] Kings are said to have banished or washed away the sins of Kali. In this case, the royal duty of banishing Kali and subduing disorder is combined with an ideology of order and it becomes the sub-text of the articulation of the imagery of kingship. Cultural discourses such as the Kali, with their motifs and tropes, played a part in the politics of power.[60] They were meant to drive in the fear of anarchy so as to make people conform to *dharma*. Simultaneously, they allude to the horizontal spread of state society within the ambit of Brāhmaṇical ideas[61] and, the indispensability of brāhmaṇas in the fashioning of dominant ideology.

The Early Medieval Context

Ruling elites from the Gupta period onwards engaged in a variety of successful techniques to supplement their strategies of political control, including the construction of genealogies, appropriation of *Itihāsa-purāṇa* tradition, patronage of art and literature and dispensing their resources on brāhmaṇas, *tīrtha*s, temples and monasteries. In literature, inscriptions, coin motifs and legends and art of the Gupta period we come across a repetitive set of imageries and visual symbols through which royalty was represented. The idealized perception of kings rivalled Gods in physical prowess, moral excellence and virtuosity. Motifs on coins, ranging from the archer to harp player, and the Goddess of fortune on the reverse, captured royal energies, skills and aspirations and reaffirmed societal values.[62] In brief, they provided visual imagery of the symbolism present in its expanded form in the inscriptions. Literary and artistic productions were imbued with contemporary notions of power.

Scholars have noted the imprint of political power on works of art, and have analysed how the visual idiom strove to make monarchical ambitions tangible. Artists, like poets, excelled in conveying multiple meanings in lithic art and used political allegory to dramatic effect to project royalty and their deeds. The famous Varāha at Udayagiri (near Bhopal) rescuing the earth (in the context of its production and other details in the relief) is seen to be an allegorical representation of Chandragupta II, who rescued the earth from the Śakas. In south India one comes across similar use of art forms. Decorative art on a temple wall at Kañchi clearly focuses on the analogy of the reigning king Pallava Nandivarman's exploits and those of the epic heroes.[63] The depictions of Krishna lifting the Govardhana and the descent of the Gaṅgā at Mahabalipuram, it is said, were related to the provision of water at the site by a Pallava king. Such investigations are informed by a concern to explore the ways in which ideas of kingship were transmitted. They focus on the connections between art and monarchical ideologies or how art was bound to dynastic purposes, especially when people in power intervened to conspicuously project that reading. Funds were lavished on religious monuments under Harṣavardhana and his contemporaries in northern India. Adityasena's generosity at Aphsad, Shahpur and Mandara hill, the Dah Parbatiya door-way ascribed to Bhāśkaravarman and Harṣa's patronage of Nālandā are cases in point. It is not difficult to imagine the political benefits that would have accrued from such patronage.[64]

Religious pluralism and the catholicity of the kings are noticed in the case of the Guptas and their contemporaries, such as the Māṭharas of Kaliṅga, Śālankāyanas of Andhra, Kadambas of Banavāsi and the Vākāṭakas of the northern Deccan. However, it was possibly not entirely unrelated to power and politics. The compulsion of royal power, as so often in the past, made it necessary for patronage to be broad based. Several dynasties addressed the problem by ensuring that members of the royal family, especially women, patronized sects other than the one sponsored by the king.[65] These were therefore as much acts of politics as piety.[66] The Maitrakas of Valabhi (the first local dynasty of Saurashtra) through land grants to brāhmaṇas, Buddhist *vihāras*, and occasionally to temples sought to legitimize their authority and extend into the countryside for resource mobilization.[67] The Śarabhapurīyas and more particularly the Pāṇḍuvaṁśīs of south Kośala, both early autochthonous families, engaged in a multipronged strategy of donations to brāhmaṇas, *vihāras*, and temples and the construction of motifs and images invoking analogy with epic-purāṇic heroes and deities. These were intended to sanction status to the rulers.[68] Dynasties of humble origin such as those mentioned above, and most of them across regions in early medieval India had similar origins, had to repeatedly announce their new-found status to win acceptability and respect within local society and outside.[69] Ramtek, in Vidarbha, under the Vākāṭakas was shaped into an impressive sacred centre. The cluster of sanctuaries at the site is envisaged to have communicated 'the prestige and sovereignty of the royal family that had built them'. The incorporation of popular cults like that of Varāha and Narasiṁha would have gone a long way in uniting the people of the realm 'into a community of worship' and enhanced the royal family's leadership role in the community of believers.[70] The peripheral location of Ramtek was important. While royal activities helped to integrate it with the mainstream, it enabled the king to be omnipresent. Vākāṭaka inscriptions focused on the virtues of the king and disseminated the image of the ruler as the restorer of ideal dharmic *Kṛtayuga*. The prestige of these rulers was partly based on donations to brāhmaṇas and local temples. By superimposing Sanskritic rituals Brāhmaṇical ideology was spread among the populace.[71]

The emergence of temples was indeed an important development during this period and could not have been possible without corresponding developments in the spheres of religion and culture. The growing importance of *Bhakti* and the influence of purāṇic religion together with the spread of state society and, flowing from it, the political compulsions of the new ruling lineages contributed to the new phenomenon.[72] Outside Gangetic northern India and its fringes early temples were built in Saurashtra, Vidarbha, Chhattisgarh, Orissa, and Tamil Nadu, among others. Buddhist monasteries in these regions too were recipients of royal patronage. Sculptural art began to get integrated with the decorative scheme of temple architecture. Episodes from the epics and *purāṇa*s came to adorn temple walls, pillars of *maṇḍapa*s or halls attached to the *garbhagṛha* and even door-jambs at Kanchipuram, Mahabalipuram, Bhubaneswar, Sirpur, and Rajim.[73] It can be argued that because of the requirements of political validation and the growth of rural economy and caste society there was a heightened awareness about epic-purāṇic ideas and, this engagement is reflected in artistic developments. Continued manifestation of these ideas can be gleaned from the epigraphical material. Rulers claimed to have followed the laws of Manu and studied the Vedas, epics, and *purāṇa*s.[74] In general, the symbols and imageries representing contemporary notions of power show a gradual spread of forms and styles associated with Gupta norms. The inscriptions of the Śarabhapurīyas, Pāṇḍuvaṁśīs, Kadambas, and Pallavas are among those with strong traces of such influence. They were the forerunners of later day elaborate complex *praśasti*s.

With the establishment of state society local societies were marked by a disjunction between the small ruling elite, quickly Sanskritizing itself, and a numerous subject population whom they tried to successfully control. A theory of authority was necessary. It was constructed drawing partly from transregional Brāhmaṇical tradition enshrined in Vedic-śāstric-epic-purāṇic literature, and partly based on local indigenous tradition. By the logic of *Bhakti* local folk deities came to be transformed into major temple Gods through the largesse of kings and the connivance of brāhmaṇas. Viṣṇu and Śiva representing pervasiveness suited the requirements of expanding society and polity. Particularly Viṣṇu because of his association with protection, prosperity and fecundity was a favourite with several early dynasties.[75] Notwithstanding the Sanskritizing trend in culture, the local/regional flavour was never completely replaced or subsumed. In Orissa while the autochthonous deities were raised to a higher level of ritual elaboration and universalized in course of the transformation of tribal chieftains to 'Hindu' kingship, their visual manifestations, priests, and rituals were allowed to coexist with the superimposed Brāhmaṇical practices.[76] That the names of *Rāmāyana* characters in Karnataka were localized can be seen in the expressions Lakhan, Site, and Suppankhi in the inscribed panels at Pattadakal.[77] The appropriation of the ancient lineage traditions and other symbols inherited from the Saṅgam period by the early medieval dynasties in Tamiḷakam[78] represent the same process of incorporation of indigenous elements. Similarly, in south Indian inscriptions the rendering of the *praśasti* section in Sanskrit and the operative part in regional languages can be partly explained in terms of royal need to tie legitimacy both down and sidewise. There was an interesting interface between regional and transregional processes in early medieval India. The flow of goods, persons and information through a variety of exchange networks created cultural arenas that went beyond those defined by the regions or sub-regions, while undoubtedly related to them.[79]

The genealogical portions and *praśasti*s in the epigraphical material provide evidence for the elements that went into the making of the image or self-image of kingship from the Gupta period onwards. In the context of south India this aspect of courtly ideology has been worked in great details.[80] The curious origin myths, grand dynastic traditions, inflated genealogies, and kṣatriya lineage, it is said, lent prestige to the dynasty as a whole and emphasized inheritability of virtues, typical of caste ideology.[81] Claims to *Chakravartin* status, the warrior and donor images glorified individual rulers in focusing on their political, military, and cultural dimensions. The performance of Vedic sacrifices by early members of the lineage, we are told, had transgenerational impact and could elevate the status of subsequent rulers.[82] As mentioned above local traditions and stereotypes from Sanskrit literature were fused in the courtly constructions. These images sought to sanctify the rulers' claims to rule. The ideologues saw to it that they suited the cultural milieu of the times so as to project the monarch as the omphalos of the socio-political order. These self-perceptions have been situated in the wider context of the multi-centred hierarchized polities, and it is argued that the idioms and symbols made sense to a people immersed in śāstric-purāṇic tradition and temple-based *Bhakti* ideology.[83] After all, the function of genealogies, like other state rituals and ceremonies, was to strengthen royal authority.[84] The short dynastic genealogies of the Guptas expanded to full-blown eulogistic genealogies during the early medieval period. The size of the *praśasti*s under the Cōḷas in the eleventh century was quite impressive. The *praśasti* in the inscription of Virarajendra, the son of Rajendra Cōḷa, in a temple at Kanya Kumari is the most striking. The *praśasti* of Virarajendra and his ancestors are represented in 419 out of its 444 lines, engraved on six pillars. This is the best but certainly not the only example of its kind. It is envisaged that the eulogistic genealogies in the copper plates and temple inscriptions in advertising the message of great kingship possibly took over the socio-political function of *Carita* literature and obviated the need for it during the eighth to eleventh centuries.[85] At this point one may seek to understand the relationship between text and context. Was the former reflective of the latter?

Ideas were not always defined by or reflective of socio-cultural conditions, but by a process of continuous dissemination of a set of symbols and ideas, through multiple agencies, values could be instilled and internalized. Ideas and material culture mutually influenced each other. In societies in transition ruling elites tried to intervene and effectively transform ground realities by constantly mediating in the negotiations in the cultural domain.[86] The post-Gupta centuries witnessed the spread of śāstric-epic-purāṇic ideas in a situation of the operation of comparable socio-political processes across regions. These ideas and 'invented traditions', mediated by brāhmaṇas, temples, monastic establishments, and translocal transactional networks, played an important role in cultural transmission and reproduction.[87] Societies in the course of absorbing these ideas were changing somewhat in the process.

The simultaneous emergence of *tīrtha*s and local/translocal states and, the association of chiefs and kings with many of these sacred centres by way of participation in the rituals and ceremonies or extending munificence clearly bring out their interrelationship. *Tīrtha*s emerged mostly in regions outside Gangetic northern India, that is, Rajasthan, Gujarat, Maharashtra, Madhya Pradesh, Chhattisgarh, Andhra Pradesh, Orissa, and Jharkhand. A closely related development was the proliferation of shrines and temples. Ruling lineages in early medieval times patronized the construction and maintenance of temples as it was becoming an important agency of political validation. Temples were endowed with sacred traditions by *Mahātmya*s and *Sthala Purāṇa*s as well as the *bhaktas*, leading to the growth of pilgrimage networks.[88] Royalty sought to channelize such institutions for political purposes and patronage became an important means for doing so. Inscriptions attest to temple building activities by numerous chiefs in tribal frontiers. The instances of the association of temples with tribes are quite large. The Cheñchus at Srisailam, Boyās at Draksharama, Sabaras at Puri, and Kurubas at Tirupati, should suffice to illustrate the point.[89] In the process of transforming the world of the tribes Brāhmaṇical tradition was also changing in accommodating their inheritance, in a situation of mutual interaction. The linkages between *tīrtha*s, acculturation, and state formation are brought into relief by a number of studies. In Andhra Pradesh, for example, the strategic location of Śaivite and Vaiṣṇavite cult centres and *mathas* atop hills and on passes across the Eastern Ghats facilitated the integration of tribes.[90] Folk Gods were made incarnations of Śiva and Viṣṇu and the goddesses were universalized as their consort or as manifestations of Durgā and Kāli in the course of the transformation of folk deities, through village deities, to tutelary deities of ruling families.[91] *Tīrtha*s as centres of integration of tribal and pastoral people/areas became sites of political interest. Inscriptions from Rajasthan, Chhattisgarh, and Orissa indicate the building of temples for autochthonous deities by local kings.[92] The cults of Ekaliṅgaji, Danteśwarī, and Jagannātha make the more general point about 'kings and cults'.

A fine example of the inherent relationship between the sacred centre and political authority is provided by the simultaneous evolution of the cult of Jagannātha and a regional kingdom in Orissa under the Later Eastern Gaṅgās. The history of Orissa from around the Gupta period onwards was characterized by the rise of indigenous chiefs together with their local tutelary deities to translocal importance.[93] While the autochthonous deities provided the necessary connectivity with the tribes in transition and bridged the gap between them and the emerging ruling elite, undergoing a synchronous process of change from chieftainship to kingship, the superimposition of Brāhmaṇical rituals on local cults helped their incorporation in the pantheon of pan-Indian deities.[94] The movement towards the formation of a regional polity began under the Bhaumakaras, was carried forward by the Somavaṁśīs, their successors, and finally actualized under the Gaṅgās. The making of a regional state was supplemented by a similar process of consolidation in the sacred realm.

The Jagannātha cult was a synthesis of various elements which brought together deities with a strong territoriality, that is, Vīrajā-Durgā of Jajpur, Śiva-Liṅgarāja of Bhubaneswar and Purushōttama-Jagannātha of Puri. An inscription of 1216 represents Anangabhima III as the son of Purushōttama, Rudra and Durgā.[95] The coming together of important sub-regional deities, with Viraja and Lingaraja having already been influential deities during the Bhaumakaras and Somavaṁśīs respectively, paved the way for political consolidation.[96] As the cult of Jagannātha evolved from Purushōttama and Lakṣmi, through Purushōttama, Rudra, and Durgā, to Jagannātha, Balabhadra, and Subhadrā it forged both horizontal and vertical linkages. The shift from early kingdom to imperial kingdom/regional state was accompanied by a change in the ideological domain. The construction of the Jagannātha temple and the emergence of Jagannātha as the tutelary deity of the Eastern Gaṅgās demonstrate this. The political advantages accruing from these developments are obvious and that the ritual policy of the Gaṅgās was politically motivated emerges from the fact that

Anantavarman Cōḍagaṅgā in spite of sponsoring the monumental temple for Jagannātha at Puri continued to be a Śaiva in personal faith.[97] Anangabhima III dedicated the state to Jagannātha, the *rāṣṭradevatā*, in 1230 and ruled under his orders as his subordinate (*rāuta*).[98] The Sūryavaṁśī Gajapatis, who succeeded the Gaṅgās in the middle of the fifteenth century, further elaborated the Gaṅgā strategy and ruled not just as the *rāuta* (deputy) of Jagannātha, but as his servitor (*śevaka*).[99] The surrender of the state to the regional deity and the proclaimed close affinity with the cult allowed kings to denounce political opposition or non-compliance with royal orders as treason (*drōha*). This marked a significant shift from earlier forms of legitimation and sought to place the ruler and his actions beyond the range of criticism and, deriving from it, make his position unassailable. After the fall of the Gajapatis in the mid-sixteenth century the imitation of the 'Puri model' by states in the hinterland in the seventeenth–eighteenth centuries and competition among the *raja*s or 'little kings' in the south (Kaliṅga and adjoining territories) to inherit and appropriate the Gaṅgā-Gajapati ideological legacy unambiguously demonstrate the continued depth and extent of the reach of the Jagannātha cult as well as its political importance.[100]

A comparable process of legitimation through cultic integration and state formation has been discerned in the case of Mewār. The interrelatedness of the changes in the religious and political processes bearing on the transformation of a local ruling lineage into a regional power attracts attention. Popular local goddesses such as Araṇyavāsinī, Ghaṭṭavāsinī, and Vaṭayaksinidevī were gradually incorporated into the cult of Vindhyavāsinī, who subsequently found a place in the cult of Ekaliṅgaji. Finally, in the fifteenth century the Guhila king, like the Gajapatis of Orissa, adopted the title *Ekaliṅganijaśevaka* (Ekaliṅga's personal servitor) so as to strengthen the basis of his power.[101] Besides suggesting a correspondence between the stages of political development and the evolution of legitimation apparatuses in early medieval and medieval Mewār, Ulrike Teuscher moves on to elaborate the latter.[102] She posits that in the fifteenth century there was a borrowing of elements from Orissa and Vijayanagara, to bolster the self-perception of the king, and that is best illustrated in the title of the personal or first servant of Ekaliṅgaji, which the king bore, and the Navarātri festive celebrations.

The Rājarājeśwara temple built by Rājarāja at Tanjore has been the subject of some fascinating studies which emphasize its socio-political functions. G.W. Spencer in an important contribution argued that patronage to the temple instead of representing the power of a despotic ruler was actually an effective device to strengthen royal power.[103] Monumentality apart, the frescoes and records of Rājarāja's patronage on the walls of the temple reflect contemporary ideas of power. The convergence of the Cōḷa religious and political centres at Tanjore together with its transactional network invested it with additional visibility. James Heitzman in carrying the story forward has argued that the transactional networks of the imperial temple bound the core, intermediate and important places in the peripheral regions as well as the king and local leaders in a cooperative (not necessarily static) relationship, while providing the king with an enhanced leadership profile.[104] Both Spencer's and Heitzman's analyses focus on the question of royal identification with the central deity, with the consequence of making royal power more tangible.[105] The temple is hence believed to have conveyed a political message, that is, the message of royal greatness, emphasizing the centralized role of the king in a segmented political system. It needs to be said that what we notice at Jagannātha, Ekaliṅgaji and Rājarājeśwara is more a comparable reading of socio-cultural values than a direct transplantation of the same everywhere.

Temples located outside the core such as those at the borders too in given historical situations played significant roles in socio-cultural transformation and political validation. The temples at Simachalam and Draksaram, in Andhra Pradesh, by virtue of their location became sites of contestation between rival dynasties during the late early medieval centuries and beyond. It is borne out by the inscriptional records of the contending parties on the walls of these temples.[106] Temples such as these hugely benefited from these struggles by emerging as the legitimizer of competing families and their overlapping claims. In the thirteenth century the Yādavas of Devagiri sponsored the two sacred centres: Pandharpur and Ramtek, situated at the borders of their kingdom. In investing at these ancient sites which were experiencing the transition to full-fledged Vaiṣṇava cultic centres, from their earlier association with a pastoral deity orVarāha-Narasiṁha worship, they were actually aligning themselves with and tapping the religious movement of the times, that is, Vaiṣṇava *bhakti*. It could yield significant political dividends in terms of enhanced prestige and community following.[107] The pilgrim networks connecting these temple centres of Krishna and

Rāma respectively may have facilitated their integration with the core of the kingdom. Having said that, it may be mentioned that temples acquired and played important political roles in regional and sub-regional settings depending on how historical forces converged at those sites. The relationship between the royal devotee and the sacred centre was not necessarily political in all instances, nor were all temples imbued with a political role. The relationship between kings and temples was not always the same.[108] While some like the Gaṅgāikondacholapuram complex died prematurely, others such as Jagannātha Puri continued to retain their importance, admittedly though depending on how the temporal domain constantly defined and redefined its relevance vis-à-vis itself.[109]

Epilogue

Recently there has been criticism of the legitimation theory/theme as a relevant category of analysis. Both Sheldon Pollock and Daud Ali have voiced their reservations against straight line arguments or assumptions characterized by mechanical functionalism, and seem to urge the need to work it out through historical analysis of concrete situations.[110] Although Pollock's criticism emerges from his engagement with the problem of explaining the use and spread of Sanskrit as the language through which power was expressed for about a millennium in early South and South-East Asia and Daud Ali's from his concern with the diverse complexities of courtly culture in early medieval India, they raise larger questions. Some of these are arguably genuine concerns, difficult to disagree with, suggesting the need for greater focus on issues such as the audiences and their response to legitimatory apparatuses, the effectiveness of the deployed strategies, the forms of communication as well as their reach and efficacy. However, questioning the theme as an area of legitimate academic endeavour seems to border on cynicism,[111] and such opposition may not be entirely unrelated to the understanding that precolonial India had no viable political structures and authority was elusive. If the issue of legitimation is no more important then how does one explain social and political mobility of individuals and groups, shifts in patronage, and more importantly one may ask what happens to the concept of Sanskritization and the explanation of change within that framework? Ideology is perceived to be a more nuanced conceptual category which could perhaps substitute legitimation, which sees culture as being reflective.[112] However, though ideology and legitimation are intricately and inextricably tied to one another, yet the former is an inclusive and far more comprehensive concept than the latter. Legitimation unmistakably represents aspects of ideology, but certainly not the whole of it. Thus, the substitution of one with the other would mean the loss of specificity of the analytical category. Alongside, it seems that the actual problem is not so much with the term/category, but with the facile assumptions of some of the studies in the area.

So where does the consideration of the changing forms of patronage and legitimation and the voices of dissent leave us? It seems that unlike what is at times assumed, a new legitimation structure was not usually imposed, nor was it easy to do so, but was designed to accommodate, incorporate and tap what was already available in local societies.[113] There was constant appropriation of the local and localization of translocal cultural flows. Legitimation entailed negotiations and integration of competing traditions. In Orissa and Bengal brāhmaṇas legitimated aspects of local beliefs and religious practices.[114] Such recognition instead of treating common people as docile pawns in the games that the elite played concedes them with agency. It also rejects the simple divisive perception of the cultural domain in terms of 'great' and 'little' traditions, urging instead the acknowledgement of change through continuity.

Brāhmaṇas, monastic establishments, temples and *tīrtha*s or played a vital role in the process of cultural communication and socialization and, flowing from it, were vehicles of political legitimation in settled and developing areas.[115] Land grants to brāhmaṇas in the centre and outlying regions of the kingdoms helped the extension of state power insofar as they propagated Vedic-śāstric-epic-purāṇic ideas, *varṇa* ideology and the ideal of Hindu kingship, and in the process familiarized people with the norms of state society.[116] The growing importance of temples in socio-religious life is amply borne out by the staging of dance dramas, recital of *purāṇa*s, celebration of festivals, among other activities, in their premises. The temple was the site of community gathering, rituals and education, a place where people imbibed values.[117] The performance of *vrata*s, deriving from the authority of the *purāṇa*s, *kathā*s and recitals of religious texts as well as community performance in processions and ritual observances transmitted Brāhmaṇic-purāṇic ideas and notions of authority.[118] From copper plate land grants and inscriptions on stone to sculptural art and monumental architecture were employed to touch a chord with the people.[119] Language, symbols and idioms played a significant part in the negotiations in the cultural domain. The texts and art forms reveal the process of the constitution of political ideology that was at once complex and nuanced. Messages repeated over and over again provide a certain credence to it and that explains why repetitive messages were being transmitted through different channels. The land grants, among other things, by asserting the state's rights entered into multiple levels of engagement and helped in constituting notions of legitimacy. In constituting authority the state also constituted its subjects. The internalization of values is visible in the poets' and scribes' use of Vedic-śāstric ideas in their compositions, including the draft of land transaction documents, and artists' rendering of epic-purāṇic episodes in stone. One can see that, conflicts and contestations apart, the brāhmaṇas succeeded in establishing their modes and codes. Similarly, the pan-Indian spread of Sanskrit is indicative of the effectiveness of traditional communication systems.

We do not have alternative accounts which contradict the self-representations of royalty and their moral claims to authority,[120] but then one may ask what constituted consent and who had to provide it to lend legitimacy to those in power? It could have been achieved through a variety of alternatives or a combination of some of the devices discussed above. People's participation in the coronation ceremony or the local notables' acceptance of state recognition or peoples' acceptance of standardized royal claims depicted in contemporary or near contemporary literature, could have symbolized approval.[121] States try to bind in the men of substance among the subjects through public actions demonstrative of their consent with the intention of publicizing the confirmation of their legitimacy to a wider audience. The continuous references to the brāhmaṇas and śramaṇas in the Aśokan inscriptions, *kuṭumbins* as addresses in the land grant charters in the middle of the first millennium AD,[122] and the region-specific substantial peasants and notables such as the *mahattaras*, *mahāmahattaras*, *gāvuṇḍas*, *nattārs*, *heggaḍes*, *pergaḍḍes*, and *reḍḍis* later on seem to have served similar functions. The addresses shared that state's confidence and authority.[123] The continuous representation of the Kākatīya queen Rudramā-devī as a male (though there was no effort to mislead the people) in name, clothing, attributes as well as epithets depict the force of constructed political tradition, which associated legitimate political power with masculine features.[124] Popular narratives of the state in a regional/sub-regional context provide insights into the percolation of royal claims in society and the domain of popular perceptions. In the case of Mewar some effort has been made to capture it and what emerges clearly reflects on the process of acknowledgement of royal claims and, implicitly consent to the ruling family.[125] In Orissa the continued use of the cult of Jagannātha by contenders and pretenders to power even during the seventeenth–eighteenth centuries bears testimony to its pervasiveness and transgenerational influence.[126]

Times of greater or lesser engagement may have occurred, but there was a continuous production and refinement of the structure of legitimation, and an ongoing evolution of styles across regions. Legitimation is after all hard work and there is a need to understand how power works and the ways in which people in power struggled to retain it. There were alternative, competing ideas other than the dominant forms, but they are harder to retrieve because of the normative or optative nature of our sources. While ascribing agency to both the hegemon and hegemonized in the construction of political processes, there is no doubting the larger picture of domination that goes beyond individual intentions or regional specificities. The legitimation theme has, despite differences, rightly gained wide acceptance in Indian studies in the last three decades. Such studies, besides providing insights into the structure of polity, have revealed some important historical trajectories along which regional traditions and identities were formed (though everyone may not have been included in it) over centuries. They have shown that India's cultural past, as elsewhere, was not bereft of the rituals of power, involving among others, visuals, mendacity and propaganda. Not that all questions have been answered satisfactorily, but that at least some interesting questions have been posed to keep the theme open for discussion is a matter of satisfaction.

Notes

1. For example, there have been criticisms of the legitimation theme. See the discussion in Sheldon Pollock, 'The Sanskrit Cosmopolis, 300–1300 CE: Transculturation, Vernacularization and the Question of Ideology', in Jan E.M. Houben (ed.), *Ideology and Status of Sanskrit: Contributions to the History of the Sanskrit*

Language, New York, E.J. Brill, 1996, pp 197–247; idem., *The Language of the Gods in the World of Men: Sanskrit Culture and Power in Pre-Modern India*, New Delhi, Permanent Black, 2007 and Daud Ali, 'Introduction', in his *Courtly Culture and Political Life in Early Medieval India*, Cambridge, Cambridge University Press, 2004.

The relative neglect of the early historical period, among other issues, in legitimation studies has been discussed. See Upinder Singh, 'Early Medieval Orissa: The Data and the Debate', in Martin Brandtner and S.K. Panda (eds), *Interrogating History: Essays for Professor Hermann Kulke*, New Delhi, Manohar, 2006, pp. 189–211.

2. This is the usual, often-cited Weberian distinction between power and authority.

3. For discussion see I.W. Mabbett, 'A Survey of the Background to the Variety of Political Traditions in South-east Asia', and idem., 'Introduction: The Comparative Study of Traditional Asian Political Institutions', in his (ed.), *Patterns of Kingship and Authority in Traditional Asia*, London, Routledge, 1985.

4. For a discussion of the range of methods employed to achieve cohesiveness and effectiveness of a system in the ancient past see Anton Powell (ed.), *Classical Sparta: Techniques Behind Her Success*, London, Routledge, 1980; also see M.I. Finley, *Politics in the Ancient World*, Cambridge, Cambridge University Press, 1984 (reprint), pp. 24–49.

5. David Beetham, 'Introduction', in *The Legitimation of Power*, London, Macmillan, 1991.

6. A detailed examination of the problem, including a reassessment of the ideas of Max Weber, is available in David Beetham, *The Legitimation of Power*.

7. In the early medieval situation, for example, the use of the lord's era or a humbler title than that of the overlord or participation in the courtly ceremonies of the lord and the request for making a land grant(s) by the subordinate *samanta*s would constitute indicators of consent.

8. See B.D. Chattopadhyaya, 'Political Processes and the Structure of Polity in Early Medieval India: Problems of Perspective', Presidential Address, Ancient India Section, Burdwan Session, *Pracedings of the Indian History Congress* (hereafter *PIHC*), 1983, p. 32.

9. For its social dimensions see Romila Thapar, 'Social Mobility in Ancient India with Special Reference to Elite Groups', in R.S. Sharma and V. Jha (eds), *Indian Society: Historical Probings*, New Delhi, People's Publishing House, 1977 (2nd edn.), pp. 95–123; idem., *Cultural Transaction and Early India: Tradition and Patronage*, New Delhi, Oxford University Press, 1987.

10. R.S. Sharma's *Aspects of Political Ideas and Institutions in Ancient India*, Delhi, Motilal Banarsidass, 1991 (3rd edn., 1st edn. 1959) is the earliest work to identify stages in ancient Indian polity and focus on the role of ideas.

11. See D.D. Kosambi, 'Ancient Kosala and Magadha', *Journal of the Bombay Branch of the Asiatic* Society (*JBBRAS*), 1952, especially pp. 191–6; idem., 'Social and

Economic Aspects of the Bhagavad Gītā', *Journal of the Economic and Social History of the Orient* (hereafter *JESHO*), vol. IV, 1961, 198–224; R.S. Sharma, *Aspects of Political Ideas and Institutions*, and 'Material Background of the Origin of Buddhism', in Mohit Sen and M.B. Rao (eds), *Das Kapital Centenary Volume, A Symposium*, New Delhi, 1968, pp. 59–66; Surajit Sinha, 'State Formation and Rajput Myth in Tribal Central India', *Man in India*, vol. 42, 1962, pp. 35–80; Romila Thapar, 'Social Mobility in Ancient India...' and 'Origin Myths and the Early Indian Historical Tradition', in D. Chattopadhyaya (ed.), *History and Society*, Calcutta, 1978, pp. 271–94; Burton Stein, 'Integration of the Agrarian System of South India', in R.E. Frykenberg (ed.) *Land Control and Social Structure in Indian History*, Madison, 1969, pp. 175–213 and idem., 'The Segmentary State in South Indian History', in R.G. Fox (ed.), *Realm and Region in Traditional India*, New Delhi, 1977, pp. 3–51; G.W. Spencer, 'Religious Networks and Royal Influence in Eleventh Century South India', *JESHO*, vol. 12, 1969, pp. 42–56; and N.B. Dirks, 'Political Authority and Structural Change in Early South Indian History', *Indian Economic and Social History Review* (hereafter *IESHR*), vol. 13, no. 2, 1976, pp. 125–57.

12. For a good discussion, see B.D. Chattopadhyaya, 'Confronting Fundamentalisms: The Possibilities of Early Indian History', *Studies in History*, vol. 18, no. 1, 2002, pp. 103–20.

13. Kosambi, 'Ancient Kośala and Magadha' and '*Social and Economic Aspects of the Bhagavad Gita*', reiterated in his *The Culture and Civilization of Ancient India in Historical Outline*, New Delhi, Vikas Publishing House, 1981 (6th impression), 5.5 and 7.3–7.4.

14. *Aspects of Political Ideas and Institutions*, idem., 'Form Gopati to Bhupati', in D. Chattopadhyaya (ed.), *Marxism and Indology*, Calcutta, 1981, pp. 263–73.

15. Supra nos 11 and 13. For a recent statement on Kosambi's writings see B.D. Chattopadhyaya, 'Introduction' in B.D. Chattopadhyaya (ed.), *D.D. Kosambi, Combined Methods in Indology and Other Writings*, New Delhi, Oxford University Press, 2002, also see Romila Thapar, 'The Contribution of D.D. Kosambi to Indology', in idem., *Interpreting Early India*, New Delhi, Oxford University Press, 1992, pp. 89–113.

16. For example, see V.K. Thakur, 'Social Roots of the *Bhagavad-Gītā:* A Note on the Role of Ideology in the Early Medieval Society', in his *Historiography of Indian Feudalism*, Patna, Janaki Prakashan 1989, Appendix II, pp. 104–18; Kesavan Veluthat, 'The Temple-Base of the Bhakti Movement in South India', *PIHC*, Waltair Session,1979, pp. 185–94. For a comprehensive treatment of the subject see R.S. Sharma, 'The Feudal Mind', in his *Early Medieval Indian Society: A Study in Feudalisation*, Kolkata, Orient Longman, 2001, pp. 266–82.

17. See R.N. Nandi, *Social Roots of Religion in Ancient India*, Calcutta, 1986.

18. For a critique of the iron-productivity-surplus-complex society paradigm see Shereen Ratnagar, 'Archaeology and the State', in *Indian Historical Review* (hereafter *IHR*), vol. 22, no. 2, 2000, pp. 157–66. For a detailed discussion, see

'Editor's Introduction' in B.P. Sahu (ed.), *Iron and Social Change in Early India*, New Delhi, Oxford University Press, 2006.

19. See, for example, Kumkum Roy, *The Emergence of Monarchy in North India, Eighth to Fourth Centuries* BC, New Delhi, 1994; B.D. Chattopadhyaya, '"Autonomous Spaces" and the Authority of the State: the Contradiction and its Resolution in Theory and Practice in Early India', in Herausgegeben von Dieter Schuh, Bernhard Kolver *et al.* (eds), *The State, the Law and Administration in Classical India*, Munich, R. Oldenbourg Verlag, 1997, pp. 1–14.

20. See H. Kulke, 'The Integrative Model of State Formation in Early Medieval India: Some Historiographic Remarks', in M. Kimura and A. Tanabe (eds), *The State in India: Past and Present*, New Delhi, Oxford University Press, 2006, pp. 59–81. For a critique of the dominant historiography see B.D. Chattopadhyaya, 'State and Economy in North India' Fourth Century to Twelfth Century', in Romila Thapar (ed.), *Recent Perspectives of Early Indian History*, Bombay, Popular Prakashan, 1995, pp. 309–46.

21. H. Kulke, 'The Early and the Imperial Kingdom: A Processural Model of Integrative State Formation in Early Medieval India', in idem. (ed.), *The State in India 1000–1700*, New Delhi, Oxford University Press 1995, pp. 233–62.

22. See Romila Thapar, *From Lineage to State: Social Formations in the Mid First Millennium* BC *in the Gaṅgā Valley*, New Delhi, Oxford University Press, 1984; idem., 'The Mouse in the Ancestry', and 'Death and the Hero', in idem., *Cultural Pasts: Essays in Early Indian History*, New Delhi, Oxford University Press 2000, pp. 680–95 and 797–806; B.D. Chattopadhyaya, *The Making of Early Medieval India*, New Delhi, Oxford University Press, 1994, chs 1, 3, 5 and 8; idem., *Studying Early India: Archaeology, Texts and Historical Issues*, Delhi, 2003, chs 3, 4, 7, and 8; H. Kulke, *Kings and Cults: State Formation and Legitimation in South and Southeast Asia*, New Delhi, Manohar, 1993; B. Stein, *Peasant State and Society in Medieval South India*, New Delhi, Manohar, 1980 and supra n. 10; G.W. Spencer, supra n. 11; James Heitzman, *Gifts of Power: Lordship in an Early Indian State*, Delhi, Oxford University Press,1997.

23. The differences have not been adequately grasped or consciously ignored. For a recent example, see D.N. Jha, *The Feudal Order: State, Society and Ideology in Early Medieval India*, New Delhi, Manohar, 2000, pp. 23–4 and n. 144.

24. For a critique of the segmentary state model see B.D. Chattopadhyaya, 'Political Processes and the Structure of Polity', pp. 41–4. Also see D.N. Jha, 'Validity of the Brāhmaṇa-Peasant Alliance and the Segmentary State in Early Medieval India', *Social Science Probings*, vol. 1, no. 2, 1984, pp. 270–96.

25. See James Heitzman, 'State Formation in South India, 850–1280', *IESHR*, vol. 24, no. 1, 1987; idem., 'Ritual Polity and Economy: The Transactional Network of an Imperial Temple in Medieval South India', *JESHO*, vol. 34, no. 1, 1991, pp. 23–54; and reiterated in *Gifts of Power*, chs 4 and 5.

26. See B.D. Chattopadhyaya, 'Geographical Perspectives, Culture Change and Linkages: Some Reflections on Early Punjab', Presidential Address, Ancient

Section, *Proceedings of the Punjab History Congress,* 27th session, 1995, idem., '"Autonomous Spaces" and the Authority of the State'; H. Kulke, 'Fragmentation and Segmentation versus Integration? Reflections on the Concepts of Indian Feudalism and the Segmentary State in Indian History', *Studies in History*, vol. 4, no. 2, 1982, pp. 237–63; idem., 'The Early and the Imperial Kingdom'.

27. See Ibid.

28. See B.D. Chattopadhyaya, 'Introduction', *The Making of Early Medieval India*; Kulke, 'The Integrative Model of State Formation in Early Medieval India'.

29. For a recent assessment of the writings on the state in early India see B.P. Sahu, 'Ways of Seeing: History and Historiography of the State in Early India', in this book and Martin Brandtner and S.K. Panda (eds), *Interrogating History: Essays for Hermann Kulke*, Delhi, Manohar, 2006, pp. 63–82.

30. L. Dumont, 'Conception of Kingship in Ancient India', *Contributions to Indian Sociology*, vol. 6, 1966, pp. 48–77; Heesterman, *The Inner Conflict of Tradition, Essays in Indian Ritual, Kingship and Society*, New Delhi, Oxford University Press, 1985.

31. A good detailed critique is available in Jean-Claude Galey, 'Reconsidering Kingship in India: An Ethnological Perspective', in idem. (ed.), *Kingship and the Kings,* London, 1989, pp. 123–87; also see Ronald Inden, *Imaging India*, Oxford, Basil Blackwell, 1990, ch. 5; and B.P. Sahu, 'The State in Early India: An Overview', *PIHC*, Aligarh Session, 1994, pp. 88–98.

32. It seems to me that there is great merit in the concept of 'little kings', but that does not make kingship illusory or ephemeral.

33. See Romila Thapar, *Aśoka and the Decline of the Mauryas*, Delhi, Oxford University Press, 1961, pp. 144ff.

34. H. Kulke and Dietmar Rothermund, *A History of India*, London, Routledge, 1999 (3rd edn.), pp. 65–6.

35. See Romila Thapar, *The Mauryas Revisited*, Kolkata, K.P. Bagchi, 1987; G. Fussman, 'Central and Provincial Administration in Ancient India: The Problem of the Mauryan Empire', *IHR*, vol. 14, nos 1–2, 1988, pp. 43–72.

36. See Romila Thapar, 'Literacy and Communication: Some Thoughts on the Inscriptions of Aśoka', in idem., *Cultural Pasts*, p. 447.

37. See Rock Edict XIII in the Kalsi text.

38. See Kesavan Veluthat, 'The Sannathi Inscriptions and the Questions they Raise', *PIHC*, Calicut Session, 1999, pp. 1081–6.

39. For a discussion see Thapar, 'Literacy and Communication', pp. 439–52.

40. Ibid., see Separate Rock Edicts I and II.

41. For a comparable reading of royal records, though in a different location and time, see Sunil Kumar, 'Assertions of Authority: A Study of the Discursive Statements of two Sultans of Delhi', in Muzaffar Alam, Francoise 'Nalini' Delvoye, and Mare Gaborieau (eds), *The Making of Indo-Persian Culture*, New Delhi, Manohar, 2000, pp. 37–65.

42. Māt inscription of the time of Huvishka, *JRAS*, 1924, pp. 397 ff. cited in Bhaskar Chatterjee, 'Religion and Polity in the Kushana Age', *Journal of Indian History*, 1976, p. 512.

43. See B. Puri, 'Ideology and Religion in the Kushāṇ Epoch', in B.G. Gafurov *et al.* (eds), *Central Asia in the Kushāṇ Period*, Vol. II, Moscow, 1975, pp. 183–90; Bhaskar Chatterjee, 'Religion and Polity in the Kushāṇa Age', pp. 511–15.

44. A.K. Narain, 'The Kushana State: A Preliminary Study', in H.J.M. Claessen and Peter Skalnik (eds), *The Study of the State*, The Hague, 1981, pp. 251–73.

45. See R.C.C. Fynes, 'The Religious Patronage of the Sātavāhana Dynasty', *South Asian Studies*, vol. 11, 1995, pp. 43–50.

46. See H.P. Ray, *Monastery and Guild: Commerce under the Sātavāhanas*, New Delhi, Oxford University Press, ch. 5.

47. Ibid., p. 207.

48. See B.D. Chattopadhyaya, 'Transition to the Early Historical Phase in the Deccan: A Note', in B.M. Pande and B.D. Chattopadhyaya (eds), *Archaeology and History (Essays in Memory of Sri A. Ghosh)*, Vol. II, Delhi, 1987, pp. 727–32; H.P. Ray, *Monastery and Guild*, ch. 5 and Conclusion.

49. On the basis of the remarkable correspondence between the content of the Hāthigumphā inscription and the visual imagery of sculpture at the site it has been suggested that the Udayagiri-Khandagiri complex was as much a product of power and politics as piety. B.P. Sahu, 'Authority and Patronage in Early Orissa', in K.K. Basa and P. Mohanty (eds), *Archaeology of Orissa*, Vol. II, Delhi, 2000, pp. 431–40.

50. See M.G.S. Narayanan, 'The Cult of War as Class Ideology in the Saṅgam Age in South India', *PIHC*, Dharwad Session, 1988, pp. 109–13; T.K. Venkatasubramanian, *Societa to Civitas: Evolution of Political Society in South India*, Delhi, 1993.

51. See Rajan Gurukkal, 'Towards the Voice of Dissent: Trajectory of Ideological Transformation in Early South India', *Social Scientist*, nos 236–7, 1993, pp 2–22.

52. See R. Champaklakshmi, 'Ideology and the State in South India', Mamidipudi Venkatarangaiah Memorial Lecture, Andhra Pradesh History Congress, 13th Session, Srisailam, 1989.

53. See Sibesh Bhattacharya, 'Political Authority and Brāhmaṇa-Kṣhatriya Relationship in Early India—An Aspect of the Power Elite Configuration', *IHR*, vol. 10, nos 1–2, pp. 1–20.

54. For a critique of Louis Dumont's and J.C. Heesterman's positions supra n.30; B.P. Sahu, 'The State in Early India', p. 90.

55. See R.S. Sharma, 'Varna in Relation to Law and Politics', *Aspects of Political Ideas and Institutions*; ch. 16; and Romila Thapar, 'Society and Law in the Hindu and Buddhist Traditions', in idem., *Ancient Indian Social History: Some Interpretations*, New Delhi, Orient Longman, 1984, pp. 26–39.

56. See, for example, *Manusmriti,* VII, 201–2; VIII, 41 and 46. For more details see Sibesh Bhattacharya, 'Pluralism and Visible Path (*Pratyaksha Mārga*) an Early Indian Idea of Polity', Presidential Address, Ancient India Section, Mysore Session, *PIHC*, 1993, pp. 42 ff.

57. See Richard W. Lariviere, 'Dharmaśāstra, Custom, "Real Law" and "Apocryphal" Smritis', in Herausgegeben von Dieter Schuh, Bernard Kolver *et al.* (eds), *The State, the Law and Administration in Classical India*, pp. 97–109.

58. See Arnold Kunst, 'Use and Misuse of Dharma', in Wendy Doniger O'Flaherty and J.D.M. Derrett (eds), *The Concept of Duty in South Asia*, New Delhi, 1978, pp. 3–17; also see the Preface in the same volume.

59. See B.P. Sahu, 'Conception of the Kali Age in Early India: A Regional Perspective', *Trends in Social Science Research*, vol. 4, no. 1, 1997, pp. 27–36.

60. The idea of *arājaka* and *matsyanyāya* could have had similar implications. They constituted post-facto rationalization of the state.

61. B.P. Sahu, 'Conception of the Kali Age'.

62. See B.S. Miller, 'A Dynasty of Patrons: The Representation of Gupta Royalty in Coins and Literature', in idem. (ed.), *The Powers of Art: Patronage in Indian Culture,* Delhi, Oxford University Press, 1992, pp. 54–64.

63. See F.M. Asher, 'Historical and Political Allegory in Gupta Art', in B.L. Smith (ed.), *Essays on Gupta Culture*, Delhi, Motilal Banarsidass, 1983, pp. 53–66.

64. F.M. Asher, *The Art of Eastern India, 300–800*, Minneapolis, 1980, pp. 66–7.

65. A.K. Narain, 'Religious Policy and Toleration in Ancient India with Particular Reference to the Gupta Age', in Smith, *Essays on Gupta Culture*, pp. 17–51.

66. Such trends continued in early medieval Tamil Nadu and Orissa. See K.A.N. Sastri, *The Cōḷas*, Madras, 1984 (rpt), pp. 645–6. For simultaneous patronage of several local deities besides Shiva under the Early Eastern Gaṅgās see Mary F. Linda, 'Temples of Stone, Centres of Culture: Sacred Space in Early Medieval Kaliṅga', in Srinivasan *et al.* (eds), *Urban Form and Meaning in South Asia*, Minneapolis, University of Minneapolis, 1993, p. 156.

67. Nandini Sinha, 'Early Maitrakas, Landgrant Charters and Regional State Formation in Early Medieval Gujarat', *Studies in History*, vol. 17, no. 2, 2001, pp. 151–73.

68. B.P. Sahu, 'Inscriptions and their Changing Context: From the Śarabhapurīyas to the Pāṇḍuvaṁśīs in Early Medieval South Kośala', paper presented at the International Conference on 'Text and Context in Orissa and Beyond', at Salzau/Kiel, 10–13 May 2000; idem., 'Rituals, Royalty and Rājya in Early Medieval Eastern India', in H. Kulke and U. Skoda (eds), *State and Ritual in India*; Margo Kitts *et al.* (eds), *Ritual Dynamics and the Science of Ritual: State, Power and Violence*, Wiesbaden, 2010, pp. 665–81.

69. The changing epithets from *sāmanta* to *mahāsāmanta* or *mahārāja* indicated shift in status. It was common to several early medieval local dynasties.

70. See Hans Bakker, 'Throne and Temple: Political Power and Religious Prestige in Vidarbha', in idem. (ed.), *The Sacred Centre as the Focus of Political Interest,* Groningen, 1992, pp 83–100; idem., 'Memorials, Temples, Gods and Kings: An Attempt to Unravel the Symbolic Texture of Vākāṭaka Kingship', in A.W. Van Den Hoek, D.H.A. Kolff, and M.S. Oort (eds), *Ritual, State and History in South Asia (Essays in Honour of J.C. Heesterman),* Leiden, 1992, pp. 7–19.

71. For a comparable situation in Orissa see H. Kulke, 'Royal Temple Policy and the Structure of Medieval Hindu Kingdoms', in A.C. Eschmann, H. Kulke, and G.C. Tripathi (eds), *The Cult of Jagannāth and the Regional Tradition of Orissa,* New Delhi, 1978, pp. 125–38; idem., 'The Early and the Imperial Kingdom'.

72. See, B.D. Chattopadhyaya, 'Historical Context of the Early Medieval Temples of North India', in idem., *Studying Early India,* Delhi, 2003, pp. 153–71. Also see Devangana Desai, 'The Patronage of the Lakshmana Temple at Khajuraho', in Miller, *The Powers of Art,* pp. 78–85.

73. See Devangana Desai, 'Social Dimensions of Art in Early India', Presidential Address, Ancient India Section, Gorakhpur Session, *PIHC,* 1989, pp. 21–56; B.P. Sahu, 'Profiling Dakṣiṇa Kośala: An Early Historical Sub-Region?', in H. Kulke and G. Berkemer (eds), *Centres Out There? Facets of Sub-Regional Identities in Orissa,* Delhi, Manohar, 2011, pp. 39–59.

74. See, for example, the Asanpat inscription of Satrubhanja and Midnapore plate of Somadatta, in Snigdha Tripathy, *Inscriptions of Orissa,* Vol. I, Delhi, 1997, pp. 172, 201–2.

75. Similarly, Śhivaism with its focus on family and kin ties may have endeared itself to people in transition from tribalism to complex society. See K.M. Shrimali, 'Religion, Ideology and Society', Presidential Address, Ancient India Section, Dharwad Session, *PIHC,* 1988, p. 79.

76. Supra n. 69.

77. Devangana Desai, 'Social Dimensions of Art in Early India', pp. 34–5.

78. See G.W. Spencer, 'Heirs Apparent: Fiction and Function in Chola Mythical Genealogies', *IESHR,* vol. 21, no. 4, 1984, pp. 422–9.

79. See B.P. Sahu, 'Brāhmaṇical Ideology, Regional Identities and the Construction of Early India', Presidential Address, Ancient Section, *Proceedings of the Punjab History Conference,* 33rd Session, Patiala, 2001, pp. 12–26; also in *Social Scientist,* nos 338–9, 2001, pp. 3–18.

80. The most comprehensive work is by Kesavan Veluthat, *The Political Structure of Early Medieval South India,* New Delhi, Orient Longman, 1993. For earlier efforts, see Dirks, 'Political Authority and Structural Change'; G.W. Spencer, 'Heirs

Apparent'; D. Sridhara Babu, *Kingship: State and Religion in South India According to South Indian Historical Biographies of Kings*, Gottingen, 1975. For other regions, see Hans Bakker, 'Throne and Temple', and Romila Thapar, 'The Mouse in the Ancestry'.

81. Little surprise therefore that there was a shift from *yajña* to *vaṁśa* in early medieval times. See N.B. Dirks, 'Political Authority and Structural Change', pp. 144–51.

82. Ibid., p. 139.

83. See Kesavan Veluthat, 'Religious Symbols in Political Legitimation: The Case of Early Medieval South India', *Social Scientist*, nos 236–37, 1993, pp. 23–33.

84. G.W. Spencer, 'Heirs Apparent'.

85. See H. Kulke, 'Historiography in Early Medieval India', in George Berkemer, Tilman Frasch, H. Kulke, and J. Lutt (eds), *Explorations in the History of South Asia (Essays in Honour of Dietmar Rothermund)*, New Delhi, South Asia Institute, 2001, pp. 81–2.

Change in genealogical claims, despite their usually repetitive messages, is associated with important changes in the fortunes of the dynasty. For example, see Georg Berkemer, 'Orissa Revisited: A View from the South', in H. Kulke and B. Schnepel (eds), *Jagannāth Revisited: Studying Society, Religion and the State in Orissa,* New Delhi, 2001, pp. 255–7.

86. Hans Baker, supra n. 70; B.P. Sahu, supra n. 68 and 73.

87. For a perceptive discussion of the role of invented traditions see Eric Hobsbawm's 'Introduction', in Eric Hobsbawm and T. Ranger (eds), *The Invention of Tradition,* Cambridge, Cambridge University Press, 1992.

For the Indian situation see B.D. Chattopadhyaya, 'Festivals as Ritual; An Exploration into the Convergence of Rituals and the State in Early India', in H. Kulke and U. Skoda (eds), *Section IV: State and Ritual in India,* in M. Kitts *et al.* (eds), *State, Power and Violence*, Wiesbaden, 2010, pp. 627–45.

88. The *Cidambaramahātmya* and *Ekaliṅgamahātmya* are good examples. See Kulke, 'Functional Interpretation of a South Indian Mahātmya' in idem., *Kings and Cults*, pp. 192–207; Nandini Sinha, *State Formation in Rajasthan: Mewar during the Seventh-Fifteenth Centuries,* New Delhi, 2002, chs 5 and 6.

89. See Vijay Nath, 'From Brahmanism to Hinduism: Negotiating the Myth of the Great Tradition', Presidential Address, Ancient India Section, *PIHC*, Calcutta Session, 2001, pp. 43–4; P.S. Kanaka Durgā and Y.A. Sudhakar Reddy, 'Kings, Temples and Legitimation of Autochthonous Communities: A Case Study of a South Indian Temple', *JESHO*, vol. 35, no. 2, 1992, pp. 145–66.

90. M.L.K. Murty, 'Environment, Royal Policy and Social Formation in the Eastern Ghats, South India, AD 1000–1500', Presidential Address, Historical Archaeology, Epigraphy and Numismatics Section, *PIHC*, Warangal Session, 1992, pp. 621–6.

91. Ibid., pp. 624–7.

92. H. Kulke, 'Royal Temple Policy,' Nandini Sinha, *State Formation in Rajasthan*, Ch. 5; K.S. Singh, 'Hinduism and Tribal Religion: An Anthropological Perspective', *Man in India*, vol. 73, 1993, pp. 1–16.

93. For the early medieval centuries, see Kulke, 'Early State Formation and Royal Legitimation in Late Ancient Orissa', in M.N. Das (ed.), *Sidelights on History and Culture of Orissa*, Cuttack, 1977, pp. 104–14; for the earlier period, see B.P. Sahu, 'Early State in Orissa: From the Perspective of Changing Forms of Patronage and Legitimation', in B. Pati, B.P. Sahu, and T.K. Venkatasubramanian (eds), *Negotiating India's Past (Essays in Memory of Professor P.S. Gupta)*, New Delhi, 2003, pp. 29–51.

94. In India one form was superimposed on the other without displacing the former, each reinforcing and supplementing some of the other's relevance. See D.D. Kosambi, 'Social and Economic Aspect of the Bhagavada Gita'.

95. *SII*, no. 1329, cited in H. Kulke, 'King Anangabhima, the Veritable Founder of the Gajapati Kingship and of the Jagannātha Trinity at Puri', in idem., *Kings and Cults*, pp. 19–20.

96. For a discussion of political processes, see S.K. Panda, *The State and the Statecraft in Medieval Orissa under the Later Eastern Gaṅgās (AD 1038–1434)*, Calcutta, 1995, ch. 6.

97. H. Kulke, *Jagannātha-Kult Und Gajapati-Konigtum*, Wiesbaden, 1979, p. 229.

98. Supra n. 95, pp. 20–3.

99. Supra n. 97, pp. 233–4; also see Kulke, *Kings and Cults*, pp. 35–6.

100. See H. Kulke, 'Rathas and Rājās: The Car Festival at Puri', in *Kings and Cults*, pp. 66–81; Georg Berkemer, 'Orissa Revisited: A View from the South', in *Jagannāth Revisited*, pp. 253–70.

101. See Nandini Sinha, *State Formation in Rajasthan*, ch. 5.

102. Ulrike Teuscher, *Konigtum in Rajasthan: Legitimation in Mewar des 7. Bis 15. Jahrhunderts*, EB-Verlag, 2003 (see the Summary in English, pp. 272–87). For mutual cultural borrowings and adaptations across regions and political systems, especially political motifs, see B.D. Chattopadhyaya, *Representing the Other? Sanskrit Sources and the Muslims (Eighth to Fourteenth Century)*, Delhi, Manohar, 1998, ch. 2.

103. G.W. Spencer, 'Religious Networks and Royal Influence in Eleventh Century South India'.

104. James Heitzman, 'Ritual Polity and Economy: The Transactional Network of an Imperial Temple in Medieval South India'.

105. Other studies have also come to similar conclusions. For example, see R. Champakalakshmi, 'Urbanization in South India: The Role of Ideology and Polity', Presidential Address, Ancient Indian Section, *PIHC*, Srinagar Session, 1986, pp. 81–4. Some earlier examples of such royal identification can be seen at the temple of Kukkureśvara Mahādeva built by king Kukkureśvara in Mewar

and Rājasiṁheśvara built during the reign of Rajasimha Pallava. Similarly the correspondence between Kośaleśvara, the Śiva temple at Baidyanath (western Orissa), and the Somavaṁśīs who called themselves the Lords of Kośala (*Kosalendra*) cannot be missed.

106. See Georg Berkemer, 'The Centre Out There as State Archive: The Temple of Simhachalam', in Bakker (ed.), *The Sacred Centre as the Focus of Political Interest*, pp. 119–30; Kanaka Durgā and Sudhakar Reddy, 'Kings, Temples and Legitimation of Autochthonous Communities'.

107. Hans Bakker, 'Ramtek: An Ancient Centre of Viṣṇu Devotion in Maharashtra', in idem. (ed.), *The History of Sacred Places in India (Being Volume III of Panels of the VIIth World Sanskrit Conference)*, Leiden, E.J. Brill, 1990, pp. 62–85.

108. The importance of land grants to brāhmaṇas and temples as a part of the legitimation strategies has been highlighted in recent writings. However, in the post-tenth century there seems to have been a shift in the pattern of patronage insofar as the temples emerged as the major recipients of royal donations in Tamil Nadu, Karnataka, Andhra, and Orissa. See R.N. Nandi, 'Growth of Rural Economy in Early Feudal India', Presidential Address, Ancient India Section, *PIHC*, Annamalai Session, 1984, pp. 33–7; R. Champakalakshmi, supra n. 105; Murty, 'Environment, Royal Policy and Social Formation'; Upinder Singh, *Kings, Brāhmaṇas and Temples in Orissa (300–1147 CE)*, New Delhi, 1994, ch. 5 and Conclusion.

109. Besides the devices already mentioned the successor states in Orissa following the Gaṅgā-Gajapati rule engaged in the production of a regional historiography, that is, the *Māḍalā Pañji* (temple chronicle), which, among other things, produced a transdynastic history so as to legitimize the reigning Khurda dynasty (as the legitimate inheritors of the Gajapati legacy) and *Vaṁśavalis* for similar purposes. These performed functions similar to the *Itihāsa-purāṇa* tradition and *Carita* literature of the earlier period. See Kulke, *Kings and Cults*, op. cit., essays 9 and 10. Also see Romila Thapar, 'Society and Historical Consciousness: The *Itihāsa-Purāṇa* Tradition', in idem., *Interpreting Early India*, New Delhi, 1992, pp. 137–73.

110. Supra n. 1.

111. David Shulman in the course of reviewing a recent monograph remarks that 'similarly with 'legitimation': I am no longer sure that this overworked Weberian term really explains anything useful and would like to suggest a ten-year moratorium on its use among South Asianists so we clear our minds and think of something new', *Studies in History*, vol. 19, no. 2, 2003, p. 280.

112. Personal communication with Dr Daud Ali.

113. The structure of polity was correspondingly integrative. It was not fully settled, but continuously developing in a situation of expanding state society.

114. See Kunal Chakrabarti, *Religious Process: The Purāṇas and the Making of a Regional Tradition*, New Delhi, 2001, chs 5 and 6.

115. Brāhmaṇas and temples have also been perceived as checks on rival *sāmantas* and peasant-warrior power. See H. Kulke, 'Royal Temple Policy and the

Structure of Medieval Hindu Kingdoms'; M.L.K. Murty, 'Environment, Royal Policy and Social Formation'.

116. The absence of evidence for the association of royalty with the construction of the early temples together with the evidence of their location in clusters near Brāhmaṇic settlements, especially in the context of Kaliṅga has been interpreted to suggest that they were sponsored by the brāhmaṇas in the initial stages. Mary F. Linda, 'Temples of Stone, Centres of Culture', supra n. 66.

117. These activities explain the extensive patronage to temples in the first half of the second millennium AD. Supra n. 108.

118. Vijay Nath, 'From Brāhmaṇism to Hinduism'; Kunal Chakrabarti, *Religious Process*.

119. See H. Kulke, 'Some Observations on the Political Functions of Copper-Plate Grants in Early Medieval India', in Bernhard Kolver *et al.* (eds), *The State, the Law*, pp. 237–43; G.W. Spencer, 'Religious Networks and Royal Influence'; James Heitzman, 'Ritual Polity and Economy'; and Georg Berkemer, 'The Centre Out There as State Archive'.

120. However, for an interesting juxtaposition of alternative narratives in the context of Sultanate history, see Sunil Kumar, 'Assertions of Authority: A Study of the Discursive Statements of Two Sultans of Delhi', in Muzaffar Alam *et al.* (eds), *The Making of Indo-Persian Culture*, pp. 37–65.

121. For a theoretical discussion, see David Beetham, *The Legitimation of Power*, pp. 18 ff.

122. See Ranabir Chakravarti, '*Kuṭumbikas* of Early India', in V.K. Thakur and A. Aounshuman (eds), *Peasants in Indian History*, Patna, pp. 179–98.

123. For example, see Kesavan Veluthat, 'Landed Magnates as State Agents: The Gāvuḍas under the Hoyśāḷas in Karnataka', *PIHC*, Gorakhpur Session, 1989, pp. 118–23; also in B.P. Sahu (ed.), *Land System and Rural Society in Early India*, New Delhi, 1997, pp. 322–28; B.D. Chattopadhyaya, *Aspects of Rural Settlements and Rural Society in Early Medieval India*, New Delhi, 1990, Chs. 2 and 4.

124. Cynthia Talbot, 'Rudramā-devī, the Female King: Gender and Political Authority in Medieval India', in David Shulman (ed.), *Syllables of Sky*, New Delhi, 1996, pp. 391–430.

125. Nandini Sinha, *State Formation in Rajasthan*, ch. 6.

126. It also bears on the dimension of competition and contestation. See Georg Berkemer, 'Orissa Revisited'; B. Schnepel, *The Jungle Kings: Ethnohistorical Aspects of Politics and Ritual in Orissa*, New Delhi, Manohar, 2002, chs 2 and 6.

The *Chāmu cītaus* (Royal letters) issued by the Khurda kings (inheritors of the Gajapati legacy) were intended to address this situation of assertion of authority by the constituent units of the erstwhile Gaṅgā-Gajapati supra-regional kingdom. See H. Kulke, 'Kṣetra and Ksatra: The Cult of Jagannāth of Puri and the Royal Letters (*chāmu cītau*) of the Rājas of Khurda', in idem., *Kings and Cults*, pp. 51–65.

III

The Shaping of Regional Rural Societies

9

Mapping the Patterns of Regional Land Systems and Rural Society*

Geographical boundaries and rural landscapes in early India were neither static nor undifferentiated. There was continuous fragmentation of habitats with settlements encroaching into and separating woodlands and forests. The ongoing formation of new rural settlements led to the extension of agrarian space in erstwhile tribal frontiers and virgin territories. In some cases earlier tribal hamlets could be transformed into peasant villages. It also implied increase in the density of settlements in already settled areas. Thus, a space segment is not an immutable, uniform historico-geographic unit. It has always been a conglomeration of smaller diverse segments, encompassing different types of settlements and levels of socio-political organization. *Vana/araṇya* and *janapada/kṣetra* have been juxtaposed in north Indian literature. While the former represent forest or jungle, the latter are identified with well-settled, inhabited space with plough agriculture. The same contrast in Tamil literature may be seen in the distinction between *vanpulam* (jungle tracts/pasture lands) and *menpulam* (paddy land).[1] It has been postulated that 'this dichotomy of *vana* and *kṣetra* is not mutually exclusive, but is rather complementary or a continuum, similarly as the continuum from tribe to caste'.[2] The continued manifestation of *janapada*s since their first emergence in the Doab in the later Vedic period and the appearance of new ones like Kāmarūpa, Gauḍa, Kaliṅga and Dakṣiṇa Kośala, among numerous others, in the

*Originally published as a part of the Editor's Introduction in *Land System and Rural Society in Early India*, Delhi, Manohar, 1997. This is an extensively revised version.

first millennium AD, suggesting the emergence of regions, derived form such processes of continuous spatio-historical transformation.

An understanding of the hierarchy of regions—nuclear regions, areas of relative isolation and areas of isolation—explains partly, if not entirely, their chronologically phased formation. It is generally recognized that the distinction between these categories was not unalterably fixed and the nuclearity or otherwise of a region is linked to how historical factors converge on it. It would be interesting to study the pattern of the evolution of agrarian regions in India and the history of rural settlements and rural society in relation to it. In the absence of adequate detailed studies on rural settlements in the early historical period, and this being largely true for the early medieval situation as well, the two aspects may be studied together so as to lend the discernible patterns amenable to wider correlations.

EXPANDING AGRARIAN FRONTIERS

The emergence of peasant farming, artisanal production, varied settlements, and state societies in the mid-first millennium BC have been explained in terms of the long-term dynamics of change starting with Ṛg Vedic pastoralism, through the inchoate stage of development in the later Vedic period. In such analyses the evidence in Vedic literature and early Pāli sources have been normally used, admittedly though for the later Vedic context and beyond the available archaeological data have been culled, compared and correlated to present a more comprehensive picture. The perspective provided by archaeological cultures, especially those succeeding the Harappan civilization, some of them overlapping with the Late Harappan and others having an independent origin, assume importance in the context of the shift from the primacy of Vedic literature to a greater reliance on archaeological evidence to understand the long-term history of the evolution of regions, settlements and peasant units of production. The plurality of archaeological cultures between the later part of the second millenium BC and the middle of the first millennium BC; manifested in the black and red ware (BRW), Ochre Coloured pottery (OCP), copper-hoards, Painted Grey ware (PGW) and Black slipped ware,[3] suggests the possibility of contacts and interactions between different cultures, and mutual adaptations and adjustments as well. The non-Sanskritic terms associated with agricultural activities in Vedic texts supports this line of argument.[4] Similarly, interactions between the Upper and Middle Gangetic plains, it is said, produced not only the deluxe Northern Black Polished Ware (NBPW) but also gave rise to such languages as Pāli and Prākrit.[5] Such analyses transfer the focus from invasion, physical movement and 'colonization', involving ethnic groups, to interactions and entanglements as the agent of change.

The spread of iron technology with considerable chronological variance into culture regions is important as a marker of the transition to full-fledged sedentary agriculture. This seems to have happened at various points of the first millennium BC in the varied zones. However, the origins of agriculture, emergence of first farming communities and settlements predate the use of iron in these regions. To say this, however, does not mean that there was continuity in the evolution and spread of cultures and settlements across the disparate regions. While some kind of continuity is noticed in the Upper and Middle Gangetic plains there are discernible breaks or disjunctures in the history of settlements in the Deccan and western and central India.[6] The chalcolithic sites suffered desertion and decay at various stages in time and the same areas were not reoccupied until the fifth–third centuries BC.

In the Upper and Middle Gaṅgā plains pre-Iron settlements are known and their role in the emergence of Iron Age sites is beginning to be grasped.[7] A study of settlement patterns in Kanpur district,[8] in the Upper plains, shows a steady increase in the number of sites from the chalcolithic to the NBPW/early historic period. There is a marked enlargement in the size of settlements and spatial extent of the occupied area over time. In the NBPW period land which was well drained but away from the rivers as well as lakes was also occupied. In the later part of the NBPW period even less hospitable tracts were colonized, pointing perhaps to increased population pressure. It has been pointed out that during this entire period the Yamuna between Agra and Allahabad was largely uninhabited owing, it seems, to the unattractiveness of the soil in terms of agriculture. One may add that the Mathura area remained pastoral for centuries and that may perhaps explain the absence of stable sites. In a recent analysis of the emergence of complex society in the Middle Gangetic plains,[9] which takes cognizance of the pre-Iron Age cultures in a long-term perspective, it is posited that unlike in the Doab (Kanpur and Allahabad districts) there were no settlement clusters or nucleated villages in the region prior to 500 BC. The density of settlements, their relationship to one another over an area, and the study of change through time help up to generalize about cultural processes, but such studies are far and few between. Notwithstanding the limitations of analytical archaeological[10] studies and the problems involved in the correlation of archaeological and literary evidence, it is generally agreed that agriculture and pastoralism co-existed in the Ṛgvedic and later Vedic societies. While the former was primarily pastoral but familiar with agriculture, in the latter the relative importance of these forms of subsistence was reversed.

R.S. Sharma and Romila Thapar, despite their differences in the overall reconstruction of the stages leading up to and including the pre-Mauryan period, show how through the convergence of a variety of historical factors the process of *janapada* formation acquired a greater socio-political visibility during the sixth-fifth centuries,[11] especially in the Middle Gaṅgā plains. It was a period characterized by agrarian expansion, introduction of iron tools for facilitating production, proliferation in the number and variety of settlements, invention of metallic money and the extension of communication and trade networks. The period also marked the beginnings of stratified society. The opening of trade routes seems to have helped the greater use of iron as the metal was not always available locally. The spread of plough cultivation, paddy transplantation and knowledge of varieties of rice (*śāli* being a generic term), wheat, barley, sesamum, mustard, lentils, plantation, and mangoes indicate the crystallization and consolidation of sedentary peasant farming. Wet paddy cultivation and the attendant increase in yield led to the proliferation of settlements. The spread of rural economy and spurt in agrarian settlements is indicated both by early Pāli texts and the distribution of NBPW sites in Bihar and eastern Uttar Pradesh. On the basis of the explored and excavated data an increase in the size and number of settlements has been postulated, though all the sites may not be as early as 500 BC. Pāṇini's work and Pāli literature refer to various types of settlements, including *grāma*, *nigama*, *nagara*, and craft settlements of potters and carpenters. The classification and preparation of fields, and demarcation of village space into *kṣetra*, *vaṭhu*, *gocāra*, and so on, suggest the increasing preoccupation with land and cultivation. It has been characterized as the peasant mode insofar as free peasants dominated production. Slavery was known, but it was incidental and largely confined to the domestic sector.

Land clearance was not only a consequence of the transition from tribalism to peasant economy but was also related to population rise. Demographic change led to fissioning of communities. A part of the social unit or a younger generation would break away and form a new nucleus in another cultivable wasteland. Although the establishment of new settlements in the process is known as early as the PGW culture in the Doab,[12] it seems to have gained momentum during the age of the Buddha. Historical examples of the process are attested in early Buddhist sources.[13] The role of iron in this transformation has been a much debated issue. In the face of the fact that iron was known in the Gaṅgā valley centuries before the spread of settlements and that no discernible changes are marked in the crop patterns between the BRW-chalcolithic and NBPW and related phases one group of scholars argue against positing any causal link between iron technology and the spread of agriculture and settlements and, flowing from it, the rise of complex state societies.[14] The other group of historians led by Sharma point to the shift in the method of cultivation, rising yields and the unprecedented proliferation of settlements, crafts and artifacts with the introduction of iron for productive purposes.[15] The point of inference, however, is that while it is difficult to deny the transformative potentiality of iron technology, it may not be very useful to reduce the explanation of societal processes of change to a factor, in this case technological determinism, howsoever important. In doing so, it is said, one is actually oversimplifying the process of agricultural production. Developments may be situated in the wider context of environment, land-types, and patterns of land use across regions; and the interrelationship between the gamut of other variables.[16]

The processes under discussion came into their own and blossomed fully in the Gaṅgā valley during the Mauryan period. By the third century BC we see certain commonness in the material culture of Gangetic northern India and the fringes of central India. Over the last two decades there has been a departure in the characterization of the Mauryan state and society from the earlier view, which assumed a certain measure of material and cultural uniformity for the subcontinent,[17] deriving largely from the paradigm of centralized pan-Indian empire. It is steadily being recognized that an empire by its very nature accommodated a variety of social formations and the transition to the early historical phase in the region south of the Vindhyas acquired momentum during and after the Mauryas.[18]

In spite of the difficulties in accepting the *Arthaśāstra* as being reflective of the realities of the Mauryan period much of the reconstruction of the contemporary agrarian economy is based on it. The *Arthaśāstra* recognized that the basis of the state's wealth and power lay in agricultural production; hence every effort had to be made to maximize it. The concern is evident in the details dealing with the founding of new rural settlements (*janapadaniveśa*). Details with regard to reclamation of wasteland, preference for śūdra cultivators in newly settled areas, employment of sharecroppers, crops, agricultural taxes and village administration suggest a thriving rural economy.[19] Discussions on types of land, organization of production, including the provision allowing the state to ask the peasants to produce extra crops in situations of emergency, reflect on aspects of agriculture as well as settlements.[20] The possibility of the use of prisoners of war, besides slaves and hired labourers, in extending the orbit of peasant activity has been conceded. The increase in the number of settlements and quality of material culture during the period is demonstrated in the archaeological record of the later phase of the NBPW culture.

It is becoming increasingly evident from recent writings that the post-Mauryan period extending up to the Guptas was seminal in various ways for the Deccan and south India. It marks the transition from pre-state to state societies bringing in its wake other concomitant changes. However, for long the period was characterized as a 'Dark Age', largely owing to the absence of imperial formations, in what appears to be empire-centred discourses. Even within the dominant historiography the agrarian dimensions of the epoch have not received the attention they deserve.[21] Agrarian history tends to be subsumed under discussions on towns, metallic money, craft production, inter-regional trade, and maritime commerce, which then are assumed to explain the broad contours of the period. The fact that even in a recent publication, intended to be a survey of research on early India, the post-Mauryan space is occupied by a chapter on trade is suggestive of the problem.[22] Crafts, trade and urban centres need to be located in the context of their rural hinterland and agrarian foundations. The dearth of focus on the agrarian history of this period, marked by enormous extension of the peasant frontier beyond the north Indian plains, reinforces the impression of a break between the early historical and early medieval periods. Deriving from this gap in our understanding, the two phases located at the opposite ends of the post-Mauryan period appear to be sharply dissimilar and the concentration on non-agricultural activities during *c.* 200 BC–AD 300 has helped to enhance the perceived contrast.

In fact, the post-Mauryan period was the formative period for most of the Deccan and south India. The archaeological data from early historical settlements, bearing on stratigraphy and life ways, in these regions provides ample evidence for it. Continued manifestation of 'locality'/*janapada* formation is discernible in the disparate data from the various regions.[23] Together with the archaeological evidence, the epigraphic material and locality circumscribed coins of various individual chiefs and those of the Mahāmeghavāhanas, Mahārathis, Mahābhojas, Kuras, Ānandas, Sadās, and others, suggest the emergence of a ruling stratum in various areas in the Deccan, Andhra, and Orissa.[24] An almost analogous picture of the gradual evolution of plough agriculture and peasant society has been obtained for ancient Tamiḷakam through a judicious mix or archaeological data and Saṅgam literature.[25] Parts of the Deccan and the eastern coast emerged into historical limelight. Kaliṅga, the Godavari-Krishna deltaic zone and the Tamil coast acquired a visible political profile. The shifts in the power centres on the east coast, however, indicate the complex interplay of historical forces and caution against notions of unilinear development.

The trajectories of internal transformation across regions were not uniform. The differences may be understood in terms of the processes that went into shaping them. In Vidarbha, Andhra, and Karnataka the megalithic cultures appear to be crucial to any long-term explanation of the unfolding of historical society. These cultures exploited local minerals and agricultural resources and also yield evidence for craft production, exchange networks and internal differentiation, which subsequently got elaborated in historical times. Many of the megalithic communities began with a preference for mineral rich areas but gradually expanded into the riverine and flood plains, indicating the diversification of the resource base and a greater reliance on agriculture.[26] At this stage of development they experienced the Mauryan interaction, which is seen as a quickening impulse in the movement towards the early historical times. The transition in the varied regions thus, derived from the changes coming from within local societies and the interactions consequent upon the horizontal spread of the Mauryan state. The autochthonous chiefs were accommodated in a relationship of subordination to the 'metropolitan state' for the manipulation of labour and transfer of resources. If interaction constituted the dynamics of change, it was propelled by the Mauryan concern for revenue maximization. However, the structure of the Mauryan state and economy necessitated differential levels of interaction with the peripheries.[27] The regional resource potential and the stage of historical development being the determining factors in the nature and intensity of interactions, the end results were understandably varied.

The western Deccan shows evidence for settlements from the Mauryan period onwards. Developments in much of Andhra and Karnataka seem to have been different. Settlements spread in these regions during the second-first centuries BC, and more particularly by the late first-early second centuries AD.[28] Even the agriculturally unattractive south Konkan experienced occupation by the late first century BC. The westerly trade from Bharuch and Sopara opened the northern Deccan to communication from Andhra and Karnataka. The overland route connecting the lower Krishna and Bharuch and Ujjain was dotted by a number of settlements. The northern Deccan ecologically and culturally seems to be different from Andhra and Karnataka. While the latter provide evidence for megalithic settlements the former was marked by its absence. There seems to have been an earlier and heavier concentration of settlements in the northern Deccan. The scanty evidence from Orissa seems to be largely the consequence of its transitory character during the post-Mauryan times.[29] Pāli texts of this period mention three types of settlements, one of which stood on the periphery of the countryside or forest frontier. Such areas were potential zones for rural expansion. All sites yielding early historic artifacts may not have been urban centres after all, contrary to what is usually assumed. Some may well have been overgrown, prosperous rural settlements. The lead provided by H. Sarkar and B.D. Chattopadhyaya perhaps needs to be pursued.[30] It is ultimately the cultural ensemble that defines a site. The problem is compounded, as is widely recognized, by the urban bias of early historical archaeology. Rural studies have received no attention and we usually end up with general statements on the town and country relationships. A study of Kathiawar reveals the occupation of many new areas through the Mauryan and post-Mauryan centuries. Agriculturally productive areas, it is said, show a greater density of settlements.[31] The spatio-temporal pattern of settlements suggests that farming was more successful in the region in the early historic period, particularly since the first century BC.

The proliferation of settlements, monasteries and rock-cut activities in the Deccan presupposes surpluses from contemporary artisanal production, trade, and agriculture. Iron ploughshare and irrigation-based agriculture seems to have augmented agricultural operations in many regions. Areas of concentration of agrarian settlements can be seen in the river valleys and the Krishna-Tungabhadra Doab.[32] The lower Krishna valley and the coast were areas of attraction and therefore more densely settled. *Āhāra* as a territorial unit finds mention in the Sātavāhana inscriptions from various areas. *Āhāra* means food, and the term in a territorial sense possibly tried to differentiate the food-producing eco-zones from other kinds of terrains. Such units of production were dispersed and spread over parts of Gujarat, Maharashtra, and Karnataka.[33] Excavation reports indicate the cultivation of a variety of crops, including paddy, wheat, millet, and lentils. Dhānyakataka, an important place-name in Andhra, alludes to rice cultivation. The *Gāthā-Saptaśati* records rice and mango cultivation and betel-leaf plantations.[34] Two major cash crops, coconut grown in northern Konkan and pepper in Malabar, are reported during this period. The *Gāthā-Saptaśati* and a Nasik inscription refer to some hydraulic contrivances.[35] Similarly, the Sudarśana lake in Gujarat, the canal at Nagarjunakonda in Andhra, Khāravela's restoration of a water channel in Kaliṅga, and Cōḷa Karikaḷa's embankment enterprise in the Kaveri delta bear testimony to contemporary concern for water resources. However, in Mauryan and post-Mauryan times state initiative in irrigation seems to have been marginal and small-scale irrigational works like *kūpa* and *bandha* based on local initiative seem to have been the normal prevailing condition.[36]

The *gahapatis* emerge as a powerful category patronizing religious establishments. Amaravati and Sanchi provide evidence for such rural donors. Some of the inscriptions at Sanchi even record donations by villages.[37] Rural settlements are mentioned in the context of land donations to ascetics and monasteries.[38] The monasteries in the Deccan emerged as important centres of knowledge dissemination and cultural integration, providing cohesion to society.[39] The phenomenon of land-grants, with all its implications for ownership rights in land and/or control over produce, made its first appearance during this period.

The 'epicentre' seems to have shifted from the Gangetic plains to areas peripheral to it in the post-Mauryan phase. These regions exhibited early patterns of socio-economic transformation. Pulsating trade and urbanization notwithstanding, agriculture continued to be the dominant economic pursuit, and rural society, perhaps, the hub of social reproduction all through.

Historical and geographic transformation of space continued unabated and manifested itself in the protracted rise of secondary states. The Aśokan edicts refer to the troublesome forest (*aṭavi*) people of central India. About six hundred years later the Allahabad *praśasti* of Samudragupta mentions the emergence of forest kingdoms (*aṭavika-rājyas*) in the same region. The appearance of *rājya*s in a forest tract shows the distance it had travelled in socio-political terms since the Mauryan times. Expressions such as *Pulindarāja rāṣṭra* in an inscription from Bundelkhand, belonging to the Gupta period, shed light on local state formation and are important for mapping such transition. Pulinda like sabara is a generic term for tribes in early Indian literature. Again, the perpetuation and survival of the *Gaṇasaṁgha* polities in the Punjab till about the fourth century suggests uneven socio-economic integration as well as the co-existence of varied cultural milieus. However, as elsewhere, here too the internal transformation and final dissolution of the *Gaṇa-saṁgha* tradition have been located in the long history of the networks of linkages and interactions with the Gangetic plains and Taxila and beyond.[40] Post-Gupta Punjab experienced the process of state formation in the hills, within the framework of Brāhmaṇical ideology. Continued manifestation of the process is noticed in the land-grant charters. Between *c.* AD 400 and 650 about fifty kingdoms surfaced in Maharashtra, eastern Madhya Pradesh, Andhra, Orissa, and Bengal.[41] It is a continuous but substantially forested terrain. The emergence of state societies in pre-state tracts is a significant marker of transition in the rural landscape. State formation and socio-economic transformations move in tandem. The state does integrate society, though it also splits up communities. The expanding frontiers of state society and the corresponding rise in the land-grants and temple building activities during Gupta and post-Gupta times bring out their obvious interrelatedness.[42] The transition came from within autochthonous societies, and was neither just a matter of colonization nor had it anything to do with fragmentation from an 'epicentre'. The early medieval centuries are replete with examples of ruling lineages emerging from autochthonous foundations as a consequence of such processes of change.[43] Internal transformation of local societies continued into the medieval centuries in central and north-eastern India.[44]

During the 200 years of Vākāṭaka rule pockets in central India and the northern Deccan experienced the spread of rural settlements. Out of the 131 settlements listed in their inscriptions many are believed to have come up during this period.[45] The Vidarbha region, constituting the eastern half of the Vākāṭaka dominions, opened up. The dissemination of Sanskritic culture and attendant acculturation are discernible in the records.[46] Similar processes of socio-economic and political change in the region around Narmada can be delineated from the copper-plates of the chiefs of Valkha (identified with Bagh).[47] These inscriptional sources illuminate the drive towards the establishment of new rural settlements in central India, almost simultaneously with the opening up of Vidarbha. The absence of detailed boundary delineations of gift lands in the records is quite instructive insofar as it suggests the early stage of agrarian activities in the concerned areas, and the possibility of agrarian expansion through encroachment.

The expansion in the agrarian base doubtless came through the interplay of several concomitant developments: introduction of plough agriculture, spread of iron technology, concern for water resources and irrigational devices, and so on, but growth in turn bred tensions and led to occasional setbacks. The *Harṣacarita* not only beautifully encapsulates the contrast between Srikaṇṭha *janapada* (parts of modern Haryana) and the Vindhya forest region, but also provides evidence to show that economic growth was not entirely frictionless. Early forms of resistance come through in the common folks' representation to the king on tour against the local lords (*bhōgapatis*) and officials' oppression, as well as the 'zealous foresters violently seizing the axes of trespassing wood-cutters'.[48] The 'Kalabhra interlude' seems to have provided non-brāhmaṇas in south India the opportunity to appropriate the *ekabhōga-brahmadeyas*. Indirect evidence for it is registered in the records of the Pallavas and Chāḷukyas. Positive proof for non-brāhmaṇa resistance to the expansion of *brahmadeyas* comes from the Dalavaypuram plates of the early Pāṇḍyas.[49] The juxtaposing of the negative injunctions against misappropriation of *brahmadeyas* with the extolling of the merits of protection in the imprecatory verses in land-grant charters concedes the possibility of opposition to land-grants. The precedence accorded to *Rājaśāsanas* over other sources of law in early medieval India, it is said, was aimed at preventing and resolving such situations.[50] Even later the efforts of peasants and/or the local dominant castes to extend agriculture were resisted by the neighbouring tribes. The Bhil revolts in the history of Mewar point to the imperfections and problems in the socio-cultural integration of a region.[51]

The formation of agrarian bases at the locality and sub-regional levels was an ongoing process and it introduced a new kind of comparable socio-political structure throughout. The spread of Vedic-śāstric-purāṇic ideas, as gleaned from epigraphic records and sculptural art in Tamil Nadu, Orissa, Maharastra, and other regions[52] from the sixth–seventh centuries onwards strengthened the authority of the ruling lineages, while simultaneously legitimizing the social order and facilitating cultural integration over wider areas. The spread of *tīrtha* clusters across regions and their recognition and eulogization in the *purāṇas* clearly bear it out. The induction of tribal deities into the purāṇic pantheon allowed for their integration into the *tīrtha* tradition. Consequently, through the connectivity that pilgrimage networks provide and the connivance of the brāhmaṇas their elaboration and universalization was ensured.[53]

The post-Gupta centuries were characterized by the formation of sub-regional agrarian bases, best manifested in the rise of numerous ruling lineages across the country; subsequently leading to the emergence of regional agrarian and state structures from around the ninth/tenth century onwards. Bengal under the Pālas and Senas, Orissa under the Somavaṁśīs and Later Gaṅgās, Western Gaṅgā and Hoyśāḷa Karnataka and Tamil Nadu during the Pallava, Pāṇḍya, and Cōḷa times amply exhibit these developments within the respective regions. Usually the post-Gupta period has been treated as a different phase in early Indian history, which then admits of two sub-phases, with the tenth century constituting some kind of a dividing line. The fourth–seventh centuries mark the transition to the early medieval stage insofar as they anticipate many of the later developments. It is, however, not our intention to argue for a rigid schema of uniform validity all over the country. Historical evolution in Assam, Kerala, and Rajasthan, for example, show dissimilar spatial and temporal trajectories. Nevertheless, on the basis of the available regional trends some broad patterns are discernible, and it may be surmised that from the seventh century onwards the varied regions experienced the operation of comparable historical processes.[54] These processes seem to have further accelerated around the tenth century and after.

The study of regional agrarian histories has been varied and disparities can be easily noticed both in terms of the quality and quantity of historical output. While in the case of Tamil Nadu, Kerala, Karnataka, Bengal, and Assam aspects of agrarian economy have been worked out at some length and in Andhra, Orissa, and Rajasthan some beginnings have been made, we are less fortunate about the other regions insofar as the necessary details are concerned.

Tamil Nadu may be taken as a case study because of the availability of a number of imaginative, rigorous analytical works on the region. The agrarian map of the Tamil country began to change from the time of the Pallavas. The rise and spread of settlements unequivocally show the spread of agriculture. The patronage extended to tank building activities is yet another marker of agrarian expansion. There seems to have been a correspondence between the increase in irrigational works and the rise in the number of *nāḍu*s (agrarian localities) between the seventh and tenth centuries. Reclamation of land affected by floods and breaches in the embankment of the Kaveri began under Parāntaka I and continued well into the times of Kullōtuṅga.[55] Fallow lands were similarly brought under cultivation. A micro-study of a taluk too suggests that the Pallava period constituted a turning point in the history of the proliferation of settlements in the region.[56] The phased growth may be seen in the gradual spread of settlements from the wet to the dry zones under the Cōḷas. A recent study reveals the pattern of agrarian expansion in the region and suggests that the southern Kaveri delta witnessed hectic activity in the post-tenth century.[57] The Pāṇḍyan territory (Vaigai-Tamraparni valleys) opened up during the seventh–ninth centuries, and more particularly from the ninth century onwards. The intensive occupation and use of the upper reaches of the Tamraparni, it is said, reflects conscious state policy towards an area for strengthening its own economic foundations.[58] The emergence and proliferation of *nāḍu*s through the Pallava-Cōḷa periods were inextricably linked to expanding agrarian pursuits. In contrast to the smaller *nāḍu*s in the river valleys, the less fertile tracts were characterized by larger *nāḍu*s with lesser density of settlements. Some kind of a peak was attained in different areas in course of the eleventh–twelfth centuries[59] and beyond it there was a slowing down of the process.

The picture obtained for some other regions, though not synonymous, is very close to the pattern of development in Tamil Nadu. The intra-regional variations and the phased development of sub-regions are discernible in the context of early medieval Orissa and Kāmarūpa.[60] In Orissa, the deliberate royal choice of certain sub-regions for development as agrarian resource bases during the ninth–eleventh centuries, as in Tamil Nadu, attracts attention.[61] There is a perceptible rise in the number of settlements in the Brahmaputra valley in the post-tenth century. The fact that about fifty settlements are reported for this period as against thirteen for the earlier phase is very striking.[62] Andhra in the post-Ikṣvāku phase exhibits the phenomenon of land-grants, but interestingly all these early dynasties and their grants were confined to coastal Andhra.[63] It is a pattern that is largely corroborated in the developments in pre-eighth century Orissa. Not that the areas of Telengana and Rayalaseema in Andhra were economically barren, but evidently they opened up to agriculture on a large scale in subsequent times. The history of agriculture and irrigation, especially the care bestowed on the construction of tanks and reservoirs, in Warangal under the Kākātiyas[64] and the attendant visible profile of the Reḍḍis points to the gradual agrarian integration of the region.

The trends available for Assam, Bengal, Karnataka, and Rajasthan endorse the picture of burgeoning rural economy during the period under discussion. While a study on irrigation in Rajasthan alludes to a general growth in agricultural production through royal initiative in irrigation works,[65] another contribution confined particularly to the Abu-Sirohi belt in south-western Rajasthan shows the growth of rural settlements[66] and the growing complexity of rural society over time. The reclamation of waste lands, inducements such as the initial exemption from taxes in newly settled areas, geographical spread of rural settlements and the concern for man-made water resources, particularly tanks, characterized the country-side of Karnataka.[67] The formation of agricultural guilds, non-brāhmaṇa corporate bodies and the rise of substantial non-brāhmaṇa peasants as exemplified in such terms as *ūrar, uḍaiyān, oḍeya, eḷame, nāttār, gāvuṇḍa*, and so on,[68] in south India indicate the process of agrarian change in the later half of the first and early centuries of the second millennium. Evidence for land improvement programmes and large-scale irrigational works in Kerala during the same period is not forthcoming, though small-scale reclamations by tenants are attested. Developments in Kerala charted a different course, with temples emerging as the nucleus of extensive agrarian corporations.[69] Regional variations in course of the transformations can be seen in the adoption of different modes. While in Bengal, for example, large groups of brāhmaṇas, were settled to change and open up a tribal pocket,[70] in Assam settlements stood largely isolated and seem to have experienced a gradual expansion in their agrarian space.[71] Although there were broad patterns of agreement, there were features of a specific nature as well; showing the individual path of development in the regions.

Aspects of Rural Settlements

Rural settlement patterns, as so often today, were not the same all over. There were distinctions even between geographically proximous regions. For Bengal the possibility of a unity of homestead (*vāstu*) and farm land (*kṣetra*) has been negated,[72] whereas in the case of Assam an exactly opposite pattern has been worked out. In other words, while the rural folk lived in compact groups in Bengal, in Assam their habitations were widely scattered.[73] Again, as against the clusters of villages in Bengal in the Gupta period, we have the picture of dispersed settlements in Assam at least up to the ninth–tenth centuries. Variations across regions can also be seen by comparing changes over time. Whereas Assam in the early centuries of the second millennium appears to be a loosely structured primarily agrarian society, Rajasthan during the same period was characterized by hierarchies in rural settlements and bustling mercantile activities, and thus, presents a very different picture.[74]

The increasing density of settlements and the greater utilization of agrarian space over time find reflection in the increasingly complicated and detailed boundary delineations of donated land, especially from the ninth–tenth centuries onwards. It is borne out by epigraphic evidence from regions such as Tamil Nadu, Andhra, Orissa, and Assam.[75] There is evidently a shift in the boundary marks from trees, stones, ant-hills and the conventional unspecified *catuḥsīmā* to adjoining settlements and plots owned by others.[76] Landmarks such as rivers, tanks, wells, orchards, marshy land, cattle track, cremation ground, temples, and *maṭhas*[77] not only provide insights into rural settlement geography but also give us an idea about the constituent elements of the villages. It may be of some interest to note that early medieval villages mostly derived their names from local flora, mineral resources or even occupational associations.[78] Villages having Prākrit names and named after trees, autochthons and so on are generally considered to have had a greater antiquity, and correspondingly those with Sanskritized names and having a migrant population, including brāhmaṇas, were supposedly later settlements.

Notwithstanding the continued extension of the peasant frontier, there were spaces outside the orbit of plough agriculture and organized state intrusion across regions. Certain Pāṇḍya records, especially those from the dry zone mention pastoral groups and pastoral headmen who were entrusted with the security of the local villages. Inscriptions and Hero stones from the same upland areas of Tamil Nadu refer to the coeval existence of pastoral groups, headmen, cattle raiding and heroic activities in the later half of the first millennium along with the Pallava and Pāṇḍyan states.[79] The *vīragals*, a type of hero stone, belonging to the Rāṣṭrakūta period, were situated on the periphery of their dominion and are mostly concerned with cattle raids. Such areas were inhospitable for agriculture and best suited to pastoral activities.[80] Instances such as these, suggesting the co-existence of pastoralism side by side with agriculture show the uneven nature of development within regions. The normally invisible pastoral sector cannot be discounted and it poses a challenge to historians. Subsistence activities need not be viewed in terms of cultivation alone. The continued importance of pastoralism needs to be recognized and addressed. Large-scale lamp endowments and gift of cattle for their upkeep in Tamil Nadu and Andhra reveal that these livestock were maintained by shepherds and cowherds in the service of the temple.[81] All through Indian history pastoralists and cultivators have lived in a relationship of symbiosis. Similarly, tribes and forests too played an important role in the life of the peasants. The mention of forest route (*vanamārga*) in one of the inscriptions of the Guhilas of Kiṣkindhā is an interesting piece of information revealing the possible tribal-non-tribal linkages.[82] The interaction between people of the valley and hills in Kāmarūpa for the exploitation of forest products in the form of wood, cane, bamboo, cotton, and so on, has been worked out.[83] And such cases can be multiplied.

The frequent references to different types of water resources in the context of land donations and burgeoning rural settlements drive home their importance for irrigational purposes and the role they played in transforming the countryside. In some cases administrative divisions were named after rivers.[84] That the pattern of the geographical distribution of settlements was related to water resources and the agrarian potentiality of the landscape has been persuasively argued in a comparative study of the Sabarmati and Godavari basins during the Rāṣṭrakūta period.[85] Evidently there was a correspondence between the increase in man-made water resources and the spread of settlements. South India during the Pallava-Cōḷa periods, Telengana under the Kākātīyas and the northern Deccan during the Rāṣṭrakūta times illustrate the point. In the Tamil country the villages had water management committees (*ēri-variyams*) to look after the construction and maintenance of tanks, reservoirs, and canals. By the turn of the first millennium *araghaṭṭas* were in vogue in parts of Rajasthan. The *Harṣacarita*, in an earlier context, mentions irrigational devices such as the *Udghaṭaghaṭi* and *ghaṭiyantra*, which were perhaps in operation in the Haryana region and adjoining territories. A work on rural settlements shows that the significant landmarks in rural Bengal were rivers and ponds, in south-eastern Marwar they were wells, and in southern Karnataka tanks constituted them.[86] These contrasts are then highlighted to bring out the distinctions between rural settlements of the varied regions. Irrigation was not the only area of concern. Early medieval texts like the *Kṛṣiparāśara* and *Kāśyapiyakṛṣisūkti*, among others, deal with the entire range of issues related to agriculture.

The early medieval centuries were characterized by immense dynamism in terms of the proliferation of crops and cereals, including the introduction of new crops (betel leaves, areca nuts, oranges, and so on), improvement in agricultural techniques, awareness of plant preservation methods and expansion of irrigational facilities.[87] Rising agricultural productivity provided the basis for the emergence of *hāṭṭas*, local fairs, and nodal points such as *maṇḍapikās*, *peṇṭhās*, and *nagarams*, which in turn lubricated the mobilization, exchange and distribution of resources. The turn of the millennium coincided with the emergence of supra-local polities. The economic and political changes appear to have been interrelated developments. A recent work focusing largely on Karnataka beautifully demonstrates the concomitant processes in the agrarian world during the early medieval centuries. The story of agrarian growth is discussed with reference to agricultural techniques, expansion of cultivable area, crop production, population, temples and the emergence of market economy, in the wider context of their relationships with contemporary society and polity.[88]

Rural settlements in early medieval India were the hub of all activity. Ironically however, rural settlement studies are in their infancy. This somewhat curious lapse may have much to do with the fact that the study of early medieval rural settlements so far was subsumed under general studies on economy and society. The importance of the study of rural settlement geography in the larger context of contemporary society and polity is beginning to be recognized. This, however, is not to suggest the total absence of earlier works in the area. A.S. Altekar's study[89] of the origin and growth of villages in western India is a pioneering work in the field, but is understandably circumscribed by the intellectual climate of his times. A.K. Choudhary's work on villages in north-eastern India is an important contribution[90] insofar as it for the first time focused on the constituents of villages and the typology of rural settlements. *Grāma* was the usual term for villages. However, all rural settlements were not of the same kind and we come across a variety of terms such as *pallī*, *pāṭaka*, *padra*, *ghoṣa*, denoting typological distinctions between rural settlements.[91] While *pallī* normally meant a tribal village, *pāṭaka* stood for a part of a village or a hamlet adjoining a larger village. Settlements of herdsmen were called *ghoṣa*s. Works of comparable interest are available for the northern Deccan and central India under the Vākāṭakas.[92] Linguistic analyses of place-names and suffixes mentioned in the land charters have led to interesting derivations in terms of the hierarchy of settlements, size variations, and their functional associations. Such analyses are indubitably useful, but it is good to remember that inferences based on place-names are tricky exercises and accepting them on their face value has its pitfalls.[93]

Place-names normally outlive the historical context of their origin. Owing to the convergence of several factors, settlements could change and assume different dimensions. Sarkara-*padraka* of the Śarabhapurīya records came to be known as Sarkara-*pāṭaka* by the time of the Pāṇḍuvaṁśīs. Similarly, again in Dakṣiṇa Kośala we come across the transformation of Khala-*padraka* into Khala-*vaṭika* between the sixth–seventh and fifteenth centuries.[94] However, the persistence of old names, despite changes in the character of settlements, in many cases tends to complicate matters. Settlements were not static, and the typological distinctions between categories were not unchangeable. The history of Kalikaṭṭi, a village in south Karnataka during the Hoyśāḷa period, over a hundred years beautifully sums up the inherent possibilities of change in rural settlements in the early medieval set-up.[95] Although it was initially administered by a series of *sāmantas*, at a certain stage it came to be associated with groups linked to the royal court and finally it was converted into an *agrahāra*.

In Lalgudi taluk, in Tamil Nadu, shifts in the site of settlements broadly within the same geographical area have been noticed. For example, many Pallava settlements stood at a distance from early historic sites. Such examples point to the changes in landscape profile and suggest the usefulness of the study of settlement complexes[96] as against individual sites in an area, for wider correlations. The formation of *taniyūrs*[97] with major *brahmadeya* and temple settlements as its nucleus, and the acquisition of several hamlets (*piḍāgais*) or revenue villages under its jurisdiction, or the coming together of numerous hamlets to form a big village in the Cōḷa period suggest the existence of settlement clusters rather than dispersed habitations. They also illustrate the alterations in agrarian space and the introduction of a hierarchy among settlements. There are instances of separation of hamlets from villages as well as their addition to new ones, indicating the emergence of new realignments. During Rājarāja II's time nine hamlets were brought together to constitute a big village.[98] Without getting into details it may be surmised that both the processes of fusion and bifurcation of rural landscape were in operation.

Rural settlement studies relate to the relationship of the habitation area to other spatial features of a settlement, and the changing profile of segments of space over time. Such aspects have received detailed treatment in the work of Chattopadhyaya, which marks a departure from the dominant historiography on many counts.[99] The perception of rural society as isolates has been questioned and it has been situated in the context of the contemporary processes of change. The evolution and the making of hierarchies among rural settlements with some of them emerging as nodal points, owing to political intervention from the top or compulsions of mobilization and circulation of resources have been revealed.[100] The strategic geographical location or favourable socio-economic make-up of settlements too may have contributed to the formation of hierarchies. Changes such as these had a bearing on the relations between settlements.

Generally a distinction is made between brāhmaṇic and non-brāhmaṇic villages and it is posited that they differed from each other both at the level of administration and social organization. While *sabhā* represented the brāhmaṇic settlement, the *ūr* was the corporate body of an ordinary village in south India.[101] These distinctions have their own merit and are helpful insofar as they exhibit differentiation between rural settlements, but as some recent studies have shown one has to go beyond it and look for the social composition in the habitations so as to have an idea of the growing complexity of social organization in the villages and their immense variety.[102] Brāhmaṇas may have been the dominant category in some, whereas in others a section of non-brāhmaṇas may have been important and yet in some other instances a wide social cross-section, including brāhmaṇas, may have constituted the substantial landowning group. The stage and scale of the introduction of brāhmaṇas in a settlement would have had much to do with its social organization. The donation of a few plots in a settled village would have made no substantial difference to its organizational structure except for extending the network of linkages of the village.[103] Brāhmaṇic settlements and temple land in most regions formed only a part of the total area under cultivation, but the ratio between such donated areas and tax-paying ordinary villages remains to be worked out for the different regions. A study on south-western Rajasthan shows that only one out of the ten villages discussed was an *agrahāra* with full exemptions.[104] Similarly, it is tentatively suggested that four-fifths of the settlements in the Cōḷa country were non-brāhmaṇic villages.[105] The brāhmaṇic settlements have been the focus of investigations for a long time now,[106] and the non-brāhmaṇic rural settlements and their spatial and chronological distribution have to be part of any future agenda on early medieval agrarian history.

Changing Rural Societies

The concept of 'the Indian village community', with its focus on co-operation and harmony has been criticized for corresponding to the Brāhmaṇic perception of it, and its inability to accommodate conflict and change.[107] The idea has been addressed within the dominant historiography and despite its rejection of the Asiatic Mode of Production,[108] it envisages closed, self-sufficient villages in the context of early medieval India. However, it distinguishes itself from the earlier usage of the idea at least on two counts: first, by arguing that such entities emerged owing to a particular configuration of historical forces in the early medieval situation, and secondly by recognizing and addressing differentiation and exploitation in rural society.[109] The community ownership of land as the basic form of landholding has been consistently questioned.[110] Researches within and outside the dominant historiography over the last forty years have demonstrated that rural society was sufficiently differentiated during the early historical and early medieval times. While the *gahapatis* and *kuṭumbins* were the well to do categories as against the *bhṛtyah* and *dāsas* (wage workers and servile groups) earlier, many categories of peasants, tenants and agricultural labourers as well as rich landed sections across regions illuminate the historical scene during the early medieval times. It has been said that inter-village relations were essentially intra caste relations, whereas intra village relations were inter-caste relations.[111] N. Karashima has shown on the basis of inscriptional evidence that every village in Tamil Nadu did not have all the necessary occupational groups to ensure their self-sufficiency, and that social interdependence functioned beyond the boundaries of individual settlements during the Cōḷa period.[112] Cremation grounds, tanks and temples were not common to every settlement and that necessitated inter village co-operation in everyday life. The social composition as well as the constituents of villages was different across space and time. Change over time had bearing on land relations, size and nature of settlements, and their placement in the settlement hierarchy. Flowing from it, it is generally agreed that it is time the focus shifted from 'the village community' to its plural form, that is, 'village communities'.

The study of rural society in the round began with the early writings of D.D. Kosambi and R.S. Sharma in the later part of the 1950s and through the 1960s.[113] The story within that framework was carried forward in the next two decades.[114] Early historical society was seen to be a vaiśya-śūdra society insofar as these categories were perceived to be the producers of wealth and suppliers of labour. The brāhmaṇas and kṣatriyas were the recipients of gifts and taxes.[115] The iniquitous process was accentuated in the early medieval centuries 'marked by the formation of two major classes related to prevailing mode of production: the landed intermediaries, including a hierarchy of ruling landed aristocracy, and a large body of peasantry which was mostly dependent and impoverished'.[116] The increasing subjection and immobility of the peasantry, their misery and suffering, and the resultant peasant protests attracted the notice of historians in their efforts to lay down the structural contours for understanding rural society.[117] Through the 1980s and later historians have been concerned with the understanding of society, particularly rural society, in all its complexity. Differentiation within the dominant and subject strata has attracted their attention. Evidence from Buddhist literature elaborates and disturbs the *varṇa* centred analysis for the early historical times and suggests that the *gahapatis* were an inclusive category in terms of their *varṇa* affiliation. However, they were internally differentiated as some worked their land themselves, while others employed extra familial labour.[118] There were yet others who did well in the towns. Similarly, Saṅgam literature makes a difference between those who were ploughmen and others who engaged cultivators in early Tamiḷakam.[119] Donative inscriptions from western India, Sanchi, and Bharut, for example, too disturb the conventional Dharmaśāstra ordering of society. They focus on people belonging to numerous occupations and places, but are conspicuous by their silence on their *varṇa* affiliations. In large parts of north India the *kuṭumbins* emerged as a middle peasant group during the fourth–seventh centuries, which owned their land and mainly used family labour to work it.[120] The presence of the *dāsas, karmakāras*, share-croppers and hired labourers elaborates the story of differentiation in rural society.

The post-Gupta period witnessed the gradual eclipse of the *gahapatis*/*gṛhapatis* and *kuṭumbins*, and the rise of many region-specific rich peasant groups. It was also marked by greater differentiation within the subject peasantry, and the numerous terms used for them across regions easily reinforce it.[121] In Bengal in the said period we do come across well-to-do peasant groups such as *mahattara* and *mahāmahattara*. Orissa too provides evidence for these categories. *Mahattaras* have been reported from the sixth–seventh centuries onwards also from Kathiawar. The context of their occurrence in the inscriptions suggests that they as rural notables were the principal representatives of their local societies, and the state found it convenient to address them. The *veḷḷāḷas* and *gāvuṇḍa*s were the corresponding groups in Tamil Nadu and Karnataka respectively. References to *prabhu-gāvuṇḍa*s and *prajā-gāvuṇḍa*s in the inscriptions, as the prefixes clearly suggest, indicate internal differentiation within the category.[122] Similar differences between the rich and medium peasants existed within the inclusive term *veḷḷāḷa*s too. It has been pointed out that in Tamil nadu in the early centuries of the second millennium peasant villages (*ūr*) experienced the emergence of private holdings at the cost of communal ownership of land.[123] The rise of men of substance in non-*brahmadeya* settlements is seen from the use of titles such as *kilān* and *uḍaiyān,* connoting a sense of ownership. The *brahmadeya* settlements were already characterized by private ownership of land and social stratification since the middle of the first millennium. North India during the same period witnessed an intensely differentiated peasantry and menial categories, with the sharecroppers and village artisans in between, as is alluded to by the lexiconized Sanskrit terms for peasants and the agricultural workforce.[124] Agrarian growth, rising productivity and the forging of agrarian regions was inextricably related to the evolution of a permanent stock of landless agricultural labour, usually within the fold of the untouchables.[125] Rural society encompassed diverse groups: from the grades of *sāmanta*s, through the officials, including *kāyastha*s, and intermediate region-specific rich peasants, to the subject peasantry, tenant cultivator and the untouchables. The local notables or men of substance were identified and incorporated into the administrative structure to facilitate the extension of authority of the regional states into the countryside.

Notes

1. See Guenther D. Sontheimer, 'The *Vana* and the *Kṣetra*: The Tribal Background of Some Famous Cults', in G.C. Tripathi and H. Kulke (eds), *Eschmann Memorial Lectures*, vol. 1, Bhubaneswar, Utkal University, 1987, pp. 125–7.

2. Ibid., p. 128.

3. See K.N. Dikshit, 'The Ochre Coloured Ware Settlements in the Gaṅgā Yamuna Doab', in D.P. Agrawal and D.K. Chakrabarti (eds), *Essays in Indian Protohistory*, Delhi, B.R. Publications, 1979, pp. 285–99; B.B. Lal, 'The Copper Hoard Culture of the Gaṅgā Valley', *Antiquity*, vol. 46, 1972, pp. 282–7; T.N. Roy, *The Ganges Civilization*, Delhi, Ramanand Vidya Publications, 1983; V. Tripathi, *The Painted Grey Ware: An Iron Age Culture of Northern India*, Delhi, Concept Publishing House, 1976; and for a recent statement D.K. Chakrabarti, *The Oxford*

Companion to Indian Archaeology: The Archaeological Foundations of Ancient India, New Delhi, Oxford University Press, 2006.

4. See Romila Thapar, 'The First Millennium BC in Northern India (up to the end of the Mauryan Period)', in idem. (ed.), *Recent Perspectives of Early Indian History*, Bombay, Popular Prakashan, 1995, p. 95.

5. See R.S. Sharma, 'Material Background of the Genesis of the State and Complex Society in the Middle Gangetic Plains', *Social Science Probings*, vol. 10, nos 1–4, 1993, p. 26; idem., *The State and Varṇa Formation in the mid-Gaṅgā Plains,* Delhi, Manohar, 1996.

6. See M.K. Dhavalikar, 'Chalcolithic Cultures: A Socio-Economic Perspective', in K.N. Dikshit (ed.), *Archaeological Perspective of India Since Independence*, New Delhi, Books & Books, 1984, pp. 63–80; Supriya Varma, 'Changing Settlement Patterns in Kathiawar', *Studies in History*, vol. 6, no. 2, 1990, pp. 137–61 and Sharma, *The State and Varna Formation*, pp. 7–10.

7. Supra, n. 3. See also Sharma, ibid.

8. Makkhan Lal, *Settlement History and the Rise of Civilization in the Gaṅgā-Yamuna Doab,* Delhi, 1984; also see his 'The Development and Dispersal of Agricultural Settlements in the Gaṅgā-Yamuna Doab (2nd and 1st Millennium BC)', *Proceedings of the Indian History Congress* (hereafter *PIHC*), Goa session, 1987, pp. 730–40.

9. See Sharma, supra n. 5.

10. The construction of hierarchy of settlements on the basis of surveys, surface measurements of sites and modern ethnographic/demographic parallels, in the absence of excavations, are tricky endeavours. We can have no idea of the spatial distribution of an earlier culture at multi-cultural sites by applying such methods.

11. See R.S. Sharma, *Material Culture and Social Formation in Ancient India*, Delhi, Macmillan, 1985; Romila Thapar, *From Lineage to State: Social Formations in the Mid-first Millennium BC in the Gaṅgā Vallley*, New Delhi, Oxford University Press, 1984.

12. Supra, n. 8.

13. See Thapar, *From Lineage to State*, ch. 3.

14. For clear statements see Makkhan Lal, 'Iron Tools, Forest Clearance and Urbanization in the Gangetic Plains', *Man and Environment*, vol. X, 1986, pp. 83–90; and D.K. Chakrabarti and N. Lahiri, 'The Iron Age in India: The Beginning and Consequences', *Puratattva*, vol. 24, 1993–4, pp. 12–32.

15. See R.S. Sharma, 'Material Background of the Genesis of the State and Complex Society', pp. 1–27, including the chart on pp. 14–15 and Supriya Varma, 'Changing Settlement Patterns in Kathiawar'.

16. See B.P. Sahu, 'Introduction', in idem. (ed.), '*Iron and Social Change in Early India*, New Delhi, Oxford University Press, 2006; Shereen Ratnagar, *Makers and Shapers: Early Indian Technology in the Home, Village and Urban Workshop*, New Delhi, Tulika, 2007; and O.P. Singh, 'Iron Technology and Social Change in

Peninsular India: An Archaeological Perspective', PhD dissertation, Department of History, University of Delhi, 2007.

17. For a reassessment of the nature and structure of the Mauryan state see Romila Thapar, *The Mauryas Revisited*, Calcutta, K.P. Bagchi, 1987, pp. 1–31.

18. See, for example, S. Seneviratne, 'Kaliṅga and Andhra: The Process of Secondary State Formation in Early India', *Indian Historical Review* (hereafter *IHR*), vol. 7, nos 1–2, 1980–1, pp. 54–69 and idem., 'Pre-State to State Societies: Transformation in the Political Ecology of South India with Special Reference to Tamil Nadu', presented at seminar on State Formation in Pre-Colonial South India, Centre for Historical Studies, Jawaharlal Nehru University, New Delhi, March 1989.

19. R.P. Kangle, *The Kauṭilya Arthaśāstra*, pt. II, Delhi, Motilal Banarsidass, 1988 (rpt), 2.1.

20. See S. Bhattacharya, 'Land-System as Reflected in Kauṭilya's *Arthaśāstra*', *The Indian Economic and Social History Review* (hereafter *IESHR*), vol. 26, no. 1, 1979, pp. 85–95.

21. The works of D.N. Jha and D.R. Das are exceptions in some ways. However, while Jha understandably concentrates almost entirely on the evolution of the revenue system, Das provides useful information without really explaining the historical processes. See D.N. Jha, *Revenue System in Post-Maurya and Gupta Times*, Calcutta, Punthi Pustak, 1967; D.R. Das, *Economic History of the Deccan*, Delhi, 1969.

22. See Romila Thapar (ed.), *Recent Perspectives of Early Indian History*, Bombay, Popular Prakashan, 1995.

23. A good discussion of the process of 'locality' formation is available in B.D. Chattopadhyaya's 'Transition to the Early Historical Phase in the Deccan: A Note', in B.M. Pande and B.D. Chattopadhyaya (eds), *Archaeology and History: Essays in Honour of A. Ghosh*, vol. II, Delhi, Agam Kala Prakashan 1988, pp. 727–32.

24. See ibid., S. Seneviratne, 'Kaliṅga and Andhra'; Aloka Parasher-Sen (ed.), *Social and Economic History of Early Deccan: Some Interpretations*, New Delhi, Manohar, 1993, ch. 2; and B.P. Sahu, 'The Early State in Orissa: From the Perspective of Changing Forms of Patronage and Legitimation', in B. Pati, B.P. Sahu, and T.K. Venkatasubramanian (eds), *Negotiating India's Past: Essays in Memory of Partha Sarathi Gupta*, New Delhi, Tulika, 2003, pp. 29–51.

25. See M.G.S. Narayanan, 'The Role of Peasants in the Early History of Tamiḻakam in South India', *Social Scientist*, vol. 16, no. 9, September 1988, pp. 17–34; Rajan Gurukkal, 'Towards the Voice of Dissent: Trajectory of Ideological Transformation in Early South India', *Social Scientist*, vol. 21, nos 1–2, Jan.–Feb. 1993, pp. 2–22; idem., *Social Formations of Early South* India, New Delhi, Oxford University Press, 2010, sections 2 and 3; and T.K. Venkatasubramanian, *Societas to Civitas: Evolution of Political Society in South India* (*Pre-Pallavan Tamiḻakam*), Delhi, 1993.

26. See H.P. Ray, 'Bharhut and Sanchi: Nodal Points in a Commercial Interchange', in Pande and Chattopadhyaya (eds), *Archaeology and History*, vol. II, pp. 623–5 and her 'Early Historical Settlement in the Deccan: An Ecological Perspective', *Man and Environment*, vol. 14, no. 1, 1989, p. 104. See also Seneviratne, 'Kaliṅga and Andhra'.

27. See Romila Thapar, *The Mauryas Revisited*.

28. See H.P. Ray, 'Early Historical Settlement in the Deccan', pp. 105–6.

29. See B.P. Sahu, 'Situating Early Historical Trade in Orissa', K.M. Shrimali (ed.), *Indian Archaeology since Independence*, Delhi, ASHA, 1996, particularly pp. 99–101.

30. See H. Sarkar, 'Emergence of Urban Centres in Early Historical Āndhradeśa', in Pande and Chattopadhyaya (eds), *Archaeology and History*, vol. II, especially pp. 634–6; and B.D. Chattopadhyaya, 'Urban Centres in Early Bengal: Archaeological Perspectives', *Studying Early India: Archaeology, Texts and Historical Issues*, New Delhi, Permanent Black, 2003, pp. 66–101.

31. See Supriya Varma, 'Changing Settlement Patterns in Kathiawar', particularly pp. 152–3.

32. For details see B. Rajendra Prasad, 'Early Historic Āndhra Deśa: A Perspective', Presidential Address, Section I, *Proceedings of the Andhra Pradesh History Congress*, vol. 18, pp. 8–12.

33. H.P. Ray, 'Early Historical Settlement in the Deccan', p. 106. For the spatial and chronological distribution of the term *āhāra* and its variants see D.N. Jha, *Revenue System in Post-Mauryan and Gupta Times*, pp. 141–3.

34. *Gāthā-Saptaśati,* edited and translated by R.G. Basak, Calcutta, Asiatic Society of Bengal, 1971, 1.9, 6.43, 6.67–8, etc.

35. See V.K. Jain, 'Dynamics of Hydraulic Activity in Mauryan and Post-Mauryan Times', in *PIHC*, Delhi Session, 1992, pp. 162–9.

36. Ibid. Also see S. Bhattacharya, 'Land, Soil, Rainfall, Irrigation: Some Aspects of the Backdrop of Agrarian Life in the *Arthaśāstra of Kauṭilya*', *IESHR*, vol. 15, no. 2, 1978, pp. 211–19.

37. See H.P. Ray, 'Bharhut and Sanchi', p. 627.

38. See for example Lüders' list, *Epigraphia Indica* (hereafter *EI*), vol. 10, no. 1124 and *EI*, vol. 8, pp. 73ff.

39. See H.P. Ray, *Monastery and Guild: Commerce under the Sātavāhanas*, New Delhi, 1986.

40. See B.D. Chattopadhyaya, 'Geographical Perspectives, Culture Change and Linkage: Some Reflections on Early Punjab', Presidential Address, Ancient Section, Punjab Historical Conference, Patiala Session, March 1995, also in idem., *Studying Early India*, pp. 48–65.

41. R.S. Sharma, *Urban Decay in India c. 300–1000*, Delhi, 1987, p. 168.

42. See B.D. Chattopadhyaya, 'Historical Context of the Early Medieval Temples of North India', in idem., *Studying Early India*, pp. 153–71. See also

Vijay Nath, 'Tīrthas and Acculturation: An Anthropological Study', *Social Science Probings*, vol. 10, nos 1–4, 1993, especially pp. 37–42.

43. For examples see B.D. Chattopadhyaya, 'Origin of the Rajputs: The Political, Economic and Social Processes in Early Medieval Rajasthan', *IHR*, vol. 3, no. 1, 1976, pp. 59–82; and H. Kulke, 'Early State Formation and Royal Legitimation in Late Ancient Orissa', in M.N. Das (ed.), *Side-Lights on History and Culture of Orissa*, Cuttack, Vidyapuri, 1977, pp. 104–14. See Romila Thapar, *Clan, Caste and Origin Myths in Early India*, New Delhi, Indian Institute of Advanced Study, 1992.

44. See Surajit Sinha, 'State Formation and Rajput Myth in Tribal Central India', *Man in India*, vol. 42, vol. 1, 1962, pp. 35–80; K.S. Singh, 'A Study in State Formation among Tribal Communities', in R.S. Sharma and V.N. Jha (eds), *Indian Society: Historical Probings*, New Delhi, People's Publishing House, 1977 (2nd edn.), pp. 317–36. See also relevant papers in Surajit Sinha (ed.), *Tribal Polities and State Systems in Pre-Colonial Eastern and North-Eastern India*, Calcutta, K.P. Bagchi, 1987; and J.B. Bhattacharjee, *Social and Polity Formations in Pre-Colonial North East India*, New Delhi, Har-Anand, 1991.

45. See K.M. Shrimali, *Agrarian Structure in Central India and the Northern Deccan (c. AD 300–500)*, New Delhi, Munshiram Manoharlal, 1987, particularly pp. 22–8 and maps 2–4.

46. Ibid., p. 27. H. Kulke argues for Vidarbha experiencing local state formation under the Eastern Vākāṭakas. Idem., 'Some thoughts on State and State Formation under the Eastern Vākāṭakas', in H. Bakker (ed.), *The Vākāṭaka Heritage: Indian Culture at the Crossroads*, Groningen, Egbert Forsten, 2004, pp. 1–9.

47. See K.V. Ramesh and S.P. Tewari (eds), *A Copper-Plate Hoard of the Gupta Period from Bagh, Madhya Pradesh*, New Delhi, Archaeological Survey of India, 1990; also K.M. Shrimali, 'Land Relations in Central India, *c.* AD 350–*c.* AD 450', (mimeographed).

48. *The Harṣa-Carita of Bana*, trans. E.B. Cowell and F.W. Thomas, Delhi, 1993 (rpt), ch. 7, pp. 208–9; also see M.S. Randhawa, *A History of Agriculture in India*, vol. 1, New Delhi, Indian Council of Agricultural Research,1980, p. 430.

49. See Rajan Gurukkal, 'Non-Brāhmaṇa Resistance to the Expansion of Brahmadeyas: The Early Pāṇḍya Experience', *PIHC*, Annamalainagar Session, 1984, pp. 161–3.

50. See R.S. Sharma, '*Rājaśāsana:* Meaning, Scope and Application', *PIHC*, Calicut Session, 1976, pp. 76–87.

51. See Nandini Sinha, 'State and the Tribe: A Study of the Bhils in the Historic Setting of Southern Rajasthan', *Social Science Probings*, vol. 10, nos 1–4, 1993, pp. 55–67.

52. For example, see Rajan Gurukkal, 'Towards the Voice of Dissent'; Kesavan Veluthat, 'Religious Symbols in Political Legitimation: The Case of Early Medieval South India', *Social Scientist*, vol. 21, nos 1–2, Jan.–Feb. 1993, pp. 23–33; and B.P. Sahu, 'The State in Early Orissa'.

53. See Vijay Nath, 'Tīrthas and Acculturation'.

54. For a discussion of the historical processes see B.D. Chattopadhyaya, 'Introduction', in *The Making of Early Medieval India*, New Delhi, Oxford University Press, 1994.

55. See R. Tirumalai, 'Land Reclamation of Flood-Damaged and Sand-Cast Lands—A Study in Prices, Rentals and Wages in Later Chōḷa Times (from AD 1070 to AD 1210)—Based on Srirangam Inscriptions', *Journal of the Epigraphical Society of India*, vol. 11, 1984, pp. 65–87; M.D. Sampath, 'Agricultural Guild', in D.C. Bhattacharya and Devendra Handa (eds), *Prāci-Prabhā: Perspectives in Indology*, New Delhi, 1989, particularly pp. 67–8.

56. See K.V. Raman and P. Shanmugam, 'Settlement Pattern in Lalgudi Taluk', in N. Karashima (ed.), *Socio-Cultural Change in Villages in Tiruchirapalli District, Tamil Nadu*, India part I, Tokyo, ILCAA, 1983, pp. 2–12.

57. R. Champakalakshmi, 'The Study of Settlement Patterns in the Chola Period: Some Perspectives', *Man and Environment*, vol. 14, no. 1, 1989, pp. 91–101.

58. Ibid., p. 95.

59. Ibid.

60. B.P. Sahu, 'Aspects of Rural Economy in Early Medieval Orissa', *Social Scientist*, vol. 21, nos 1–2, Jan.–Feb. 1993, pp. 48–68; and Chitrarekha Gupta, 'Evolution of Agrarian Society in Kamarupa in Early Medieval Period', *IHR*, vol. 19, nos. 1–2.

61. Sahu, 'Aspects of Rural Economy', particularly pp. 54–5.

62. See N. Lahiri, *Pre-Ahom Assam: Studies in the Inscriptions of Assam between the 5th and the 13th Centuries AD*, New Delhi, Munshiram Manoharlal, 1991, pp. 106–7.

63. See P.K. Mohan Reddy, 'Agriculture in Ancient Andhra', *Proceedings of the Andhra Pradesh History Congress*, vol. 18, pp. 16–19.

64. See Y. Gopal Reddy, 'Agriculture under the Kākatīyas of Warangal', *Itihas*, vol. 1, no. 1, 1973, pp. 57–71; C. Talbot, *Precolonial India in Practice: Society Religion and Identity in Medieval Andhra*, New York, Oxford University Press, 2001; and Neeraj Sahay, 'Environment, Settlement History and the Emergence of an Agrarian Region in Early Medieval Andhra', unpublished PhD dissertation, University of Delhi, 2009.

65. B.D. Chattopadhyaya, 'Irrigation in Early Medieval Rajasthan', *Journal of Economic and Social History of the Orient* (hereafter *JESHO*), vol. 16, pts 2–3, 1973, pp. 298–316.

66. Nandini Sinha, 'Rural Society and State Formation in Early Medieval South-Western Rajasthan', *PIHC*, Aligarh Session, 1994, pp. 123–31.

67. See K.S. Shivanna, 'Some Aspects of the Agrarian System During the Hoyśāḷa Period', in *Śrikantika: S. Sastri Felicitation Volume*, Mysore, 1973, pp. 292–8; and Shivanna and G.R. Rangaswamiah, 'Agriculture During the Gaṅgā Period', in the same volume, pp. 299–303. See also A. Settar, 'Aspects of Agricultural Expansion

in Early Medieval Southern Karnataka', in K. Veerathappan (ed.), *Studies in Karnataka History and Culture*, Mysore, 1987.

68. See Kesavan Veluthat, *The Political Structure of Early Medieval South India*, New Delhi, Orient Longman, 1993, ch. 6; M.D. Sampath, 'Agricultural Guild', pp. 67–74; Kesavan Veluthat, 'Landed Magnates as State Agents: The Gāvuḍas under the Hoyśāḷas in Karnataka', *PIHC*, Gorakhpur Session, 1989, pp. 118–23, and idem., 'The Nature of Agrarian Corporations in South Canara Under the Alūpas and Hoyśāḷas', *PIHC*, Delhi Session, 1992, pp. 108–14.

69. See Rajan Gurukkal, 'The Socio-Economic Milieu of the Kerala Temple: A Functional Analysis c. 800–1200 AD', *Studies in History*, vol. 2, no. 1, 1980, pp. 1–13. Also Kesavan Veluthat, *Brāhmaṇa Settlements in Kerala*, Calicut, Sandhya Publications, 1978; and idem., *The Early Medieval in South India*, New Delhi, Oxford University Press, 2009, part II.

70. See B.D. Chattopadhyaya, *Aspects of Rural Settlements and Rural Society in Early Medieval India*, Calcutta, Centre for Studies in Social Sciences, 1990, pp. 28–9.

71. See Chitrarekha Gupta, 'Evolution of Agrarian Society in Kāmarūpa'.

72. See Chattopadhyaya, *Aspects of Rural Settlements*, pp. 21–4.

73. See N. Lahiri, 'Landholding and Peasantry in the Brahmaputra Valley c. 5th–13th Centuries AD', *JESHO*, vol. 33, 1990, p. 164 and idem., *Pre-Ahom Assam*, pp. 93–5.

74. See Chattopadhyaya, *Aspects of Rural Settlements*, pp. 77–83. Also see idem., 'Markets and Merchants in Early Medieval Rajasthan', *Social Science Probings*, vol. 2, no. 4, 1985, pp. 413–40; also in idem., *The Making of Early Medieval India*.

75. See R. Champakalakshmi, 'The Study of Settlement Patterns in the Chola Period'; B.P. Sahu, 'Aspects of Rural Economy'; N. Lahiri, *Pre-Ahom Assam*, pp. 106–7; and Neeraj Sahay, 'Environment, Settlement History and the Emergence of an Agrarian Region in Early Medieval Andhra'.

76. Ibid. See also Shyam N. Lal, 'An Aspect of Rural Landscape in the Rāṣhtrakūta Kingdom', *PIHC*, Mysore Session, 1993, particularly pp. 91–2.

77. For such details in a regional context see Annapurna Chattopadhyay, 'Some Aspects of the Village in Ancient Bengal: Size and Periphery', *PIHC*, Aligarh Session, 1994, pp. 108–14.

78. See, for example, R.N. Misra, 'Village Life and Settlements in the Light of Vākāṭaka Inscriptions', in Pande and Chattopadhyaya (eds), *Archaeology and History*, p. 645.

79. See Rajan Gurukkal, 'Aspects of Warrior Power in Localised Agriculture: The Case of the Pāṇḍya Region during the Early Medieval Period', *PIHC*, Srinagar Session, 1986, pp. 195–6; S. Gunasekaran, 'Cattle Raiding and Heroic Tradition: Sedentary Pastoralism in Upland Tamil Nadu (Sixth to Tenth CE)', *IHR*, vol. 34, no. 1, 2007, pp. 91–124.

80. See V.S. Elizabeth, 'Hero-stones in the Rāṣḥṭrakūta Period: Their Implications for Society and Polity', *PIHC*, Gorakhpur Session, 1989, pp. 828–30.

81. See, for example, M. Krishna Kumari, *History of Medieval Āndhradeśa*, Delhi, Gyan Publishing House, 1989, pp. 47–52; and B.K. Pandeya, *Temple Economy under the Cōḷas*, New Delhi, Bahri, 1984, pp. 41–3.

82. Cited in Nandini Sinha 'State and the Tribe', p. 62.

83. See Gupta, 'Evolution of Agrarian Society in Kamarupa'.

84. In early medieval Orissa there were administrative units such as Oṅgataṭa *viṣaya* and Telataṭa *viṣaya* which were named after the rivers Oṅg and Tel respectively. See S.N. Rajaguru's *Inscriptions of Orissa*, vol. IV, Bhubaneswar, Orissa State Musuem, 1966, line 4, p. 106 and line 25, p. 192.

85. See Lal, 'An Aspect of Rural Landscape in the Rāṣḥṭrakūta Kingdom', pp. 89–100.

86. Chattopadhyaya, *Aspects of Rural Settlements and Rural Society in Early Medieval India*.

87. See, for example, L. Gopal, 'Technique of Agriculture in Early Medieval India (*c.* AD 700–1200)', *University of Allahabad Studies*, 1963–4, pp. 1–37 and Sharma, *Urban Decay in India*, pp. 172–4. For the rise of local markets see R. Chakravarti, *Trade and Traders in Early India*, Delhi, Oxford University Press, 2002.

88 See R.N. Nandi, *State Formation, Agrarian Growth and Social Change in Feudal South India c. AD 600–1200*, Delhi, Manohar, 2000, chs 3–8.

89. A.S. Altekar, *A History of Village Communities in Western India*, Bombay, Oxford University Press, 1927.

90. A.K. Choudhary, *Early Medieval Village in North-Eastern India: AD 600–1200*, Calcutta, Punthi Pustak, 1971.

91. For detailed discussions, see ibid., ch. 3.

92. See Shrimali, *Agrarian Structure in Central India and the Northern Deccan*; and Misra, 'Village Life and Settlements in the Light of Vākāṭaka Inscriptions'.

93. For a discussion of some of the problems, see V.M. Jha's review of K.M. Shrimali's *Agrarian Structure in Central India and the Northern Deccan,* in *Social Science Probings*, vol. 5, nos 1–4, 1988, pp. 150–2.

94. See S.K. Acharya, 'Rural Settlements in South Kośala', *The Journal of Orissan History*, vol. 13, 1995, particularly pp. 49–51.

95. For a meticulously reconstructed picture of the successive changes in the village see Chattopadhyaya, *Aspects of Rural Settlements*, ch. 4.

96. For settlements in Lalgudi taluk see n. 56. On the issue of the study of settlement complexes in the early historic context see Chattopadhyaya, 'Urban Centres in Early Bengal'.

97. See R. Champakalakshmi, 'The Study of Settlement Patterns in the Cōḷa Period', p. 98.

98. K.V. Raman and P. Shanmugam, 'Settlement Pattern in Lalgudi Taluk', supra n. 56, p. 6.

99. Chattopadhyaya, *Aspects of Rural Settlements.* See also Kishore K. Singh, 'Changing Landscape of Rural Settlements in Early Medieval India', a review article, in *Social Scientist*, vol. 21, nos 7–8, Jul.–Aug. 1993, pp. 79–88.

100. See Chattopadhyaya, *Aspects of Rural Settlements*, ch. 3 and 'Conclusion'.

101. For details see Veluthat, *The Political Structure of Early Medieval South India*, chs 6 and 7.

102. For details of the argument see Chattopadhyaya, *Aspects of Rural Settlements*, ch. 2, particularly pp. 51–7. For early medieval south India see N. Karashima, 'The Village Communities in Chōḷa Times: Myth or Reality', *Journal of the Epigraphical Society of India*, vol. 8, 1981, pp. 85–96.

103. See, for example, Nandini Sinha, 'Rural Society and State Formation in Early Medieval South-Western Rajasthan', especially p. 128.

104. Ibid., p. 129.

105. See Y. Subbarayalu, 'The Place of Ūr in the Economic and Social History of Early Tamilnadu, AD 750–1350', in A.V. Narasiṁha Murthy and B.K. Gururaja Rao (eds), *Rangavalli: Recent Researches in Indology*, Delhi, 1983, p. 171.

106. Pushpa Niyogi's *Brāhmaṇic Settlements in Different Sub-divisions of Ancient Bengal*, Calcutta, R.K. Maitra, 1967; Kesavan Veluthat, *Brāhmaṇ Settlements in Kerala*, Calicut, Sandhya Publications, Calicut University, 1978; Shanthakumari Leela, *History of the Agrahāras in Karnataka, 400–1300*, Madras, New Era Publications, 1986; Swati Datta, *Migrant Brāhmaṇas in Northern India*, Delhi, Motilal Banarsidass, 1989; and Upinder Singh's *Kings, Brāhmaṇas and Temples in Orissa: An Epigraphic Study (300–1147 CE)*, New Delhi, Munshiram Manoharlal, 1993, are some of the important works.

107 For a good discussion of the varied uses of the idea, see Louis Dumont, 'The Village Community From Munro to Maine', *Contributions to Indian Sociology*, vol. 9, 1967, pp. 67–89. Also see B.P. Sahu, *Land System and Rural Society in Early India*, Delhi, Manohar, 1997, pp. 33–6.

108 For example, see R.S. Sharma, *Aspects of Political Ideas and Institutions in Ancient India*, Delhi, Motilal Banarsidass, 1991, pp. 77–86; also B. Hindess and P.Q. Hirst, *Pre-Capitalist Modes of Production*, London, Routledge and Kegan Paul, 1975, pp. 197–9.

109. See Sharma, *Indian Feudalism*, pp. 52 and 103–5, and idem., *Early Medieval Indian Society: A Study in Feudalization*, Delhi, Orient Longman, 2001, ch. 6, pp. 186–213.

110. For a discussion of the debates on the question of land ownership, see Sahu, *Land System and Rural Society*, pp. 28–33.

111. See Jan Breman, *The Shattered Image: Construction and Deconstruction of the Village in Colonial Asia*, Amsterdam, Centre for Asian Studies, 1988.

112. Karashima, 'The Village Communities in Chōḷa Times'.

113. Kosambi, 'Introduction to the Study of Indian History'; R.S. Sharma,

'Stages in Ancient Indian Economy', in idem., *Light on Early Indian Society and Economy*, Bombay, Manaktalas, 1966, pp. 52–89.

114. For example see B.N.S. Yadava, *Society and Culture of Northern India in the Twelfth Century*, Allahabad, Central Book Depot, 1973; and Suvira Jaiswal, *Caste: Origin, Function and Dimensions of Change*, Delhi, Manohar, 1998.

115. R.S. Sharma, *Śūdras in Ancient India (A Social History of the Lower Order down to circa AD 600)*, Delhi, Motilal Banarsidass, 1980 (2nd edn); idem., 'Problems of Peasant Protest in Early Medieval India', *Social Scientist*, vol. 16, no. 184, 1988, also in his *Early Medieval Indian Society*.

116. B.N.S. Yadava, 'Problem of the Interaction Between Socio-Economic Classes in the Early Medieval Complex', *IHR*, vol. 3, no. 1, 1986, p. 44.

117. Supra nos 113 and 114; also see Nandi, *State Formation, Agrarian Growth*, ch. 8.

118. Uma Chakravarti, *The Social Dimensions of Early Buddhism*, New Delhi, Oxford University Press, 1987; idem., 'In Search of the Peasant in Early India: Was the Gahapati a Peasant Producer?', in her, *Everyday Lives, Everyday Histories: Beyond the Kings and Brāhmaṇas of Ancient India*, New Delhi, Tulika, 2006, pp. 101–18.

119. M.G.S. Narayanan, 'The Role of Peasants in the Early History of Tamiḻakam', in *Social Scientist*, vol. 16, no. 9, 1988, n.15, p. 29; also in Sahu, *Land System and Rural Society*.

120. R. Chakravarti, '*Kuṭumbikas* of Early India', in V.K. Thakur and A. Aounshuman (eds), *Peasants in Indian History*, Patna, Janaki Prakashan, 1996, pp. 179–98.

121. See B.N.S. Yadava, 'The Problem of the Emergence of Feudal Relations in Early India', Presidential Address, Ancient India Section, Bombay Session, *PIHC*, 1980, pp. 19–78.

122. See Chattopadhyaya, *Aspects of Rural Settlements*, chs 2 and 4; also see Veluthat, 'Landed Magnates as State Agents', pp. 325–32.

123. N. Karashima, 'Alur and Isanamangalam', in idem., *South Indian History and Society (Studies from Inscriptions AD 850–1800)*, New Delhi, Oxford University Press, 1984.

124. B.N.S. Yadava, 'Historical Investigation into Social Terminology in Literature: A Problem of the Study of Social Change (Mainly in the Context of Early Medieval North India)', General President's Address, Warangal Session, *PIHC*, 1993, pp. 1–35.

125. See V.N. Jha, 'Stages in the History of Untouchables', *IHR*, vol. 2, no. 1, 1975, pp. 14–31; Also Irfan Habib, 'The Peasant in Indian History', General President's Address, Kurukshetra session, *PIHC*, 1982, pp. 14–15 and 18.

10

Agrarian Changes and the Peasantry in Early Medieval Orissa*

The agrarian history of early medieval Orissa has either been provided a matter-of-fact treatment or perceived within the framework of Indian feudalism. The spread of plough agriculture and extension of the orbit of peasant activity need to be located in the context of the specificities of the region and its network of linkages with other parts of the country. The 800 years from the middle of the fourth century AD to the early part of the twelfth century constitute the formative period in the history of the region insofar as they experienced intense socio-economic transformations across the varied sub-regions. There were concomitant political developments and a series of local/sub-regional states emerged in different parts of present-day Orissa. The economic foundations of these polities were strongly rooted in agriculture. The area under cultivation steadily expanded during these centuries. However, during this formative period developments within the region were uneven and segmented. The increasingly ambitious political experiments of the Bhaumakaras, Somavaṁśīs, and the Later Eastern Gaṅgās were gradually possible largely because of the continuous economic and socio-cultural integration of wider areas in the region. The related issues are the indicators of agrarian change, nature of changes, the status of the peasantry and the role of the brāhmaṇas. One may begin the discussion, of necessity, with a brief statement of the geography of the land of Orissa.

*Originally published in V.K. Thakur and A. Aounshuman (eds), *Peasants in Indian History*, Patna, Janaki Prakashan, 1996, pp. 283–311. This is an extensively revised version.

Geographically, the land of Orissa can be divided into two distinct units: (i) the hills and (ii) the plains.[1] The hill division includes the northern uplands spread over Mayurbhanj, Keonjhar, Sundergarh, and the Pallahara sub-division of Dhenkanal district and the middle mountainous region stretching over the hilly tracts of the districts of Koraput, Kalahandi, Phulbani, and Ganjam. Rivers like the Brahmani, Baitarani originate in and traverse over parts of the northern uplands, which are an extension of the Chhotanagpur plateau. The middle mountainous zone is a part of the Eastern Ghats. The Tel, Vamsadhara, Indravati, and the Kolab are the major rivers that flow through the region. The soil in either of these geographical sub-divisions is not very conducive for agriculture. The Plains include the coastal plains, the major river valleys and the erosional plains of the Mahānadī and the Tel in western Orissa. The coastal plains comprise the undivided districts of Balasore, Cuttack, Puri, and parts of Ganjam. The Suvarnarekha, Budhabalanga, Baitarani, Brahmani, Mahānadī, and the Rishikulya join the Bay of Bengal on this littoral. The rivers have formed deltas. However, the middle coastal plains covering the districts of Puri and Cuttack are the widest and not unnaturally, therefore, have frequently been the bone of contention between competing powers. All major sub-regional states in early medieval Orissa gravitated towards this area. The pull of the area of attraction was very material. The coastal plains are thus centred largely on the Mahānadī delta. The erosional plains of the Mahānadī valley, comprising the present day undivided districts of Sambalpur and Bolangir in western Orissa and parts of Dhenkanal district in the central part of the state, is the other fertile sub-region. The Tel, Ong, and other tributaries of the Mahānadī flow in this area. It may be mentioned that the river valleys and flood plains are narrow and elongated. The sub-soil water-table in these areas is lower than that of the coastal plains.[2] However, beyond the coastal plains they are the other good agricultural pockets in the region.

The mountainous nature of the greater part of the region[3] influenced the formation and expansion of local and sub-regional polities in the early medieval times. The fertile coastal plains, with a richer agrarian base compared to the undulating, erosional plains of western Orissa and the river valleys, provided a focal point and have been the hub of socio-cultural development throughout. Usually, the states in the upstream river valleys, in the hilly and upland areas, acknowledged the lordship of those based in the coastal plains. These 'areas of attraction' were usually separated by frontiers and natural boundaries and were known variously as Kaliṅga, Koṅgōda *maṇḍala*, Dakṣiṇa (South) Toṣala, Uttara (North) Toṣala, Dakṣiṇa Kośala, Khiñjali *maṇḍala*, Kodalaka *maṇḍala* and Khijjiṅga *maṇḍala*.

State Formation across Local Societies

The period between *c.* AD 400 and 1000 was marked by the rise of several dynasties at the local and sub-regional levels. The Māṭharas and their contemporaries (Vāsisṭhas and Pitṛbhaktas) ruled parts of Kaliṅga between *c.* AD 350 and 500. The Māṭharas had Sripura as their capital.[4] At its peak their kingdom extended from the Badanadi in the north to Krisnāveṇi in the south.[5] To the west of the Māṭhara kingdom in modern Bastar region of Chhattisgarh and parts of Kalahandi and Koraput districts of Orissa the Nalas rose to power.[6] They ruled during the fifth-sixth centuries AD. After the fall of the Māṭharas and their contemporaries, the Śailōdbhavas emerged as their successors in the northern half of their territory during the last quarter of the sixth century AD, and the Early Eastern Gaṅgās succeeded in the south. The Sailodbhava territory known as Koṅgōda *maṇḍala* was situated in the lower valley of the Rishikulya river. It converged with modern Ganjam district and the adjoining parts of Puri district. The Phulbani forest complex in the west and Mahendragiri in the south defined its limits.[7] The early Eastern Gaṅgās emerged on the political scene at the close of the fifth century AD. They began their rule around Mahendra mountain and their capital Kaliṅganagara was situated on the bank of the Vamsadhara,[8] in Srikakulam district of Andhra Pradesh. Almost simultaneously (fifth–sixth centuries AD), the Śarabhapurīyas appeared on the political map of Dakṣiṇa Kośala—comprising northern Chhattisgarh and the Sambalpur-Kalahandi tract in western Orissa.[9] This area was subsequently ruled by the Pāṇḍuvaṁśīs and Somavaṁśīs. The forest complex of Phulbani was the natural frontier between Koṅgōda *maṇḍala* and Dakṣiṇa Kośala.

The inscriptions shed light on few more contemporary dynasties. The Manas ruled to the north of the Māṭharas, beyond the Mahānadī, in Uttara Toṣala in the last quarter of the sixth century AD.[10] The Vigrahas are known from the Sumaṇḍala and Kaṇās plates.[11] These inscriptions provide information about three rulers in the family and further suggest that Lokavigraha ruled over South Toṣala in the southern Mahānadī delta. A copper plate inscription at Terasinga near Asurgarh in Kalahandi district reveals the rule of a king named *Mahārāja* Tuṣṭikara in that area in the fifth/sixth century AD.[12] In the eighth century AD, a branch of the Early Eastern Gaṅgās ruled from Svetaka, identified with Chikiti area in Ganjam district.[13] They came to be known as Śvetaka Gaṅgās and their kingdom was located to the south-west of Koṅgōda *maṇḍala*. The archaeological data and the inscriptional evidence in and around Sitabinji in Keonjhar district, in the north, suggest that the locality was ruled by some Bhañja rulers during the fourth–sixth centuries AD.[14]

The Bhaumakaras who began their rule around AD 736 had Uttara Toṣala, comprising the northern delta of the Mahānadī and the Brahmani delta, as their core territory. They ruled from their capital Jajpur (in Cuttack district) and expanded to have their sway over almost the entire coastal region. Toṣala and Koṅgōda formed their core territories, although several dynasties in the upstream river valleys acknowledged their sovereignty.[15] These dynasties include the Śulkis of Kōdalaka *maṇḍala* in the Brahmani valley of present Dhenkanal district, Bhañjas of Khiñjali *maṇḍala* in the Baud valley region of the Mahānadī[16] between South Kośala and Toṣala, Tuṅgas of Yamagarta *maṇḍala* and the Nandodbhavas of Airāvata *maṇḍala*. The last two states were carved out of Kōdalaka *maṇḍala* after the eclipse of the Śulkis.[17] All these dynasties thrived during the ninth–tenth centuries AD. The Ādi Bhañjas ruled over Khijjiṅga *maṇḍala* almost contemporaneously. It comprised Mayurbhanj district, parts of Keonjhar district and some portions of Singhum in south Bihar/Jharkhand.

There are a few Bhañja inscriptions with names of kings who cannot be related to either the Ādi Bhanjas of Khijjiṅgakoṭṭā or the Bhañjas of Khiñjali *maṇḍala*. Some of these records belong to the eighth/ninth century AD. There are two unrelated Nettabhañjas. One issued a grant from Angulkapāṭṭaṇā (Angul) and the other is known by his Banatumva charter (near Bhanjanagar in Ganjam).[18] Similarly, we come across another ruling family known as the Mayūras of Boṇāi *maṇḍala*. They seem to be contemporaries, and possibly also *sāmanta*s, of the Bhaumakaras. The Boṇāi *maṇḍala* comprised Boṇāi and a part of Panposh sub-division of Sundergarh district. This line of rulers with *Varāha* titles appeared in the middle of the tenth century AD.[19] However, they had a very short rule.

In the early stages of their rule the Somavaṁśīs were confined to South Kośala. However, by the middle of the tenth century AD, they had captured Khiñjali *maṇḍala* and the coastal parts of the Bhaumakara territory. For the first time they brought together South Kośala, Khiñjali *maṇḍala*, Kōdalaka *maṇḍala*, both the Toṣalas and Koṅgōda *maṇḍala*. In the process they laid the basis for the formation of a regional kingdom, which was further actualized under their successors, the Later Eastern Gaṅgās. Under the Gaṅgās all the coastal sub-regions, that is, Kaliṅga, Koṅgōda, Uttara Toṣala, and Dakṣiṇa Toṣala were integrated for the first time. Their sway extended over central and western Orissa as well.

Before moving on to the issue of agrarian changes and related aspects, it will be useful to briefly turn to the problem of the nature of these states. The states that emerged from around AD 700 onwards were mostly expansive and appear to have been well perched on relatively sound economic foundations. The very longevity of these states, the list of officials and designations, the presence of regular and irregular troops, and mention of a number of taxes, administrative units and the high sounding epithets of the kings found in the inscriptions of these dynasties seem to reflect this reality. In contrast one comes across fewer taxes, lesser number of officials, humbler official designations and a weak association of kingship with divinity and pompous titles as in the case of the Māṇas, Vigrahas, Nalas, Māṭharas, and the Śarabhapurīyas, all of whom flourished between the fourth and the seventh centuries AD. The rulers of these dynasties normally used the title *Mahārāja*. The Māṭharas did not raise the number of their officials even at the height of their territorial expansion.[20] The Śarabhapurīya charters also reveal similar tendencies. The evolution of the draft of their copper plate charters is very instructive[21] insofar as they record gradual elaboration in both style and content. These features can possibly be explained in terms of the said historical phase being an early stage in the evolution of polities in the region.[22] The fact that the Māṇas and the Vigrahas failed to consolidate themselves in Toṣala in the sixth century AD, whereas subsequently others like the Bhaumakaras flourished in the same region reinforces this understanding.[23]

Orissa, as seen above, is a mountainous region, being a part of the Eastern Ghats and an extension of the Chhotanagpur plateau and the central Indian complex. The region is broadly characterized by thick forests and river valleys that open into the coastal plains. Contacts with the plains opened the forest areas to caste-peasant based influences. The potentialities of the coastal plains and the river valleys were realized through socio-political and technological factors.

Inscriptions provide evidence for the rise of about twenty small and big states in early medieval Orissa. Admittedly, the taxes are known in their remission. However, they unmistakably suggest the various items of taxation and possibly their collection from the peasants. Various officials are mentioned by designation[24] and occasionally by their names in the contemporary land-grant charters. The grants are addressed to the officials in all cases. This suggests the existence of an administrative apparatus. Further, numerous land-grant charters of the early medieval ruling dynasties mention that the *cāṭas* and *bhaṭas* were prohibited from entering the gift villages. It drives home the fact that the states maintained coercive machineries. The states emerged in areas which had no previous experience of organized political systems.[25] It needs no emphasis that the transition to statehood *ipso facto* presupposes a viable sedentary agrarian base. What follows is a discussion of the different facets of the growth of rural economy.

The Growth of Rural Economy

There is evidence for land-grants in tribal areas, jungles or hilly tracts and also the grant of uncultivated land, implying that such grants were made to open up virgin soil and to extend cultivation.[26] Several dynasties such as the Śulkis, Tuṅgas, Naṇḍōdbhavas, Mayūras, Bhañjas of Khijjiṅgakoṭṭā, and the Khiñjali Bhañjas ruled over forest tracts and hilly terrains. Land-grants in forest areas were made by the rulers of these dynasties and the Somavaṁśīs and the Gaṅgās as well. The grants of Jayastambadeva of Kōdalaka *maṇḍala* besides other rights delegated the rights to fishing and hunting,[27] suggesting the proximity of the gift area to water resources and forests. The Hindol plate of Subhakaradeva, the Bhaumakara ruler, similarly transferred hunting rights and thickets to the donee.[28] There is also some reference to deer and wild animals in the neighbourhood.[29] Yasobhanjadeva of Khiñjali *maṇḍala* donated a village with its trees, creepers, thickets, and forest along with rights to fishing and catching tortoises.[30] In the donative charters of the Somavaṁśīs there are references to forests (*araṇya*) and forest products. The Kudopali plates of Mahabhavagupta record the donation of forest land (*araṇya*).[31] The only copper-plate inscription from Kelga records that the beneficiary was given the right to collect ivory (*hastidanta*), tiger-skin (*vyāghracharma*), various animals living in the forest (*nanāvanachāra*), and tortoises (*kachapa*).[32] It also records the transfer of forest area together with a settlement (*sapadra-araṇyaka*).[33] Indubitably, the donee had been assigned land in a forest tract. The Sonepur plates of Somesvaradeva mention various trees such as mango (*āmra*), *madhuka,* palm (*tālika*), and tamarind (*tentalika*) along with the taxes.[34] They also refer to shrubs and creepers (*sa-gulma-latā*) and various other trees (*nanāvṛkṣa*) and again make a joint reference to the transfer of forests and a settlement.[35] The importance of the donation of cows together with milkmen (*go-gauḍa*)[36] in such forest tracts in a general context of agrarian expansion needs no emphasis. Another Somavaṁśī grant transferred two villages along with the right to kill snakes (*ahidaṇḍa*) and elephants (*hastidaṇḍa*).[37] It may be of some interest that the donated villages were situated in an administrative unit called Airāvatta *maṇḍala*. Further, it may be mentioned that the right to kill snakes and elephants were made over to the grantees in some other cases too under the Somavaṁśīs. The Nuapattana plates of Dharmaratha record a donation where the land was first cleared and made cultivable (*kostād-akarsya khaṇḍa kṣetra*).[38] It is pertinent to mention that most of their land-grant charters refer to mango and *madhuka* trees. Palm (*tāla*) and teak (*śisu*) trees also find mention in their inscriptions.[39] All these Somavaṁśī grants belong to the eleventh century AD, especially the second half of it. The Gaṅgās also made some grants in inhospitable jungle areas. Anantavarman donated a village which was in the midst of jungles, rocks, and trees.[40] The Asankhali plates of Narasiṁhadeva II mention the donation of two plots of land which were cleared of their forest cover and made cultivable.[41] The expression *krittāraṇya-bhū-bhāga* possibly refers to the clearance and cultivation of land originally covered with forest.[42] Georg Pfeffer provides information about a large sub-division of Brāhmaṇas known as Balarāmagōṣṭhi who are settled in an area which must have been on the 'tribal frontier' in the past.[43] The grant of land to Brāhmaṇas in tribal and forest areas suggest that conscious efforts were made to extend the orbit of agriculture. Unless such lands were brought under cultivation they would have been of no use to the donees.

We come across land-grants which were made according to the maxim of bringing virgin soil under cultivation or the custom of reclaiming fallow land. The operative expression is *bhūmichhidra-pidhāna-nyāya*, which may mean the same as *bhūmichhidranyāya*, a term which is also found in the inscriptions of other regions.[44] This term occurs mostly in the grants of the Bhaumakaras[45] and the Śulkis.[46] It is also found in the Narasampatnam plates of Vajrahasta.[47] These instances lead us to envisage a steady extension of the area under cultivation.

The land-grant charters usually give some indication of the location of the donated plots and villages insofar as they mention the administrative units in which they were situated. The other details such as the transfer of various rights to the donees tell us if the donated area was in a settled or a forested tract. Apparently, the transferred rural settlements and lands were demarcated because one comes across the expression *chatuḥsimā* in the epigraphs. The details of the boundaries are, however, not specified in several charters of various dynasties, including some of those of the Somavaṁśīs.[48] This provided the opportunity for encroachment and expansion, more so in the forest and hilly tracts. Through the ages peasants have cleared and encroached on neighbouring forest lands. It is pertinent to mention that as seen above many of the ruling families also donated land in forest areas and virgin soils. The fact that normally village boundaries have not been very specifically defined with reference to other settlements may also suggest that the land donations were possibly made in areas with sparse settlements, leaving scope for the extension of agriculture and the spread of rural economy.

The names of many villages, *khaṇḍa*s, *pāṭaka*s, and *visaya*s appear to be non-Sanskritic which may suggest that they were located in 'backward' areas[49] or localities in their formative period of evolution. It may also imply the slow and gradual spread of Brāhmaṇical culture into these areas. Not all rural settlements were of the same kind. We come across suffixes such as *grāma, pallī, vāṭaka/pāṭaka*, and *padraka/padara* in the inscriptions of various dynasties.[50] A *pallī* is normally understood as some kind of a hamlet or tribal settlement.[51] A *vāṭaka* may be the local variation of the term *pāṭaka,* which stands for a part of a village or a hamlet which formed a part of a larger village. It is suggested that the rise in the number of *pāṭaka*s within the same village boundary was an indication of agrarian expansion.[52] A *padara* in Oriya language denotes a small settlement with a cluster of houses in the vicinity of a *grāma* (village). Admittedly, settlements could grow and develop into big peasant villages and yet continue to use the earlier suffixes. However, on the basis of the fact that there were an immense number of settlements with these suffixes; it may be envisaged that there was a mushrooming of rural settlements in the early middle ages. It is an indicator of the spread of peasant farming and village economy.

Most of the contemporary ruling dynasties had an autochthonous origin[53] and the tribal influence on the cultural ethos of the land has been considerable.[54] Inscriptions of the period refer to the Savaras, the Gonds, and the Khonds. In the Narasinghpur charter of Udyotakesari Mahavabhagupta IV there is reference to a Savara woman.[55] A grant of the Early Eastern Gaṅgā king Devendravarman bears reference to a *savaramahattara*.[56] The early rulers of South Kośala possibly had a Savara origin.[57] The Antirigam plates of Jaya Bhañjadeva, dated to the twelfth century AD, mention the defeat and capture of the Khond chief of Kullada by Pratap Bhañja.[58] The Deogaon charter of the Somavaṁśīs is addressed to various officials, including the *Goṇḍapati* (leader of the Gonds).[59] Royal families such as the Śulkis, Tuṅgas, and the Nandōdbhavas, ruling in and around present Dhenkanal district, assumed the title of *Śakala-Goṇḍramādhi-pati*. Some rulers in this sub-region assumed the title of *Astādasa-Goṇḍramādhi-nātha*.[60] It is said that the term Goṇḍrama was probably used owing to the predominance of the Gond tribe over the other aboriginals in this part of the region.[61] In fact, a major part of the district of Dhenkanal is covered with jungles and hills. Hilly tracts are noticeable on the northern and southern parts of the Brahmani valley. Kulke[62] postulates that the river valleys have been centres of integration of tribal elements. Socio-cultural and political integration, however, went hand in hand with the economic transformation of these areas, which in turn was rooted in the introduction and extension of plough agriculture.

There are some instances of collective grants which mostly date from the time of the Bhaumakaras. The number of recipients in such grants varied between 200 and 300. The Māṭharas provide the early evidence for land-grants to numerous brāhmaṇas through the same charter. The Bobbili plates of Chandavarman[63] and the Ningondi grant of Prabhanjanavarman[64] mention two separate donations to brāhmaṇas of various *gotras* and *charanas*. Vinitatunga II issued the Talcher plates recording the grant of land to two brāhmaṇas.[65] The Talcher plates of Gayadatunga mention that he apportioned out a village among three brāhmaṇas.[66] In one of the grants of Gayadatunga eleven brāhmaṇa beneficiaries are listed.[67] Mahabhavagupta I granted the village of Vakavedda to four brāhmaṇas in his Patna plates.[68] Three brāhmaṇas figure as donees in a grant of Devananda of the Nandodbhava family.[69] The Neulpur plate of Bhaumakara king Subhakaradeva I, placed in the ninth century AD, records a grant of two villages to 200 brāhmaṇas.[70] The Bardula plates of Mahasivagupta record the gift of a village named Vatapadraka to a dozen brāhmaṇas.[71] Five rural settlements are the object of a grant to fifteen brāhmaṇa donees in the Sirpur stone inscription of the time of Mahasivagupta.[72] The Banatumbva plates of Nettabhañjadeva refer to fourteen brāhmaṇa beneficiaries.[73] The Dasgoba plates of Rajaraja III refer to the gift of Korada village to seventy-five donees. The area donated to each one of them is categorically mentioned.[74] Three hundred brāhmaṇas appear as donees of a grant of Vajrahasta III.[75] Such grants may have been prompted by the desire of the donors to extend and strengthen Brāhmaṇical influence in and around the donated areas and in the process to integrate these areas and their surroundings with mainstream socio-cultural life. Consequently, it could ensure the extension and consolidation of royal power and influence over these stretches. The establishment of brāhmaṇa colonies resulted in the dissemination of Brāhmaṇical culture and the opening of tribal enclaves, especially those bordering on river valleys; to what is described as 'Hindu'/Brāhmaṇical way of life.[76]

Instances of scattered donations of land are there. Kanakabhañja donated two *pāṭakas*, Jamarapura and Sihipura, in Vabulavendaka to Harivamsa.[77] Mahabhavagupta IV Udyotakesari, the Somavaṁśī ruler, gave away the village called Kontalanda to Sankarasarma, while his uterine brother was granted the village named Lovakarada.[78] The two villages were about four miles apart. Similarly, the Kelga plates of Somesvaradeva of the same dynasty record the donation of two villages at two different places to a father and son.[79] The practice of granting land scattered over varied distances either to the same donee or the members of the same family may have been motivated by the desire for a wider spread of Brāhmaṇical culture and life-styles. The Talcher copper-plate inscription of Gayadatungadeva mentions that villages were purified by the sound of the *Veda*s chanted by the brāhmaṇas.[80] Such grants also make the point that villages were neither closed or isolated.

The land-grants were neither spontaneous acts nor random in their distribution. There appears to be a pattern and design underlying the donations. It is but natural that rulers of states at the locality and the sub-regional levels had to make their donations within their limited areas and did not have much of a choice. But the Bhaumakaras, Somavaṁśīs and the later Eastern Gaṅgās who gradually and successively integrated an ever increasing number of sub-regions were under no such compulsion. Nevertheless, a certain pattern or a thrust area emerges in the case of each of these dynasties. The Śulkis, Tuṅgas, and the Nandōdbhavas, who were contemporaries and *sāmantas* of the Bhaumakaras, donated land to the brāhmaṇas mostly in and around present day Dhenkanal district. A good number of the Bhaumakara grants are located in the same area.[81] Thus, the sub-region formed by the upper Brahmani appears to have opened up considerably during the time of the Bhaumakaras. The immigrant brāhmaṇas seem to have played a significant role in changing the political economy of the region by introducing plough cultivation in place of the tribal practice of slash-and-burn. Almost all the villages mentioned in the Somavaṁśī donative charters between *c.* AD 880 and 930 are situated in and around Bolangir district. Even subsequent to their territorial expansion and the unification of their sub-regional kingdom in the upper Mahānadī valley with the coastal territories of the Bhaumakaras and their *sāmanta* states, and the establishment of the first regional kingdom in Orissa, the Bolangir area continued to attract their attention. During *c.* AD 930–1120 the Somavaṁśīs made more than twenty grants, a large number of which was concentrated in western Orissa, especially in Bolangir district. Numerous villages have been mentioned in these land-grants and most of them have been identified in the present district of Bolangir and the adjoining areas.[82]

The choice of areas for land-donations to immigrant brāhmaṇas may have been dictated by the desire and need to extend the resource base of the state. The immigrants had to create a minimum of a Brāhmaṇical milieu in and around their settlements in order to survive, and do well. This involved the transformation of undeveloped areas and their transition to the caste-peasant base. Even during the period of the Later Eastern Gaṅgās a certain pattern is discernible; the donative records of the Gaṅgās reveal that their activities were basically confined to the coastal plains. Their copper plate grants and temple inscriptions are found mainly in the modern undivided districts of Ganjam, Puri, and Cuttack.[83] In the case of the Gaṅgās the pattern of the distribution of land-grants may have been largely influenced by political compulsions.[84]

The enumeration of different types of land in detail, which we notice phase-wise in the variegated areas since the time of the Māṭharas of Kaliṅga, may also be an indicator of the emergence and consolidation of a sedentary agricultural population, because the detailed, meticulous divisions and enumeration of land types is usually related to the increasing preoccupation with land and cultivation. In the inscriptions we come across terms such as *kṣetra* (cultivable land), *khila-sunya* (cultivable land), *kedāra* (corn field) and *śasya-bhumi* (corn land), all of which refer to agricultural land. There are various other terms such as *khila, vāstu, vātika, gō-prachara, gō-patha, tala bhūmi, araṇya, nisidhi-bhūmi,* which refer to uncultivable land, waste land, homestead land, gardens, pastures, cattle tracks, groves, jungles, and burial grounds.[85] The description of the different types of land and the separation of agricultural land from the other categories is very suggestive of the growing importance of agriculture.

Early medieval Orissa, in fact, was characterized by immense dynamism. It witnessed the proliferation of crops and cereals. There was an increasing awareness about irrigation and expansion of irrigational facilities. The number of rural settlements increased immeasurably. These developments together gave rise to local *hāṭṭa*s. Since the time of the Māṭharas and their contemporaries an increasing number of rural settlements are referred to in the inscriptions of the various dynasties. The donative charters of the Śailōdbhavas, Bhaumakaras, and contemporary ruling lineages, as well as the Somavaṁśīs record numerous rural settlements.[86] So do the Later Gaṅgā inscriptions speak about several such settlements.[87] The *khaṇḍakṣetra*s and the *pāṭaka*s denoting a part of the village or its extension could always develop into full-fledged villages over time. Local state formation, agrarian expansion and the spread of rural settlements were simultaneous processes in operation.

Water bodies of various kinds have been mentioned in the inscriptions of this period. The Śailōdbhava capital was situated on the bank of river Sālia and many villages of the time have been identified with places located in the Rishikulya river valley.[88] Similarly, the Mahānadī, Tel, and their tributaries such as Mora-nadi, Vyaghra-nadi, Amvada-nadi, Balat-nadi, have been often mentioned in the donative charters of the Bhañjas of Khiñjali *maṇḍala*, ruling from Dhṛtipura, and the Somavaṁśīs.[89] The gift villages were situated on the banks of these rivers. One frequently comes across the expression *sa-matsya-kachhapa* (together with fish and tortoise) in the copper-plate records of the time, which clearly suggests the proximity of the gift villages to water sources. The donor's concern for the easy availability of water for various purposes, including irrigation, is clearly attested. The Somavaṁśī records invariably mention the Mahānadī and the Tel.[90] Administrative divisions were also named after rivers. Oṅgataṭa *viṣaya*[91] was so named after the river Ong and Telatata *viṣaya*[92] was so called after the river Tel. The records of the Early Eastern Gaṅgās refer to *taṭakas*[93] (ponds) which may have been used for bathing and irrigational purposes. The grant of land near the *taṭakas* clearly implies their use for irrigation. The Kama-Nalinakshapur plates of Jayavarman mention *puṣkariṇi* and *sarāh* (pond/lake) while defining the boundaries of the gift village. The word *vāpi* is referred to in a temple inscription of the time of the Bhaumakaras.[94] There are occasional references to the term in the Somavaṁśī records.[95] We also come across evidence pointing to the use of *kupas* (wells).[96] It has been pointed out that the term *vāpi* is derived from the root *vāp* which means 'to sow'.[97] Therefore, these water sources besides other things were also meant for irrigating gardens and fields. The Later Eastern Gaṅgā records yield more evidence of the local irrigational facilities such as *baṇḍha, puṣkariṇi, golapuṣkariṇi,* and *vāpi.* In the early medieval period irrigational facilities seem to have been expanded. These man-made and natural sources of water aided the extension of agriculture and sustained the productivity of the land.

One is struck by the increasing reference to the number and variety of cereals, crops, fruits and flowers during this period. Hiuen Tsang makes a very general observation when he speaks of the abundance of grains in this region.[98] However, the Bhaumakara and the Later Gaṅgā inscriptions yield evidence for paddy cultivation.[99] It may be pertinent to mention that Orissa is a natural habitat zone for rice. Wild rice grows in abundance in the Jeypore tract (Koraput district).[100] Besides rice, barley (*yava*), wheat (*godhuma*) and sugarcane (*iksu*) were also produced.[101] The reference to weavers in the Bhaumakara and the Śulki grants[102] and the mention of *salmalīvṛkṣa*[103] in various epigraphs of our period bear testimony to cotton cultivation. Inscriptions of the period of the Later Eastern Gaṅgās refer to the donation of perpetual lamps to temples with provisions for the regular supply of oil.[104] Castor oil is specifically mentioned. Possibly oil seeds like sesamum, mustard and castor were grown. Betel leaf, mango, palm, coconut, and palmyra (*jāmbu*) have been mentioned in numerous records of the Bhaumakaras, Somavaṁśīs and the Gaṅgās.[105] We also come across different useful trees like tamarind, *madhuka, nimba, jāmbu, kadamba, arjuna,* banyan, and so on.[106] Mango, *madhuka* and tamarind trees are frequently referred to in the Somavaṁśī records. Inscriptions of our period shed light on various kinds of flowers.[107] *Mālati* (jasmine), *malli* (white lily), *madhuka,* and lotus appear as the more sought after flowers. The Brāhmaṇic superimpositions and consequent high ritual elaboration of the autochthonous deities and the proliferation of temples evidently explain the avid interest in floriculture. The very existence of occupational categories such as the *tāmbulika* (betel-leaf grower), *gauḍika* (manufacturer of jaggery), *mālākara* (gardener/garland maker), *gaṇḍhika* (perfumer), *puspalaka* (flower arranger), *śauṇḍhika* (distiller), *taiḷika* (oilman), and *tantuvāya* (weaver) bear eloquent testimony to the spread of cultivation and the practice of horticulture in early medieval times. The spread of Brāhmaṇical culture, mushrooming of rural settlements, introduction of plough cultivation on an extensive scale, the expansion and better utilization of various forms of irrigational facilities and the proliferation of and increase in agricultural products and produce were interrelated aspects. Together, they contributed towards agrarian growth.

The gradual formation of an agrarian region and rising productivity led to the emergence of village *hāṭṭa*s (markets/fairs). The earliest available reference comes from Jajpur and it dates to the time of the Bhaumakaras.[108] The Baud plates of Nettabhañja assigned to the early ninth century AD, inform that Angulakapāṭṭaṇā (Angul), owed its prosperity to the merchant community who traded in various articles.[109] Under the Somavaṁśīs, Sonepur (Suvarṇapūra), on the confluence of the Tel and the Mahānadī, emerged as a *pāṭṭaṇā* or trading centre. The Later Eastern Gaṅgā inscriptions refer to the *hāṭṭas* more often.[110] The articles of trade included among other things, textiles, perfumes, sugarcane, oil, betel leaves, coconut, salt, earthen vessels, bronze goods, conch shell, bangles, and ornaments.[111] Thus, the marketable surplus of the villages was exchanged at the *hāṭṭa*s and commercial centres. These rural institutions provided a meeting ground for the peasants, craftsmen and merchants. It is from the second half of the eighth and the early part of the ninth century AD that we notice the emergence of these centres of exchange. Their genesis was certainly linked to the contemporary agrarian growth. Both food-grains and commercial items brought for sale reflect the immediate rural context of the exchange centres. There is no mention of items which could be of distant origin. Almost all the items appear to be locally produced and were largely meant for local consumption. The range of spatial interaction evidently remained confined to the immediate rural surroundings.

From the middle of the first millennium AD, there was an immense acceleration in the process of change and it continued during the succeeding centuries. It extended the frontiers of peasant production immensely. However, among the indicators of growth in peasant farming the rise of about twenty states, each with an independent agrarian base, at the level of a locality or a sub-region, indubitably attracts attention. Numerous peasant settlements arose in the region between the rise of the Māṭharas and the ascendency of the Later Gaṅgās. They were the hub of bustling activity. The territorial and cultural integration of the region, first actualized under the Somavaṁśīs and subsequently sustained and elaborated by the Gaṅgās,[112] was possible largely because of the unprecedented broadening of the agrarian frontier and the phase-wise integration of larger areas with mainstream peasant activity. The step-wise political and cultural integration that Kulke[113] has so convincingly argued about thus had a strong material foundation. The spread of agriculture, especially wet paddy cultivation, helped the grand political experiments of the Bhaumakaras and beyond. The transition from tribal chieftainship to 'Hindu'/Brāhmaṇical kingship and pre-state to state society hinged on the peasantization of the tribes and the introduction of the caste-peasant base.[114]

Of Brahmanas and Peasants

The brāhmaṇas as harbingers of socio-cultural change played a very important role in the introduction and spread of plough agriculture in the backward areas of Orissa. This helped to generate the necessary surplus for the rise of the sub-regional kingdoms. Orissa was one region which attracted the largest number of brāhmaṇas from outside during *c.* AD 400–1200. During the same period there is no evidence of the migration of brāhmaṇas from Orissa to any other part of the country.[115] This trend can possibly be explained by the fact that Orissa with its large stretches of backward, hilly areas had a massive tribal content and during the said period many such pockets were experiencing the transition to state-society. The brāhmaṇas may not have been pioneering cultivators themselves; however, they could and certainly seem to have helped in bringing virgin soil under cultivation. They were largely instrumental in unleashing the process of peasantization of the autochthons. The transition from tribal chieftainship to 'Hindu'/Brāhmaṇical kingship was actualized with the connivance of the brāhmaṇas. They helped the legitimation of the assumed or accrued status of the rulers. The rituals that were performed and the myths that were created in the process resulted in the spread of Brāhmaṇical life-ways and the universalization of autochthonous culture. The local tribal priests and the in coming brāhmaṇas coexisted in a situation where there was enough for both to do. While one tied legitimacy down, the other did it side wise. The brāhmaṇas, who came from various parts of northern India, disseminated the knowledge of the calendar, agricultural seasons, plough agriculture, the utility of cattle for cultivation, and so on.[116] Much of the codified knowledge on agriculture in the *Arthaśāstra*, *Bṛhat-Saṃhitā* and comparable texts seems to have been spread by them.[117] The dissemination of Brāhmaṇical culture with its *varṇa*, *jāti* and gender hierarchies led to the gradual disintegration of tribal egalitarianism and the emergence of a degree of division of labour and social stratification. In addition, in course of the acculturation of the autochthons, the brāhmaṇas inculcated in them a sense of loyalty to the established socio-political order. In brief, they were indoctrinated so as to ensure their habitual subservience and the perpetuation of the new order, upheld by the tribal chiefs turned 'Hinduised' kings. Thus, the peasantization of the tribes, their acculturation and indoctrination were being carried out simultaneously.

The brāhmaṇas, therefore, played a very constructive role in early medieval Orissa. They were not only instruments of socio-cultural change, but precisely for the same reason also indispensable to the whole process of state formation at the locality and sub-regional levels. In course of the process of state formation in the early middle ages, the brāhmaṇas legitimized kingship and in various ways were the pace-makers of royal authority.[118] Instances of large scale land donations are rare.[119] Mostly single villages or different types of individual rural settlements were donated to the immigrant brāhmaṇas. Besides, there are references to the donation of plots of land (*khaṇḍakṣetra*) under the Somavaṁśīs, *pāṭakas* by the Bhañjas of Khiñjali *maṇḍala*, and *timpiras* (a certain measure of land) during the time of the Śailōdbhavas. Further there are instances of a few *halas* of land, spread over more than one village, being transferred to the donee.[120] It may be added that collective land-grants could result in fragmentation of holdings and smaller individual shares. The Dasgoba plates provide a very good example. The grant enumerates seventy-five assignees and their individual shares.[121] More than sixty beneficiaries received one *gṛha vati* each. The generally modest land-donations unambiguously show that the brāhmaṇa donees were mostly humble landlords. In the light of this reality and the decisive role that the brāhmaṇas played in the internal transformation of the sub-regions and the attendant process of state formation, it becomes difficult to perceive them as forces responsible for the decentralization of the state or the parcellization of its sovereignty during the said period. In peripheral areas, such as Orissa, where the transition to organized state/class society actually took place in the post-Gupta period, the possibility of political fragmentation 'from above' simply did not exist.[122] It was the formative period insofar as the evolution of the socio-political personality of the region is concerned.

Let us now turn to the implications of the above mentioned developments for the peasantry. The epigraphic evidence shows that the number of land-grants made to the brāhmaṇas in early medieval Orissa was considerable.[123] There is evidence for the transfer of numerous fiscal and administrative rights to the brāhmaṇa beneficiaries. Similarly, the various categories and the number of *sāmantas* appear to have expanded considerably since the time of the Bhaumakaras.[124] The entrenchment of brāhmaṇa land-holders in the villages and the consolidation of their domination through the various types of privileges and exemptions, it is said, led to the growth of a servile, dependent peasantry.[125]

In the Māṭhara grants we come across taxes like *mēya* and *hiraṇya*.[126] Villagers are instructed to render all customary services and to pay all dues to the donee. The Baranga plates of Umavarman enjoin the donee to be given all that the soil produced.[127] While the Bhaumakara charters mention *uparikara*,[128] those of the Tuṅgas and the Bhañjas emphasize *nidhi* and *upanidhi*. The Khiñjali Bhañja records occasionally also bear reference to *bhāga*, *bhōga*, and *hiraṇya*.[129] Another revenue term *kara* is frequently encountered in the Early Eastern Gaṅgā inscriptions.[130] We come across the term *kṣetrakara* in the charters of the Later Eastern Gaṅgās.[131] The Somavaṁśī epigraphs provide the names of a large number of taxes that possibly accrued to the donees. They include *bhāga, bhōga, kara, hiraṇya, uparikara, nidhi*, and *upanidhi*.[132] Moreover, the beneficiaries were entitled to receive the proceeds of the fines for the commission of ten offences (*dasāparādha*)[133] within the jurisdiction of the donated area. *Dasāparādha* included offences against family, property and *varṇāśramadharma*. In the last quarter of the tenth and the eleventh centuries AD we come across a term meaning future taxes (*bhaviṣyatkara*) in the Somavaṁśī donative inscriptions.[134] It is tempting to argue that with the conquest of coastal Orissa the Somavaṁśīs had greater avenues for resource mobilization and hence there was a spurt in the number of taxes. However, these taxes were transferred to the brāhmaṇa beneficiaries in the Bolangir region, too. Further, the entitlement to *bhaviṣyatkara* was an extraordinary right which could be used by the donees to the great disadvantage of the villagers.

Apart from the above mentioned tax privileges, the brāhmaṇa donees of the period were also entitled to levies on animals and animal products, fruit bearing trees, thickets, creepers, fishing and so on. The Early Eastern Gaṅgā, Khiñjali Bhañja and the Somavaṁśī records clearly mention the transfer of such rights.[135] In the charters of Jayastambha and Kanakabhanja, fishing and hunting rights have been listed as part of the privileges accruing to the grantees.[136] Once the local resources like jungles, trees and rivers were specifically made over to the donees the peasants were automatically deprived of their natural community rights. They were constrained and had to depend on the lord's permission for the utilization of these resources. In addition, there is evidence for the transfer of weavers (*tantuvāya*), brewers (*śauṇḍika*), cowherds (*gōkuta*) and other subjects (*prakṛtikaḥ*) together with the land. The Bhaumakaras, the Śulkis, and the Tuṅgas bestowed such grants in the ninth–tenth centuries AD.[137] Such grants are seen to provide evidence of constraints on peasants' movements. Flowing from it, the inhabitants are perceived to have been attached to the soil.

There are a few instances of the donation of more than one village to brāhmaṇa donees.[138] In such cases the recipients had to depend on tenant farmers or some intermediaries to get the land cultivated. Such donations transferred the donees into powerful landlords. There are a few deeds called *kara-śāsana*s. The term suggests that the grantees had to pay a small, at times nominal, amount as rent to the king. Some such grants were made by the Māṭharas, Early Eastern Gaṅgās,

Bhaumakaras, Śulkis, Tuṅgas, Nandōdbhavas, Khiñjali Bhañjas, and the Somavaṁśīs.[139] The word *kara* is not always used. Instead in a few cases one comes across the term *tṛṇodaka* (meaning grass and water), implying that the rent was very nominal. Admittedly, the rent fixed for such gift lands/villages, were much less than the usual rent in ordinary villages. However, the determination of these concessional rates possibly depended on the size of the donated areas and their revenue potentialities. The deeds show that the payments varied from area to area. While the Ningondi grant was made subject to the payment of 200 *pāṇas* annually in advance,[140] the Talcher plates of Gayadatunga provide for an annual cess of four *pālas* of silver.[141] Mahabhavagupta I realised eight *pālas* per annum from the donated village Vakavedda.[142] It is not easy to explain the phenomenon of *kara-śāsanas*. These grants may be accounted for in terms of either the kings' unwillingness to suffer total loss of revenue or the desire to assert their superior rights in land or both. However, the fact remains that this demand for nominal payments could also be passed on to the peasants.

The evidence on the face of it appears to be impeccable and normally on the basis of the picture that has been obtained for other parts of the country it can be argued that the multiplicity of taxes, transfer of village community rights and the surrender of judicial and administrative rights to the donees reinforced the power and position of the beneficiaries, while simultaneously increasing the burden and misery of the peasants. Apparently, Orissa presents a good case of feudal exactions and peasant subjection. However, the early medieval centuries were characterized by the step-wise transition to peasant agriculture and the broadening of the agrarian base, and the concomitant process of state formation in the various sub-regions of Orissa. It is difficult to reconcile the patronage and extension of peasant farming with the increasing number of taxes, which imply an enhancement in the fiscal burden on the peasants. The imposition of taxes subsequent to agrarian expansion in an area is quite natural. But far from being so, the land-grant inscriptions across sub-regions suggest that both the developments were simultaneous. It may be pointed out that the large number of revenue terms is mostly known in the context of their remission rather than their real collection. A very important argument made by Kulke is that the transfer of immunities and rights through donations may not always be taken at face value, for the king may not have actually exercised all these rights, and privileges himself.[143] For all one knows, such rights in most cases may have been asserted, for the first time, in an area through their remission or transfer. This may be more true of areas such as Khijjiṅga *maṇḍala,* Kōdalaka *maṇḍala*, Khiñjali *maṇḍala*, and Dakṣiṇa Kośala, among others. These areas were unfavourably endowed by nature in comparison to the coastal tracts and they experienced a belated transition to full-fledged agriculture and state society. It may be pertinent to point out that sub-regions like Kōdalaka and Khijjiṅga *maṇḍala* experienced the transfer of occupational groups together with the land. It is important to recognize the sub-regional variations, as well as the fact that land could not have been transferred *sans* its inhabitants.

Myriad revenue terms are known from the epigraphs of the Bhaumakaras and their contemporaries, the Somavaṁśīs and the Later Gaṅgās. However, in the context of time and space it seems that the frequency of some revenue terms was greater than the others. While *uparikara* is often mentioned in the Bhaumakara records, the Early Eastern Gaṅgās frequently referred to the revenue term *kara*. Similarly, we encounter the expression *bhāga-bhōga-kara* in the inscriptions of the Somavaṁśīs. The more frequent revenue terms may represent the standard, regular collections in an area. The other levies mentioned in a land-grant charter may reflect the possible avenues of resource generation rather than their actual collection.[144] Similarly, in areas experiencing socio-political transformations the possibility of a conventional or mechanical repetition of the revenue terms from developed areas may be considered.

Brāhmaṇa beneficiaries were created through the medium of land-grants in early medieval Orissa largely to aid and accelerate the process of state formation in the variegated areas. They were perceived as instruments of socio-cultural change and royal validation, indispensable to the process of state formation. Under these circumstances the emerging and nascent sub-regional states needed the cooperation of the peasantry both for revenue and the defense of the realm.[145] It may thus be assumed that in the early stages of agrarian transformation, the revenue demands by the beneficiaries could not have been excessive and/or exacting. However, the fact that the brāhmaṇa beneficiaries were created through land-grants indicates that the system was based on the 'feudal' modes of surplus expropriation. It had the potentialities of reducing peasants to different grades of dependence and servility with the passage of time.

NOTES

1. See B.N. Sinha, *Geography of Orissa*, New Delhi, National Book Trust, 1971, pp. 146–62.

2. Ibid., pp. 148–9.

3. In addition to the northern uplands and the middle mountainous zone there are numerous small hills and hillocks in almost every area barring the coastal belt. A little over one-third of the total area of the state is under the plough (36.4 per cent). The rest is uncultivated land, waste land and under the forest, see ibid., p. 52.

4. S.C. Behera, 'Māṭhara Rule in Kaliṅga (*c.* 250–550 AD)', *Journal of Indian History* (henceforth *JIH*), vol. 48, pp. 171–9.

5. Lines 2–3, Ningondi grant, in S.N. Rajaguru, *Inscriptions of Orissa* (*300–700* AD), vol. I, pt. 2, Berhampur, Orissa State Museum, 1958, p. 44.

6. Ibid., pp. 106–112; also see N.K. Sahu, *History of Orissa*, vol. I, Bhubaneswar, Utkal University, 1964, pp. 495–6.

7. S.C. Behera, *Rise and Fall of the Śailōdbhavas: History and Culture of Ancient Orissa from c. AD 550 to AD 736*, Calcutta, Punthi Pustak, 1982, p. 9.

8. The place is now in neighbouring Srikakulam district of Andhra Pradesh.

9. The find of Śarabhapurīya inscriptions and coins in Kalahandi district would suggest that historically some parts of it were also a part of South Kośala.

10. D.K. Ganguly, *Historical Geography and the Dynastic History of Orissa*, Calcutta, 1976, pp. 187–8.

11. S.N. Rajaguru, *Inscriptions of Orissa* (*c. 600–1100 AD*) (henceforath *IO*), vol. II, Bhubaneshwar, Orissa State Museum, 1960, pp. 113–16 and 120–3.

12. S.C. Behera, *Interim Excavation Reports*, Sambalpur, Sambalpur University, 1982, p. 4; also see Rajagurau, *IO*, vol. II, pp. 81–5.

13. Ibid., pp. 364–8.

14. See B.P. Sahu, 'Prehistoric and Early Historic Archaeology of Orissa', unpublished MPhil dissertation, Department of History, University of Delhi, Delhi, 1979; S. Tripathy, *Inscriptions of Orissa* (henceforth *IO*), vol. VI, Bhubaneswar, Orissa State Museum, 1974, pp. i–ii; idem., 'A Note on the Asanapat Stone Inscription', *Journal of Orissan History*, vol. 1, no. 2, p. 7.

15. See U. Subuddhi, *The Bhauma-Karas of Orissa*, Calcutta, Punthi Pustak, 1978.

16. The Bhañjas of Khiñjali have been divided into two branches—the earlier and the later Bhañjas of Khiñjali. The Bhañjas issued their inscriptions from Dhṛtipura (somewhere in Sonepur-Baud area) and the later Bhañjas issued them from Vañjulvaka (in Ganjam district) after being pushed out by the Somavaṁśīs in course of their territorial expansion, see Tripathy, *IO*, vol. VI, pp. xi–xxvii.

17. A. Joshi, *History and Culture of Khijjiṅgakoṭṭā under the Bhañjas*, New Delhi, Vikas, 1983, p. 72.

18. Tripathy, *IO*, vol. VI, pp. XXVIII–XXIX.

19. A. Joshi, *History and Culture of Khijjiṅgakoṭṭā*, pp. 64–7; also see *Journal of the Bihar and Orissa Research Society* (henceforth *JBORS*), vol. VI, pt. 3, pp. 241–5.

20. See N.K. Sahu, *History of Orissa*, vol II, p. 496; Behera, *Interim Excavation Reports*, p. 31.

21. See A.M. Shastri, The Śarabhapurayīas', *Prachya Pratibha*, vol. 5, no. 1, pp. 11–14.

22. The early history of the region between *c.* 300 BC and *c.* AD 350 is characterized by uneven patterns of growth. There is evidence for certain developed pockets. However, beyond this the details of socio-cultural development are wanting and a coherent, uninterrupted historical sequence is not available everywhere, see B.P. Sahu, 'Ancient Orissa: The Dynamics of Internal Transformation of the Tribal Society', *Proceedings of the Indian History Congress* (henceforth *PIHC*), 45th session, Annamalainagar, 1984, pp. 148–60.

23. The geography and resource potential of an area only provide possibilities or set limitations; they do not necessarily determine the rate and stage of development. The nuclearity of a region is determined by how historical factors converge on it. It is, therefore, a historical-chronological category, see B.D. Chattopadhyaya, 'Political Processes and Structure of Polity in Early Medieval India: Problems of Perspective', Presidential Address, Section I, *PIHC*, 44th session, Burdwan, 1983, p. 41.

24. A.P. Sah, 'Feudatories and Beneficiaries in Medieval Orissa (*c.* AD 600–1200)', *Journal of Indian History* (henceforth *JIH*), vol. 54, pp. 531–7; idem., *Life in Medieval Orissa*, Varanasi, Chaukhamba, 1976, pp. 42–59.

25. One is aware of the Maurya rule in Kaliṅga and Khāravela's brief tenure. However, on matters relating to the nature and extent of these polities, their material bases and long-term consequences, the details are wanting, supra n. 22.

26. The point has been made by D.D. Kosambi (*An Introduction to the Study of Indian History*, Bombay, Popular Prakashan, 1990 (rpt), pp. 313–14) and R.S. Sharma (*Indian Feudalism c. AD 300–1200*, Delhi, Macmillan, 1980 (rpt), pp. 32–5; also his *Social Changes in Early Medieval India: c. AD 500–1200*, New Delhi, People's Publishing House, 1969, pp. 15–16).

27. *JBORS*, vol. II, pp. 409–16.

28. *JBORS*, vol. XVI, line 19, p. 78.

29. Ibid., line 35, p. 79.

30. Tripathy, *IO*, vol. VI, lines 20–1, p. 204.

31. Rajaguru, *IO*, Vol. IV, line 11, p. 238.

32. Ibid., lines 4–5, p. 277.

33. Ibid., line 6, p. 277.

34. Ibid., lines 26–8, p. 270.

35. Ibid., lines 48–9, p. 272.

36. Ibid., line 30, p. 270.

37. *JBORS*, vol. XVII, lines 39 and 41, p. 17.

38. Sanjeeb K. Behera, 'Some Aspects of the Landgrants of the Somavaṁśīs of Orissa: c. AD 882–1120', unpublished MPhil dissertation, Jawaharlal Nehru University, New Delhi, 1989.

39. The grants in the coastal region in contrast do not refer to shrubs, creepers, jungles, etc.

40. *Epigraphia Indica* (hereafter *EI*), vol. III, pp. 18–22.

41. S.K. Panda, 'The Pattern of Land and Agriculture in Medieval Orissa', *PIHC*, 41st session, Bodh Gaya, 1980, p. 271.

42. *EI*, vol. XXX, p. 112.

43. 'Puri's Vedic Brāhmins: Continuity and Change in their Traditional Institutions', in A. Eschmann, H. Kulke, and G.C. Tripathi (ed.), *The Cult of Jagannāth and the Regional Tradition of Orissa*, Delhi, Manohar, 1978, p. 425ff.

44. These terms are discussed in Sharma, *Indian Feudalism*, pp. 30–1; also, see Sah, 'Feudatories and Beneficiaries in Medieval Orissa', pp. 80–1; D.C. Sircar, in *EI*, vol. XXIX, pt. IV, p. 86.

45. For example, see Taltali Plate, *Indian Historical Quarterly* (henceforth *IHQ*), vol. XXI, no. 3, line 33, p. 219; Hindol plate, *JBORS*, vol. XVI, line 19, p. 78; Dhenkanal Plates, *JBORS*, vol. II, lines 28–9, p. 423.

46. See *JBORS*, vol. XVI, pp. 409 and 416.

47. *EI*, vol. XI, lines 55–6, p. 151.

48. The situation is different in the case of the Later Eastern Gaṅgās. Their records mention various *grāmas* in the context of defining the boundaries of the gift lands/settlements. For example, see the Kendupatna Plates of Narasiṁha II, *EI*, vol. XXVIII, p. 189.

49. For a general survey, see Sah, 'Feudatories and Beneficiaries in Medieval Orissa', pp. 14–17; B.K. Rath, *Cultural History of Orissa*, Delhi, Sundeep, 1983 (see appendix on list of villages).

50. These suffixes occur quite frequently in the records of the Bhañjas of Khiñjali and the Bhañjas of Khijjiṅgakoṭṭā.

51. A.K. Choudhary, *Early Medieval Village in North-Eastern India*, Calcutta, 1971, p. 45.

52. Ibid., pp. 47–8.

53. See H. Kulke, 'Early State Formation and Royal Legitimation in Late Ancient Orissa', in M.N. Das (ed.), *Sidelights on History and Culture of Orissa*, Cuttack, Vidyapuri, 1977, pp. 104–14.

54. The tribals constitute 23.11 per cent of Orissa's population even today, as against the national figure of 7.5 per cent, see *Annual Plan 1982–83 Orissa* (Draft), Bhubaneswar, Government of Orissa (Planning and Co-ordination Department), 1981, p. 109.

55. Rajaguru, *IO*, vol. IV, lines 18–21, pp. 227–32.

56. Ibid., vol. II, line 25, p. 65.

57. S.P. Tiwari, *Comprehensive History of Orissa* (*Dakṣhiṇa Kośala under the Śarabhapurīyas*), Calcutta, Punthi Pustak, 1985; Sah, 'Feudatories and Beneficiaries in Medieval Orissa', p. 137.

58. *EI*, vol. XIX, p. 43.

59. B.K. Rath, supra n. 49.

60. S. Tripathy, 'Royal Titles of Trikaliṅgādhipati and Samasta Goṇḍramādhipati of Early Medieval Orissa Epigraphs', *Orissa Historical Research Journal* (hereafter *OHRJ*), vol. XXXI, nos 2–4, pp. 151–60.

61. Ibid., p. 159.

62. Kulke, 'Early State Formation and Royal Legitimation', pp. 106–07.

63. *IO*, vol. I, pt. 2, lines 7–8, p. 26.

64. Ibid., line 8, p. 45.

65. *EI*, vol. XXXVIII, lines 18–20, p. 131.

66. *EI*, vol. XXXIV, lines 27–8, p. 100.

67. Cited in Sah, 'Feudatories and Beneficiaries in Medieval Orissa', p. 73.

68. S.N. Rajaguru, *IO*, Vol. IV, lines 10–11, pp. 106 and 110.

69. S.N. Rajaguru, 'Tamra Plate of Devanandadeva', *OHRJ*, vol. XV, line 30, p. 120.

70. *EI*, vol. XV, pp. 1–8.

71. *IO*, vol. IV, lines 11–14, p. 56.

72. Ibid., lines 16–19, pp. 72 and 78–9.

73. *IO*, vol. VI, lines 23–8, p. 247.

74. *EI*, vol. XXXI, lines 128–45, pp. 250–2 and 260–1.

75. *EI*, vol. XXXVIII, p. 143.

76. Such donations under the later Eastern Gaṅgās, possibly, could have been politically motivated. See, for example, H. Kulke, 'Royal Temple Policy and the Structure of Medieval Hindu Kingdoms', in A. Eschmann *et al.* (ed.), *The Cult of Jagannātha*, p. 125 ff; idem., 'Fragmentation and Segmentation versus Integration: Reflections on the Concept of Indian Feudalism and the Segmentary State in Indian History', *Studies in History*, vol. IV, no. 2, pp. 247–8.

77. Swati Datta, *Migrant Brāhmaṇas in Northern India*, Delhi, 1989, p. 201.

78. S.N. Rajaguru, *IO*, vol. IV, lines 34–49, pp. 227–8.

79. B.P. Mazumdar, 'Epigraphic Records of Migrant Brāhmaṇas in North India (AD 1030–1225)', *Indian Historical Review*, vol. V, nos 1–2, p. 74.

80. Cited in Sah, 'Feudatories and Beneficiaries in Medieval Orissa', p. 124.

81. The Hindol, Dhenkanal, Talcher (two sets). Santigrama and Taltalai charters, for example, came from this area. A good number of villages referred to in the epigraphs have also been identified in Dhenkanal district, see Subuddhi, *The Bhauma-Karas of Orissa*, pp. 86–94.

82. See B.K. Rath, *Cultural History of Orissa*, appendix on list of villages.

83. See S.K. Panda, 'Orissa: Its Geography and Patterns of Settlement under

the Later Eastern Gaṅgās, AD 1038–1434', *JIH*, 1981, especially the chart on the distribution of Brāhmaṇical settlements, pp. 150–9.

84. It may have been dictated, as H. Kulke posits, by the desire and need to curb the power of the 'feudal' forces, supra n. 76.

85. For the early period see D. Das, *The Early History of Kaliṅga*, Calcutta, 1977, pp. 224 and 254; for the later period, see Panda, 'Orissa', pp. 271–2, also see chart on types of land, pp. 273–4.

86. Supra notes 81 and 82. For a general picture, see Sah, 'Feudatories and Beneficiaries in Medieval Orissa', pp. 71–4; Datta, *Migrant Brāhmaṇas*, pp. 37–61.

87. Supra notes 48 and 83; also S.K. Panda, 'Economic Conditions in Orissa in the later Eastern Gaṅgā Period: AD 1038–1434', unpublished MPhil dissertation, Jawaharlal Nehru University, New Delhi, 1978.

88. S.C. Behera, *Rise and Fall of the Śailōdbhavas*, Calcutta, Punthi Pustak, 1982, p. 19.

89. S. Tripathy, 'Some Bhañja and Somavaṁśī Place Names', *Studies in Indian Place Names*, vol. 3, pp. 12–19.

90. For example, see Rajaguru, *IO*, vol. IV, line 11, p. 191; line 25, p. 192; line 38, pp. 228 and 233.

91. Ibid., line 4, pp. 106 and 110.

92. Ibid., line 25, p. 192.

93. S.N. Rajguru, *IO*, vol. II, line 10, p. 25; line 17, p. 104; line 22, p. 154; line 20, p. 294; etc.

94. *EI*, vol. XXVIII, verse 5, p. 182.

95. S.N. Rajguru, *IO*, vol. IV, line 5, p. 101; line 2, p. 236.

96. S.N. Rajguru, 'Kalibhana Plates of Janamejaya Mahabhavagupta', *IO*, vol. IV, line 5, p. 101.

97. R.S. Sharma, *Urban Decay in India (c. 300–c. 1000)*, Delhi, Munshiram Manoharlal, 1987, p. 173.

98. Cited in Sah, 'Feudatories and Beneficiaries in Medieval Orissa', p. 93.

99. For the Bhaumakaras, see the Hindol Plates of Subhakara Deva, *JBORS*, vol. XVI, line 34, p. 79; for the Gaṅgās, see Panda, 'The Pattern of Land and Agriculture in Medieval Orissa', p. 275.

100. Wild rice has also been obtained from the neolithic context at Baidipur (Mayurbhanj District), see Vishnu Mittre, 'Palaeobotanical Evidence in India', in F.R. Allchin and D.K. Chakrabarti (eds), *A Source-Book of Indian Archaeology*, Vol. I, Delhi, Munshiram Manoharlal, 1979, p. 293.

101. *EI*, vol. XXVIII, line 147, p. 257.

102. For example, see *JBORS*, vol. II, pp. 409, 346; ibid., vol. XVI, p. 81.

103. S.N. Rajguru, *IO*, vol. I, pt 2, lines 6–7, p. 45; *IO*, vol. II, line 16, p. 71; etc.

104. S.K. Panda, 'The Temples of Medieval Orissa: A Socio-Economic Study', *Journal of Ancient Indian History*, vol. 13, pp. 141–2.

105. A.K. Rath, 'Horticulture in Ancient and Early Medieval Orissa', in idem., *Studies in Some Aspects of the History and Culture of Orissa*, Calcutta, Punthi Pustak, 1987, pp. 123–35; Sah, 'Feudatories and Beneficiaries in Medieval Orissa', pp. 95–6.

106. For example, see S.N. Rajguru, *IO*, vol. II, lines 13–16, p. 71, and lines 16–19, p. 114. Also see A.K. Rath, *Studies in Some Aspects of the History and Culture of Orissa*.

107. A.K. Rath, 'Floriculture in Early Medieval Orissa', pp. 113–22.

108. *EI*, Vol. XXVIII, verse 6, p. 182.

109. S. Tripathy, *IO*, Vol. VI, lines 6–12, p. 227.

110. The Gaṅgā inscriptions do not refer to the establishment of new *hāṭṭas*, implying that they perhaps predated the Gaṅgās. For *hāṭṭas*, see, for example, the Kendupatana Plates of Narasiṁhadeva II, *EI*, Vol. XXVIII, pp. 189, 193, and lines 203–8, p. 191; also S.K. Panda, 'Trade and Commerce of Medieval Orissa: *c.* 1000 AD–1500 AD', *JIH*, pp. 21–8.

111. Ibid., p. 23; Sah, 'Feudatories and Beneficiaries in Medieval Orissa', p. 108.

112. It may be remembered that these experiments at integration were not perfect, and did not produce a homogeneous regional state, see H. Kulke, *Jagannātha Kūlt and Gajapati-Konigtum*, Wiesbaden, 1979, pp. 228–9.

113. Ibid.

114. The transition could be possible with the diffusion of Brāhmaṇical cultural norms and ways of life either through the brāhmaṇas themselves or its immitation by peasants in the neighbourhood. Cultural contacts facilitated the transition to peasant economy. Admittedly, the transition did not necessarily always take place on a simple tribe-peasant axis.

115. Swati Dutta, supra n. 77, pp. 113–14; B.P. Mazumdar, supra n.79, p. 71.

116. Sharma, *Indian Feudalism*, pp. 222–3.

117. Sharma, *Urban Decay in India*, p. 170.

118. Kulke, 'Royal Temple Policy and the Structure of the Medieval Hindu Kingdoms', p. 132; idem., 'Fragmentation and Segmentation versus Integration', pp. 247–8.

119. For example, see Datta, *Migrant Brāhmaṇas*, p. 202.

120. *EI*, vol. XXV, lines 10–12, p. 197.

121. *EI*, vol. XXXI, lines 128–45, pp. 260–1, also see table, pp. 250–2.

122. R.S. Sharma seems to have recognized this aspect long back, 'Land System in Medieval Orissa (circa 750–1200)', *PIHC*, 23rd session, Aligarh, 1960, p. 95.

123. Though the inscriptions record numerous feudal/*sāmanta* designations and titles the actual instances of vassals and officials as beneficiaries are very few.

124. For a general survey, see A.P. Sah, 'Feudatories and Beneficiaries in Medieval Orissa', pp. 33–5; idem., *Life in Medieval Orissa*, pp. 35–42.

125. R.S. Sharma, 'How Feudal was Indian Feudalism?', *Social Scientist*, vol. 12, no. 2, 1984, pp. 28–31; B.N.S. Yadava, 'The Problem of the Emergence of Feudal

Relations in Early India', Presidential Address, Ancient India section, *PIHC*, 40th session, Bombay, 1980, pp. 22–48.

126. See the Tekkali plates, Dhavalapeta Plates and the Vrihatproshta grant of Umavarman and the Komarti plates of Chandravarman, (Author), *IO*, Vol. I, no. 2.

127. Ibid., p. 176; also see the Sripuram Plates of Anantavarman, ibid., lines 13–17, p. 32.

128. Supra n.15, p. 103.

129. For example, see the Antirigam plates of Yasabhanja, (Author), *IO*, vol. VI, line 21, p. 204.

130. For example, see (Author), *IO*, Vol. II, pp. 25, 30, 210, 221, 232, etc.

131. A.K. Panda, *Four Hundred Years of Orissa: A Glorious Epoch*, Calcutta, 1987, p. 203.

132. B.K. Rath, *Cultural History of Orissa*, chapter on Administration and Revenue.

133. See the Kalibhana plates of Janamejaya, the Chaudwar Plates of the same ruler and the Orissa State Museum plates of Yayati, (Author), *IO*, vol. IV.

134. See the Khandapara plates, Narasiṁhapur plates, and the Sonepur plates of Somesvaradeva and the Ratnagiri plates of Somavaṁśī Karna, (Author), *IO*, vol. IV.

135. Supra nos 27–37.

136. *JBORS*, vol. XVI, pp. 409, 416; (Author), *IO*, vol. VI, p. 241.

137. *JBORS*, vol. XVI, line 18, p. 78; ibid., vol. II, p. 409, lines 2021, p. 415 & line 28, p. 423; *Indian Historical Quarterly*, vol. XXI, no. 3, line 32, p. 219.

138. For a convenient list of these exceptional grants see Swati Datta, *Migrant Brāhmaṇas*, pp. 202–3; Sah, 'Feudatories and Beneficiaries in Medieval Orissa', p. 77.

139. See D.C. Sircar, 'Kraya-Śāsana and Kara-Śāsana', in idem., *Studies in the Political and Administrative Systems in Ancient and Medieval India*, Delhi, Motilal Banarsidass, 1974, pp. 66–75.

140. (Author), *IO*, Vol. I, pt. 2, line 15, p. 45.

141. *Journal of the Asiatic Society of Bengal*, vol. XII, ns, lines 32–33, pp. 293–4.

142. *EI*, vol. III, lines 19–20, p. 102.

143. Kulke, 'Fragmentation and Segmentation versus Integration', p. 247.

144. In the early stages of agrarian transformation, in large parts of Orissa, it is difficult to envisage intense exactions.

145. Kulke, 'Early State Formation and Royal Legitimation', pp. 108–9.

11

Shifting the Gaze

Facets of Sub-regional Agrarian Economies*

PRELIMINARIES

I met Professor D.C. Sircar almost thirty years ago for the first and last time at the forty-first session of the Indian History Congress at the University of Bombay, in 1980. I was aware of some of his influential writings and the esteem in which he was held by scholars as one of the most meticulous epigraphist-historians of ancient and early medieval India in the country, but what left an imprint on my young mind was his frankness and concern for the future of the discipline. His publications have been numerous, and the history of Orissa occupies an important position among them. It is some aspects of the early medieval agrarian history of that region, especially the modes and contexts of articulation of rural life across sub-regions that I wish to engage with here.

The perceptive and wide ranging studies of the agrarian history of early medieval India by D.D. Kosambi and R.S. Sharma set the agenda for the writing of alternative histories. In using the expression alternative history one does not mean any kind of moving away from the dominant concerns in the discipline, least of all suggest anything diametrically opposite, but doing the same thing differently by asking new questions and shifting the terrain of discussion. These tendencies are integral to the writing of some historians since the middle of the 1970s, admittedly though they became clearly manifest in their works from the 1980s onwards, and those of others later.[1] Kosambi and Sharma's

*This chapter was originally a paper presented at the National Seminar on Inscriptions and the Agrarian History of India (D.C. Sircar Birth Centenary Seminar), organized by Asiatic Society, Kolkata, 16–17 November 2007.

works marked the beginning of analysis and explanation of land and rural society within incorporative concepts. They shifted to addressing agrarian life in the round.[2] However the early search for an explanatory framework inaugurated a trend where land grants were seen to have brought about agrarian expansion as well as the feudalization of the early medieval production process.[3] These have also been seen to have led to the alienation of resources on the part of the state. The transfer of customary rights, rights to forced labour, and so on, are envisaged as signalling peasant subjection. The transfer of the peasants along with the land is perceived to represent the subjection and misery of these categories. Generalizations within this perspective centring on the idea of closed, self-sufficient, natural economy of the times, like most pioneering works homogenizes human experiences and does not take into serious consideration the uneven evolution of rural societies in the historical regions. Recent historiography has shifted towards understanding major societal processes of change in early India not in terms of monolithic macro generalizations or any epicentric perspective, but at the level of the uneven social formations and cultural patterns obtained and encountered across regions in the sub-continent. The point could be pushed to make the argument, which should be obvious, that regions in the past as in the present were not undifferentiated entities, but constituted by varied sub-regions and localities. The processes that operated across regions and sub-regions were local state formation and the emergence of ruling lineages, agrarian expansion and peasantization of the autochthons and other interrelated concomitant developments; leading to the evolution of regional political structures, social stratification and caste formation, and new agrarian orders. The comparable patterns over the regions, notwithstanding the range of variations, and the transregional social and cultural networks shaped early medieval India.[4]

Our understanding of aspects of agrarian history of early medieval Orissa is largely based on generalized studies which focus on the region as a whole, liberally drawing on material cutting across time and space to present a relatively uncomplicated narrative.[5] Much of these works, historiographically important as they may be, usually do not analyse the material at the micro or sub-regional and local level, in spite of the early perceptive observations by R.S. Sharma.[6] Problems apart, Upinder Singh's *Kings, Brāhmaṇas and Temples in Orissa: An Epigraphic Study,* AD *300–1147* is the only exception. Some of these limitations were inherent to my earlier works too.[7] In the absence of such studies the problems and specificities of rural society and economy do not emerge with clarity. Early medieval Orissa was characterized by the horizontal spread of local state formation, implying socio-economic transformation of spatial segments and cultural change.[8] The simultaneous processes are visible in the emergence of numerous ruling lineages during the fourth–twelfth centuries. The polities were, as else where, characterized by monarchy clearly showing the dominance of Brāhmaṇical ideology, and more importantly the Brāhmaṇical mode of socio-political integration. The purpose of this study is to make sub-regional comparisons so as to highlight the more general point that before offering generalizations at the regional level, not to speak of wider correlations, one ought to take cognizance of the patterns obtained at these levels and be more cautious. The quantity of material varies greatly for the two sub-regions under consideration—Kaliṅga and Khijjiṅgakoṭṭā. While early historical Kaliṅga has a more visible socio-political profile, the corresponding history of Khijjiṅgakoṭṭā if not absent is not sufficiently clear. However, it is hoped that such a comparative study would enrich our knowledge of the early medieval agrarian order. About the choice of the sub-regions all that can be said at the moment is that they are situated at two ends of the region of Orissa, outside the Puri-Cuttack-Balasore core territories, and happen to be parts of larger pre-modern cultural entities. Kaliṅga provides a long continuous history on the eastern littoral, while Khijjiṅgakoṭṭā was not equally fortunate; largely owing to its hilly terrain.

Kaliṅga: The Littoral Experience

The earliest manifestation of some form of state society in early Kaliṅga is visible under the Mahāmeghavāhanas, Khāravela being the best known in the family. Though the stages leading to this are elusive in the archaeological record, it seems to have largely derived from the changes coming from within local society as well as the interaction with Gangetic northern India during the Nanda-Maurya times and after. The Aśokan Major Rock Edicts at Dhauli and Jaugada suggest that the Mahānadī and Rishikulya deltas were bustling with activity during the Mauryan period. Aśokan Kaliṅga broadly extended from the borders of Cuttack-Puri districts to modern Ganjam-Srikakulam districts. It is necessary to mention that the region Kaliṅga had varying spatial connotations at different points in time, and probably included northern Andhra, that is, at most the area up to the Godavari delta along the coast.[9] The process of locality or *janapada* formation continued after Khāravela and his successors.[10] For the most part early historical Kaliṅga was a loosely structured primarily agrarian society, where the contours of inequality were blurred unlike in later societies.

The phenomenon of land grants, which have been perceived to be both the cause and consequence of state formation,[11] provide names of rural settlements, boundary markers of donated spaces, revenue terms, administrative divisions, officials, segments of rural society, among other information, from the fourth–fifth centuries onwards. We come across seventeen copper plate grants belonging to the Māṭhara, Vāsiṣṭha, and Pitṛbhaktah families, ruling almost contemporaneously in parts of Ganjam district in Orissa and northern coastal Andhra during late fourth/early fifth and sixth centuries. In the north they were succeeded by the Śailōdbhavas and in the south the emergence of the early Eastern Gaṅgās displaced some of them.[12] Towards the later part of the Śailōdbhava rule in the middle of the eighth century the north Ganjam area witnessed the rise of the Gaṅgās of Śvetaka, most probably a collateral branch of the early Eastern Gaṅgās. That brings the history of Kaliṅga up to the end of the ninth or beginning of the tenth century.

The object of land grants made by the Māṭharas, Vāsiṣṭhas, and Pitṛbhaktas were mostly single villages largely in the Ganjam and Srikakulam areas. Most of these grants made to brāhmaṇas relate to the founding of *agrahāras*, including some collective grants. The Ningondi grant of Prabhanjanavarman, Andhavaram plates of Anantasaktivarman, Siripuram plates of Anantavarman, Baranga plates of Nandaprabhanjanavarman, and Koroshanda plates of Visakhavarman record many brāhmaṇas as the recipients of royal patronage. In some cases the names of four, nine or eighteen donees are mentioned, while in others they are just spoken about in the plural. Such grants may have been associated with the spread of Vedic-śāstric ideas and the extension and consolidation of royal power. Insofar as the former is concerned the donative charters do attest to it. In the background of our knowledge of the early history of Kaliṅga and the fact that entire *grāmas* or villages, and not uncultivated or forest tracts, were the object of donation it would be difficult to argue that virgin territories were being opened up or that agrarian expansion was the only basic motive of these grants. There is evidence to show that brāhmaṇas were already there in the donated areas. While the Ragolu plates suggest that some homestead land was donated in place of the earlier *agrahāra*, and that it was situated between two lands belonging to the brāhmaṇas (*vipra-kṣetra),* the Siripuram grant mentions the gift of the village Tontapara, which had already been an *agrahāra*, to eighteen brāhmaṇas. Such evidence however should not be construed to imply that the creation of *agrahāra*s had no bearing on the spread of agriculture and agrarian growth. The reference to Thirty-six *agrahāra*s occurs in the Bṛhatprostha plates of Umavarman and the Bobbili plates of Candavarman, especially in the context of the granted land being similar to the Thirty-six *agrahāras.* All that one can infer at the moment is that it very much appears to have been a conventional expression, suggesting the existence and/or knowledge of several other *agrahāra*s.

In addition to the *grāma*s there were some *vāṭaka*s or *pāṭakas*, *cheda*, and *pallī*. While the Ragolu plates refer to the making of a *vāṭaka*, most likely a part of a village, the Ningondi grant mentions *grāma-cheda* in the context of delineating the boundaries of the donated settlement. *Cheda* in this case may mean the border area of a village inhabited by a community of artisans. The inference is strengthened by the reference to Kumbhāra-*cheda* in a Śailōdbhava charter later (Khurda plates of Madhavarāja). One of these records (the Chicacole plates of Nandaprabhanjanavarman) was issued from Sarā-*pallī*, the temporary victorious residence of the royal donor. Efforts at defining the boundary of a gift village are rather rare. One such instance mentions other *agrahāra*s, ditches, anthills, bridges, plots (*kṣetra*s), tanks (*taṭaka*s), well (*vāpi*) and river (Ragolu plates). Though far and few between such occurrences perhaps help us to locate the constituents of a village, howsoever indirectly. Similarly, the administrative divisions within which the rent free settlements were situated are not mentioned in all cases. *Viṣaya* and *bhōga* were the more popular territorial divisions, though we have evidence for *madaṁba* (two cases) and *pañcāli* (only once) as well. The rare references to boundary marks and administrative units in which the donated villages were situated may be the consequence of the early stage in the practice of land grants, and may have a bearing on the question of the density of settlements. Similarly, the reference to other *agrahāras* in the context of defining the boundaries of donated settlements would suggest their clustering.

Usually the *agrahāras* were exempt from all taxes (*sarva-kara-parihṛta*). The local inhabitants, mostly peasants, are urged to serve the donees as per custom, and in a few instances they have been asked to render to the donee *mēya* (due in kind) and *hiraṇya* (due in cash). Interestingly, there are some instances of *kara-śāsanas*, that is, revenue paying grants. The Bobbili plates fix it at two hundred *pāṇas*, the Ningondi plates again place it at the same amount and the Siripuram plates allude to a tax paying *agrāhara*, which was exempted from such payment on the occasion of being re-granted. D.C. Sircar[13] in a paper on the theme argued that all donated settlements were not necessarily revenue free. One is not sure whether the gift villages paid as much as the non gift settlements or the burden on them was lighter, though it has been suggested that these annual payments made in advance in the case of *kara-śāsana*s were nominal.[14]

Brāhmaṇas are quite ubiquitous in the epigraphic records under discussion. They are the recipients of the grants and it is their *gotra*s and the different branches of Vedic studies that they engaged in comes through in these material. However, they yield no information about the immigration of brāhmaṇas, perhaps suggesting their local availability or just an absence in the early history of forging land grant documents in the sub-region. All the brāhmaṇa donees were not of the same competence economically. Those who were assigned a village were certainly more privileged than those who received collective grants insofar as the latter had to share it with others. Similarly, revenue-free *agrahāra*s were perhaps better than *kara-śāsanas.* However, in these cases the quality of the land and size of the settlement would have also mattered. The Srungavarapukota plates of Anantavarman refer to the transfer of a village to a brāhmaṇa who was already the *bhōgika* of Acantapura-*bhōga.* It suggests that some brāhmaṇas were more substantial than others, and that some of them held administrative positions. In any case it was not the brāhmaṇas but the peasants who tilled the land. The spread and percolation of dharmaśāstra ideas, particularly the *Manusmṛti*, can be seen in the profuse use of the suffix *varman* by members of the ruling lineages. In grant after grant the *kuṭumbin*s have been addressed, intimated about the transfer of rights, and asked to attend to the donees. The category *kuṭumbin* during this period has been identified with the middle peasant, who essentially worked with family labour.[15] Besides the *kuṭumbin* some of the charters provide interesting facts related to rural life. We come across the term *bhōjaka* in the Ragolu and and Bobbili plates. The expression has been rendered to mean tenants,[16] however the fact that these people like the *kuṭumbins* are being addressed and intimated, immediately following the former, may suggest that they were possibly better off than tenants. The Ragolu plates of Saktivarman, different from the one continuously mentioned above and issued by Nandaprabhanjanavarman, bear the term *gṛhapatikan* in place of the usual *kuṭumbins*. This may be a conventional expression or suggest the continued existence of the *gṛhapatis*. Aspects of the social transformation of the times seem to have been captured in the ways in which rulers perceived and presented themselves. While Saktivarman of the Māṭhara dynasty is described as *vasiṣṭhīputra* (son of Vasiṣṭhī), Anantasaktivarman the grandson dropped the matronymic appellation for the patronymic appellation *bappa-bhaṭṭāraka-pāda-prasād-āvapta-śarīra-rājya-vibaha* (who obtained the body, kingdom and prosperity through devotion at the feet of the lord the father). Significantly, one of the three early lineages described themselves as Pitṛbhaktas, and in their plates they are presented as *bappa-bhaṭṭāraka-pāda-bhaktaḥ* (devotee at the feet of his father). Evidence such as these may suggest that along with the spread of monarchy, Brāhmaṇical ideology, with its principles of *varṇa*/caste and patriarchy, too gained ascendancy.

It is generally agreed that the early Eastern Gaṅgās of Kaliṅganagara rose to power in south Kaliṅga by the end of the fifth century. Starting from humble beginnings they moved on to forge an imperial kingdom, which continued till the middle of the fifteenth century. Their epigraphic records before the twelfth century have been classified into three phases.[17] The early thirteen inscriptions ranging from the Jirjingi plates of Indravarman I, dated 39 Gaṅgā era, to the Tekkali plates of Indravarman III, dated 154 of the said era or the middle of the seventh century, belong to the first phase. The provenance of their records suggests that their orbit of activities extended from southern parts of Ganjam district in Orissa to Vishakhapatnam district in Andhra Pradesh.

The brāhmaṇas as usual were the beneficiaries in most cases, barring two instances where deities and religious establishments were the recipients of *dev-āgrahāras*. There are five collective grants to brāhmaṇas, their numbers ranging from two to thirteen (Chicacole plates of Indravarman). In a few cases there is reference to several brāhmaṇas without specification of the numbers. They seem to have come from places in close proximity to the grants. Mostly *grāmas* were donated. However there are references to certain *halas* of land, one to two and a half, also being transferred. In one case a village was gifted along with the *vāṭaka* (Chicacole plates of Indravarman), while in another land had to be purchased by the king from the *agrahārikas* for purposes of donation (Urlam plates of Hastivarman). There is reference to a *hala* of gifted land adjoining the *rājā-taṭaka-kṣetra* (Achyutapura plates of Indravarman). Such lands would have been privileged cultivable areas with easy access to irrigation. The boundaries of the donated land mention ant-hills, numerous trees, well (*vāpi*), stream and tanks (*taṭakas*). Interestingly, one tank is named *kṣhatriya-taṭaka.* The increasing incidence of water bodies as markers of rural space is worth noting. The occurrence of these boundary marks in relation to a *hala* of land or more being donated give us some idea about agricultural practices and water bodies within the village. The grants carried exemptions (*sarva-kara-pariharena*), and the peasants were asked to obey the donee and pay him *bhāga* and *bhōga.* Six *halas* of land, with four cottages, were constituted into an *agrahāra* and donated to the temple of Nārāyaṇa for the performance of bali, *charu* and *satra*, and repairs (Narasiṁhapalli plates of Hastivarman). The mention of the cottages would imply the transfer of their occupants as well. Again it is the *kuṭumbins* who emerge prominently as the addressees continuously in grant after grant. The *amātya, bhōgika, hastyādhyaksha,* and *mahāmahattara* or their sons emerge as being involved in the shaping of the land grant charters (Chicacole and Purle plates of Indravarman).

The early dynasties of Kaliṅga were followed by the Early Eastern Gaṅgās of Kaliṅganagara in the south and the Śailōdbhavas in the north. The Śailōdbhava territories comprised northern parts of Ganjam district and parts of Puri district. Their kingdom Koṅgōda *maṇḍala* largely covered the area around the Chilka lake. These areas had an earlier history of minor kingdoms, that is, the Muḍgalas and Vigrahas had preceeded the Śailōdbhavas. They had issued the earliest land grants in the *maṇḍala.* Thirteen of the total sixteen Śailōdbhava copper plate charters record land donations. In five cases certain measures of land, known as *timpiras,* were the object of grant, in two instances half the village was granted and in half a dozen cases a *grāma* was transferred. The Banpur grant of Dharmaraja provides evidence for the gift of three *timpiras* of land in a locality called Suvarnaralondi and another plot of two and one-fourth *timpiras* at the village of Madhuvataka to Prabuddhacandra for the maintenance of a religious establishment. The grant of plots in two separate areas is an interesting case of dispersed grants to religious establishments. Further, it also mentions that the donee would enjoy the donation till his death; implying thereby that all land donations were not in perpetuity. Two of the grants are collective grants. While the Cuttack Museum plates of Mādhavavarman mention the gift of twenty-three *timpiras* to twenty four Brāhmaṇas, the Parikud plates of Madhyamaraja record the grant of twelve *timpiras* of land to twelve brāhmaṇas. The names of the beneficiaries in both cases are given at length. The Nivina grant of Dharmaraja specifies the boundaries of the gift village. Besides the name of a village to the east and the name of a tank (Pavadisila-*gaḍi)* to the south there are references to *vanarais* and *trikutas*. About the first we are still in the dark but if the meaning of *trikuta* as a junction of three villages, as suggested, is accepted, then the area would emerge as one bustling with clusters of villages. The Puri plates of the same ruler mention the grant of two *timpiras* of land in Kiniya-cheda in a certain *grāma*, indicating that *cheda* meant a section of a village. In the context of the boundaries rows of trees, a tank (*taṭaka*) and the house of a bronze-smith (*kāṁsakāra*) at the end of the road are detailed. These markers within the settlement clearly suggest what happened to be the constituents of the village.

Notwithstanding the transfer of individual *grāmas*, the evidence for the donation of half a village or more than one *timpira* of land or even collective grants, involving a *timpira* each to individual brāhmaṇas would suggest that the grants were not quite substantial. The reference to *akṣaya-nivi dharma* in the Ganjam plates of Madhavarāja and the usual expression like *a-candr-arka-sama-kalam* suggest the perpetuity of the donations. Similarly there are indications that the grants were unhindered and not to be impinged upon. For example, the Parikud plates of Madhyamaraja bear the expression *sarva-pīḍā-varjita.* However, the actual privileges of the brāhmaṇa grantees do not emerge specifically. It is not quite clear what kind of impact a brāhmaṇa donee or donees with some units of rent free land in a village would have had on agrarian relations. Nevertheless, their capacity, especially when they were a dozen or more, to disseminate Vedic-śāstric-purāṇic ideas can be easily perceived. These grants by their very nature do not appear to have been made to open up the agrarian frontiers. The grants themselves would have helped the process of the reaching out of royal authority. The dynasty's concern for legitimacy can be seen in the carefully crafted self-images of kingship in their records. Beginning from the origin myth, through the allusions to the performance of Vedic sacrifices to the appropriation of epic characters make it obvious. Terms such as *pāṭaka/vāṭaka, cheda*, and *āhāra* occur in some of the inscriptional records. *Āhāra* is encountered in the context of situating the gift village or a part of it. Two sets of copper plates (Niviṇa and Kondedda) mention the *visaya* Khinding-*āhāra*. The term was wide spread in the Sātavāhana kingdom and adjoining territories to the north. The expression also meant food and by derivation the said territorial unit may have been called so to denote a food producing area. *Cheda* occurs in the Puri plates of Dharmaraja, which bears that two *timpira*s of land in Kiniya-*cheda* in a certain village were donated. Similarly, the Khurda plates of Madhavarāja mention the transfer of Kumbhāra-*cche*(*da*) in Arahanna village to a brāhmaṇa. The context of its occurrence makes it amply clear that *cheda* stood for a section of a village. Further, while in one case a village is shown as being a part of a certain *pāṭaka* (Buguda plates), in another instance a land grant is made from the victorious Matrcandra-*pāṭaka* and it involved the transfer of five *timpiras* of land in Uṣā-*vāṭaka grāma* (Ranpur plates). In yet another situation some *timpiras* of land in Madhu-*vāṭaka* grama are issued to the donee (Banpur grant). From these it may be deduced that settlements changed over time and *vāṭaka*s could move on to become *grāma*s. Some of them could have been important enough to be victorious camps, and perhaps in some other cases, as in the first instance mentioned above, place-names had outlived the context of their origin.[18]

In all the land grant charters discussed above, barring the one to a religious establishment, the brāhmaṇas as the recipients of land and important members of society occupy a significant position. The *gotra, pravara, caraṇa*, and Vedic schools to which they belonged are mentioned in some of the grants, if not all. Interestingly the family history of the donee is mentioned in the Buguda grant of Mādhavavarman. The donee bhaṭṭa Vamana is said to have been the son of Adityadeva and the grandson of Vamana. *Karaṇa*s as a part of the officials addressed in the context of the transfer of land are referred to continuously. It is necessary to make the point because the Kāyasthas in the region are known as karaṇas and their historical roots may be traced to the seventh–eighth centuries. Among the addressees the karaṇas are followed by the brāhmaṇas and the expression *janapadān* (*sakaraṇa-vyvahārin-brāhmaṇa-purōgadi-vaishayika-janapadān*), in the same context may mean the other inhabitants. The earlier presence of the brāhmaṇas in Kongoda *maṇḍala* is thus unmistakable. The royal officials usually addressed were *śrisāmanta, mahāsamanta, mahārāja, rājanaka, rājaputra, antaraṅga, daṇḍanāyaka, viṣayapati, tadāyuktaka* as well as present and future *vyavahārins,* as also those of the *cāṭa, bhaṭa*, and *vallabha* categories. The names of various people with the designation or suffix *bhōgin* or *bṛhadbhōgin*, who many a time happened to be a *sāmanta,* occurs along with the mention of the professionals such as writers/composers and engravers who were associated with the making and execution of the land grant charters.

The emergence of the Gaṅgās of Śvetaka synchronized with the decline of the Śailōdbhavas, and they ruled over the northern parts of Ganjam district. They were a collateral branch of the early Gaṅgās of Kaliṅganagara. Their fifteen land grant charters carry the narrative forward to the end of the ninth or the beginning of the tenth century. Fourteen of these record gifts to brāhmaṇas and one is to a temple and brāhmaṇas. Only two charters record donations to more than one individual, four in one case and eleven in the other. The land transfers comprised mostly villages, but *khaṇḍa-kṣetras* (pieces of land) and certain measures of land, called *murajas,* were also donated. The village Pherava seems to have been transferred together with Asvattha-*ccheda.* The boundaries of about half the gift lands are demarcated. In one charter the eastern boundary was constituted by a *puṣhkaraṇi* (pond), the northern by a *karmakāra-ccheda,* the western by a *sara* (lake), and to the south was Skandasarma's-*cheda* (Kama-Nalinakshapur plates of Jayavarman). Another grant similarly specifies the boundaries with reference to the western face of the tank as far as the river, the *bhōgapāṭaka* land of *vṛhadbhōgika* and till the middle of the river bed (Bishamagiri plates of Indravarma). Others refer to trees, embankments, tanks, *araṇya* and Kaliṅga-*mārga.* The easy availability of water bodies as reference points could be both because of their importance to rural life as well as the high water table in the region owing to the presence of rivers and its closeness to the sea. The mention of others' plots while delineating the boundaries of gift lands points to the growing importance of land and agriculture, as well as the rising density of occupation in settlements in some areas. The references to *araṇya* reveal the settlement (*janapada*) and forest continuum, the latter providing a range of resources and possibilities to the villagers in terms of fire-wood, forest products, grazing of cattle and extension of agriculture. One of the grants seems to be a *kara-śāsana* (Ganjam plates of Prithivivarmadeva). It reads that the beneficiary had to pay an annual rent of four *pāla*s of silver. As in the past so also now the gift lands were constituted into *agrahāra*s and declared to be made in perpetuity.

Brāhmaṇas and local inhabitants (*janapadān*) are continuously mentioned. Some of the brāhmaṇas appear to have been men of substance. Two records provide evidence for the ancestry of the brāhmaṇa donees and it has been argued that the beneficiary in both Durgakhandin or Durggakhandika was the same person because the father appears to be common, that is, *bhaṭṭa* Vo(Bo)dhana or Vo(Bo)dhuna. One of the donees in the Indian Museum plates of Indravarman was Durgakhandin and his possible identification with the above discussed donee has been suggested.[19] If the identification holds true then the brāhmaṇa would have been a very well-to-do person. There are a few references to brāhmaṇa *mahattara*s (Badakhimedi plates of Jayavarman, plates of same name of Bhupendravarma), the term occurring for the first time in the region. The fact that we come across the *kuṭumbin*s in several grants of the dynasty as significant members of rural society, the emergence of the *mahattaras* points to further differentiation and hierarchization in the countryside. Some brāhmaṇas were actually men of substance, placed above the *kuṭumbins*.[20] In addition it may be mentioned that the Chicacole plates of Eastern Gaṅgā Devendravarman (Gupta Era 183) provide evidence for the charter being written in the presence of *mahattara* the Savara Nandisarman. Nandisarman would normally suggest a brāhmaṇa name, but just in case he was a savara then the social composition of the *mahattaras* would be enlarged. The *kāṁsakāra* (brazier), once also mentioned as *kāṁsara-kulapūtraka*, (Badakhimedi plates; Bishamagiri plates)comes to light in relation to the engraving of copper plate charters. We may reiterate that there has already been reference to the *karmakāra-cheda*. These allude to the gradual emergence of professional groups/castes in the context of the regions in early India.

The foregoing discussion by focusing on factual details tries to highlight the patterns of development in the agrarian world of early medieval Kaliṅga. It experienced local and sub-regional state formation, agrarian expansion and social change almost simultaneously from the middle of the first millennium. The spread of plough agriculture, growth of settlements, including their *cheda*s and *vāṭaka*s, their growing density, use of different forms of water resources and differentiation within the peasantry, suggesting agrarian prosperity and enhanced complexity, were interrelated aspects. What was at play was not necessarily linearity but changes across spaces within Kaliṅga. The relationship between the king and the brāhmaṇa was central to the multiple processes of societal change. The spread and entrenchment of Vedic-śāstric-epic-purāṇic ideas can be seen in the inscriptional records of the Māṭharas and their contemporaries, Early Eastern Gaṅgās, Śailōdbhavas and the Śvetaka Gaṅgās. Patronage over time had shifted from rock-cut monuments at Udaygiri-Khandagiri to śāstric-purāṇic ideology, autochthonous deities and temples to establish a cord with the subjects and create larger community identities. However, patronage was not evenly dispersed, and it ranged from a few measures of land to a whole village. Admittedly, land grants constituted only a small part of the total area under cultivation, and that should help us to envisage the scale of change in rural society.

Khijjiṅgakoṭṭā: Pattern of the Jungle Territory

At this point we may shift our attention to Khijjiṅgakoṭṭā *maṇḍala.* The sub-region comprising parts of Mayurbhanja and Keonjhar districts in north Orissa came into prominence under the Ādi Bhañjas in the tenth–eleventh centuries. It is a generally forested, mineral rich area. Compared to the coastal tracts the area yields scattered and weaker evidence. Viratgarh or the mound of Khiching situated about 150 kilometres to the north-west of Baripada on the Orissa-Jharkhand border in Mayurbhanja, and Sitabinji in Keonjhar district are the two important sites in the terrain. The former was excavated in the 1920's and has yielded unstratified early historic antiquities,[21] while the latter site bears a tempera painting showing a royal procession. The name of the king is mentioned as *mahārāja* Śri Disabhanja. There are archaeological ruins in the neighbourhood. Both these sites, among others, in these districts have produced Puri-Kuṣāṇa coins, which are also available in the coastal districts and broadly placed in the second–fifth centuries AD. The probability of a trade route traversing from the Singbhum area in Jharkand to littoral Orissa and Andhra through the territory under discussion looks feasible, largely because of the local mines. The next important piece of evidence from the area under discussion is the Asanpat Natarāja image inscription of Satrubhañja, dated to the sixth–seventh century.[22] His parents *Mahārāja* Manabhañja and the queen Mahādevi Damayanti of Naga lineage are mentioned in it. He bears the epithet *Vindhyāṭavinātha* or the lord of Vindhyāṭavi, suggesting a state in the hilly forest region in Keonjhar district. It essentially records the achievements of Satrubhanja, including his donations at holy places in Bengal, Bihar and both the Toṣalis in Orissa, among others. His generosity is manifest in the patronage he extended to recluses from Brāhmaṇical to Buddhist, Jaina, and other communities, and gift of lakhs of cows and *hiraṇya.* He is said to have studied the *Bhārata, Purāṇa, Itihāsa, Srūti,* grammar, and so on, and finally built a temple for god. The kings effort to reach out to various communities, the circulation and even dominance of Brāhmaṇical and purāṇic ideas, including gift making, and association with god and temple suggest the movement towards a complex society in the locality. There may have been variations in scale but these changes in a jungle kingdom would have been possible owing to change in local inheritance and wider interactions leading to cultural adaptations.[23] Besides, the jungle state surely needed some sedentary agrarian foundation, implying peasantization and other related developments.

The Ādi Bhañja inscriptions provide continued manifestation of the aforesaid processes. On the basis of the place names mentioned in the land grant inscriptions and their find spots it appears that Khijjiṅga *maṇḍala* included parts of Keonjhar and Mayurbhanja districts in Orissa and Singbhum in Jharkhand. About half a dozen donative charters record grants to brāhmaṇas. These are all made to individual donees. There are three others of a non-religious nature. Some of the epigraphs do mention about the father and grand father of the beneficiary, while some refer to their immigrant status along with their place of origin (both the Adipur plates of Narendrabhañja). For example, the second Adipur plate of

Narendrabhañja informs that the recipient came from Oḍra *viṣaya*, and the Kesari plate of Satrubhanja records that the migrant brāhmaṇa hailed from Madhyadeśa. One notices the gift of *grāmas* or villages in all cases. However, the boundaries or *chatuḥsimā* have not been specified in any land grant. It may suggest sparse habitation and settlements, together with the possibilities of the extension of the agrarian frontier in a situation of undefined land transfers. That is how it has happened all through Indian history. There are interesting place names such as Vṛhat-sarai, Svalpa-sarai, Jamvu *padraka-grāma*, Brāhmaṇa vasti, Pagurasila *pāṭaka-grāma* and Panchapalī. Some of these may help us to map the possible changes in the spatial dimensions of rural settlements. *Palī* stands for a hamlet, *padraka* for a small habitation with fewer houses, and *pāṭaka* for a part of a village. Some of these from modest beginnings could always grow into villages. V(B)asti represents an inhabited spatial segment, and if that is true there is the unusual evidence of a Brāhmaṇa vasti village being gifted to a *sāmanta* (Bamanghati plate of Rajabhanja). Very few privileges and exemptions were transferred to the donees. In some instances the grant was made along with water and land (*sa-jala-sthala*), or bushes and creepers, and rarely we come across evidence indicating that with all obstacles removed or free from all oppressions the grant was made (Adipur plate of Durjayabhanja, Adipur plate of Narendrabhañja). Luckily, one of the land grant charters bears more details of the privileges conferred on the brāhmaṇa donee. In addition to mentioning the revenue terms such as *uparikara* and *uddeśa*, it further states that the weavers, cowherds, brewers and other people (*tantuvāya-gokuṭa-śauṇḍik-ādikam-prakṛtika*) were transferred with the land (Adipur plate of Narendrabhanja). The grant was made in keeping with the principle of *bhūmicchidra-apidhāna-nyāya*, which may mean bringing virgin land under cultivation. Despite references to the exemptions and the presence of certain occupational groups it needs to be reiterated that it is only one piece of evidence. The rulers do not refer to the mines, minerals or forest products of the *maṇḍala*. Usually they did not assume pompous titles, and described themselves as inhabitants of Khijjiṅgakoṭṭā (*Khijjiṅga-koṭṭā-vāsi*). The records of the major dynasties in central coastal Orissa do not seem to refer to this area, not to mention making grants there. The backward, forested sub-region seems to have been in an early stage of development.

Discussion

Complexities in the domain of rural society and rural settlements in Khijjiṅga *maṇḍala* were not of the same scale as obtained for Kaliṅga or even the adjoining territories. Kaliṅga finds reference in the inscriptional records of several contemporary ruling lineages across the country. Parts of a settlement or even plots of land, known by various terms, were donated there. The density of settlements was greater and the history of migrant donees was not too visible. Sub-regional specificities or dissimilarities notwithstanding, there were comparable economic and socio-political processes across the sub-regions. The forward movement of the peasant frontier, varieties of rural settlements, spatially and socially, and the spread of Brāhmaṇical ideology and epic-purāṇic ideas were some of the common mutually interacting societal processes of change. However, having said that, the uneven patterns across spaces can not be brushed aside. Nor can for that matter some of the issues relating to agrarian expansion and the movement of brāhmaṇas be glossed over. Brāhmaṇas seem to have been already there in rural settlements in Kaliṅga as can be gleaned in the references to them in the list of addressees continuously. Besides, in the period under discussion there are no references to migrant brāhmaṇas from distant places in the area under discussion. Brāhmaṇas indubitably came to Orissa in large numbers[24] but not always and not to every sub-region or kingdom at all times. Thus, there was unevenness in the spatial and temporal spread of migrant brāhmaṇas. That rural society had acquired a measure of complexity from the middle of the first millennium AD onwards can be seen from the hierarchy of peasants and occupational/caste groups, not to speak of the dominant land owning *sāmanta* and/or *bhōgi* categories. The modest land donations, mostly up to a *grāma,* in both the areas under study attract attention. The quantum of grant surely impacts the extent of socio-economic churning, notwithstanding the total number of grants; which are spread over several centuries. Besides, it may be useful to remember that the granted area was only a modest part of the total area under cultivation.[25] In fact, agrarian expansion does not emerge to be the sole motivation for the land grants. In Kaliṅga most of the donations were made in settled habitations. References to certain measures of land, pockets or parts of a settlement clearly allude in that direction. The story may be different in the comparatively backward

Khijjiṅgakoṭṭā *maṇḍala* with its experience of migrant brāhmaṇas and the usual transfer of full settlements or *grāma*s in all cases. Issues of royal legitimation and ideology appear to have been as much or more important in these transactions. Brāhmaṇas like temples and *maṭhas* later were significant negotiators in the domain of ideas and cultural values.

It emerges that the study of historical subregions can and should be an area of concerted engagement. Kaliṅga all through provides a history of gradual, phased evolution of the agrarian structure, rural settlements and rural society. This holds true for Kaliṅga as a whole or even the two halves of Kaliṅga, that is, south and north Kaliṅga, the latter being also known by other names such as Kongoda *maṇḍala* and Dakṣiṇa Toṣali. Admittedly, we have not gone fully into the tenth century and beyond, which is possible. In fact, an uninterrupted narrative can go on to include parts of the imperial kingdom of the Gaṅgās (twelfth–fifteenth centuries) or even the Gajapatis (mid fifteenth–mid sixteenth centuries). Thus, the study of sub-regions based on inscriptions holds the possibility of providing a long-term vision of history. The picture is dissimilar in the case of Khijjiṅgakoṭṭā *maṇḍala* insofar as it is not continuous, staggered and the evidence quite thin. It may have to partly do with the physiography of the area and partly how historical forces converged there. The donation of *grāma*s in all cases to migrant individual brāhmaṇas, without delimitation of their boundaries, attracts attention. The exemptions provided to the recipients of land-grants were strikingly few, barring one noticeable exception. The Adipur plate of Narendrabhañja records the transfer of *uparika* and *uddeśa* along with weavers, cowherds, brewers and other inhabitants. The combined evidence for low density of settlements, few revenue and administrative terms and the shifting of occupational groups together with the land, among others, fits in well with the late evolution of political society in a jungle kingdom. A comparative study of sub-regions unmistakably demonstrates the problems of differentiated spaces, their uneven patterns of growth even within a region; and the problems in the shaping and construction of regions in early medieval/medieval India.[26] Besides, it also helps us to transcend modern administrative and political boundaries, focus on historical spatial entities and address and resolve state-specific sub-national stereotypes. It is this movement away from the larger, standardized, grand neat pictures towards an understanding of the regional intricacies that has been phrased as 'shifting the gaze'.

Notes

1. B.D. Chattopadhyaya, 'Origin of the Rajputs; The Political, Economic and Social Processes in Early Medieval Rajasthan', *The Indian Historical Review*, vol. 3, no. 1, 1976, pp. 59–82; idem., 'Political Processes and the Structure of Polity in Early Medieval India', Presidential Address, Ancient India Section, *Proceedings of the Indian History Congress*, Burdwan session, 1983; idem., *Aspects of Rural Settlements and Rural Society in Early Medieval India,* Calcutta, Centre for Studies in Social Sciences, 1990; H. Kulke, 'Early State Formation and Royal Legitimation in Late Ancient Orissa', in M.N. Das (ed.), *Side Lights on History and Culture of Orissa*, Cuttack, Vidyapuri, 1977, 104–14; idem., 'Fragmentation and Segmentation *versus* Integration: Reflections on the Concept of Indian Feudalism and the Segmentary State in Indian History', *Studies in History*, vol. 4, no. 2, 1982, 237–63; idem., 'The Early State and the Imperial Kingdom: A Processural Model of Integrative State formation in Early Medieval India', in idem. (ed.), *The State in India, 1000–1700,* New Delhi, Oxford University Press, 1995, 233–62; B.P. Sahu (ed.), *Land System and Rural Society in Early India,* Delhi, Manohar 1997, 1–58; C. Talbot, *Pre-Colonial India in Practice, Society, Region and Identity in Medieval Andhra*, New York, Oxford University Press, 2001.

2. D.D. Kosambi, *An Introduction to the Study of Indian History*, Bombay, Popular Prakashan, 1956; R.S. Sharma, *Indian Feudalism c.* AD *300–1200*, Calcutta, Macmillan, 1965.

3. Ibid. R.S. Sharma, *Urban Decay in India (300–1000),* New Delhi, Munshiram Manoharlal, 1987; idem., *Early Medieval Indian Society: A Study in Feudalization*, Calcutta, Orient Longman, 2001; B.N.S. Yadava, *Society and Culture of Northern India in the Twelfth Century*, Allahabad, Central Book Depot, 1973; idem., 'The Problem of the Emergence of Feudal Relations in Early India', Presidential Address, Ancient India section, *PIHC,* Bombay session, 1980, pp. 19–78.

4. See B.D. Chattopadhyaya, *The Making of Early Medieval India,* New Delhi, Oxford University Press, 1994; idem., 'State and Economy in North India: Fourth Century to Twelfth Century', in Romila Thapar (ed.), *Recent Perspectives of Early Indian History,* Bombay, Popular Prakashan, 1995, 309–46.

5. See for example A.P. Sah, *Life in Medieval Orissa (c.* AD. *600–1200)*, Varanasi, 1976; R.C. Misro, *Rural Economy and Society of Ancient Orissa (c.* AD *400–1000)*, Calcutta, Punthi Pustak, 2002.

6. Sharma, *Indian Feudalism*, Appendix I.

7. B.P. Sahu, 'Agrarian Changes and the Peasantry in Early Medieval Orissa (*c.* AD 400–1100)', in V.K. Thakur and A. Aounshuman (eds), *Peasants in Indian History (Essays in Memory of Professor R.K. Choudhary)*, Patna, Janaki Prakashan, 1996, pp. 283–311.

8. Kulke, 'Early State Formation and Royal Legitimation in Late Ancient Orissa'; B.P. Sahu, 'Arguing for Feudalism from Below: A Study in Orissa Setting

(*c.* AD 400–1100)', *PIHC,* Calcutta session, 1990, 141–50; and U. Singh, *Kings, Brāhmaṇas and Temples in Orissa: An Epigraphic Study,* AD *300–1147,* New Delhi, Munshiram Manoharlal, 1994.

9. For a recent comprehensive discussion see Martin Brandtner, 'Representations of Kaliṅga: The Changing Image and Geography of a Historical Region', in H. Kulke and B. Schnepel (eds), *Jagannātha Revisited: Studying Society, Religion and the State in Orissa,* New Delhi, Manohar, 2001, pp. 179–210.

10. B.P. Sahu, 'The Early State in Orissa: From the Perspective of Changing Forms of Patronage and Legitimation', in B. Pati, B.P. Sahu, and T.K. Venkatasubramanian (eds), *Negotiating India's Past: Essays in Memory of Partha Sarathi Gupta,* New Delhi, Tulika, 2003, pp. 29–51.

11. For example, see Chattopadhyaya, 'State and Economy in North India'; Kulke, 'Early State Formation and Royal Legitimation in Late Ancient Orissa'.

12. S. Tripathy, 'Introduction', in her *Inscriptions of Orissa,* vol. I, Delhi, 1997.

References to inscriptions in Kaliṅga are to Tripathy, 1997 and S.N. Rajaguru, *Inscriptions of Orissa (c. 300–700),* vol. I, pt 2, Berhampur, Orissa State Museum, 1958, and, idem., *Inscriptions of Orissa (c. 600–1100),* vol. II, Bhubaneswar, Orissa State Museum, 1960.

13. Sircar, '*Kraya Śāsana* and *Kara Śāsana*', in idem., *Studies in the Political and Administrative Systems in Ancient and Medieval India,* Delhi, Motilal Banarsidass, 1974, pp. 66–75.

14. Tripathy, *Inscriptions of Orissa,* vol. I.

15. See R. Chakarabarti, '*Kuṭumbikas* of Early India', in Thakur and Aounshuman (eds), *Peasants in Indian History,* pp. 179–98.

16. See Rajaguru, *Inscriptions of Orissa,* vol. I, pt 2.

17. U. Singh, *Kings, Brāhmaṇas and Temples.*

18. For details of the argument, see A.K. Choudhary, *Early Medieval Village in North-Eastern India (AD. 600–1200),* Calcutta, 1971; B.D. Chattopadhyaya, *Aspects of Rural Settlements.*

19. U. Singh, *Kings, Brāhmaṇas and Temples,* ch. 3.

20. Chattopadhyaya, *Aspects of Rural Settlements,* ch. 2.

21. P. Acharya, *Studies in Orissan History, Archaeology and Archives,* Cuttack, 1969.

22. See Rajaguru, *Inscriptions of Orissa,* vol I, pt 2.; Tripathy, *Inscriptions of Orissa,* vol. I.

Reference to inscriptions in this section are to S. Tripathy, *Inscriptions of Orissa,* vol. VI, Bhubaneswar, 1974.

23. For rich discussions of the conceptual dimensions of the issue, see Chattopadhyaya, 'State's Perception of the "Forest" and the "Forest" as State in Early India', in B.B. Chaudhury and Arun Bandopadhyaya (eds), *Tribes, Forest and Social Formation in Early Indian History,* Delhi, 2004, pp. 23–37; B.D. Chattopadhyaya, 'Space, History and Cultural Process: Some Ideas of the Ingredients of Subregional

"Identity"', in H. Kulke and Georg Berkemer (eds), *Centres Out There? Facets of Subregional Identities in Orissa*, New Delhi, Manohar, 2011, pp. 21–38.

24. See Swati Datta, *Migrant Brāhmaṇas in Northern India, c.* AD *475–1030*, Delhi, 1989.

25. Even in Tamil Nadu with its numerous land-grants it is suggested that the donated area amounted to about 20 per cent of the area under cultivation. See Y. Subbarayalu, 'The Place of Ur in the Economic and Social History of Early Tamilnadu, AD 750–1350', in A.V.N. Murthy and B.K. Gururaja Rao (eds), *Rangavalli: Recent Researches of Indology*, Delhi, 1983, pp. 171–7.

26. For the larger argument, see B.P. Sahu, 'Profiling Dakṣiṇa Kośala: An Early Historical Sub-Region?', in H. Kulke and Georg Berkemer (eds), *Centres Out There?*, pp. 39–59; B.P. Sahu, 'Brāhmaṇical Ideology, Regional Identities and the Construction of Early India', Presidential Address, Ancient Section, Punjab History Conference, Patiala, March 2001, *Social Scientist*, vol. 29, nos 7–8, 2001, 3–18; and Chattopadhyaya, 'Introduction', in idem., *The Making of Early Medieval India*.

12

Dissent and Protest in Early Indian Societies

Some Historiographic Remarks*

Dissent is generally defined as emotional resentment of individuals against the established order though there is little conscious effort towards a systematic social action, while in protest, despite its commonality in terms of emotional unhappiness with dissent, there is a difference in kind insofar as it usually involves groups and the degree of concerted social action is greater and planned, including mobilization largely owing to the spread and depth of awareness. Protest against the cultural ends and institutional means of achieving them in specific societies is at the root of all social movements. Movements in terms of their typology are categorized as reform movements, transformatory movements and revolutions. Reform movements in seeking to change some aspects of the societal goals and the means to achieve them so as to make life tolerable, while accepting the larger contours of the established order are perceived to be operating within the constitutional or normative order of society. In reality they involve change in society through acceptable or legitimate means resulting in some form of patch works so as to make the old order function better. Nevertheless, the resentment against the existing order is quite visible. Movements involving more intense sense of deprivation and manifesting greater collective opposition to, even rejection of, contemporary societal norms, traditions and institutions

*This essay was originally the Keynote Address, at the National Seminar on Social Protest Movements in Orissa since Early Times, organized by Department of History, Berhampur University, Berhampur, 12–14 March 2011.

with bearing on changes of a structural nature are characterized as transformatory in nature. A total rejection of the cultural ethos and basic structures of society, leading to it being turned upside down, is a movement of a higher kind and is called a revolution.[1] There is no unilinear relationship between the typologies of movements discussed above. The motives, the means of actualizing them and the final consequences in the annals of contestations and negotiations enable one to determine the nature of the movement.

It may be useful to ask what is that Indian societies have protested against through time. We need to address the question whether there has been a singular tradition common to the country since the Harappan civilization or Vedic times, or if what is seen as a common pool of ideas and values was constituted through continuous multilateral networks of interactions and change across regions. In fact, there is no monolithic cultural tradition, it is a veritable mosaic. Our cultural antecedents are several, including the autochthonous inheritances. Flowing from it, all social protests and opposition to values and institutions need to be located in the varied regional contexts. Like the harmonic, cooperative view of Indian society earlier the conflict perspective focusing on antagonistic cooperation, contradictions and tensions assumed a dominant position from the later part of the 1960s through the 1980s when the peasant and his world became central to analytical studies in social sciences. Maximization of tax/rent, subjection and exploitation of the peasantry across societies through economic and extra economic means, it is said, led to protests of varied intensities. It needs to be remembered that often it is not one causative factor but several which lead to social eruptions such as protests. Similarly, in the shaping of regional cultural landscapes through processes of interaction conflict was only one form of manifestation among many others. For pre-modern times historians painstakingly cull their material from texts and inscriptions, often privileging the latter for a variety of standard reasons. However, inscriptions, including the land-grant charters, are also texts of a kind and may not necessarily reflect the historical reality in its entirety. Finally, to conclude these qualifying statements it needs to be said, what should be obvious, that in Indian history protest movements usually after peaking have got integrated with general society, changing society by a bit in the process. Differentiation and integration have been integral to Indian tradition throughout.

Barring a few instances of revolt against the king by the subject population, normally led by the brāhmaṇas, which one encounters in the Buddhist Jātaka stories[2] most of the material relating to what have been described as peasant protests come from the early medieval centuries. The spread of the *brahmadeyas* in the second half of the first millennium AD is usually perceived to have been a peaceful process. It may be plausible to suggest that agrarian expansion and the movement of Brāhmaṇical ideology must have built on and not entirely escaped opposition and conflict. Intrusion of these ideas and institutions would have carefully blended coercion and persuasion. One of the earliest evidence of resistance and encroachment of *brahmadeyas* is recorded in the Dalavaypuram plates of the early Pāṇḍyas.[3] It mentions that an *ekabhōga-brahmadeya* was appropriated by the native śūdras and the act was supported by the neighbouring clan leaders. The king's intervention had to be sought to regain the old possessions. Interestingly, the encroached *ekabhōga-brahmadeyas* in the process of being restored were converted into corporate *brahmadeyas*;[4] against which there is no evidence for violation and appropriation. The Koragas who have been recognized as a primitive tribe live in the Udupi and Dakṣiṇa Kannada districts of Karnataka and the Kasaragod district of Kerala. In the locally popular story Hubbāśika, a Koraga king of yore, is said to have ruled the same territory. The masters of the land subsequently following a misfortune caused by the Brāhmaṇical upper castes and their representatives lost it all to become a depressed class. Notwithstanding the local variations among the versions preserved and cherished by the Koragas, and the divergence among scholars about the date and origins of Hubbāśika, it is interesting that the account finds corroboration in the Brāhmaṇical tradition; adding again to the variations in the available versions. The convergence in the essential details of the narrative across different versions and parties, presumably antagonistic, attracts attention insofar as it lends historicity to the event.[5] The attachment to the glorious past, out of which they were cheated through an act of treachery, serves to not only compensate for their toiling present but may also be seen to constitute an expression of protest against their lived experiences.

Peoples' protests against their oppressors found ventilation in the course of royal movements too. The country folk while greeting Harṣa on the move also complained against the *bhōgapatis* and oppressive officials in charge of the villages, and desired the protection of their crops and ripe grains.[6] A clearer case of revolt is seen in the case of the Kaivartas of Bengal under the Pālas. *Rāmacarita* of Sandhyakara Nandi in narrating the achievements of Ramapāla describes his suppression of the Kaivarta revolt, first led by Divyoka and later by his nephew Bhima at the end of the eleventh century.[7] Alienation of land and heavy taxation appear to have triggered the rebellion. The revolt ultimately transformed the status of the Kaivartas from *antyaja* (untouchable) to sat śūdra and seems to have allowed them to shift from fishing to agriculture in terms of occupation. This transformation is articulated in later day literature.[8] Admittedly, it is not easy to discern the aims and objectives of the revolt, which was fought hard on both sides and its nature has also been debated.[9] It is said that what has been depicted in the *Rāmacarita* was not a peasant revolt but a conflict over the large Varendra region, which included parts of Rajshahi, Malda, Dinajpur, Bogra, and Rangpur districts of Bengal, between the autochthonous Kaivartas and the reigning Pālas who enlisted the support of several *sāmantas*. Interestingly, a few of them were located in the Varendra region. In brief, it is envisaged as a struggle between an expanding, intrusive state and assertion of indigenous rights and local autonomy.

Coercion by the *bhōgapatis* leading to the misery of the peasant proprietors is recorded in the *Subhāṣita-ratnakoṣa.* Similar instances of oppression are reported in the *Rājataraṅgiṇi* and *Lekhapaddhati.* Circumstances as mentioned in the texts resulted in protests and conflicts. Evidence for peasant suffering and the consequent desertion of the villages, as a mark of protest, has been brought to light by B.N.S. Yadava[10] from literary texts largely located in northern India. Through the ages it has been a potent weapon of the weak. It has been suggested that in contemporary literature there is evidence to show that expressions of disaffection were largely led by the economically non-privileged brāhmaṇas. Similarly, the Ḍāmaras in Kashmir before becoming a part of the status quo were armed peasants in upheaval against the *sāmantas* and the king.

North India does not provide much material for our understanding of social protest during the early medieval period. Most of it comes from outside the Gangetic valley. The possible reason for that may be the operation of the numerous processes of change, including state formation, agrarian expansion, peasantization of the autochthons, among others,[11] precisely outside that orbit during the same period. Tamil Nadu under the Cōḷas presents several examples of reactions to oppression and suffering by the people especially during the late twelfth and thirteenth centuries. The Pāṇḍyan invasion was followed by agitations (*kṣobham*) in parts of Tanjore district, the heart of the state. There was turmoil during the reign of Rajaraja III. Kulottunga III too was confronted with peasant struggles against brāhmaṇa and veḷḷāḷa landlords. He issued prohibitory orders decreeing that these struggles should end and that the violators of the order should be heavily fined.[12] Temple records were destroyed and deeds lost leading to the renewal of titles in many cases. Cases of self-immolation, including those by *devadasis*, are also reported. Expressions such as *rājadroha* and *rājadrohins* in the inscriptional records of the times are self explanatory. Evidently, the last phase of the Cōḷas was marked by social cleavage and ruptures. Karnataka and adjoining Rayalaseema in Andhra Pradesh have also yielded epigraphic data bearing on the issue and R.N. Nandi[13] has analysed them in their varied contexts. A mid-thirteenth century inscription refers to the refusal of the *gauḍa* peasants to accept new brāhmaṇa landlords with the conversion of their village to a brāhmaṇa free-holding. What ensued was the pillaging of the village by the king's army. In many cases *vīragals* or hero-stones were erected to honour the memory of the deceased who laid down their lives fighting for the cause of the community against brāhmaṇa freeholders and feudatories on matters relating to land and irrigation tanks. Examples of *sāmanta*-brāhmaṇa conflicts as well as the state being party to some of these dating to the twelfth–fourteenth centuries have been lucidly discussed by Nandi.

Notwithstanding all the evidence for dissent and protest or everyday forms of resistance that have been put together, there is hardly any incontrovertible proof for organized peasant revolt. Two copies of the same inscription dated AD 1429 have been reported from two different places (Aduthurai and Kil-paluvur) in Tiruchirapalli district and they significantly record the first clearly attested peasant revolt in Tamil Nadu.[14] It is said to have been an open revolt by the lower peasantry against the landlords and government officials, including the local Vijayanagara Governor. The spark for this outburst was provided by the introduction of a new measuring rod, which was to the peasant's disadvantage. Similarly, inscriptions from South Arcot and Thanjavur districts bear testimony to revolts of the Valaṅgai and Iḍaṅgai groups against the brāhmaṇa and veḷḷāḷa landlords as also the government.[15] The thirteenth to the fifteenth centuries have been envisaged as a transitional period witnessing socio-economic changes after the decline of the Cōḷa state. Particularly the thirteenth–fourteenth centuries experienced several overlapping changes. The change in Cōḷa expansionist policy led to soldiers turning to agriculture, which had a bearing on land sale. Recovery of the state's tax dues simultaneously led to the sale or auction of agricultural land. There was a concomitance of economic prosperity, deriving from overseas trade, and the power acquired by the hill-tribes, artisans, and merchants from the thirteenth century onwards. It was a period which coincided with the formation of *jātis* in the Tamil country. The oppression by the Vijayanagara administrators was supported by the brāhmaṇa and veḷḷāḷa landlords who sided with them, and this was met by popular revolts. It is in the context of a society in transition and the fashioning of a new social formation that the above said conflicts have been situated.[16] The coming of the Nāyaka system towards the end of the fifteenth century in Tamil Nadu seems to signify the new order.

The information for peasant resistance, especially those up to the thirteenth century, has not necessarily been perceived within a homogeneous perspective. Whereas R.S. Sharma and Yadav situate them within the larger framework of Indian feudalism by focusing on rising taxes, forced labour, restrictions on community rights, and the increasing suffering and misery of the peasantry, R.N. Nandi locates them in agrarian growth, better agricultural technology, more crop production, and the emergence of markets and towns. It is argued that there was prosperity propelled by the dynamism of the early medieval times, but that it fell short of the overlapping claims of the peasants, brāhmaṇa donees, *sāmanta*s and the state. Each wanted to benefit most from the growth of rural economy, leading to multi-cornered confrontations.[17] The envisaged trajectory of socio-economic transformations in early medieval Karnataka finds corroboration in several regional studies. It may be in the fitness of things to mention that besides the contradictions generated within the womb of the contemporary social formations, natural and man-made calamities such as famines, floods, and the ravages of war too contributed to people's deprivations and resentment. Inscriptions of Kulottunga II and Rajaraja III dated to the late twelfth and first half of the thirteenth century refer to famines caused by drought, along with widespread food scarcity.[18] There are many records mentioning floods in the Kaveri which laid waste huge tracts of temple land. Cases of the desertion of villages owing to famine conditions have also been captured in the epigraphic material. There is an instance of the brāhmaṇa beneficiaries' land being occupied in their absence during famine and the Cōḷa feudatory had to be invoked to restore their land to them through a renewal of the grant.[19] The gradual expansion of agrarian economy, growing population, *hāṭṭa*s, *peṅṭhā*s, and *maṇḍi*s, and towns from the seventh–tenth centuries onwards; across regions beyond Gangetic northern India generated its own pressures.[20] For this to happen it took a few centuries and not surprisingly therefore the evidence for protest surfaces only at the beginning of the second millennium. That said, it needs to be recognized that the available information has an uneven spread. It may have to do with regional cultural traditions, social structures, and the early or late evolution of historical societies and so on. Besides, we are dealing with what may be termed as official sources.

Historians have addressed the question of the meagre, if not absence of, evidence. The spread of the *Gītā* and Bhakti movements, which focused on duty and not rights, *varṇa* and gender hierarchy in the case of the former and total surrender at the feet of the lord by the *bhakta* and illusory equality in the latter instance, it is said, had much to do with people's voices being muted. Tantricism and the mother goddess cults similarly in the tribal frontiers seem to have negotiated and reconciled contestations.[21] Temples as meeting places and melting pots of varied influences, centres of *kathā, kīrtana,* collective performances and cultural communication and transmission played an important role in engendering a sense of conformism. The spread of state societies and local state formation from the middle of the first millennium AD onwards in pre-state areas; within the framework of Brāhmaṇical ideology also facilitated the spread of Vedic-epic-purāṇic-śāstric ideas.[22] These ideas along with the caste system and its logic of inheritability of virtues and the theory of *karma* created generations after generations who were averse to questioning the status quo. In brief, systematic ideological interventions in the cultural domain are believed to have domesticated the masses. Buddhist *vihāra*s and Jaina *basadi*s too were not impervious to changes such as these.[23]

Efforts at indoctrination, to feed into the strategies of domination apart, social protest nonetheless found articulation in the garb of religious movements. The Bhakti movement in its early stages was critical of the established religions, Buddhism and Brāhmaṇism alike; it rejected abstract metaphysics and was usually indifferent to caste norms. In its productive phase between the seventh and ninth centuries Bhakti represented a spirit of equality. It was quite remarkable that Nantanar, the paṛaiya, could enter a temple even after undergoing a series of ordeals. The willingness to dispense with rituals, priests, and discriminations based on caste and gender highlight the protest inherent in the movement against the order based on *varṇāśramadharma.*[24] With the emergence of *maṭhas,* temples as landed magnets and *ācharyas*; and the eclipse of the Aḷvār and the Nāyanār Bhakti saints the movement suffered in terms of its counter hegemonic character and there was a gradual return to orthodoxy by the tenth century. The Vīraśaiva or Liṅgayat movement which acquired visibility around the end of the twelfth and the beginning of the thirteenth century in north-west Karnataka gradually spread to other parts of Karnataka and Andhra Pradesh. It is envisaged to have been the product of the emerging contradictions discussed above insofar as it voiced opposition to Brāhmaṇism and was an overtly fraternal association cutting across caste distinctions and drawing its social support from the peasants, artisans, manufacturers, and traders.[25] Their strategy involved the creation of alternative cultural and ritual symbols, rejection of the Vedic rituals, pilgrimage, child marriage, including the ceremony of the sacred thread. The leaders of the movement encouraged interdining and intermarriage, involving even the untouchable converts; and permitted widow remarriage. They respected the trinity of the *guru,* Śiva *liṅga,* and *jaṅgama* (his wandering mendicant). Beyond a point, however, it lost its vigour and began to resemble the caste system based on social inheritance, ascribed qualities and cleanliness of profession. What is significant, however, is that the Vīraśaiva movement did not show signs of cleavage almost until the seventeenth century.

The *sant* movement in northern India usually associated with the names of Kabir, Namdev, Raidas, and Dadu, the great *sant*s of the fifteenth–sixteenth centuries, straddled the seventeenth and eighteenth centuries as well. The movement was iconoclastic, nonconformist and radical giving vent to popular aspirations during the first three centuries, including the seventeenth century. Its popularity was based on a following cutting through caste, regional and linguistic boundaries among lower caste people. It was against Brāhmaṇical dominance and caste hierarchy, and the followers of the *sants* wished to alter the terms of their subordination.[26] In course of the eighteenth century like other comparable movements this also suffered sectarianization and Hinduization. These instances make the more general point that resistance movements after a point could not sustain their radical tempo and became a part of everyday life.

As one moves into early Orissa unmistakable evidence for conflicts and social ruptures is rather weak, though the medieval times were marked by literary and religious movements, which are said to have subsumed varying shades of social radicalism and protest. Lest one gets the impression that it was an entirely harmonious society, it needs to be mentioned that despite the absence of evidence it does not require great imagination to visualize that the relationship between the non-producing, brāhmaṇa free-holders, *sāmanta*s and the state on the one hand and the grades of peasants (*mahāmahattara, mahattara, kuṭumbin, prakṛtika, prativāsin,* and so on) on the other; even in the best of times would have been one of antagonistic co-operation. In the inscriptions of the high state officials of the Imperial Gaṅgās in Kaliṅga one notices the occurrence of titles which possibly have something to do with the real or imagined enemies of the state. A Telugu inscription from Srikurmam dated AD 1321 recording the donation of a perpetual lamp uses some significant titles for the donor. It reads *kaliṅggarakṣapalaku meli bhaṁjana* (he who crushes the insurrections for the protector of Kaliṅga), *kaṃḍavāla* (= *khaṇḍāpāla*) *sīrascedana* (he who splits the skulls of the sword-bearers), *komddumarḍḍana* (killer of the Khoṇḍs), and there are other terms which have been translated as deliverer of heroes and lion of the mountains.[27] This can simply be dismissed as *praśasti* or eulogy material or seen to somewhat represent the donor who crushed his enemies and was the victorious ally of his lord. In the latter case there are possible pointers to popular unrest and trouble from the Khonds. A local traditional account mentions that Pratapa-Bhanja, the ruler of Gumsur (Khiñjali *maṇḍala)*, captured the Khoṇḍ chief of Kulada during the twelfth century and built a big fort there at great expense. There is yet another inscription from Srikurmam dated to the end of the thirteenth century referring to its defense by Naraharitirtha, the governor of Kaliṅga, against an attack of the Sabaras. These instances manifest the hostility of the tribes against aspects of state society, overtly pointing to the fact that socio-political integration was not a smooth, unhindered process but involved contestation as well. However, unlike

Andhra, Kaliṅga does not seem to have experienced the commemoration of heroes who died fighting for the community or the institution of hero-stone.[28]

The entrenchment and spread of the Oriya vernacular in course of the fifteenth and sixteenth centuries, best manifested in the writings of Sāralā Das and what is traditionally known as the *pañca-śakhās* who not only rendered the *Mahābhārata,* and *Ramayana,* in the regional language but also went on to enrich it with many more literary productions. Besides the important contributions of scholars of Oriya literature, R.K. Das is perhaps the earliest historian to conceive of the said literary efflorescence in terms of social protest. He saw this new knowledge production as constituting some kind of an inversion of the established norms and values insofar as they represented the autochthonous and folk tradition of the region as against the dominant Brāhmaṇical order. The use of the vernacular, four of the *pañca-śakhā* coming from a śūdra and not brāhmaṇa or upper caste background, the importance accorded to the sabara, non-brāhmaṇa, priests in the legendary origin of Jagannātha in their writings, their encounters with the brāhmaṇa guardians of society and the opposition and persecution they suffered at their hands for questioning caste hierarchy and making religious texts available to the common people; taken together has been perceived to constitute a sustained protest movement in the garb of the ascendancy of the vernacular.[29] Almost agreeing with Das, B.K. Mallik over the years has attributed radical qualities to these literary figures and their works, which supposedly produced far reaching consequences. In the process Mallik seems to have absorbed Das to the point of having consumed him almost entirely. It is not just that their views on the issue are similar; together they have opened up an area which is full of possibilities. Mallik differs from Das insofar as he formalized the thesis by marshalling new literary evidence from time to time, and refined aspects of the argument through a series of publications, including a monograph.[30] The movement is seen to have been spearheaded against *varṇa* society, dominated by Brāhmaṇism, and Sanskrit language and literature. The overt opposition to the literary products and humiliation of the authors for democratizing literature, including what was perceived as sacred, the regional adaptation of the *Mahābhārata* and its social implications for women and peasants, and society at large; and their contribution to the forging of local and sub-regional identities have been discussed at length.

It may be useful to remember that issues such as mass literacy and the movement under discussion having led towards it need to be treated with caution. In the pre-print cultures production of copies of manuscripts was neither easy nor cheap. Even today just about 17 per cent of the population has access to higher education in the country, and here the context is fifteenth–sixteenth centuries Orissa which might have been a largely face to face society. Among the *pañca-śakhās* Jaganath Das was a brāhmaṇa and the son of a *purāṇa paṇḍā*, while Balaram Das who claims to be a śūdra was son of Somnath Mahapatra, a minister of the *rājā*. Given their family backgrounds they might have been familiar with the traditional learning in Sanskrit and subsequently brought it to bear on their effective use of the vernacular. Sanskrit being the language of official communication and public discourse in Orissa was nothing unique. It was so in large parts of the subcontinent and beyond through the first millennium AD and a little after, a situation which has been beautifully captured under the expression 'the Sanskrit cosmopolis', from where the vernaculars started taking over largely in the first half of the second millennium.[31] The gradual shift towards the vernaculars and their ascendancy had much to do with the making of cultural regions and regional identities.[32] Certain social groups desiring a voice and visibility gradually create new languages and texts, or in other words there may have been a concomitance of these processes. The creation and articulation of coherent images of vernacular domains and their symmetry with simultaneous historical processes helped in the shaping of new identities.[33] The idea of Oḍradeśa was defined by the *Utkalamahātmya* in the fourteenth century with some clarity when it described its spatial spread with reference to its four centres: Konarka, Purushōṭṭama (Puri), Ekāmra and Vīrajā (Jaipur).[34] Significantly, the people of contemporary Orissa were being referred to as Oḍḍiyar in south Indian records,[35] while Sāralā Das was providing them with a comparable identity. But it may be good to remember that it is the socio-historical processes that actually informed these developments.

Chaitanya, the Vaiṣḥnava saint-cum-reformer, arrived in the region around the same time. The *pañca-śakhās* having become his disciples renounced their castes. What attracts attention is that like the Vīraśaivas in Karnataka earlier he too had a substantial following among the brāhmaṇas, officials and high castes. Surnames or status markers of his followers such as Pandit, Patnaik, Mohanty, Ācharya, Miśra, *Dwija*,

Bipra are more than suggestive on this count.[36] It is difficult to be specific about the overall impact of the Vaiṣḥnava movement under Chaitanya spanning two decades, especially because it overlapped with that of the literati and many people came to visualize Jagannātha as the symbolic form of the union of Rādhā and Krishna. The Mahimā Dharma, the intellectual leadership for which came from Bhima Bhoi, a person from the low Bauri caste, has generated lot of scholarly interest in the last two decades largely owing to its focus on monotheism and rejection of caste and idol worship, symbols of the Brāhmaṇical order. However, it is a development of the mid-nineteenth century and it is, as they say, another story.

To conclude, it may be in the fitness of things to focus on particular constituent traits of pre-modern Oriya society and culture. The second half of the first millennium AD was characterized by extensive local state formation, agrarian expansion, peasantization of the tribes, caste formation and the universalization of indigenous local deities through cultic appropriation.[37] In short, intersecting, overlapping simultaneous processes of change were at play across localities and sub-regions (*maṇḍalas*). These processes intensified in the first half of the second millennium, leading to the emergence of the first regional/supra regional states in Orissa and beyond.[38] The spread of regional vernaculars only strengthened the growing sense of affiliation and shared bond. Whereas even today north India has communities assignable to all the four *varṇas*, the same can not be said about Orissa. Notwithstanding rare instances of claims to status, for historical reasons the kṣatriya and vaiśya *varṇas* did not take shape in the region, and as in the other parts of peninsular India in Orissa too a two tiered *varṇa* structure comprising the brāhmaṇas and non-brāhmaṇas evolved.[39] Ruling lineages with humble origins lost their assumed statuses with the eclipse of power and, even the Khandāyats' peasant-cum—militia origins would go back only to the Gaṅgā-Gajapati times. In the overall social context the status of the śūdra after all may not have been very despicable. Orissa experienced a process of Hindu/caste-tribal continuum and not 'sustained displacement' of the aboriginals from their homeland, which formed the basis of local state formation and agrarian growth. The role that the Daitas at the temple of Jagannātha at Puri and the Baḍus at Liṅgarāja temple, Bhubaneswar, go on to play as the personal attendants of the deities bears testimony to it.[40] To elaborate, even today mother goddesses (*thākurāṇis*) at many places are attended to by priests/priestesses of humble origins like muni, rāula, and māli, even at instances by the autochthons. The cult of Jagannātha captures this spirit of incorporation and assimilation remarkably well. A. Stirling in the early part of the nineteenth century observed 'there is one cause sufficiently obvious why all sects should here unite in harmony in the performance of their religious ceremonies, viz. that the temple instead of being consecrated exclusively to some form of the deity Vishnu alone, is in fact occupied, in joint tenancy, by forms of three of the most revered divinities of the Hindu faith.... All other deities too are allowed to occupy niches or temples within the precincts of the great Pagoda, and are treated with so much respect, that the most obstinate sectarian could not with any decency or consistency refuse to join in the general worship of the place.'[41] That perhaps explains why the social protests in the region shared a reverential or at most ambivalent attitude towards the cult of Jagannāth.

Notes

1. See S.C. Malik, 'Introduction', in idem. (ed.), *Indian Movements: Some Aspects of Dissent, Protest and Reform*, Simla, Indian Institute of Advanced Study, 1978; M.S.A. Rao, 'Introduction', in *Social Movements in India*, vol. I, Delhi, Manohar, 1978.

2. R.S. Sharma, 'Problems of Peasant Protest in Early Medieval India', in *Social Scientist*, vol. 16, no. 9, September 1988, pp. 3–16; also see his *Early Medieval Indian Society: A Study in Feudalization*, New Delhi, Orient Longman, 2001, ch. 7.

3. Rajan Gurukkal, 'Non-Brāhmaṇa Resistance to the Expansion of *Brahmadeyas*: The Early Pāṇḍya Experience', *Proceedings of the Indian History Congress (PIHC)*, Annamalai session, 1984, pp. 161–3.

4. Ibid.

5. It may be worth mentioning that some of the versions take the story back to the times of the early Kadambas or the legendary creation of the agrarian belt by Parasurāma in the said region.

See Kesavan Veluthat, 'From Tribe to Caste? The Koragas of South Canara', in B.B. Chaudhuri and A. Bandopadhyay (ed.), *Tribes, Forest and Social Formation in Indian History*, Delhi, Manohar 2004, pp. 51–63.

6. *The Harṣa-Carita of Bana*, trans. E.B. Cowell and F.W Thomas, Motilal Banarsidass, Delhi, 1993 (rpt), ch. 7, pp. 208–9.

7. Sharma, 'Problems of Peasant Protest'.

8. Ibid.

9. See *Rāmacaritam* trans. R.G. Basak, Calcutta, The Asiatic Society, 1969. The alternative perspective is available in Swapna Bhattacharya, 'On the Concept of *Sāmantas* in Early Medieval Bengal (*c.* 5th—13th Centuries AD)', K.K. Dasgupta *et al.* (eds), *Sraddhāñjali: Studies in Ancient Indian History (D.C. Sircar Commemoration Volume)*, Delhi, Sundeep, 1988, pp. 75–81; idem., *Land Grants and State Formation in Early* Medieval Bengal, Wiesbaden, 1985.

10. B.N.S. Yadava, 'Problems of the Interaction between Socio-Economic Classes in the Early Medieval Complex', *The Indian Historical Review*, vol. 3, no. 1, 1976, pp. 53–8.

11. See 'Introduction', by B.D. Chattopadhyaya in his *The Making of Early Medieval India*, New Delhi, Oxford University Press, 1994,.

12. See Sharma, 'Problems of Peasant Protest'; M.D. Rajukumar, 'Struggles for Rights during Later Choḷa Period', *Social Scientist*, vol. 2, nos 6–7, 1974, pp. 29–35.

13. R.N. Nandi, 'Growth of Rural Economy in Early Feudal India', Presidential Address, Ancient India section, Annamalai session, *PIHC*, 1984, especially pp. 71–7; idem., *State Formation, Agrarian Growth and Social Change in Feudal South India, c.* AD *600–1200*, New Delhi, Manohar, 2000, ch. 8.

14. See Y. Subbarayalu, 'The Peasantry of Tiruchirapalli District from the 13th to 17th Centuries', in N. Karashima (ed.), *Socio-Cultural Change in Villages in Tiruchirapalli District, Tamil Nadu, India*, Tokyo, Institute for the Study of Languages and Cultures of Asia and Africa, Tokyo University, 1983, pp. 123–32.

15. See N. Karashima and Y. Subbarayalu, 'Valaṅgai/Idaṅgai, Kaniyalar and Irajagarattar: Social Conflict in Tamil Nadu in the 15th Century', in Karashima (ed.), ibid., pp. 133–60.

16. N. Karashima, 'Emergence of Medieval State and Social Formation in South India', in his *South Indian Society in Transition: Ancient to Medieval*, New Delhi, Oxford University Press, 2009, especially pp. 14–23.

17. Sharma, 'Problems of Peasant Protest'; Yadava, 'Problems of the Interaction'; idem., 'Immobility and Subjection of Indian Peasantry in Early Medieval Complex', in B.P. Sahu (ed.), *Land System and Rural Society in Early India*, New Delhi, Manohar, 1997, pp. 329–42; Nandi, *State Formation, Agrarian Growth*, chs 3–7.

For example, for Rajasthan, Gujarat, and Tamil Nadu see Chattopadhyaya, *The Making of Early Medieval India*; V.K. Jain, *Trade and Traders in Western India (*AD *1000–1300)*, New Delhi, Munshiram Manoharlal, 1990; and R. Champakalakshmi, 'State and Economy: Circa AD 400–1300', in Romila Thapar (ed.), *Recent Perspectives of Early Indian History*, Bombay, Popular Prakashan, 1995, pp. 266–308.

18. A. Mohan Ram, 'Famines and Relief Measures under the Imperial Cōḷas, AD 850–1279', in B.D. Chattopadhyaya (ed.), *Essays in Ancient Indian Economic History*, Delhi, Munshiram Manoharlal, 1987, pp. 226–34.

19. Ibid.

20. See B.P. Sahu 'Introduction', in B.P. Sahu (ed.), *Land System and Rural Society*.

21. D.D. Kosambi, 'Social and Economic Aspects of the *Bhagavad Gītā*', *Journal of the Economic and Social History of the Orient* (hereafter *JESHO*), vol. 4, 1961, pp. 198–224; Sharma, supra n. 2.

22. See B.P. Sahu, 'Legitimation, Ideology and State in Early India', Presidential Address, Ancient India section, Mysore session, *Proceedings of the Indian History Congress* (hereafter *PIHC*), pp. 44–76.

23. Sharma, 'The Feudal Mind', in idem., *Early Medieval Indian Society*, ch. 9.

24. M.G.S. Narayanan and Kesavan Veluthat, 'Bhakti Movement in South India', in Malik (ed.), *Indian Movements*, especially pp. 54–8.

25. R.N. Nandi, 'Origin of the Vīraśaiva Movement', *Indian Historical Review* (*hereafter IHR*), vol. 2, no. 1, 1975, pp. 32–46; also see Arun P. Bali, 'The Vīraśaiva Movements', in Malik (ed.), *Indian Movements*, pp. 67–100. For its social composition see pp. 94–5.

26. R.P. Bahuguna, 'Symbols of Resistance: Non-Brāhmaṇical *Sants* as Religious Heroes in Late Medieval India', in B. Pati, B.P. Sahu, and T.K. Venkatasubramanian (eds), *Negotiating India's Past: Essays in Memory of Partha Sarathi Gupta*, New Delhi, Tulika, 2003, pp. 222–53.

27. See Georg Berkemer, 'No Heroes in Kaliṅga? On Death in Kaliṅga Inscriptions', in Elisabeth Schombucher and Claus Peter Zoller (eds), *Ways of Dying: Death and its Meanings in South Asia*, Delhi, Manohar, 1999, pp. 181–92.

28. For a persuasive argument see ibid.; for the capture of the Khond chief see *Epigraphia Indica* (hereafter *EI*), vol. XIX, 1927–8, p. 43 and for the Sabara invasion see *EI*, vol. VI, 1900–1, pp. 260 and 264.

29. R.K. Das, 'Social Protest in Medieval Orissa', in *PIHC*, Bombay session, 1980, pp. 340–8.

30. For example see B.K. Mallik, *Paradigms of Dissent and Protest: Social Movements in Eastern India (c. AD 1400–1700)*, Delhi, Manohar, 2004; idem., 'Contribution of Sāralā Dasa to the Emergence of an 'Oriya Identity' and its Localization', in H. Kulke and Georg Berkemer (eds), *Centres Out There? Facets of Subregional Identities in Orissa*, New Delhi, Manohar, 2011, pp. 123–32.

31. Sheldon Pollock, *The Language of the Gods in the World of Men: Sanskrit, Culture and Power in Premodern India*, Delhi, Permanent Black, 2007.

32. For a good example, see S. Nagaraju, 'Emergence of Regional Identity and Beginnings of Vernacular Literature: A Case Study of Telugu', *Social Scientist*, vol. 23, nos 10–12, Oct.–Dec. 1995, pp. 8–23; also see B.P. Sahu, 'Brāhmaṇical Ideology, Regional Identities and the Construction of Early India', Presidential Address, Ancient section, Panjab History Conference, Patiala, 2001, in *Social Scientist*, vol. 29, nos 7–8, Jul.–Aug. 2001, pp. 3–18.

33. The notion of Andhra's regional extent grew as the Telugu linguistic sphere gradually expanded. Besides, in the construction of us-versus-them the Orissan kings were treated as aliens in the thirteenth–fourteenth century Kākatīya inscriptions. See Cynthia Talbot, 'Inscribing the Other, Inscribing the Self: Hindu-Muslim Identities in Pre-Colonial India', *Comparative Studies in Society and History*, vol. 37, no. 4, 1995, pp. 710ff.

34. Cited in Pollock, *The Language of the Gods*, ch. 10.

35. *EI*, 27, 1947–8, p. 193, fn 4.

36. For details, see A.K. Deb, *The Bhakti Movement in Orissa*, Calcutta, 1984, pp. 73 and 256–7.

37. See H. Kulke, 'The Early and the Imperial Kingdom: A Processural Model of Integrative State Formation in Early Medieval India', in Idem (ed.), *The State in India, 1000–1700*, New Delhi, Oxford University Press, 1995, pp. 233–62; also see B.P. Sahu, Agrarian Changes and the Peasantry in Early Medieval Orissa (*c.* AD 400–1100), in V.K. Thakur and A. Aounshuman (eds), *Peasants in Indian History (Essays in Memory of Professor R.K. Chaudhary)*, Patna, Janaki Prakashan, 1996, pp. 283–311.

38. For a good study of the stages of evolution, see U. Singh, *Kings, Brāhmaṇas and Temples in Orissa: An Epigraphic Study (300–1147 CE)*, Delhi, Munshiram Manoharlal, 1994; Kulke, 'The Early and the Imperial Kingdom'. This happened in Andhra, Tamil Nadu, Rajasthan, and elsewhere too. While the imperial Gaṅgās and Gajapatis ruled over parts of Orissa and beyond, the south experienced the Vijayanagara enterprise.

39. B.P. Sahu, 'The Past as a Mirror of the Present: The Case of Oriya Society', *Social Science Probings*, vol. 9, nos 14, 1995, pp. 8–23; also idem., '*Varna, Jati* and the Shaping of Early Oriya Society', in this volume.

40. Kulke, 'The Early and the Imperial Kingdom'; A. Eschmann, 'Hinduization of Tribal Deities in Orissa: The Śākta and Śaiva Typology'; and also her 'The Vaiṣṇava Typology of Hinduization and the origin of Jagannāth', in A. Eschmann, H. Kulke, and G.C. Tripathi (eds), *The Cult of Jagannāth and the Regional Tradition of Orissa*, Delhi, Manohar, 1978, pp. 79–97 and 99–117.

41. A. Stirling, 'Orissa: Religion, Antiquities, Temples and Civil Architecture', in N.K. Sahu (ed.), *A History of Orissa*, vol. II, Delhi, 1980 (rpt), pp. 277–8.

Index

motifs and symbols 137, 192
Puri-Kuṣāṇa 85, 87, 141–2, 188–9, 291
punch-marked, cast, Sātavāhana 83–7, 136–7, 141–3, 163, 187
Roman 86, 163
Cōḷas 6, 18, 76, 115, 118, 122, 160, 190, 196, 231, 301–4
dissent and protest 301, 302
legitimation, ideology and state 190, 196
polity and state 156–7, 160
regions and constructions 6, 16, 18
regional land system and rural society 230, 231, 237, 238, 239
varṇa, *jāti* and shaping of society 76;
colonial Indology 111, 112
colonization 19, 228
Common Era 53, 69, 119, 139
communication systems 203
community
culture 33
identities and territoriality 81, 190
patronage 130, 144
performances 202
rights over natural resources 90
constitutional monarchy 112
cosmic periodization, Indian schema 47
cows, donation 257
craft specialization 87
creation myth 34
cultic appropriation and their universalization 62, 309; and extension of Brāhmaṇical ideology 11
cults, sects, castes and beliefs 10–11, 134, 145, 156, 183, 194, 198, 304. *See also* Tantricism
cultural
adaptations 291
and political reality 3
and technological attainments 9
aspirations 189
assemblage 4, 83
basis of power 51, 145
changes 2, 42
communication 20–1, 69, 202
discourses such as Kali 192
forms 53, 81, 97, 144, 180
identity 17, 97
integration 121, 144, 227, 230, 265
mosaic 5, 14, 180
networks 64, 279
pluralism 3, 15
process/traditions/values 5, 10, 54–5, 81, 83, 92, 112, 222, 304
regions 76
transformation, transmission and reproduction 158, 197, 304
Cuñcus 39
customary rights 279
customs and beliefs 9
Cuttack 48, 89, 135, 252, 254, 261, 280
cyclical change, notion of 50

Dadu 305
daitas 309
Dalavaypuram plates 229, 300
Damaras, Kashmir 301
Damayanti, Mahadevi of Naga lineage 291
dānas 68, 145
daṇḍanāyaka 86, 288
Dandi Mahadevi 48

Jaina, Jainism 134
art and antiquities 187–8
basadis 304
ethics and ethos 134
monks 131
Jajpur 171, 198, 254, 264
Jambudvīpa 12
Jammu and Kashmir, 7, 18, 42, 301
janapada 6, 14, 70, 87, 163, 219, 222, 225, 229, 281, 289
janapadān 66–7, 69, 70, 73, 288, 289
janapramukhas 74
jātidharma 37
jātis. See also caste; *varṇa*
Brāhmaṇical conception 31–43
origin 33
formation in Tamil country 303
Jaugada, Ganjam 13, 63, 135, 139
Jaya Bhanjadeva 259
Jayapurakotta 48
Jayaraja, Sarabhapuriya king 85, 164, 166
Jayastambhadeva of Kodalaka *maṇḍala* 256, 268
Jayaswal, K.P. 111, 112
Jayavarman 67, 263, 288, 289
Jaya-Vijayagumpha 134
Jayrampur plates of Achyuta 48
Jha, D.N. 46, 47, 154
Jirjingi plates of Indravarman I 284
Jithani temple 93
Junagarh inscription of Saka Rudradaman 189–90
jungle kingdoms 159, 163
Junnar 13, 189

Kabir 305
Kadambapadrullaka 90
Kadambas of Banavasi (Karnataka) 15, 20, 51–2, 193, 195
conception of Kali Age 51, 52
polity 158, 192, 193, 195
kaisara 188
kaivartas (fisherman) 71
revolt, Bengal 301
Kākatīyas of Andhra 16, 17, 18, 19, 76, 232
Kakusthavarman 51
Kalabhras 51, 229
Kalachuris 81, 93, 95
kālādhyasin (astrologer) 70
Kalahandi. *See* Asurgarh
Kalahandi-Bolangir-Sambalpur 68
Kali Age, *Kaliyuga* 19, 41, 46–56, 68, 70, 73, 192
conception in early India 20, 46–56
crisis, theory 19, 46–8, 52, 54, 154–5, 192
land-grants to brāhmaṇas, and religious establishments relationship 53
regional dimension 47
references in purāṇic literature 143
Kali deity 197
Kalikatti, Karnataka 237
Kaliṅga Jina 133
Kaliṅga purvaraja nivesitam 63
Kaliṅga, Kaliṅganagara 9, 16–17, 63, 67, 74–5, 82, 87, 131, 134, 137, 138, 145, 161, 169, 187, 219, 225, 280
agrarian change and peasantry 253, 255
the littoral experience 280–90
political structure 133
war 187
Kalivarjyas 47
Kama-Nalinakshapur plates of Jayavarman 67, 263, 288
Kāmarūpa 219, 232
Kambojas 39, 62

Rock Edicts, Major and Minor 186
royal legitimation 10, 69, 130
royal patronage 94, 155, 281. *See also* land grants; brahmanical
  of art activities 54
  and forging of royal authority 180
  and legitimation, changing forms in early Orissa 129–45, 180–81
  politics of 141
royal sovereignty 73, 137
Rudra 198
Rudramā-devī, Kākatīya queen 203
ruling dynasties and lineage 73, 75, 143, 197, 256, 279, 293, 309
rupakāras 93
rural economy 90, 194, 222, 224, 232, 303
  growth 256–65
rural settlements 88, 90–91, 165–7, 219–20, 224, 226–7, 229, 232, 233–8, 258–60, 262, 264, 266, 281, 292, 293–4
rural society in India 36, 219–41
  change 238–41

Sabarmati 235
sabhā 238
Sada, Mahāmeghavāhana 139
Sadas 225
Śailōdbhavas 64, 66, 67, 70, 169, 253, 267, 281, 282, 285, 290
  decline 288
  inscriptions 143
Saivism, Saivite 85, 95, 188, 197
  temples 84, 93, 95
Śaka-Kuṣāṇa 53
Śakas 39, 62, 193
Śakti 10
Śaktipitha 85
Śaktivarman, Mathara king 65, 284
Śālagrama 90
Śālankāyanas, Andhra 193
samāja (gathering) 16
sāmantas, *samanta*/feudatory system 53, 171, 237, 241, 254, 261, 303
  and *bhogis* 72
  brahmana conflicts 302
  hierarchy, 117, 154
Samantavarman 48
Sambalpur, Orissa 81, 86, 90, 252
Samudragupta 82, 84, 163, 228
Sanchi 53, 132, 227, 240
Sandhyakara Nandi 301
Saṅgam literature 52, 190, 195, 225, 240
saṅkhika (conch-shell dealer) 71
Sanskrit, Sanskritization 11, 20, 201, 203, 307–8
  inscription 190
Sanskritic culture 229
sant movement 305–6
Santikara 70
Santivarman, Kadamba king 51
Sarabha, *Rāja* (Sarabharāja) 164, 166
Śarabhapurīyas of Daksina Kosala 15, 19, 69
  legitimation, ideology and state, 193, 195 agrarian changes and peasantry, 236
  making of an early historical subregion, 84–85, 88–91
  polity, 158, 162–68, 172
  state formation, 253, 255
Sārala *Mahābhārata* 17, 71, 74, 307
Śaśānka 48
śāstras see vedic-śāstric-epic-purāṇic ideas
Sastri, K.A.N., 113
Sātakarṇi, Gautamiputra 51, 189
Sātkarṇi, Satavahana king, 132
Sātavāhanas
  coins 83, 163

About the Author

Bhairabi Prasad Sahu is Professor at the Department of History, University of Delhi. He has served as Sectional President (2003) and Secretary of the Indian History Congress (2006–9). At present he is a member of the Indian Council of Historical Research. His publications include *From Hunters to Breeders: Faunal Background of Early India* (1988). He has also edited *Land System and Rural Society in Early India* (1997) and *Iron and Social Change in Early India* (2006).